nelson**science**
Physics

2nd EDITION

Ken Dobson
and Martin Roberts

First published in 1995 by:
Thomas Nelson and Sons Ltd
Second edition 2002

Second edition published in 2002 by:

Nelson Thornes Ltd
Delta Place
27 Bath Road
CHELTENHAM
GL53 7TH
United Kingdom

02 03 04 05 06 / 10 9 8 7 6 5 4 3 2 1

A catalogue record for this book is available from the British Library

ISBN 0 7487 6240 X

Typeset by TechSet Ltd
Printed and bound in Spain by Graficas Estella

Contents

To our readers

This book is about physics. It is about how we can understand the universe of space, time, matter and energy. Using the ideas of physics we can invent, design and make the thousands of everyday or rare objects from corkscrews to computers, from telephones to telescopes, CDs to satellites that make up the modern world. Just a list of these useful devices would fill the book! Physics is also a vital tool for hospital doctors and nurses. It is the basis of the sources and management of energy and its discoveries have revolutionised communications. Even if we leave out the technicalities, the discoveries and ideas of physics make us think about the origin, history and future of the Earth, its living cargo and the wider Universe of stars and galaxies.

The other two books in the *Nelson Science* series, *Chemistry* and *Biology*, help you complete your understanding of science.

How to use this book

The book is divided into eight **sections** (A to H) and each section is split into Topics: A1, A2, etc. Generally each topic consists of the main text (white background) together with:

Extensions (cream background). These take some of the ideas a bit further. Your teacher will advise you which ones to read. Some of them are specific case studies with thought-provoking questions at the end.

Activities (green background). These are things you can do yourself without any special equipment. Activities that can only be done in the laboratory are in a separate Teachers' Resource Pack (see below).

Questions (various backgrounds). These are designed to help you understand the topic and test your ability to recall and interpret information. Some of the questions invite you to put forward your own ideas.

In addition there are:

- Occasional **special features** which focus on particular issues and explore them in depth.
- A selection of GCSE **examination questions** at the end of the book.
- Instructions for **practical work** and help for **investigations** in the Teachers' Resource Pack.
- You will find a range of supplementary materials at our **website** (see below).

Key skills

There are certain things that you need to learn how to do. These are called **key skills**.

The main key skills are:

- **Application of number**: measuring things, doing calculations, interpreting graphs and any information that has numbers in it.

- **Communication**: reading, writing essays and reports, making summaries, explaining things, giving talks and discussing topics.
- **Information and communications technology (ICT)**: using a computer to find information on the Internet, analysing data and presenting information by means of text, numbers and images (including diagrams and graphs).

Other wider key skills are:

- **Working with others**: collaborating with other people in carrying out investigations and discussing issues.
- **Improving your own performance**: practising techniques, repeating experiments, perfecting your other skills.
- **Problem solving**: thinking up ways of investigating things, interpreting information gained by reading or from your own investigations.

From time to time you may be tested (assessed) on the three main key skills. Our book, and the accompanying Teachers' Resource Pack, will give you lots of opportunities for practising all the key skills.

Questions and activities that provide particularly good opportunities for developing ICT skills are marked like this:

However, computers can be used in many other contexts besides the ones we have specified. Advice is given in the *Teachers' Resource Pack*.

Scientific enquiry

Scientific enquiry means the way scientists work and make discoveries. In the National Curriculum it is described as Ideas and Evidence in Science. This will underpin the whole of your physics course. In our book we give many examples. Some of the examples are historical milestones in the history of physics, others focus on modern applications of physics.

Other things to think about

Physics, like the rest of science, affects our lives in all sorts of ways. Here are some of them, and the questions they raise:

- **Spiritual and moral issues**: can we reconcile the discoveries of physics with our beliefs?
- **European dimension**: how does physics relate to our being part of Europe?
- **Environment**: what part does physics play in the environmental problems that face society?
- **Citizenship**: can an understanding of physics help us to be good members of our communities?
- **Health and safety**: how does physics affect people's physical and mental well-being?

In this book and the *Teachers' Resource Pack* we try to address all these issues in a variety of different contexts.

We hope that by the time you finish your course you will not just *know* a lot of things but also understand what it means to be a physicist, and perhaps want to study physics further.

Good luck in your study of physics!

Ken Dobson
Martin Roberts

Teachers' Resource Pack

This pack contains:

- **Investigations and experiments**, with instructions that can be photocopied and given to students, and separate notes for teachers and technicians.
- **Answers** to the questions in the textbook.
- **Advice** on how the textbook can be used for fostering and assessing scientific enquiry (ideas and evidence) and key skills.
- **Enlarged diagrams** from the textbook, which can be photocopied and used by students.
- **Grids** showing how the textbook relates to your syllabus specifications and to the main key skills.

Other books in the *Nelson Science* series

Nelson Science Chemistry by John Holman and Phil Stone, and *Nelson Science Biology* by Michael Roberts and Neil Ingram should help you to complete your understanding of science.

Website

The *Nelson Science* series has a website: www.nelsonscience.co.uk

The website contains a range of extra support for the book and your learning. It has supplementary reading materials, useful links to other websites, and opportunities for you to comment on the book and your course. The site is continually updated.

Television programmes

Channel 4 have made a series of five programmes called *Science in Focus: the nature of scientific enquiry* which accompany the *Nelson Science* series.
Faraday's Famous Inventions links directly to section E of this book. It describes how a poor and uneducated young Briton made his way in the world and produced theories and discoveries in electricity and electrochemistry which are still in everyday use.
Hubble's Expanding Universe links to section G. it describes how a not very successful American lawyer turned his first love of astronomy into a career and discovered the first evidence for the Big Bang model of our amazing universe.

Topics in the textbook that relate to the programme are marked with the Channel 4 logo:

The programmes are available as videos from Channel 4:

by post from 4Learning, PO Box 400, Wetherby, LS23 7LG;
by telephone on 08701 246444;
by fax on 08701 246446;
by E-mail from 4learning.sales@channel4.co.uk;
via the Internet at www.4learning.co.uk/shop

Thanks

Many people have helped us produce this book. We are especially grateful to the other authors of the *Nelson Science* series, John Holman, Phil Stone, Michael Roberts and Neil Ingram.

Dr Peter Main of the University of York provided expert guidance, and we are also grateful to the following for help with specific topics.

Peter Borrows, CLEAPSS School Science Service
Michael Brimicombe, Cedars Upper School, Leighton Buzzard
David Fielding, Radley College, Abingdon
Dr Ian Gray, Harrow School
Anna Grayson, geology specialist and broadcaster
Joe Jefferies, ASE Safeguards in Science Committee
Mark Tweedle, Heckmondwike Grammar School
Professor E.K. Walton, Department of Geography and Geology, University of St Andrews

Signals and codes

Human beings need information. We also send out information. This topic is about how information is coded, carried and controlled.

Picture 1 Codes for ideas.

électron	French
electrón	Spanish
Elektron	German
elettrone	Italian
ηλετρόνιο	Greek
eletron	Portugese
אלקטרון	Hebrew
电 [電]子	Chinese
elektron	Dutch
электрóн	Russian
elektrono	Esperanto
ėlĕ́ctrŏn	phonetic
ইলেকট্রন:	Bengali

Picture 2 Different codes for the same word.

CODES

The language you speak is a code, and not everybody in the world understands it! Writing is a code. Picture 1 shows how different languages have tackled the problem of putting sounds into 'pictures'. The very oldest, like Ancient Egyptian, used drawings of what the sounds meant. The word for 'house' was drawn to look like a house. But this means having a different symbol for each word. It is hard to learn, slow to write and to read, and needs thousands of different code symbols.

It is easier to break the words up into their different sound parts, and have a symbol for each of these. In English we can just about manage with 26 of these symbols – the letters of the alphabet. Of course, we do use more than 26 sounds, but we can combine letters (ee, sh, etc) to help us cope with the extra sounds. Picture 2 shows some of the codes used in the world today.

When we learn to read we are learning which sounds go with which symbols. In Western languages we 'scan' the letters from left to right. In Arabic, Hebrew and some other languages the symbols are scanned from right to left.

The earliest written books from ancient Greece show that they were read from right to left on one line and then left to right on the next, and so on. To save time, computer printers print in this way, every other line being printed backwards.

■ Carrying messages

Before writing was invented messengers needed very good memories.

Even after the invention of writing they also needed strong legs, like the messenger who carried the news of the battle of Marathon to Athens in 49 BC. He ran so hard that he died after delivering the news, and so never knew that he had just invented marathon running. But sending a messenger was a slow way of carrying information.

Light travels a lot more quickly – at 300 million metres a second. The ancient Romans used light to send messages very long distances. The Roman army built a network of signal stations criss-crossing Europe. Each station had large wooden 'flags' to send messages many kilometres across country (see picture 3).

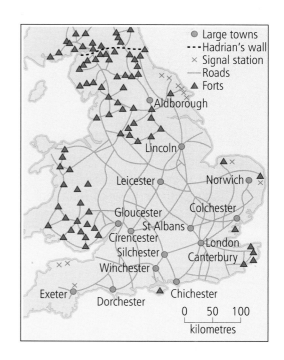

Picture 3 The Romans sent messages using light, over 2000 years ago.

To make use of 'light messages' new codes had to be invented. To have a different flag movement for each letter of the alphabet would have been a very slow way of doing it. Standard messages, like HELP!, would be given one flag movement. But even so, messages had to be kept very simple. Long, chatty letters were still sent by messengers on ship or horseback.

■ Electric messages

Electric current was discovered at the beginning of the 19th century. It was soon used as a message carrier. In fact that was its first main use, in the form of the **electric telegraph**. A new code – the **Morse Code** – was invented for this kind of message carrier (see picture 4).

Then in 1876 a Scotsman, Alexander Graham Bell, invented the first artificial **transducers**, which allowed speech to be transmitted over long distances. He had invented the **telephone**.

A transducer is a device that transfers signals from one energy system to another. For example, our ears change sound waves into electric signals that the brain can understand. Bell had found another way of changing sound signals into electric signals – the **microphone**. He also had to invent the transducer at the other end to change the electric signals back into sound – a **receiver** or **loudspeaker**. These devices are described in topic A4.

Even after the telephone was invented, light was still one of the main means of sending messages long distances. Armies and navies used flags, lamps and flashing mirrors (heliographs). They were cheap, quiet and didn't need a network of wires to carry the message.

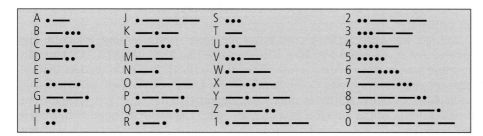

Picture 4 The earliest electric message carrier and the code it used.

Picture 5 Guglielmo Marconi.

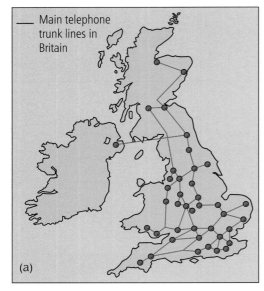

Main telephone trunk lines in Britain

(a)

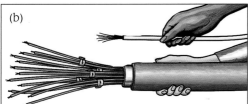

(b)

Picture 6 Modern communications are going back to using light – for very good reasons.

Then a young Italian called Guglielmo Marconi (picture 5) took up an idea that university physicists had already been experimenting with, and made it practical. He invented a message carrying system that didn't need wires – a **'wireless' telegraph**. To carry messages, this system used what we now call radio waves. These are an invisible part of the **electromagnetic spectrum**, the family of waves (see topic A7), which also includes light.

This was one of the most important inventions of the 20th century. It led to the development of radio, radar and TV, and the discovery of new facts about the universe as scientists began picking up radiation from outer space.

BACK TO LIGHT

So much information is now being sent from place to place that it is hard to find room for it. The world is getting more and more crowded with radio and TV signals, criss-crossing each other and getting in each other's way. Telephone lines can only carry so many conversations at once, even when they are specially coded.

This has forced scientists to think of other ways of sending messages. Their solution to the problem is to use light, but light sent down 'wires'. The 'wires' are made of glass drawn out into very thin fibres – **optical fibres** (see topic A6). The main 'trunk' telephone lines in the UK, which carry messages between the main cities, now carry the signals coded into pulses of light instead of electric currents (see picture 6(a)).

A standard copper cable can carry up to a thousand coded conversations at the same time. The optical fibre that replaces it can carry 11 000 conversations, using present coding systems. These can be improved to allow the cable to carry five times as many, if necessary. Using optical systems also improves the quality of the signals, so that they can carry complicated 'computer data' without losing its accuracy. The optical fibre system is also lighter and smaller (see picture 6(b)).

■ Digital codes

The world of the 21st century is a world built on information. Once upon a time information was stored in books, and the books kept in libraries. If you wanted to find out about something, you had to go to a library, look up a card index – or ask the librarian – and sit at a desk with the book. You might have had to use the book index to locate the information more precisely. Of course, books (like this one!) and libraries still exist. But more and more people are getting information using a telephone connection. The word telephone means 'distant sound', but the wire, optical fibre or cable carrying the information doesn't carry sounds. It carries electrical signals. With the right equipment you can hear it, but what you would hear is a jumble of noises that only make sense to a computer. The strange noises can be turned into written words and even pictures on the computer screen or printed out on paper. The Internet (or World Wide Web) uses telephone connections which let anyone with the right equipment get information from many thousands of 'sites', and to send and receive messages from anywhere in the world. And all for the price of a local telephone call.

All this has been done by changing a message – some writing, a picture and even sound itself – into numbers. The message has been *digitised*. We normally count in groups of ten, using a number code (decimals) based on the fact that we have ten fingers – or *digits*. Computers can only use groups of two, using a *binary* code. But the coding system is still caused digitisation.

Each letter of the alphabet has its own code. The standard code is called the ASCII system which uses 7 bits, which can count up to 128 (2^7). For example P has the code number 1010000, while p has the code 1110000.

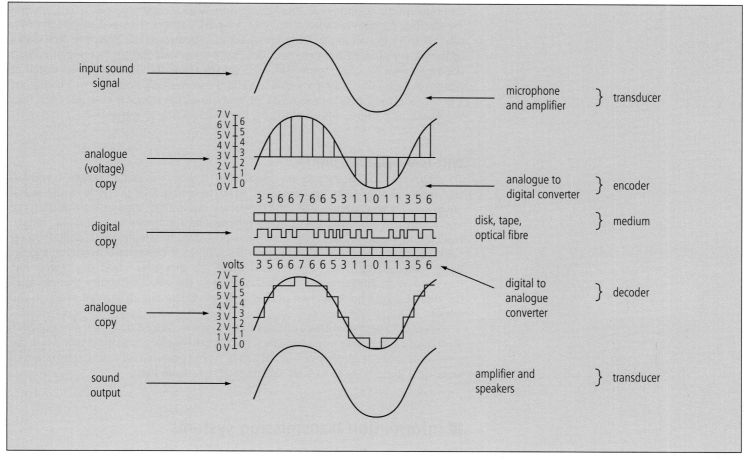

Picture 7 How sound is 'digitised' and then changed back again.

MODEMS

Suppose you want to send an e-mail to a friend in Australia. You need a computer and a telephone system. But to get the computer to 'talk' to the telephone system you need an interpreter. This is called a *modem*. When you press the letter P on a computer keyboard its ASCII code is sent into the memory until you are ready to send it as part of your message. When you send the message the computer sends out a string of pulses using the binary code. The telephone system uses a different kind of coding – the pulses have to be carried as electrical waves of rapidly changing frequency (pitch). The modem changes the pulses into these waves at the sending end, and at the receiving end another modem changes the warbling sounds back into pulses that its computer understands. This double job is called **mo***dulating* and **dem***odulating* the signal – hence **modem**.

DIGITAL MUSIC

Music can also be digitised. In fact most recorded music is now put onto compact discs (CDs) using a digital code. Soon all TV and radio stations will be broadcasting video and music signals using digital codes.

The diagram (picture 7) shows how a simple sound wave can be turned into a digital code. The sound wave is first turned into a changing electric voltage with exactly the same pattern as the sound wave. The electrical signal is called an analogue of the sound wave. The height of the wave is sampled every so often and the decimal number is then turned into a binary number. This is done much more often than is shown in the diagram which just illustrates the principle. The digits of the binary number are then sent down the telephone line as a series of pulses: the signal has become *digital*. How the pulses show the number is illustrated in picture 7. Again this is simplified for a system that can only count up to 7 using just 4 **b**inary dig**its** or **bits**. At the receiving end the digital signal is changed back into the electrical pattern, it is changed back into an analogue signal.

WHY MAKE SIGNALS DIGITAL?

The main reason that signals are digitised is to make the signal harder to spoil. A signal can be spoiled by becoming too weak to be detected properly as the signal fades away with distance. Also, the electronic equipment used in transmitting the signal can add little voltages which might swamp the weakened signal as 'noise'. How digital coding helps cope with these problems in telephones is explained on page 56. Music recorded digitally on CDs (Compact Discs) and magnetic tape is hardly affected by noise which used to be so annoying when the music was recorded as an analogue signal. This is because the small computer that changes the digital signal back into an analogue form rejects any unwanted noise in the signal.

Nowadays vast quantities of information can be stored on CDs – as CD-ROMs (Compact Disk Read-Only Memories – or DVDs (Digital Versatile Discs). But the term 'read-only' is already out of date as it is now possible for home computers to write data directly on to CDs as well as read data from them.

■ Information transmission systems

Talking to someone seems a pretty straightforward activity. You open your mouth and out comes speech. But there is more to this than you might think. A message has to go through a number of stages for it to be sent, received and understood. Picture 8 shows this: the task of sending a message is broken down into blocks where things are done to the message.

First, the message has to be encoded: *you think of something to say, then* **encode** *it into language – imagine trying to say it in French*! Then you have to make some sounds: *you breathe out a bit making a sound which you then* **modulate** *into tones and the special sounds of different parts of words (phonemes)*. Scots do this slightly differently from Lancastrians and Londoners!

Then the message travels through a **medium**: *it is* **transmitted** *by sound waves, which travel through the air as modulated longitudinal waves.*

Next your message is picked up by a device acting as a **receiver**: *the person you are talking to must have an outer ear that collects the sounds and carries them into the inner ear.*

But the human brain is not sensitive to sounds on their own: the small amount of mechanical energy they carry has to be changed into electrical signals carried by nerves. The inner ear is a **transducer**: *its mechanical sound detectors change sound waves into electrical signals sent down nerve cells to the brain.*

The signals then have to be **decoded**: *if your friend doesn't understand English all this effort has been wasted*! The message is then **stored** – *for a few seconds at least if you friend has to make a sensible reply or do something.*

Picture 8 shows that all **communications systems** have similar building blocks showing the stages messages have to go through to be sent, transmitted and received.

The inside of a TV transmitter – or even a TV set – is very complicated. So is the human brain. But it is easier to understand what they do when we break down the actions into separate smaller tasks.

■ Physics and information

This topic has given you an overview of how information is coded, stored and sent from one place to another. The next few topics will explain how physics is used in different kinds of systems to do this.

Activities

A How much information do we need?

We use writing as a code to carry a message to someone who can't hear us. Try this activity to find out about writing as a *code*.

Your group must make up a number of messages. They could be something like:

'I will meet you at Andy's Cafe at 6 pm on Wednesday', or anything else that you can think of.

Work with another group which doesn't know what your messages are. Investigate the following:

1 How many letters can you leave out of your message without making it impossible to understand?

2 What happens when you leave out all the vowels?

3 What happens if you leave out all the consonants?

4 What happens if you only let them see the bottom half of the letters?

B Finding out about codes

You can do this on your own, or as a group. Find out all you can about one of the following topics and give a short 10 minute presentation to your class about it.

1 The Pony Express.

2 The invention of writing.

3 Spy codes – trying to send secret messages.

4 Choose an animal you know something about. How does it communicate? To which other animals does it need to send messages?

5 The invention of 'wireless' – did Marconi know what he was doing?

6 How did Alexander Graham Bell come to invent the telephone?

7 Can plants send messages?

Questions

1 Name *two* devices used in your home that contain information transducers.

2 A TV set is part of an information transmission system. Look at the parts of such a system in picture 8. What jobs do these elements perform:
   a the screen,
   b the loudspeaker,
   c the aerial of a TV set?

3 Picture 8 shows the main parts of an information transmission system. Copy it out and write underneath each box what you would put in it to illustrate:
   a sending a letter,
   b how a six-month old baby communicates with its mother.

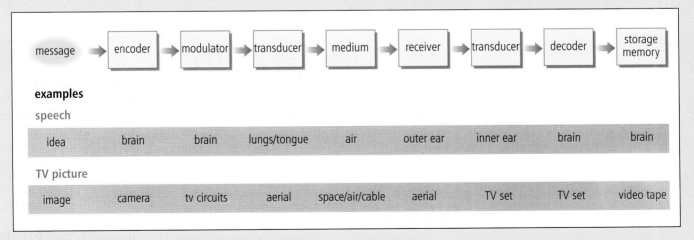

message	encoder	modulator	transducer	medium	receiver	transducer	decoder	storage memory

examples

speech

idea	brain	brain	lungs/tongue	air	outer ear	inner ear	brain	brain

TV picture

image	camera	tv circuits	aerial	space/air/cable	aerial	TV set	TV set	video tape

Picture 8 The main parts of an information transmission system.

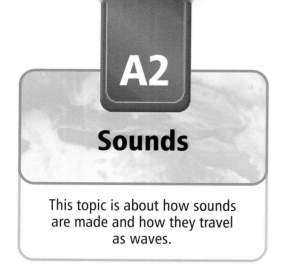

A2

Sounds

This topic is about how sounds are made and how they travel as waves.

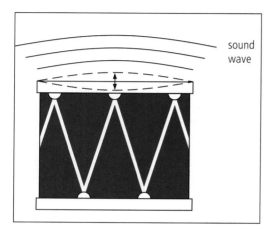

Picture 1 As the drum skin moves up and down, the air above it is squashed, then expanded.

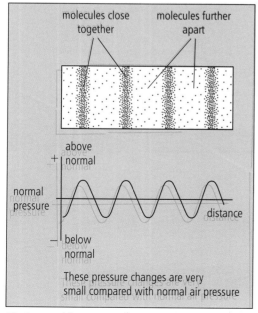

Picture 2 (a) A sound wave in air.
(b) A graph of the pressure of the air looks like this.

MAKING SOUNDS

Sounds are made when objects vibrate. As the skin of the drum in picture 1 moves up and down it also moves the air next to it. When the drum skin moves up it squashes the air in front of it. When it moves it leaves an empty space, so that the air has to expand. The result is a **sound wave** that travels through the air away from the drum.

The sound wave produced by the vibrating drum skin is a series of compressions (squashed air) and expansions. These move away from the drum, as each layer of air squashes the one next to it. Picture 2 shows what we imagine a sound wave in air to be like.

The speed at which these alternate layers of compressed and expanded air move away from the drum is the **speed of sound**. This is 340 metres per second for normal air.

Sound can also travel through other materials. It moves best when the material is very stiff, for example in metals. The speed of sound in different materials is given in table 1.

Sound is a pressure wave – it can only move through a material that can be squashed and 'unsquashed'. So sound waves can't travel through completely empty space – a vacuum. But radio waves and the waves of light can travel through a vacuum. These are *electromagnetic* waves which are so important they need a couple of chapters to themselves (see topics A7 *What is light?* and A11 *Messages through space*). There are also other kinds of waves – like the ones on water. Earthquakes produce waves too – *seismic* waves. These often carry a lot of energy and can do great damage. Seismic waves travel through the Earth and are used by geologists to find out what the inside of the Earth is like. There is more about this in topic G1 *The dynamic Earth*.

Table 1 The speed of sound in different materials.

Material (medium)	Speed in m/s (at room temperature and pressure)
air	331
hydrogen	1286
carbon dioxide	260
wood	4200 (variable)
copper	3813
iron	5000
rubber	1600 (variable)
cork	500
water	1480

HOW SOUNDS ARE DIFFERENT

We soon learn to recognise different people's voices, the sounds of moving water, the wind in the trees. Most people like music, and can easily tell the difference between one note and another, and one instrument from another. All these sounds are very different, but the differences are based on three things. What we hear is decided by:

● pitch (how high or low?): the number of vibrations the sound made per second (its frequency)

● loudness: the energy carried by the sound wave

● quality (e.g. from different instruments): the shape of the sound wave

Of course, what the wave is like is decided at the start by the type of object that is vibrating – the musical instrument, the engine of a car, etc.

Frequency and pitch

Musicians use the word **pitch** to describe how 'high' or 'low' a note is. A high-pitched note is made by something vibrating very quickly. Something vibrating slowly produces a low-pitched note. We use the word **frequency** to describe the rate at which something vibrates. It measures the number of vibrations per second, in a unit called the **hertz (Hz)**.

The human ear can hear sounds from sources which vibrate from as low as about 16 vibrations per second (16 Hz) to as high as over 20 000 Hz.

Wave shapes – amplitude and quality

But there are other differences between sounds. They can be loud or quiet. They can also be different in **quality** – which means we can tell the difference between a note played on a guitar and the same note played on a flute.

Loudness is decided by the energy in the wave. In turn, this is decided by how strongly the source of the sound compresses the air. Sound waves are pressure waves in the air. One way to show a sound wave is to draw a graph of the *change* in the air pressure caused by the wave.

Picture 3 shows some of these graphs. They show how the pressure changes with time at one point in the air for different sounds. The first two (a) and (b) show the same note, but (b) is louder than (a). The *pressure changes* in (b) are greater. This means that they have a greater effect on the ear, so we sense it as a louder sound. The amount that the pressure changes above or below normal is called the **amplitude** of the change. The bigger the amplitude the louder the sound.

Graphs (c) and (d) show notes of the same loudness and pitch made on different instruments. The waves carry the same energy, and they would be 'in tune'. But their *shapes are different*, and we hear these differences as differences in quality.

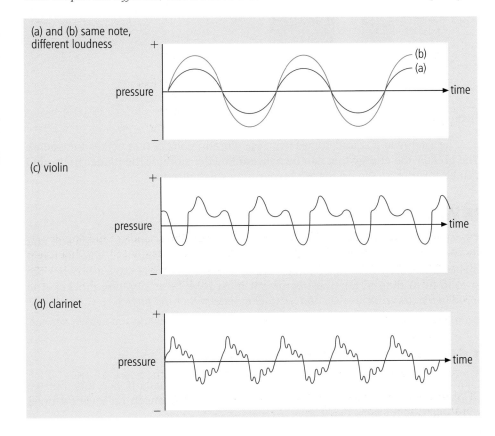

(a) and (b) same note, different loudness

(c) violin

(d) clarinet

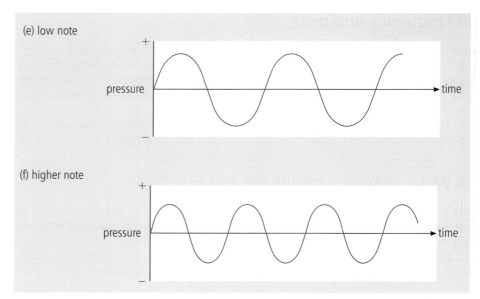

(e) low note

pressure ──────────────→ time

(f) higher note

pressure ──────────────→ time

Picture 3   These graphs show how air pressure varies with different types of sound: (a) small amplitude, (b) large amplitude, (sine wave, same frequency), (c) violin note, (d) clarinet note (same pitch and amplitude), (e) and (f) show notes of different pitch (frequency).

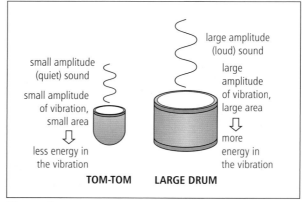

small amplitude (quiet) sound

small amplitude of vibration, small area

⇩

less energy in the vibration

TOM-TOM

large amplitude (loud) sound

large amplitude of vibration, large area

⇩

more energy in the vibration

LARGE DRUM

Picture 4

The energy in a sound comes from the vibrating object that makes the sound. The greater the energy that can be delivered by the vibrator the louder the sound can be (picture 4). Big drums are louder than small drums!

■ Wave shape and pitch

The shape of the wave can also show the frequency of the sound. Graphs (e) and (f) show notes of the same loudness but of different frequency. Note (f) has a higher pitch than note (e). You can see that there are more waves arriving per second in (f) than in (e). The instrument must have been vibrating quicker. *The more waves there are per second (frequency) the higher the pitch.*

ECHOES

Like other waves, sound can be reflected. We don't usually notice this, but we would find listening to music and speech in rooms and concert halls very strange if the walls didn't reflect sound.

Picture 5 An echo is a reflected sound wave.

Echoes are very obvious examples of sound being reflected. To hear a good echo, we must stand a few hundred metres from a cliff or hillside. When we shout, the sound travels to the reflector and bounces back (picture 5). If we are far enough away it means that we can finish a short sentence before the echo returns to us.

■ Echo ranging

If we make a short sharp sound we can time how long it takes for the sound to get to the cliff and come back again. We know that the speed of sound is 340 metres per second, so we can work out how far away the cliff is. Suppose it took 2 seconds for the sound to go there and back. This means it took 1 second to get there, so the cliff must be 340 metres away.

The same principle is used in **radar**, which uses radio waves to find the position of distant aircraft, for example. However, radio waves can't travel through water, so radar is no use under the sea. Instead, sound waves are used in **sonar** devices. They are used to find submarines, shoals of fish and to survey the bottom of the sea (picture 6).

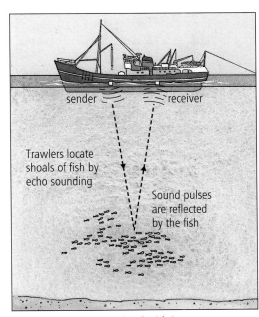

Picture 6 Using sound to find fish.

Questions

1. a What is the quietest sound you can hear?
   b Why can very loud sounds damage your ear drum?

2. What are the three main ways in which sounds can be different from each other? What are the physical causes of these differences?

3. (For musicians) How are the three differences in question 2 shown on a musical score?

4. a What is an echo? How is it produced?
   b Echo sounders are used to find shoals of fish. How do you think they work?

5. A mountain walker notices that when she shouts she hears an echo from a distant cliff. She times it and finds that it takes 2.5 seconds for her shout to be returned as an echo. How far away is the cliff? (Speed of sound in air: 340 m/s.)

6. You can work out how far away you are from a thunderstorm by measuring the time between seeing the lightning flash and hearing the thunder it makes. This works because light travels so much more quickly than sound. A worried boy counted off 5 seconds (by saying 'alpha one, alpha two …') between the flash and the thunder. How far away was the thunderstorm?

7. The diagram below (picture 7) shows three traces of sounds, shown by a cathode ray oscilloscope. Which of them: (a) would be the loudest, (b) would be the highest in pitch, (c) is likely to be made by a flute?

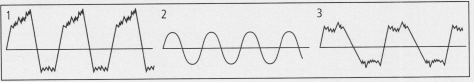

Picture 7

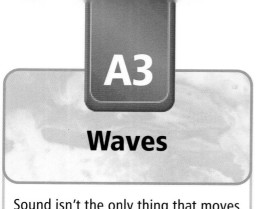

Waves

Sound isn't the only thing that moves as waves. There are waves on water, light waves and earthquake waves.

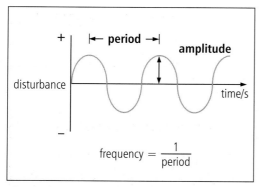

Picture 1 Amplitude and period –
(disturbance *v* time).

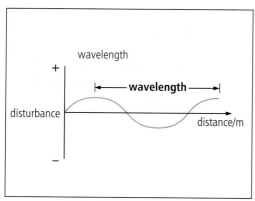

Picture 2 Wavelength and amplitude
(disturbance *v* distance).

WAVES IN SPACE

Light, and the whole electromagnetic spectrum of which it is a small part, travel through space as waves. Earthquakes set up waves which can cause great damage. They also travel right through the Earth, and scientists use them to find out what the inside of the Earth is like. Topics A8 and G1 deal more fully with these types of wave.

But whatever kind of waves they are, they are similar to each other. They all *move, carrying energy*. They all have a *pattern*, which repeats *itself*.

Picture 1 is a graph of a typical wave. It could be a water wave, a sound wave or a light wave. We can use it to explain the meaning of the key words we use to describe wave motion.

First, its **amplitude**. This is a measure of how much the wave vibrates the medium it passes through. It could be the height of a water wave, or the pressure of a sound wave.

Next we have the wave's **period**. This is the time it takes for the wave to repeat its pattern. It is the time for one **vibration** of the source of the wave.

The frequency of a wave is related to its period. The more vibrations are made in a second, the shorter is the time that each one takes. Thus, if a wave has a period of 1/100th of a second it repeats itself 100 times a second, so has a frequency of 100 Hz. That is:

$$\text{period} = 1/\text{frequency}$$

◼ Wavelength

The graph in picture 1 was of the wave changes plotted against time. If we plot these against distance instead we get an idea of the size of the wave. This is done in picture 2. The marked distance is the **wavelength** – the distance between equivalent points on the wave pattern. This could be from peak to peak, or from trough to trough.

The wavelength of a typical sound (say middle C) is about 133 cm. The wavelength of light is very much smaller. For yellow light it is about 600 billionths of a metre. Long wave radio broadcasts use a wavelength of over 1000 metres.

THE WAVE SPEED FORMULA

If a source of sound is vibrating 16 times a second it is producing 16 waves every second. At the end of that second the first wave has travelled 16 wavelengths away from the source. The wave speed is simply how far the waves move in a second. In this case it is obviously just 16 wavelengths. Picture 3 illustrates this.

If the sound source vibrated at 20 Hz, it would produce 20 wavelengths in a second. But sound travels at the same speed in air, whatever its frequency, so the waves are more squashed up – the wavelength is smaller. This is also shown in picture 3.

Thus, because the speed of sound is the same, however many waves are made each second they all have to fit into the same distance. This distance is 340 metres, in air. Looking at it mathematically:

$$\text{length of a sound wave} = \frac{\text{distance sound travels in a second}}{\text{number of waves made per second}}$$

$$\text{or:} \qquad \text{wavelength} = \frac{\text{speed}}{\text{frequency}}$$

This is usually written more neatly as:

$$\textbf{wave speed} = \textbf{frequency} \times \textbf{wavelength}$$
$$v = f\lambda$$

This formula applies to all waves.

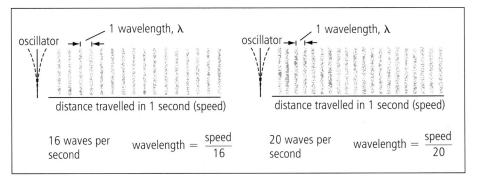

Picture 3 The speed stays the same, so wavelength gets less when frequency increases.

■ To and fro, up and down

Sound waves compress and expand the air. The particles of air move backwards and forwards in line with the direction the sound travels. Waves on a large-coil spring can also do this. These kinds of waves are called **longitudinal** waves.

When sea waves move, the water surface moves up and down as the wave moves along. Waves on a rope or a guitar string are also like this. Waves in which the carrier (medium) moves at right angles to the direction of wave movement are called **transverse** waves. Picture 4 shows these differences.

WAVES THROUGH LIQUIDS

Sound waves travel well through water. Dolphins use sound waves as a sonar to hunt their prey. Sound travels through water because sound is a longitudinal wave. Transverse waves can travel along the surface of water but not through water. This is the case for all liquids. This fact has been used to prove that the core of the Earth is liquid, because the transverse earthquakes waves don't get across to the opposite side of the Earth (see topic G1).

WAVES CAN CARRY ENERGY

Picture 5 shows the coast of Norfolk at a place where the sea cliff is slowly disappearing. The energy for this has been carried by the sea waves continually beating on the base of the cliff. The worst damage is done in storms, when the sea waves are many metres high and carry a great deal of energy.

The bigger the amplitude of a wave the more energy it carries. In fact, the energy carried is proportional to the square of the amplitude. So doubling the wave height increases the energy carried four times. See picture 6.

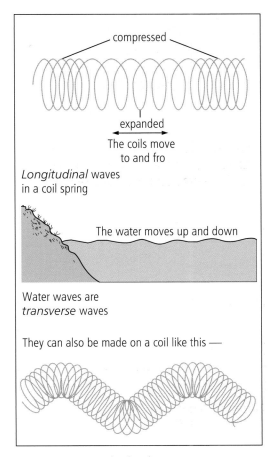

Picture 4 Longitudinal and transverse waves.

Picture 5 Coastal erosion – these houses are at serious risk!

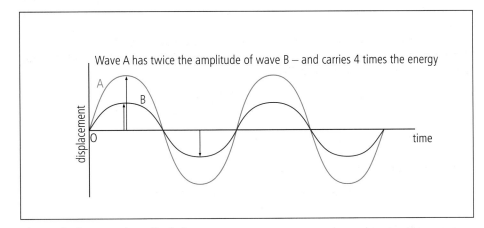

Picture 6 Energy and amplitude for a wave.

Picture 7

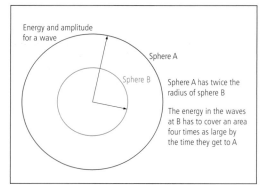

Energy and amplitude for a wave

Sphere A

Sphere B

Sphere A has twice the radius of sphere B

The energy in the waves at B has to cover an area four times as large by the time they get to A

Picture 8   Sphere A has twice the radius of sphere B.

Like ripples on a pond

Imagine a stone thrown into the middle of a pond. When it hits the water it makes a small group of water waves that move outwards from the centre (picture 7). Some of the kinetic energy lost by the stone is being carried away by the waves. As the waves spread out into an ever-widening circle the energy has to be shared over a bigger and bigger length of wave. The energy per metre length gets less and less. The same thing happens to a sound wave as it spreads out. The further away it gets from the source of sound, the less energy it carries. Its amplitude gets less and the sound becomes quieter. Exactly the same rules apply to light waves (see topic A7 *What is light?*). The further away the source of light is, the fainter it appears to the eye.

Sound and electromagnetic waves like light also carry energy. A loud sound can break your ear drum, a very bright light like the beam from an industrial laser can carry enough energy to cut through steel. When light and sound waves spread out freely the energy carried per unit area decreases according to an **inverse square law.** As they travel, the same total quantity of energy has to spread out over a bigger area (see picture 8).

This is the reason that you need to have large amplifiers and loudspeakers to fill a concert hall at a pop concert, while the same music can sound just as loud on a walkman with very small headphone speakers. And the sound from the headphones can be just as damaging to the ear!

Sound going around corners: diffraction

Sound doesn't only travel in straight lines. You can hear someone talking in a nearby room when the door is open even when you can't see directly into the room. The ability that waves have to bend around corners is called **diffraction**. Light waves and radio waves can do this as well – but see topic A8 for more about the diffraction of these kinds of wave.

Picture 9 shows what is happening. Sound is a disturbance of the air. The sound wave changes the air pressure slightly as it moves through it. At the door the edge of the wave is not cut off sharply. The pressure changes slip sideways and move out, expanding in a circle just like the ripples in a pond (picture 9). This means that the person outside the room can hear what is being said.

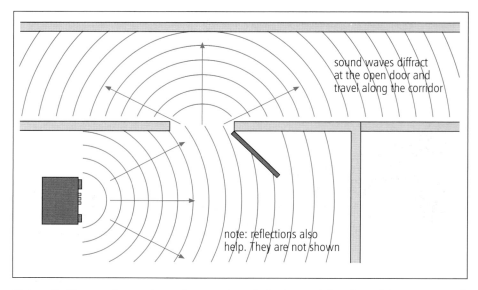

sound waves diffract at the open door and travel along the corridor

note: reflections also help. They are not shown

Picture 9   The sound waves leave the room through the door and the edges of the wave expand sideways. They **diffract**.

■ Wave reflection

Waves can also be **reflected**. They obey the simple rule shown in picture 10.

ACOUSTICS

Acoustics is the science of sound as an energy carrier. A concert hall needs to have 'good acoustics'. This means that wherever people sit in the hall they can hear the music or speech equally well. The problem that has to be solved by the architect who designs the hall is mostly due to **echoes**.

Most solid surfaces reflect sound. A good reflector bounces back the sound without taking much energy from it. A good absorber will take away most of the energy. Hard, shiny surfaces are usually good reflectors of sound; soft surfaces – like cloth and human bodies – are good absorbers. If a concert hall is full of good reflectors, the sound bounces around from wall to wall and from ceiling to floor and the listener will hear the same note, for example, many times. In a well designed concert hall the different reflections reach the ear in a balanced way – and quickly. Less than 35 ms is good. More than 60 ms is bad, the result is confusion: the music or speech is muddy and unclear (see picture 11). The hall is too **reverberant**: each sound produces an echo which takes a long time to die away.

But the opposite design is almost as bad. If the walls and ceiling do not reflect sound at all, the sound seems to vanish. It is like hearing a concert in the open air. Music and musicians sound best when there is some reflection; the small echoes add 'life' to the music – it all sounds more natural.

Picture 12 shows the interior of the Concert Hall in the city of Birmingham. The sloping board above the stage reflects sound out towards the audience. There is little echo delay, and the sound just appears louder. The walls and ceiling are made of a mixture of surfaces which reflect and absorb just the right amount of energy. The seats are made of materials which reflect and absorb sound in just the same proportions as a human body sitting in the seat would. Thus the acoustics are the same however large the audience.

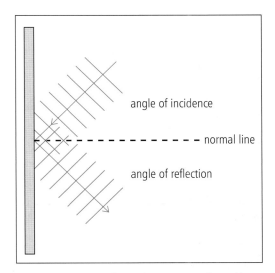

Picture 10   A set of straight waves is reflected by a straight barrier. The angles of incidence (as they hit the barrier) and reflection are the same.

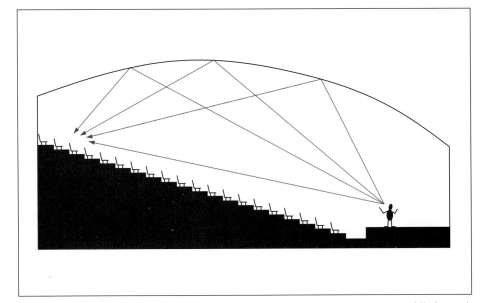

Picture 11   Sound reaches a seat in the hall via several routes. This can cause a muddled sound if there is a long delay between reflections.

Picture 12   Interior of Birmingham City Concert Hall.

IT'S ALL IN THE TIMING: RESONANCE

Things that can vibrate have a **natural frequency** of vibration. When you pluck a guitar string it vibrates to give what musicians call its **fundamental** note. When you push someone on a playground swing the swing oscillates to and fro at a rate which is decided by how long the swing is. The same thing happens in a **pendulum**, where a heavy object on a cord is set swinging.

To make a swing oscillate you have give it energy – you have to push it. To keep it swinging you push it at regular intervals – usually every time the person on the swing comes back within your reach. You are supplying energy at the same frequency as the natural frequency of the swing. In an old-fashioned grandfather clock the wound up spring or weight stores up energy when you wind it up or lift a weight. The stored energy is released by a timing system so that it gives a push to the pendulum at just the right time to keep it swinging. This matching of energy input to a natural frequency is called **resonance**.

Resonance is important in many musical instruments. When you pluck a guitar string the sound dies away as the energy of vibration in the string dies down. But a violin can keep a note going far longer. This is because it is bowed: the energy comes from the player pulling a set of horse hairs across the string. The vibration of the string at its natural frequency moves it against the bow and makes the horse hair pull it more or less strongly. The result is that energy gets into the string at the same rate as its own natural fundamental frequency. This is also resonance. Of course as violinists know things can get more complicated than this. Bowing the string in a slightly different place can make a string vibrate at other frequencies than its simple fundamental one. They can produce extra notes called harmonics.

Another resonance effect is caused by the body of a guitar or violin. The wooden body and its special shape is designed so that it can vibrate at any frequency the strings can produce. This means that it too resonates with the strings, so amplifying the sound.

Wind instruments also rely on resonance. A column of air can vibrate and does so most simply at its own natural frequency. Hold a vibrating tuning fork with the same frequency at the open end of a tube of air and you will hear the sound get louder. Energy from the vibrating fork is given to the air at just the right time and its vibrations build up in amplitude. It is just like pushing a playground swing at the right intervals. Wind instruments work like this. When someone blows across the open tube, or into a special mouthpiece, this produces a whole range of vibrations. One of them will be the same as the natural frequency of the air column – in a trombone, a flute or a clarinet, say. The air column picks up energy and vibrates strongly. And just like the horse hair bow and the violin, this vibration is fed back to the mouthpiece where a reed or a player's lips start vibrating at that frequency so that energy is delivered even more effectively at just the right frequency. This can produce a very loud sound indeed!

■ Bad vibrations

But resonance can be harmful. In an earthquake the earthquake waves may have a range of frequencies. Some of them may be the same as the natural frequency of vibration of a building. If this is so the building can pick up energy at just the right frequency to make it resonate so strongly that it falls apart.

The most famous example of resonance damage happened in Washington State, USA, in 1940. The bridge of the Tacoma Narrows was able to vibrate in time with regular gusts of wind formed by its own shape and the effect of nearby cliffs. As the wind got stronger more and more energy was given to the bridge at its own natural frequency until eventually it tore itself apart (see picture 15). More recently, the

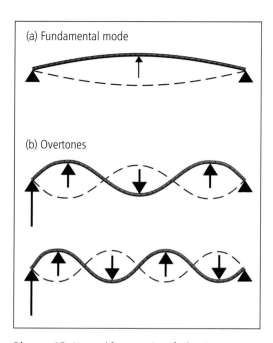

Picture 13 Natural frequencies of vibration.

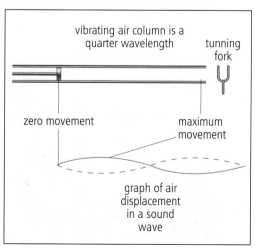

Picture 14 The frequency of the fork matches the natural frequency of the air column.

new Millennium Bridge across the River Thames in London had a natural frequency which closely matched the footsteps of people crossing it. As it started to swing people reacted by stepping even more in time with it. The energy delivered made it resonate. It wasn't enough to destroy the bridge but it had to be closed down for more engineering work.

Picture 15   The Tacoma Narrows bridge.

Picture 16   Walkers on the new Millennium Bridge found some unexpected thrills. It swayed because of resonance.

Questions

1 Explain the difference between frequency and period for a wave.

2 Give a brief outline of an experiment you could do to show:
   a   that sound waves can pass through each other,
   b   that water waves can pass through each other.

3 You should have learned that when light is reflected, 'the angle of incidence is equal to the angle of reflection'. Explain what this means. How could you test to see if sound waves obey the same rule?

4 Use the formula *wavelength = speed/ frequency*, and the data in table 1 in topic A2, to calculate the following:
   a   the wavelength of a 500 Hz note in air,
   b   the wavelength of a 1000 Hz note in air,
   c   the speed of a note of 500 Hz which is measured to have a wavelength of 0.5 metres in carbon dioxide.

5 The speed of radio waves is 300 000 000 m/s. What is the frequency of the UK Radio 4 programme which has a wavelength of 1500 metres?

Record and playback

Most of the music we hear has been recorded. Even when it is 'live', we often hear it through electrical devices of some kind.

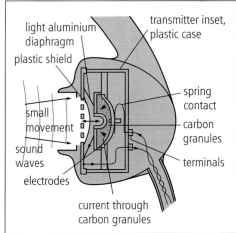

Picture 1 Carbon microphone.

Both microphones and loudspeakers are **transducers**, as explained in topic A1. Transducers change information from one energy system to another.

A microphone has the job of changing sound waves into a varying electrical current. The pattern of the changing current has to be a close copy of the pattern of the sound wave. The loudspeaker converts the changing current back into sound waves.

MICROPHONES

Picture 1(a) shows a typical microphone – the **carbon microphone**. It is still used in some older telephones, but modern ones use **electret microphones** (picture 2).

The key component in the carbon microphone is the capsule with the grains of carbon in it. When sound waves reach the microphone they make a flexible piece of steel (the **diaphragm**) vibrate. As the diaphragm vibrates the grains of carbon are squashed closer together and then moved further apart in time with the vibrations.

Carbon is a conductor of electricity. When you pick up the telephone handset a current is switched on. This current flows through the grains of carbon. When the grains are squashed closer together they conduct better. But when they move apart a little their resistance increases.

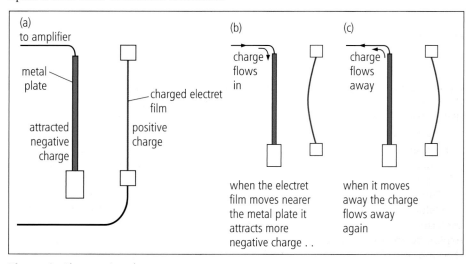

Picture 2 Electret microphone.

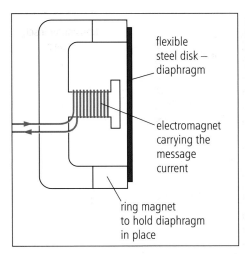

flexible
steel disk –
diaphragm

electromagnet
carrying the
message
current

ring magnet
to hold diaphragm
in place

Picture 3 Telephone earpiece. The current in the coil is a copy (analogue) of the sound. It powers an electromagnet which makes the diaphragm vibrate to reproduce the original sound.

The current through the carbon grains thus changes in the same pattern as the sound waves that affect the diaphragm. This current flows down the line to the handset of the person you are talking to. Picture 1(b) explains this.

Most ordinary cassette recorders use electret microphones (picture 2). They are also used in some telephones. The key item in this type of microphone is a very thin piece of plastic film, 12 to 25 micrometres thick. One side of the film is metallised and is connected to an electric terminal. This is usually one side of an amplifier input.

The film is made of a special plastic that is a very good insulator. The plastic is electrically charged at the factory, and is such a good insulator that it can keep its charge for 200 years.

When the sound waves reach the microphone the plastic film vibrates in tune with it. The charged film moves nearer to or further away from a metal plate which is connected to the opposite terminal of the amplifier. The charge on the film attracts opposite charge to this metal plate. When the film gets nearer it attracts more charge. When it moves away it attracts less charge.

This makes a current which is a copy of the sound wave, which flows into or away from the metal plate. This is amplified for recording or for sending down the telephone line. Picture 2 shows how an electret microphone works.

MOVING COIL DEVICES: LOUDSPEAKERS AND MICROPHONES

Pictures 3 and 4 show two kinds of loudspeaker. The simplest is the type used in the telephone **earpiece**. The key parts are the electromagnet and the thin steel disk (diaphragm). As the size of the electric current changes in the coil it changes the pulling strength of the electromagnet. The plate moves to follow the changes in strength of the electromagnet. As it does so it moves the air in front of it – to produce sound. This is, of course, a copy of the sound wave going into the microphone at the other end of the line.

The telephone earpiece is good enough for conversations but cannot reproduce musical sounds accurately. A better way of doing this is to use a **moving coil** loudspeaker (picture 4). This uses the motor effect, which is explained in topic E8. As in the telephone earpiece, the changing current flows through a coil. This time the coil is inside a strong, steady magnetic field, produced by permanent magnets.

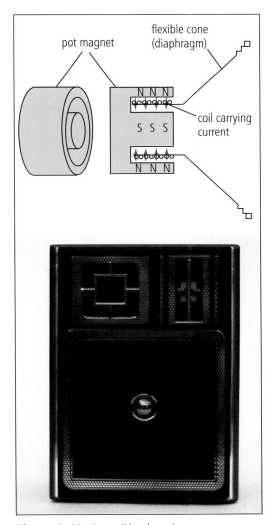

pot magnet

flexible cone
(diaphragm)

N N N

S S S

coil carrying
current

N N N

Picture 4 Moving coil loudspeaker.

As a result of the motor effect, the coil moves. Its movements are an exact copy of the changing current. The coil is connected to a large flexible diaphragm, usually made of special paper or card. This has a large area and as it moves it produces sound waves in the air. A large loudspeaker can move a lot of air, and so produce very loud sounds.

■ Moving coil microphone

In a moving coil loudspeaker a changing current in the coil reacts with a magnetic field to produce a force on the coil. The same set-up can be used to make a changing current when the coil is moved, by a sound wave, for example. This means that a movable coil placed in a magnetic field can act as a microphone. It changes a sound wave into a changing electric current that is a copy of the patterns in the sound wave. This is the principle of the **moving coil microphone**. These microphones are usually larger than the small electret microphones; they can handle louder sounds and produce better sound quality when well-made.

In a simple **intercom** system the same device can act as both loudspeaker and microphone. You will find intercoms connecting different offices in a building, at door entry ports, etc.

The basic physics of how magnetic fields and currents interact is dealt with in topic E8.

■ Headphones

These are made from two very small speakers and may be the moving coil type or may use an electret system (rather like the microphone, but in reverse). They don't need to produce sounds with a lot of energy, because they are so close to the eardrum. But they can produce enough energy to damage the ears. Doctors are worried that the use of 'personal stereos' is producing a generation of people who are all partly deaf. Headphones need to be used with great care. As a general rule, if other people can hear the music it is too loud for the wearer!

AMPLIFIERS AND ELECTRONICS

The earliest 'sound systems' relied on the energy in the sound waves alone to make the electric current and even to make recordings.

Better results are produced when extra energy is injected into the system. This is what **amplifiers** do.

An amplifier can make a weak current produced by a microphone much stronger for making recordings. This is also better for carrying messages down a long wire.

At the loudspeaker end of the system the current can be amplified still more to power large, powerful loudspeakers. Most playback systems produce a very small current from the 'record' (disc, cassette, compact disc). This needs to be greatly amplified to make the speakers work.

Picture 5 shows the main parts of a typical 'sound system'.

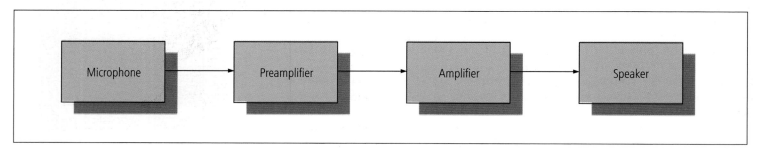

Picture 5 The main parts of a sound system.

Electric sounds

Electric instruments – like electric pianos, violins and guitars – simply do away with mechanical resonators. Instead, the small, low energy vibrating source (e.g. a guitar string) is used to produce a small electric current which is fed to speakers via an amplifier (see picture 6).

Electronic instruments (see picture 7) don't need a mechanical input. An electric current with the pattern of a sound wave is made **electronically**. The mechanical vibrations (or oscillations) that produce the sound in an 'acoustic' instrument are replaced by electronic circuits (oscillators, wave shapers, etc).

Acoustic is a word used to describe traditional instruments that produce sound using only mechanical means, like vibrating strings or air columns.

The vibrations in electronic instruments are made by circuits called **oscillators** which produce a voltage that can vary at any desired frequency. Other circuits combine the pure oscillations to make a copy of the complex waves that real instruments produce. These signals are then amplified and played through a loudspeaker.

When you press a key on the keyboard you are simply operating a switch system which makes the circuits start working.

Picture 6 An electric guitar.

Picture 7 An electronic keyboard.

STORING MUSIC

Music is stored in three main ways:

- mechanically – on 'compact' discs (CDs) or on vinyl records (LPs)
- magnetically – on magnetic tape,
- optically – on film sound tracks.

Mechanical systems record the music either in analogue or in digital form. In both, the *shape* of a material is altered. Vinyl records store the music as a long wavy groove that spirals around the disc. In a CD the information is stored in a long groove with 'holes' in it, as explained below.

The 'wave' in the groove of an LP is a copy of the sound wave of the original music (see picture 8). This is called an **analogue** of the original.

The master record is actually made on tape (see below), but it is copied onto the disc mechanically. A sharp pointed metal needle (a **stylus**) cuts the groove into soft plastic. This is then covered with a thin layer of metal to harden and preserve it. In this way a metal master is produced which is used to stamp out the discs.

The music is read off the disc by another stylus which moves through the groove as the disc turns under it on a record player. The stylus is very light. It moves up and down and from side to side as it follows the waves in the groove.

Picture 8 The 'groove' in a vinyl record.

Picture 9 A compact disc.

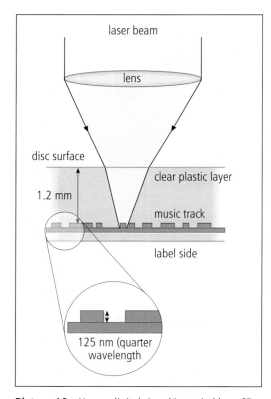

Picture 10 How a digital signal is carried by a CD.

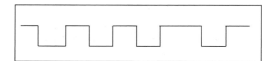

Picture 11 Ordinary numbers can be changed to binary numbers (digits) and then coded as on-off signals as shown here. When these numbers represent sound signals the pattern can be transferred to a series of holes and 'non-holes' on the surface of a compact disc.

The stylus is connected to a coil or a small magnet. The movement of these produces an electric current which is a copy of the original sound. This is then amplified and fed to the speakers.

The problem with vinyl discs is that the material has to be soft enough to be stamped, and so the grooves are easily damaged. Also, the groove has to be very long to get a reasonable amount of music stored in it, and this means that the disc has to be quite big. Thus it is easy for it to warp and distort the recording.

Digital recording is a great improvement. The information is converted to a set of numbers (digits), which are easy to store and quite hard to damage. They are binary numbers (see topics A1 and H2). The system relies on computer technology, which has always used binary numbers to store and control information.

Picture 7 in topic A1 shows how a sound wave can be converted to numbers which can be stored on a **compact** disc. It is called 'compact' because the information is stored in a small space. Two sides of an LP can be stored on one side of a much smaller compact disc.

The numbers are stored as a series of **pits** (small holes) in a strong plastic disc.

The pits are very small – about half a micrometre (millionth of a metre) wide and a fifth of a micrometre deep. They are laid in a thin spiral, beginning at the centre of the disc. The width of this spiral track is about one-thirtieth the thickness of a human hair. It is this small size that allows so much information to be stored on a small disc.

The pattern of holes forms a coded signal of '16-bit' binary numbers, each number standing for one feature of the sound wave. (A 16-bit number is a binary number between 0 and 65 536.) The diagram on page 5 (picture 7) shows how an analogue version of a sound wave can changed into a stream of numbers ('digitised') by sampling the amplitude of the wave at very short intervals. This is a job for a computer. The highest sound frequency that can be heard by a normal person is 20 000 Hz. The sound wave is sampled and changed into numbers 44 thousand times a second. In music the sound wave changes quite rapidly, and if it was sampled less often some of the quality would be lost.

The groove with the holes in it does the same job as the wavy groove in a vinyl disc. But the pattern on a CD is far too small to be made or read mechanically, using a stylus. Instead **lasers** are used.

Picture 11 shows numbers coded into pulses. The pattern can be interpreted as the volume (loudness) of a sound, say. As explained below, this pattern of pulses can be copied onto a surface to represent the stream of digits into which a sound has been encoded. In a CD the sound volume is sampled and converted into a very large number of levels – 2^{16} (65 536 levels).

The series of pits is burnt into the plastic disc using a powerful, concentrated beam of light from a laser. The track is then silvered to make it a good reflector. In use the track is 'read' by another, weaker laser.

Laser light is a very accurate beam of light. Light is reflected from the surface of the compact disc. The pit is exactly one-quarter of a wavelength deep so light getting into the pit travels a half wavelength further that light that doesn't. Light waves reflected from the pit and from the unmarked surface are out of phase and so combine to make a low signal – a digital zero. With no pit there is simply a strong signal – a digital 1 (see picture 10). Thus the reflected beam is switched on and off in the same digital pattern as the pits on the disc.

In the CD player the pattern is read by a low power laser and a small computer changes the digital stream back into an analogue pattern that can drive a loudspeaker.

The advantage of digital recording and playback is that it doesn't depend on the quality of the 'holes'. As long as the surface between the holes is smooth the numbers are the same and the result is exact.

Also, in a compact disc once the pattern is made the replay system doesn't touch it to wear it out.

Magnetic recording

Recording tape is a long piece of thin, strong plastic with a very thin layer of magnetic material on it. The magnetic material must be easy to magnetise – and demagnetise. The cheapest magnetic material is iron oxide (ferric tape), but you get better results from iron mixed with chrome or some other substance (ferrochrome and 'metal' tapes). The magnetising is done by a **recording head**, which is shown in picture 12. It is a very tiny electromagnet. The information to be recorded is sent as a changing electric current through its coil. This produces a small, varying magnetic field which magnetises the tape in the same pattern as the current in the coil.

The tape is read by the **playback head**, which is almost exactly the same as the recording head. As the tape moves under the head, it produces a changing magnetic field. This changing field is a copy of the current that made the recording.

This time, the changing magnetic field induces a current in the coil (see topic E8), which can be amplified to make a loudspeaker work.

The tape recorder also needs an **erase head**. This is similar in design to the other two heads, but the coil is fed with a very high frequency current that overwrites any signal already on the tape. The frequency of this signal is too high to be audible.

Tape recording can be either digital or analogue. The large record companies use digital recording on special, very wide tape. As explained above, the original sound is converted electronically to a series of numbers before being recorded on the tape. Thus the tape recording consists of a series of simple on/off magnetic 'bits', which are a coded form of the sound.

Noise

All sound systems, whether in transmission, recording or playback, suffer from **noise**. For example, a perfect sound at a single frequency can be sent down a wire as an analogue signal of varying electric current. The current is carried by moving electrons. But the electrons bump into each other, or are affected by metal ions. They do not swing to and fro to match the signal perfectly. This produces little spikes of current which are added to the signal and distort it. Amplifiers are not made perfectly, and can also add some distortion. Vinyl discs get scratched and can be very 'noisy'. A good record and playback system will be designed to reduce the effects of noise, by using very high quality components and/or by using special circuits (such as Dolby B, etc). The noise in a system is measured by the signal-to-noise ratio, expressed in decibels. Digital systems are much less affected by noise than analogue systems – so CDs give much cleaner sound reproduction than tape or vinyl.

SOUND AND ENERGY

Sound waves carry energy. This energy comes from the vibration of the object making the sound. The sound waves can make something vibrate – like the diaphragm in a microphone or the **ear drum** in your ear. A loud sound carries a lot of energy, which means that it can damage the ear drum by tearing it. Even a quiet sound carries enough energy if it is made close to the ear. Personal stereos inject sound energy directly into the ear and can in fact be quite dangerous to the ear drum as well as sensitive parts of the inner ear. They should be used with care.

Ultrasonic cleaning

We can use the energy in a sound wave to clean things, like clothing or instruments that need to be kept specially clean. The sound is at a very high frequency which is too high for us to hear. The sound is directed at a dirty object and its energy shakes up the small dirt particles. The dirt is shaken out but the rest of the object is unaffected. This method of cleaning is used for delicate fabrics or objects that might be damaged by chemical cleaning fluids.

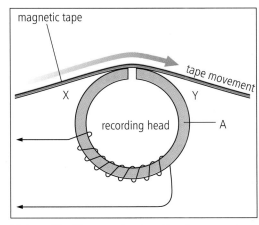

Picture 12 The recording head in a tape recorder.

Questions

1 The list below contains a number of different recording/playback devices. Sort them into two groups, headed *analogue* and *digital*:

human brain, cassette recorder, compact disc, LP record, sound film track, book, computer ROM chip, photograph, video cassette.

If you don't know, guess!

2 Give *two* reasons why compact discs are better than the older vinyl LPs. Are there any ways in which they are worse?

3 Describe what you would imagine to be the perfect 'sound system' – one that you might get for your birthday in the year 2010.

4 Explain the meaning of: analogue, digital, binary, bit, distort, transducer.

5 'There ought to be a law against playing music loudly.' Do you agree with this? Give arguments for and against this suggestion.

6 Explain either: (a) how a moving coil loudspeaker works or (b) how a carbon microphone works.

7 List *five* ways of storing information. For each way, state how that information is retrieved again.

8 'In a modern democracy, a supply of information is as important as a supply of energy.' Obviously, *energy* is vital for life. Is *information* really that important? Write a short essay (or a long one if it interests you!) giving your opinion and justifying it.

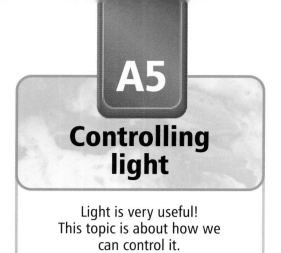

A5

Controlling light

Light is very useful!
This topic is about how we
can control it.

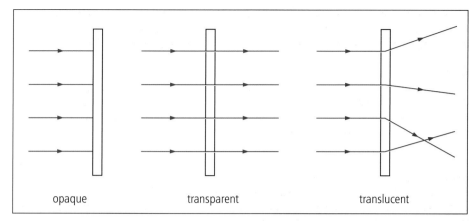

Picture 1 What happens to light in opaque, transparent and translucent materials.

opaque   transparent   translucent

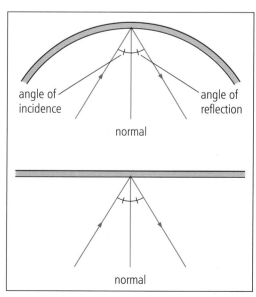

Picture 2 Diffuse reflection – light goes off in all directions.

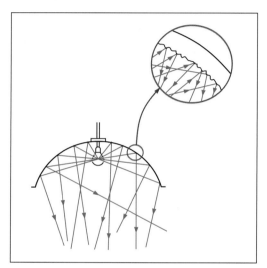

angle of incidence

angle of reflection

normal

normal

Picture 3 The law of reflection.

KEEPING LIGHT IN – OR OUT

There are some materials that light cannot pass through. They are **opaque**. We stop light getting into a camera by using a metal or plastic material that is opaque to light.

Curtains and blinds do the same thing. A material that lets light go through it is either **transparent** or **translucent** (see picture 1). A transparent material, like glass, air, water and some plastics, lets light through in straight lines. We can see things clearly through them.

A translucent material breaks up the light so that we don't get a picture of the object sending out the light. Finely scratched glass, or 'ground' glass, is like this. We use translucent materials in some light bulbs and bathroom windows.

White painted materials can reflect light so that more of it goes where we want it to, but without a glare. The insides of lampshades are sometimes painted white for this reason (see picture 2).

▩ Mirrors

Mirrors reflect light in a regular way (see picture 3 and compare it with picture 2). The light is reflected according to the rule:

the angle of incidence equals the angle of reflection.

In other words, the light rays make the same angle to the mirror going in as they do when they come away from it. We normally measure these angles between the light rays and a line at right angles to the mirror (called the **normal** line).

This means that flat (**plane**) mirrors reflect light to give a clear image. But it is a 'mirror image', in which left hands turn into right hands, and vice versa (picture 4).

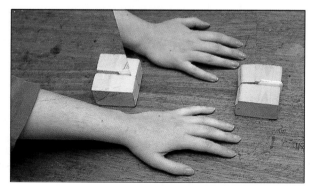

Picture 4 An image in a plane mirror. A left hand becomes a right hand.

We can work all this out using the idea that light travels in straight lines. Picture 5 shows how this idea explains why an object in front of a mirror produces an image that is as far behind the mirror as the object is in front of it.

CURVED MIRRORS

Curved mirrors produce interesting effects. They can magnify and make smaller, depending on which way they curve and how far away the object is (see picture 6). If the shiny (reflecting) side curves inward, it is a **concave** mirror. If the reflecting surface curves outwards, it is a **convex** mirror.

Concave mirrors are easy to find in everyday life. They are most often used just to straighten up beams of light, as shown in picture 7. Torches, searchlights and car headlights use mirrors in this way.

They work as they do because of the basic law of reflection, given above. The curved shape of the concave mirror changes the direction of the rays in such a way that parallel light rays coming towards the mirror are all reflected to pass through the same point. This is the **principal focus**. Light leaving the focus retraces the same path and leaves the mirror as a parallel beam. This is shown in picture 7, where the lamp filament is placed at the focus of the mirror.

You will often find convex mirrors in shops, or at the corner of the stairs in a double-decker bus. They are used to give the shopkeeper or bus conductor a **wider field of view**. This helps to stop theft or fare-dodging. This time the shape of the mirror allows light to be collected from a wide angle and reflected towards the observer (see picture 8).

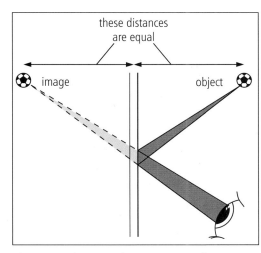

Picture 5 The image that appears in a flat mirror seems as far behind it as the object is in front.

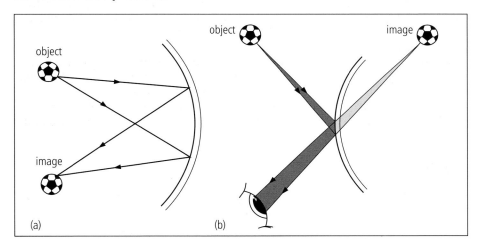

Picture 6 Curved mirrors and their effects on light.

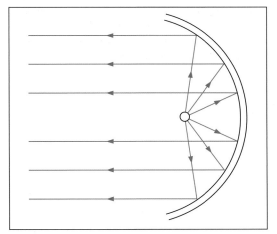

Picture 7 A curved mirror can make a parallel beam of light – as in a searchlight.

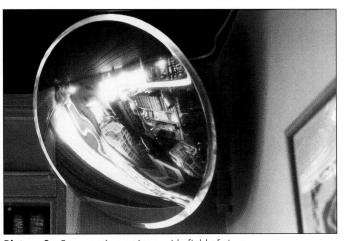

Picture 8 Convex mirrors give a wide field of view.

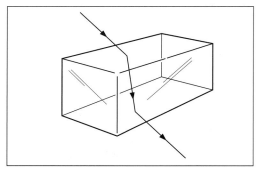

Picture 9 Refraction in a glass block.

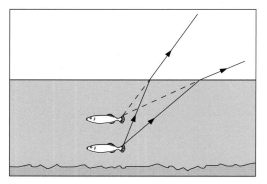

Picture 10 Why pools look shallower than they really are.

Picture 11 A straight stick looks bent in water. Why?

Picture 12 Light passing through a prism.

■ Using transparent materials

When light passes at an angle from one transparent material into another it changes direction. This is called **refraction**, and is caused by the fact that light travels at different speeds in the different materials. This effect is used in lenses and optical fibres. Topic A6 deals with how these components are used in different kinds of practical devices, like cameras, microscopes and binoculars.

REFRACTION

Picture 9 shows what happens to a ray of light as it goes from air into glass, and from glass back into air. As it goes into the denser material, it changes direction to make a bigger angle with the surface. The opposite happens on the way out.

Refraction can cause some optical illusions. For example, a pond or swimming pool always looks a lot shallower than it really is. Picture 10 shows why. The light from a pebble on the bottom is refracted, and the light *appears* to come from somewhere else, nearer the surface. This is why a straight stick looks bent when you put it in water (picture 11).

A **prism** is a block of glass or plastic with straight sides. It is usually triangular in shape. Light that enters the prism at right angles to a surface carries on unchanged. But if it goes in at an angle it changes direction due to refraction (picture 12).

But prisms are not used to change the direction of light by refraction. The reason is that white light would come out coloured. Prisms produce a spectrum of the light. How they do this is explained in topic A7.

TRAPPED LIGHT – TOTAL INTERNAL REFLECTION

Picture 13 shows light travelling out of water. See what happens as the angle the light makes with the surface is reduced.

At a certain angle the light doesn't get out at all. It is trapped inside, or **totally internally reflected**. The same thing can happen with glass.

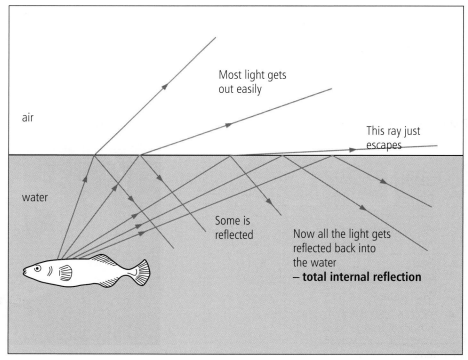

Picture 13 How total internal reflection happens.

This effect is used, in prisms, to make very good mirrors (see **binoculars**, topic A6). It is also used to send light down long thin fibres of glass – **optical fibres**. Picture 14 shows total internal reflection in action in a prism and a glass fibre. (See page 56 for more about fibre optics.)

FOCUSING AND MAKING IMAGES

One of the most useful applications of refraction is in **lenses**. Lenses are curved pieces of very clear glass. When a straight beam of light reaches them the outer part of the beam is bent inwards by refraction at both surfaces of the lens (picture 15).

This happens because the light reaches the glass surfaces at an angle. The further out from the centre of the lens the bigger the angle is. So the outer part of the beam is bent inwards more than the inner parts. The beam comes to a point (converges) before spreading out again. This effect is called **focusing**.

The lens in picture 15 is a **positive** or **converging** lens. A lens shaped 'the other way', as in picture 16, makes the light beam spread out (diverge). It is a **negative** or **diverging** lens.

The more curved the lens surfaces are, the more powerful is the lens. Picture 17 shows this.

Lenses are used to make images in various kinds of optical instruments. How they do this is described in the next topic.

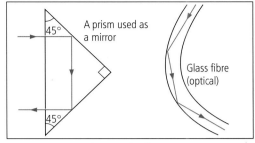

Picture 14   Total internal reflection in action.

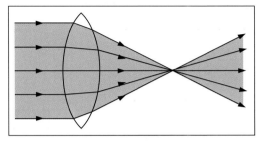

Picture 15   What a positive lens does to light.

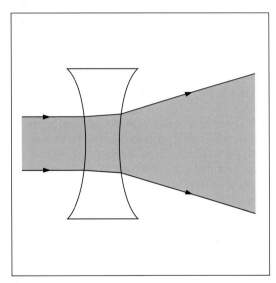

Picture 16   A negative lens makes the light spread out – or diverge.

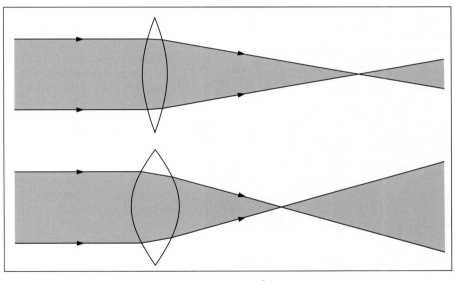

Picture 17   The more curved the lens the more powerful it is.

Questions

1 Describe and explain any application you know about that uses a concave mirror.

2 Describe and explain any application you know about that uses a convex mirror.

3 What is the *law of reflection*?

4 You can see all of yourself by standing in front of a large plane mirror. Explain, using diagrams, why the mirror doesn't have to be as tall as you are.

5 Draw diagrams to illustrate what is meant by:
  a reflection
  b refraction
  c focusing of light
  d total internal reflection.

6 Describe the difference between an object and its mirror image (as seen in a plane mirror).

7 What are the differences between *converging* lenses and *diverging* lenses?

8 Two converging lenses are made of the same type of glass. What is the main difference between the two lenses if one brings parallel rays of light to a focus closer than the other one does?

9 Some ceiling lamps have reflectors behind the bulb made of shiny mirror-like material, others are backed by a plain white reflector. Describe and explain the different effects these different backing reflectors have in the lighting of a room.

Using light

This topic explains how light is used and controlled in some everyday devices.

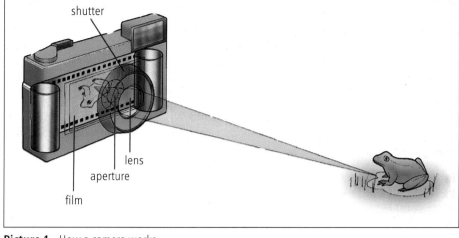

Picture 1 How a camera works.

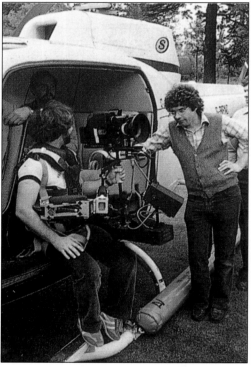

Picture 2 The screen of a TV camera senses light.

Cameras

Cameras use positive lenses to make a clear image on a light-sensitive screen. Picture 1 shows how this is done in a simple camera. A single lens of the kind that you might work with in school doesn't make clear enough pictures. In real cameras more complicated lenses have to be used.

In an ordinary camera the screen is a piece of thin plastic – the **film**. The light produces a chemical change in light-sensitive chemicals held by this film. Later, the film is **developed**, which means that another chemical is used to make the changed chemicals visible. They turn black (in a black-and-white film) or to a particular colour in a colour film.

In a **TV camera** the screen is made up of very small light-sensitive electronic devices (see picture 2). When light reaches these they produce an electronic signal. The camera is programmed so that each picture cell (pixel) is looked at in turn, or **scanned**. The signal from each pixel is sent down a cable one after the other to make a long coded message, which represents the picture on the screen. The screen is scanned completely 25 times a second. The coded signal is then recorded or broadcast directly.

Predicting the position and size of images

Optical instruments are amongst the most precise measuring devices that are used. Even in comparatively simple devices like cameras it is vital that the image is focused clearly on the film. This means that the designer must be able to predict

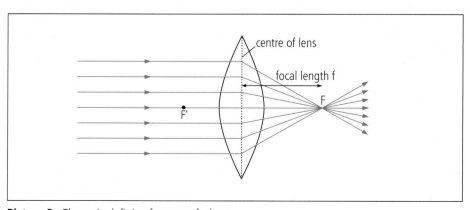

Picture 3 The main defining features of a lens.

as exactly as possible where the image of an object will appear for a range of distances of the object from the lens. For a simple lens this may be done by **ray-drawing** or by calculation using the **lens formula**.

Both methods rely on a knowledge of the **focal length** of the lens. Picture 3 shows a beam of parallel rays of light entering a lens. The beam is parallel to the main axis of the lens (its **principal axis**). The beam is brought to a focus at a point (shown as F). This point is called the **principal focus** of the lens. The distance of the principal focus from the centre of the lens is called the **focal length** of the lens. The focal length of a lens has the same value whichever direction the light enters the lens. Thus a lens has two principal foci, one on each side the lens (F and F´ in picture 3).

RAY DRAWING

Picture 4 shows an object labelled OT in front of a converging (positive) lens L. It is conventional to draw an object as an upright arrow. Light leaves the object in all directions, and some of it enters the lens. *We consider just the three rays whose behaviour we can predict by drawing.*

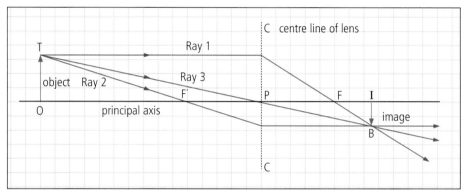

Picture 4   Finding an image by ray drawing.

Ray 1 leaves the top of the object T in a direction parallel to the principal axis, and as shown in picture 3 all such rays bend so that they pass through a principal focus. This ray must pass through F. The ray is drawn 'conventionally' – it is made to change direction at the centre of the lens, shown by the line CC. Light actually changes direction at each surface as shown on the diagrams on page 27.

Ray 2 is chosen to pass through the other principal focus of the lens – F'. At the lens it changes direction to emerge parallel to the principal axis. Why? If we imagine this ray travelling in the opposite direction we can see that it behaves exactly as Ray 1 does – it must bend to pass through F.

The point where Ray 1 and Ray 2 meet defines the arrowhead B of the image. All other rays that leave T and pass through the lens also arrive at B. If you imagine drawing similar pairs of rays from any point in the image between O and T you could build up the rest of the image between I and B. The lens maps the line OT onto the line IB.

Ray 3 is a confirming ray: the centre of a lens does not deflect light, so the ray passes straight through. It reaches B and is a useful check that you have drawn the first two rays correctly.

It is best to make the drawing to scale, using graph paper.

REAL AND VIRTUAL IMAGES AND RAYS

Picture 4 shows the formation of an image such as that produced in a camera. A sheet of film or a screen placed at I would show a real picture of the object.

Picture 9(b) (page 31) shows a ray drawing for an object that is placed closer to the lens than the principal focus. On leaving the lens the rays diverge and do not meet to form a **real image** of the object as they do in picture 4. But the eye is quite capable of bringing diverging rays together and we see a magnified image as shown. The rays only *appear* to come from this image, and it would not be possible to place a film at the image position and make a picture of it. The image is called a **virtual image**. Virtual means 'not really there'. The dotted lines used to construct the image in picture 9(b) are equally unreal, and are virtual rays.

IMAGE FINDING BY FORMULA

The distances of the principal focus, the object and the image for a lens are related by a formula:

$$\frac{1}{u} + \frac{1}{v} = \frac{1}{f}$$

where u is the object distance, v the image distance and f the focal length as defined in picture 5.

For example, when an object is placed 15 cm from a lens of focal length 5 cm the image will be found at a distance v such that

$$\frac{1}{15} + \frac{1}{v} = -\frac{1}{5}$$

This equation can be solved to give $v = 7.5$ cm. This is the result obtained by the scale drawing in picture 4.

When the object is placed closer to the lens than the principal focus the formula produces a negative value for v. This shows that the image is virtual.

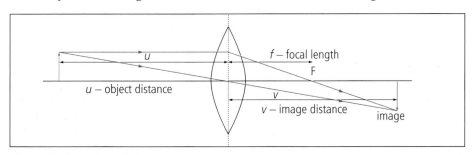

Picture 5 Formula symbols.

DIVERGING (NEGATIVE) LENSES

The rules for finding an image by drawing apply equally well to diverging lenses. The result is usually to produce a virtual image. The rays do not pass through the principal focus but appear to diverge from it. The principal focus – and the focal length – is *virtual*. Picture 6 shows an example.

When you use the formula you have to remember that the principal focus is virtual – the formula works if you assign a *negative* number to the focal length. Suppose we place an object 15 cm from a diverging lens of focal length 5 cm. The formula tells us, using the correct sign:

$$\frac{1}{15} + \frac{1}{v} = -\frac{1}{5}$$

This works out to give $v = -3.75$. The image is a *virtual* image 3.75 cm from the lens.

CURVED MIRRORS

Both the drawing and calculation methods can be used for curved mirrors as well as lenses. Picture 7 shows the rays that are drawn, with parallel rays reflecting back through the principal focus, and rays directed at the centre of the mirror being reflected such that the angle of incidence equals the angle of reflection. It is handy to know that a mirror curved to form part of a sphere of radius r has a focal length $f = r/2$.

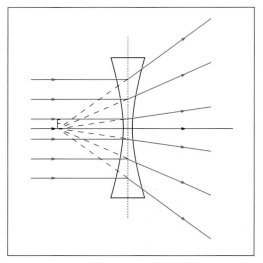

Picture 6 A diverging lens has a virtual principal focus F.

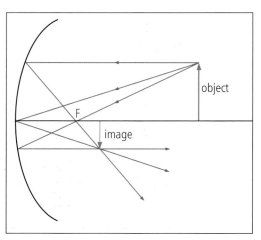

Picture 7 How a concave mirror forms an image.

The formula for lenses can be used for mirror calculations; it stays unchanged. A concave mirror focuses light to a point and is a converging device – like a converging (positive, convex) lens. A convex mirror behaves like the diverging lens. Thus a concave mirror has a positive focal length; a diverging convex mirror has to be assigned a negative value of focal length (see picture 8).

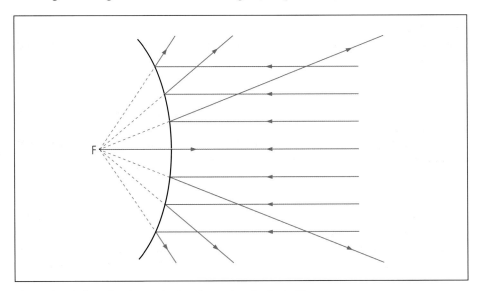

Picure 8   A diverging (convex) mirror has a virtual principal focus.

■ Seeing things bigger

When you look through a positive lens at an object some distance away it looks smaller, and the image is upside down. If you bring the lens closer and closer to the object you will reach a position where it makes an enlarged image of the object. This image is the right way up. The lens is now acting as a **magnifying glass**. Pictures 9(a) and 9(b) show what the light is doing to produce these two different kinds of image.

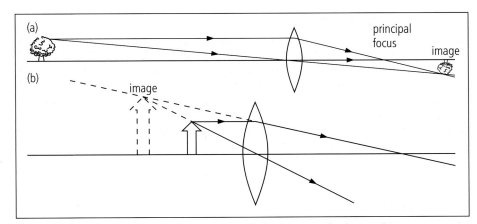

Picture 9   (a) A positive lens makes a small, upside down image of a distant object.
(b) The same lens can make a magnified, upright image of a close object. It acts as a magnifying glass.

Two positive lenses can be used to make a simple **microscope**. The first lens, placed near the object being looked at, is very powerful. It is called the **objective** lens, and it makes an upside down image of the object. This image is then viewed through another lens – the **eyepiece** lens. The eyepiece lens acts as a magnifying glass to make this first image look even bigger. Picture 10 shows what happens.

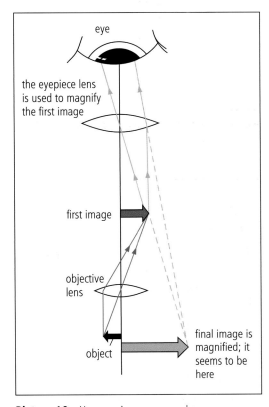

Picture 10   How a microscope works.

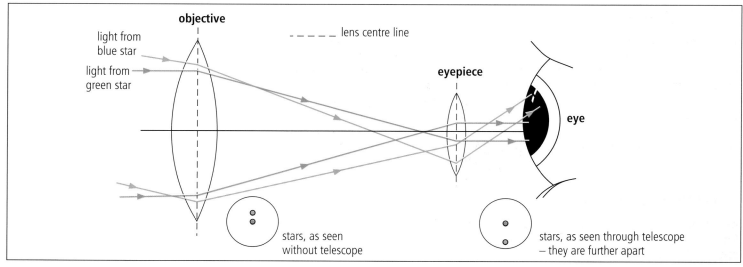

Picture 11 What a simple telescope does to light. The lenses have been drawn much thicker than they really are on this scale, so the light is drawn changing direction at their centre lines.

■ Seeing further – telescopes and binoculars

A simple **telescope** works much like a microscope, but the eyepiece is now the more powerful lens. The first, weaker lens again makes an upside down image. The eyepiece lens is more powerful. Again, you use it as a magnifying glass to look at the image made by the first lens (the objective lens). Picture 11 shows how this is done.

The first lens makes an upside down image. The second one (the **eyepiece**) works just like a magnifying glass, and so the image stays upside down. This kind of telescope is used by astronomers to look at stars and planets. They don't seem to mind that they see the universe upside down. In most astronomy books the pictures of the moon are actually printed upside down, so that they don't get confused.

Sailors don't like seeing distant ships and landfalls upside down. They may prefer to use **binoculars**. A pair of binoculars is simply two telescopes fixed side-by-side, one for each eye. They are shorter than astronomical telescopes. They also make an image which is the right way up. Both of these effects are produced by using **prisms**.

Picture 12 shows a pair of binoculars. The two prisms make the light go up and down the tube three times. This means that the binoculars need only be one-third the length of a telescope. At the same time the mirror faces of the prism swap the light rays around so that the final image is the right way up.

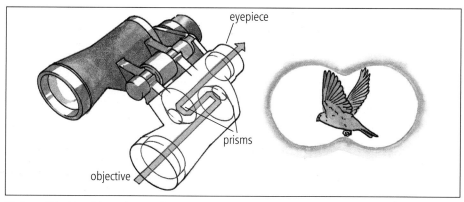

Picture 12 How binoculars work.

Seeing inside

Thin glass fibres can be used to carry a beam of light so that the light cannot escape. This is due to **total internal reflection** (see topic A5). A bundle of very thin fibres is used in medical research and in hospitals to look deep inside the human body. Picture 13 shows how the fibres are arranged.

One set of fibres carry light down into the body. The others carry reflected light back – the image of the part of the body that is illuminated.

This useful device is called an **endoscope**. They can be made small enough to slip down a vein and bring pictures back from inside a living heart or other organ. Picture 14 shows the inside of the human gut.

Communications

As explained in topic A1, thin glass fibres carrying 'light' signals are much better for carrying information than almost any other medium. There is more about optical fibres on page 56.

Picture 13 Fibres in an endoscope.

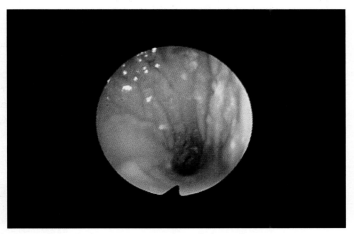

Picture 14 The human gut seen through the endoscope.

Questions

1. Copy the following diagrams (picture 15) and complete them to show what happens to the rays or beam of light, for:
   a a strong lens, b a weak lens,
   c a glass block, d a curved mirror.

2. A positive lens can be used to start a fire.
   a Explain how it can do this.
   b Why is it dangerous to leave empty glass bottles in a wood?

3. 'When you look into a river or lake and see a fish, it isn't where you think it is.' Draw a diagram to justify this statement (with you standing on the river bank and rays of light coming to you from a fish in the water).

4. What is the difference between a *transparent* material and a *translucent* material?

5. Why are 'fat' lenses more powerful than 'thin' ones?

6. Compare the human eye with a simple camera. In what ways are they similar, and in what ways are they different?

7. a Explain what is meant by total internal reflection.
   b Give three uses for total internal reflection.
   c Describe how one of the uses you have named works.

8. a Draw a ray diagram to find the position of an image for an object placed 25 cm from a converging (positive lens) of focal length 15 cm.
   b Check your result by using the lens formula.

   c Use your drawing to check that the lens has magnified the object in the ratio v/u

9. Repeat Q8 for the case where the object is placed 10 cm from the lens.

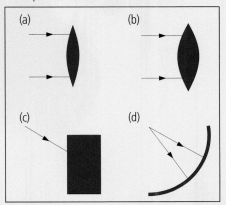

Picture 15

What is light?

We take light, and the fact that we can see it, for granted. But light has strange properties …

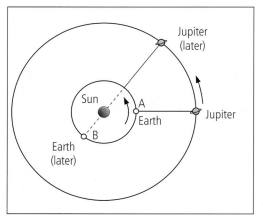

Picture 1 How Römer measured the speed of light.

Light is just the visible part of a whole family of 'radiations' that we call the **electromagnetic spectrum**. These radiations all travel through space at the same speed, 300 million metres per second (3×10^8 m/s).

THE SPEED OF LIGHT

This was first measured by a tidy-minded Danish astronomer, Olaf Römer, as long ago as 1676. He noticed that the moons of Jupiter were sometimes a few minutes late in disappearing behind the planet. The moons of Jupiter orbit at a very constant rate, and it was easy to calculate when this disappearance should take place. Römer explained why the moons were late by saying that light took time to travel.

This might be obvious to us, but at that time many scientists believed that light took no time at all to go from one place to another. But Römer said that this was not so: light had a definite speed. He said that light took longer to get to the Earth from Jupiter when the two planets were further apart.

As picture 1 shows, at its furthest point from Earth the light from Jupiter has to cross an extra distance equal to the diameter of the Earth's orbit. He measured the time difference this extra distance caused. The size of the Earth's orbit around the Sun was known fairly accurately in 1676, and so Römer was able to calculate a value for the speed of light.

His measurements of the times were not very accurate, however. His measurements gave the speed of light as only two-thirds of the modern value. But it was a start. The speed of light is now very accurately measured, and is so reliable that we use it to measure distance. Accurate surveying is done by measuring the time it takes for laser beams to travel a particular distance. The times are then converted to distances:

distance = light speed × time of travel.

Picture 2 Modern laser surveying instrument in use.

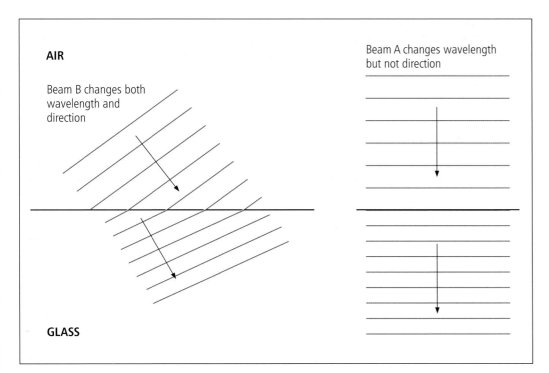

Picture 3 What happens when light moves into a different medium.

All electromagnetic waves travel at the same speed in a vacuum. Short radio waves are used in **radar** systems to measure the distances of aircraft in air traffic control.

Radar has been used to measure the distances of planets from Earth. This has given us an accurate measurement of the scale of the Solar System. The distance of the Earth from the Sun is the baseline used to measure the distances of stars (see topic G6). The distances of stars and galaxies are so great that we measure them in **light years** – the distance travelled by light in a year.

■ Changing the speed of light

When light leaves a vacuum and enters a transparent medium, like glass, it slows down. The most important effect produced by this change of speed is something that you have already studied: **refraction** (see topic A5). Picture 3 shows what happens as a set of waves reaches a glass surface, travelling from air. When the wave hits the surface at right angles (beam A) the wavelength changes, but there is no change in direction. Beam B reaches the surface at an angle, and as the leading edge slows down the rest of the wave catches up with it. The result is the change of direction called refraction.

The wave formula (see page 12) shows that as the speed is reduced the wavelength must get shorter. The frequency f of the light stays the same. The symbol for light speed is usually c.

Speed in air $c_a = f\lambda_a$, where λ_a is the wavelength of the light in air. In glass the speed reduces to c_g and a smaller wavelength λ_g is needed to match:

$$c_g = f\lambda_g$$

Thus the ratio of wavelengths equals the ratio of speeds:

$$\frac{\lambda_a}{\lambda_g} = \frac{c_a}{c_g}$$

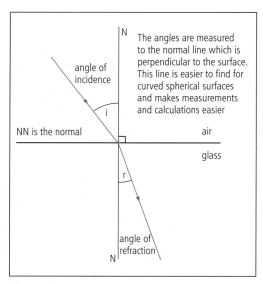

N

angle of incidence

The angles are measured to the normal line which is perpendicular to the surface. This line is easier to find for curved spherical surfaces and makes measurements and calculations easier

NN is the normal

air

glass

i

r

angle of refraction

N

Picture 4

Table 1   Refractive indices.

Material	Refractive index
air	1.0003
crown glass	1.52
flint glass	1.65
diamond	2.42
sugar	1.56
water	1.33
paraffin	1.44

REFRACTIVE INDEX

It was discovered in the 17th century that when light is refracted there is a relationship between the angles of incidence (*i*) and refraction (*r*) as defined in picture 4. The relationship is known as Snell's Law:

$$\frac{\sin i}{\sin r} = \mu$$

μ is a constant for any pair of media (e.g. air-glass) and is called the **refractive index**. We now know that μ is the ratio of the two speeds involved:

$$\mu = \frac{\text{speed in vacuum}}{\text{speed in medium}}$$

Table 1 gives some values for the refractive index between a vacuum and some transparent materials. For most purposes the speed of light in air is taken to be the same as the speed of light in a vacuum.

WHY A PRISM MAKES A SPECTRUM

In a vacuum all frequencies of light travel at the same speed. But in a medium like glass high frequency light (which we see as blue) travels more slowly than lower frequency light (such as yellow and red). Thus blue light has a higher refractive index than red light, and is bent through a greater angle. A beam of white light is thus spread out by refraction so that we can see the different colours as a **spectrum**. There is more about colour in topic A10. In the table above the refractive index is for yellow light.

MAKING LIGHT

Light usually comes from very hot objects – flames, the Sun, hot filaments. But it can also come from insects (fireflies, glow worms), from the fluorescent paint in TV tubes and some lamps, and from the glowing gases in advertising lights ('neon lights'). But all these sources produce light in the same basic way – by giving energy to atoms to make them unstable.

Picture 5 reminds you what an atom is like – a positive nucleus with some electrons around it. If an atom is given the right amount of energy, the outermost electron jumps up to a slightly higher energy level. It stays there for a while and then falls back to its normal level. When it falls back it gives back the extra energy as light.

The atoms of different elements have their electrons in different levels. Thus the light they give out is different in colour. This means we can tell what kind of element it is from its spectrum (see *Signals from Space*, page 50).

THE ELECTROMAGNETIC SPECTRUM

Picture 6 shows the main parts of the electromagnetic spectrum. It summarises how the radiations are made and how they are detected. In one way or another, all ways of making the radiations involve the movement of charged particles.

Radio waves are made by making electrons move rapidly up and down a wire – called the **aerial**. In other words, the aerial has an alternating current in it. The frequency of this alternating current is the same as the frequency of the broadcast. For a VHF (very high frequency) radio broadcast it is about 90 MHz (90 million waves a second).

The **microwaves** in a microwave oven are made by electrons which move round and round in a small metal box with no air in it (a magnetron). The device was first used in **radar** in World War II, to detect aircraft at a distance.

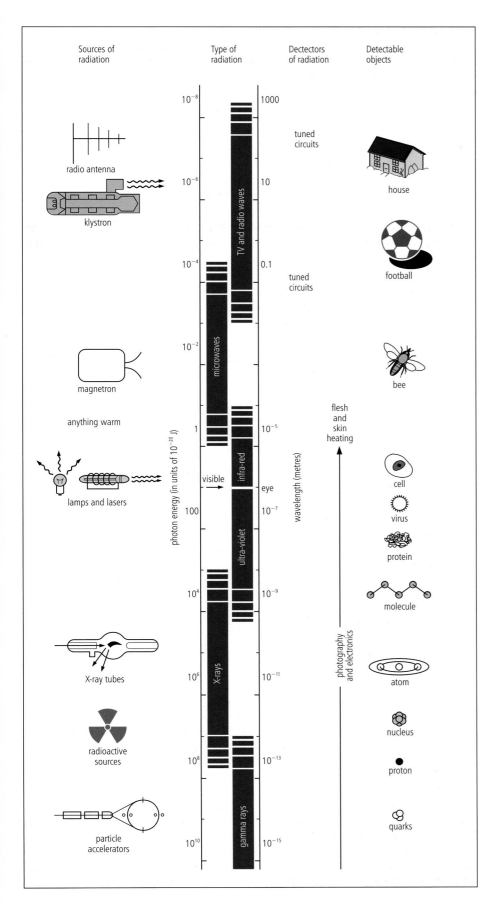

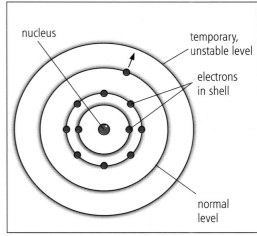

Picture 5 A simple model of the atom.

Picture 6 The main parts of the electromagnetic spectrum.

Infra-red is produced by making whole atoms vibrate inside the molecules. This happens when materials are heated, so we associate infra-red with hot objects.

The visible is a very small part of the whole spectrum. To our eyes the infra red and the ultra violet are invisible, although some animals can see them. Infra red radiation can be sensed as it heats up the skin, and we have temperature sensors for this. Ultra violet (UV) can be detected – but only painfully. It carries more energy than visible light and can damage living cells. Looking directly at the Sun is dangerous because the UV damages retinal cells. It can also damage skin cells, causing blistering and even skin cancers. But low intensity UV can help cure some skin diseases, and it helps to stimulate the production of vitamin D, which is hard to find in food. Fluorescent lamps use UV light emitted from mercury vapour. The UV is absorbed by chemicals coated on the inside of the tube and their energy is emitted in the visible region of the spectrum as white light.

As we go along the spectrum towards the **gamma ray** end, the radiations are more and more dangerous to life. This is because of the large packets of energy they carry (see page 44). The changes in the atom that produce the radiations are due to electrons involved in large energy changes, or change inside the nucleus itself (see topic F2).

■ Electromagnetic waves

Electromagnetic radiations travel as **waves**. They are called electromagnetic because when electric charges move (i.e., there is an electric **current**) they always produce a magnetic field. This is covered in topic E8. An electron is a charged particle. Thus it has an electric field surrounding it.

When electrons move to and fro or go around in circles they produce changing electric and magnetic fields. This is what the **electromagnetic radiations** are – a set of constantly changing, combined electric and magnetic fields that travel through space at 300 million metres a second. This is shown in picture 7.

This also means that they don't need anything to 'carry' them. 'Normal' waves, like water waves or sound waves, need a **medium**. Water waves need water! Sound needs air, or a liquid or solid. Sound cannot travel through a vacuum because there is nothing there 'to be waved'.

Electromagnetic waves carry their own 'waviness' with them, so they can travel through the vacuum of empty space.

The range of electromagnetic waves is shown in picture 6.

■ The discovery of radio waves

The electromagnetic theory of light was first put forward by a great Scots physicist, James Clerk Maxwell, in 1873. It was a good theory because it not only explained what scientists knew about light, it also made **predictions**.

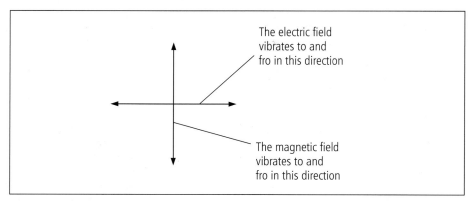

The electric field vibrates to and fro in this direction

The magnetic field vibrates to and fro in this direction

Picture 7 An electromagnetic wave has two moving fields.

Maxwell predicted that there ought to be other radiations which travelled through space at the same speed as light. These waves were not discovered until 15 years later, in 1888. They were discovered by the German scientist Heinrich Hertz, who detected what we now call radio waves. Although they had been predicted, they were discovered by accident! Radio waves can be made by electric sparks. You may have noticed this when you play a radio close to a car engine.

Hertz was working with a machine used for making static electricity. He noticed that whenever the static machine made a spark, so did a small coil of wire on the other side of the room. Energy was travelling from one side of the room to the other as radio waves. We name the unit of frequency the hertz after Heinrich Hertz.

The whole of the radio and television industry is based on these discoveries. The first radio transmitters were 'spark transmitters' and they were in use, in ships at sea, by 1902 (see picture 8). Also see topic A11 *Messages through space*.

The next topic deals with the evidence for the wave nature of light. Topic A9 then tells about some astonishing discoveries that showed, once again, that the world of physics was not as simple as it seemed.

Picture 8   One of the earliest 'Marconi transmitters' used by the Royal Navy

Activities

A   The uses of electromagnetic waves

The chart of the electromagnetic spectrum (picture 6) shows the main uses of the different parts of the electromagnetic spectrum. Use reference books or the Internet to find other uses for any section of the spectrum that interests you.

Questions

1   The famous scientist Galileo tried to measure the speed of light using two people with lanterns, standing about a mile apart from each other. One person was supposed to send a light signal back when he saw the light sent to him by the first person. Galileo tried to measure the time this took. The experiment was a complete failure. Suggest one or two reasons why it failed.

2   Design an experiment to show that infra-red (heating) rays travel at the same speed as visible light.

3   Which parts of the electromagnetic spectrum:
   a   can be used for heating?
   b   cause skin tanning?
   c   can pass through flesh but are partly stopped by bones?
   d   can cause cancer?
   e   are stopped by the ozone layer in the atmosphere?
   f   are used to find the positions of distant aircraft?

4   The speed of light is 300 000 000 metres per second (3×10^8 m/s). Use the wave formula **speed = frequency × wavelength** to calculate the following:
   a   the wavelength of MW radio waves that are broadcast at 1500 kHz.
   b   the frequency of BBC Radio 2 which is broadcast on a 'long wave' of 1500 metres.
   c   the wavelength of the waves in a microwave oven which works on a frequency of 2 450 000 000 Hz (2.45×10^9 Hz).

5   The speed of light in a vacuum is 3×10^8 metres per second. Use the data in table 1 above to find the speed of light in (a) crown glass (b) diamond (c) water.

6   A ray of pure yellow light reaches the surface of a pond at an angle of incidence of 60°. What angle does it make with the normal inside the water?

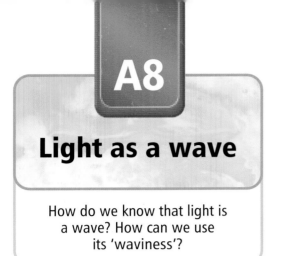

A8

Light as a wave

How do we know that light is
a wave? How can we use
its 'waviness'?

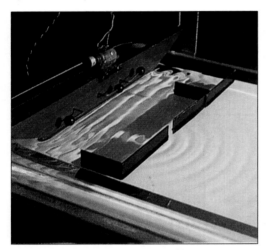

Picture 1 Waves spread out when they go through
a gap…

■ Waves

Topic A3 deals with some of the main properties of waves. Water waves and waves on ropes and springs are easy to see. We can show sound waves on an oscilloscope, and investigate how the **frequency** and **amplitude** of the waves change when we alter pitch and loudness.

Light waves are harder to investigate. Their wavelength is so small. But all waves behave in much the same way, in that they can show **diffraction** and **interference** effects. We use these effects to investigate light. They are explained below.

■ Diffraction

Picture 1 shows water waves moving through a gap in a barrier. When they reach the gap the waves spread out. This effect is called **diffraction**. Picture 2 shows what would happen if particles, like bullets, were fired at a barrier with a gap in it. The bullets that go through the gap carry on in a straight line.

When light is shone through a narrow gap it actually spreads out. This is shown in picture 3. This means that light is behaving like a wave, and not like a particle. If light travelled in straight lines, like a stream of particles, it would make a sharp shadow as shown in picture 2.

But as picture 3 also shows, light makes a more complicated pattern than you might expect. There are zones of light and dark outside the main spread of light. This effect is due to another property of waves – **interference**. This picture was made by shining light through a narrow slit.

■ Interference

Picture 4 shows what happens when waves meet. Two pulses travelling in opposite directions on a rope can pass through each other. When they meet the waves just 'add up'. Two 'up' parts of a wave (the crests) add up to make a larger crest. Two 'down' parts (the troughs) add up to make an even bigger trough. This is what you would expect.

But it might be surprising to see that when a crest meets a trough the result is a 'zero'. It is even more surprising that this also happens with light. Two light waves can meet – and the result is darkness! But this is what has happened in picture 6. The dark places are where two sets of light waves have met and cancelled each other out.

We say that when two waves meet they **interfere**. They can add up to make a bigger wave – or cancel each other out (picture 4).

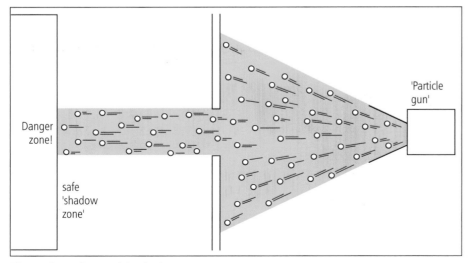

Picture 2 … but particles don't.

Picture 3 Light spreads out – like a wave.

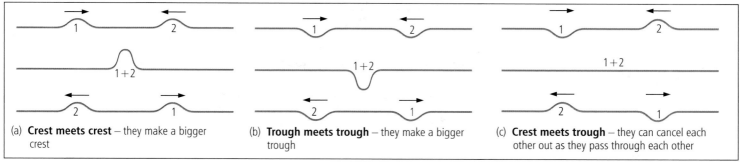

(a) **Crest meets crest** – they make a bigger crest

(b) **Trough meets trough** – they make a bigger trough

(c) **Crest meets trough** – they can cancel each other out as they pass through each other

Picture 4   What happens when waves meet.

The two-slit experiment

This experiment was first done by a doctor, Thomas Young, in the early part of the 19th century. It was the first clear proof that light travelled as a wave. At that time scientists believed that light was made of particles, like tiny bullets. They believed this so strongly that Young's work was accused of being 'absurd and illogical'. It was completely ignored for twenty years.

Picture 5 shows how you could set it up to do it yourself. When you look through the two narrow slits on the painted glass slide you will see an **interference pattern** like the one shown in picture 6. Picture 7 shows how the waves from the two slits combine. At some places they meet so that crests always meet with crests. The following troughs always meet with troughs. The result is a light patch.

At other places, the crest of wave from one slit always meets with a trough from the other slit. The result is darkness. The activities at the end of the topic are about investigating these effects with light and radio waves.

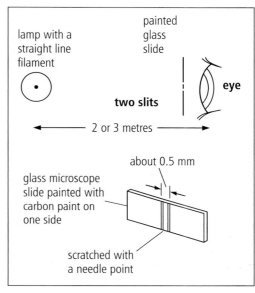

Picture 5   How to see 'Young's fringes'.

Picture 6   This is what we see in Young's two-slit experiment.

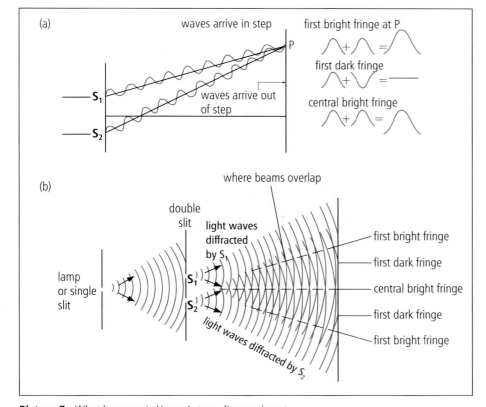

Picture 7   What happens in Young's two-slit experiment.

■ Polarised light

Light is a **transverse** wave, which means that it vibrates at right angles to the direction in which it travels (see page 13). Normally, a ray of light is a mixture of waves, all vibrating at different angles to each other, as shown in picture 8. A filter made from a special substance called **polaroid** only lets through the waves which vibrate in one direction. The light that comes through is said to be **polarised**.

If you hold another piece of polaroid film in the path of the polarised light it will let it through – but only if the film is aligned the right way. If you turn it through 90 degrees it cuts out all the light. This effect is shown in picture 9.

Polaroid **sunglasses** work because light reflected from shiny surfaces, like water or glass, is partly polarised. The glasses are made of polaroid film. They cut out the polarised light. Thus they cut down 'glare' from shiny surfaces – which in summer is usually strong reflected sunlight (picture 9).

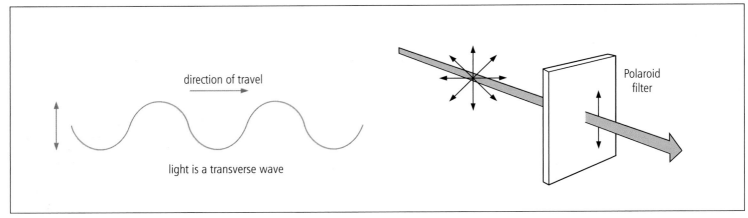

direction of travel

light is a transverse wave

Polaroid filter

Picture 8   Light can be polarised because it is a transverse wave.

Picture 9   Polaroid filters can cut out glare. When they are 'crossed' they cut out all the light.

Activities

A Looking through holes

These are experiments about the wave nature of light that you can do at home.

You will need a distant street lamp, or at least a bright torch placed about 50 metres away. You can also do this in the laboratory, by looking at a small hole lit by a bright lamp.

1 Face the spot of light and look at it through the gap between two fingers (e.g. the first and second fingers of one hand). Gradually bring the fingers closer together to make an ever narrowing slit. Just before the light from the lamp disappears you should see it broaden out. This is **diffraction**.

2 Get a piece of kitchen foil about 10 cm long by 5 cm wide. The exact size doesn't matter. With a sharp pin or needle, make a small hole in the foil. When you look through the pinhole at the light source you will also see **diffraction**, but this time there should be a more definite pattern to it. This is really worth seeing.

   The difficult bit about this experiment is finding the small pinhole in the dark. Mark it before you go out by putting a small piece of sticky paper next to it. You could go on to try the effect of making pinholes of different diameters.

3 Now make two pinholes in the foil, about a millimetre or so apart. You should be able to see through both holes together. When you look through the pair of holes at the light source you will see not only the spreading out effect (diffraction) but also an interference pattern. This is caused by light from the two separate holes combining ('interfering') with each other.

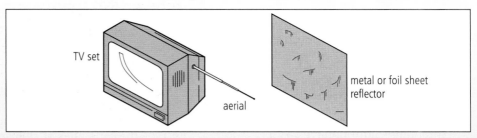

Picture 10

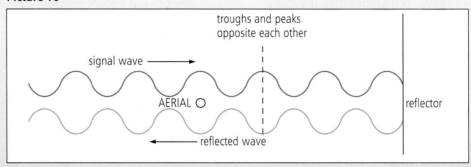

Picture 11

B Radio waves

The wavelength of light is very small. This is why we don't notice the waviness of light very often. VHF radio and UHF TV have much longer waves – about 3 metres long for radio and about half of that for TV. You can show interference between radio waves using a sheet of metal and a small radio with a telescopic aerial. The metal sheet could be a length of kitchen foil pinned to some cardboard. It needs to be about a metre square for the radio experiment; about half that will do for the TV.

1 Tune the radio to a 'weak' VHF station, or make it just off-tune for a strong one. The aerial should be horizontal, as shown in picture 10. You can tell it is weak or mistuned by the fact that the sound gets distorted now and again, especially when the speech or music is loud.

2 Hold the sheet of metal upright about 2 metres from the aerial. Walk towards or away from the aerial, moving the metal sheet closer or further from it. As you do this, you will find places where the signal is made stronger, and places where it is made weaker.

For this experiment to work, the radio or TV will have to be in line between you and the station broadcasting the signal. If you don't know where the station is you will have to find the best place by trial and error.

Picture 11 shows what is happening. The reflected wave is sometimes reinforcing the direct wave. In other positions the reflected wave cancels out the direct wave, making reception worse. The distance between successive 'cancel points' or 'reinforcement points' is half the wavelength of the radio broadcast.

Questions

1 a Explain the difference between *diffraction* and *interference*.

    b Why don't we usually notice these effects with light in everyday life?

2 Design an experiment to show (a) diffraction (b) interference using sound waves.

3 Name – or describe very briefly – two scientific discoveries which were ignored or said to be wrong when they were first made.

4 Describe an experiment you have seen or done to show that (a) water waves spread out (diffract) when they pass through a narrow opening (b) when water waves from two sources pass through each other, the 'up' part of one wave can be cancelled by the 'down' part of the other wave.

5 Explain what *polarised* light is. Why do 'polaroid' sunglasses cut down glare on bright sunny days?

6 What evidence is there that light is a wave? Describe some experiments and show how they support this idea.

7 You are given a box which gives out some mysterious, unknown 'rays' when you press a switch on it. The rays make a certain kind of paint glow. How could you test if these rays were waves? (They might be particles.)

Light as a particle

Sometimes light behaves as a wave, but sometimes it's more like a particle.

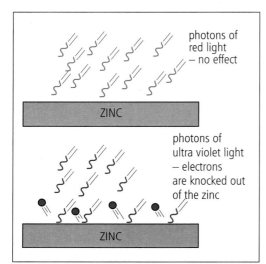

Picture 1 Light arrives in packets of different energies.

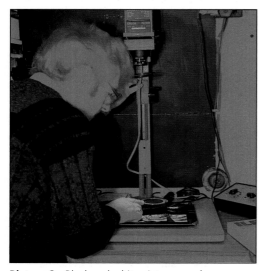

Picture 2 Black and white pictures can be developed in red light but not in blue light. Why?

■ A beautiful theory spoiled by an awkward fact

Maxwell's theory (page 38) joined together light, electricity and magnetism. It explained why elecromagnetic radiations travel through space as waves, with a speed of 300 million metres a second. As a scientific theory it was one of the great successes of 19th century science.

It was also of immense practical importance. It dealt not only with light, but with new discoveries like radio and X-rays. But we now know that it doesn't tell us everything about electromagnetic waves.

In 1905 the certainties of 19th century physics were shattered. Albert Einstein came up with some surprising additions to the theory of light. One was his **theory of relativity** (see topic B9). The other was the idea that light might *travel as a wave*, but when it met matter it seemed to behave like a particle!

PARTICLES OF LIGHT?

Isaac Newton believed that light was made up of particles of different colours – but he was wrong. As time went on, his theory didn't match the evidence. Experiments carried out in 1801 by Thomas Young proved without any doubt that light was a wave (see topic A8).

■ The photoelectric effect

But in 1905 Einstein asked physicists to think about a simple experiment that could be done with a zinc plate and some ultra-violet light.

When you shine UV light on the zinc, it gives off electrons. This is the principle of the **photocell**. Photocells are used to detect light and to read the signals coded on to sound films in cinemas.

The strange thing about the experiment with zinc is that it doesn't work when you shine *visible* light on to the zinc plate. However bright you make the light, no electrons are produced. But the very weakest trace of UV light will produce electrons, which shoot out of the metal at speed.

Einstein argued that this simple effect could only be explained by a particle theory of light, as follows.

EINSTEIN'S EXPLANATION

Light hits the metal as small particles, which are now called **photons**. Each photon carries some energy. If it carries enough energy, it can knock an electron out of the metal. It takes a definite amount of energy to do this, depending on the metal.

If the photon doesn't carry enough energy then the electron stays in the metal. Each photon of UV light *does* carry enough energy to knock an electron out of zinc. Photons of visible light don't carry enough energy – they are too feeble, and however many you throw at the metal they produce no effect. (See picture 1.)

It is rather like a coconut shy. To get a coconut out of its cup needs some energy. A lightweight ball travelling at a certain speed simply doesn't have enough energy. A faster ball, or a more massive ball travelling at the same speed, would. Slow throwers could throw millions of light balls at the coconuts and not win one. One heavy ball travelling at the same speed would get a result – if it hit the coconut, of course. This is illustrated in picture 3.

But this analogy is slightly misleading. Wooden balls can travel at different speeds and have different masses. All photons travel at the same speed – the speed of light. They do not carry any mass. The difference between photons of different colour is simply how much **electromagnetic energy** they carry.

Einstein worked out that the energy, **E**, carried by a photon of light depended on its frequency, **f**.

$$\text{photon energy} = \text{a constant} \times \text{frequency}$$
$$E = hf$$

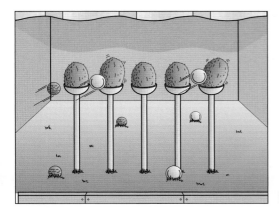

Picture 3 The coconut analogy.

The constant, **h**, is called the **Planck constant** after the German physicist Max Planck. Planck had been able (in 1900) to explain how hot objects emitted light in exactly the way they did only by assuming that the energy of the hot object existed in small packets. These packets are now called **quanta**, and this was the first inkling of quantum physics, which is now seen as one of the most fundamental ideas in all physics. Einstein extended the idea to say that it also described the way that light energy was sent and received. You will notice that the particle (photon) theory of light has to use the wave theory as well. It needs to use the **frequency** of the wave.

The higher the frequency of a wave the shorter is its wavelength. Blue light has a shorter wavelength than red light, and each photon of blue light carries more energy than a photon of red light. Photons of short-wave ultra-violet rays and X-rays carry even more energy. This is why they are so dangerous to living material.

All this should not really be a surprise to you, living at the beginning of the 21st century. But it is hard to imagine something that is both a wave (spread out over space) and a particle (all in one small space). Yet both models of how light behaves are useful. You will find that science magazines and TV programmes use both theories of light, as they see fit. They use whichever one seems to give the best explanation for what they are talking about.

WAVES OR PARTICLES?

Photography, sun-tanning, the retina of the eye and the physics of the ozone layer all need the particle theory to explain what is going on. In each of these cases, a little packet of energy is delivered to make something happen. If the packet isn't big enough, nothing happens. This is why you can develop a black-and-white photograph in red light. The photons of red light do not carry enough energy to affect the light-sensitive chemicals in the photographic paper (see picture 2).

Radio broadcasts, aerials and the action of lenses all need the wave theory to explain how they work. You will learn more about this if you take more advanced courses in physics.

Both theories are 'right', because they are backed up by experiments. They also make good predictions about new effects. Scientists have stopped being worried by the fact that they seem to contradict each other.

THE WAVE–PARTICLE DUALITY

Just to make things fair, we now know that 'real' particles, like electrons and alpha particles, can also behave like waves. Electrons can diffract and interfere, just like light waves. The **electron microscope** uses electron waves to see very small objects, just as ordinary microscopes use light waves.

Electron waves are not electromagnetic waves. They do not travel at the speed of light, for example. They are **matter waves**.

Activities

A Theories and models

This activity asks you to think about science in general. Do it as a group.

1 First, 'brainstorm' to write down seven or eight scientific theories or laws that you have learned about.

2 Put them into three lists:
    (a) Definitely true (b) Possibly true
    (c) Definitely false.

3 Discuss whether it is correct to put any theory into list (a).

B Photography and light

Investigate which colours of light affect a piece of photographic paper. Use 'black and white' paper or architects' 'blueprint' paper. You can get various colours by using good filters, but it may be better to use a spectrum made by a prism or by a diffraction grating. You will also need special chemicals to develop and fix the prints you make.

Plan what you are going to do carefully, then check your plan with your teacher.

Use the theory of photons to explain your results.

Questions

1 Black and white photographs (prints) are made from paper containing light-sensitive chemicals. These chemicals turn black when light gives them energy. But red light doesn't affect these chemicals. Suggest why this is.

2 Why do X-rays and ultra-violet rays damage living cells, while ordinary visible light doesn't?

3 Give three differences between photons and electrons.

4 The following are types of electromagnetic radiation. Put them in order of photon energy, with the photons of highest energy first (see picture 6, topic A7):

    microwaves infra-red ultra-violet green light gamma rays X-rays

5 Write a page or two summarising the evidence for saying that light is both a wave and a particle.

Light and colour

The world is full of colour.
What makes colours?
How can we see them?

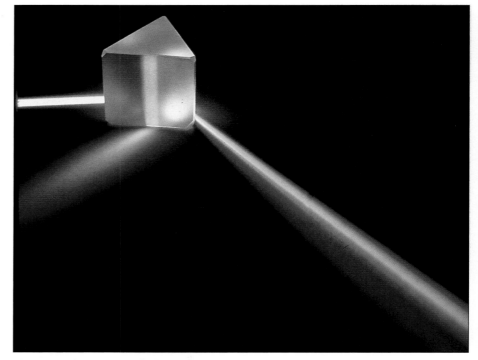

Picture 1   The spectrum of white light.

SPLITTING UP LIGHT

White light is a mixture of colours. When we pass white light through a prism the colours become separated out into a **spectrum** (see topics A7 and A9). Picture 1 shows a prism splitting up white light. The same effect can be produced by tiny drops of water, and causes the **rainbow**.

Keen-eyed people say they can detect seven colours in this spectrum. In order, they are red, orange, yellow, green, blue, indigo and violet. You can remember this by the sentence 'Richard Of York Gave Battle In Vain'. Light from the sun, or any white hot object, also includes invisible radiations, like ultra-violet and infra-red. See topic A7.

■ How prisms separate colours

When light goes from air into glass it slows down. This is why it changes direction – it is **refracted** (see topic A5). All electromagnetic waves travel at the same speed in a vacuum. They slow down when they enter a transparent medium, like glass. This change of speed causes refraction.

But the different colours of the spectrum travel at **different** speeds in glass. For example, violet light travels more slowly than red light. This means that it is refracted more, so that its direction is changed more than red light. The other colours fit in between, depending on their speeds in glass. Light of different colours is thus spread out into the spectrum. This spreading out is called **dispersion** (picture 2).

If you collected all the seven colours of the spectrum and joined them together again you would once more see white light.

■ Primary colours

This effect may not be a surprise to you, but what might be surprising is that you can recreate white light by using just three colours – **red, green** and **blue**. Picture 3 shows three beams of light shining onto a white screen.

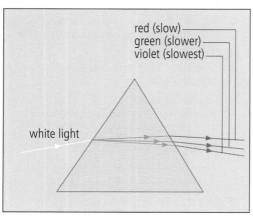

red (slow)
green (slower)
violet (slowest)

white light

Picture 2   Light of different colours travels in different paths.

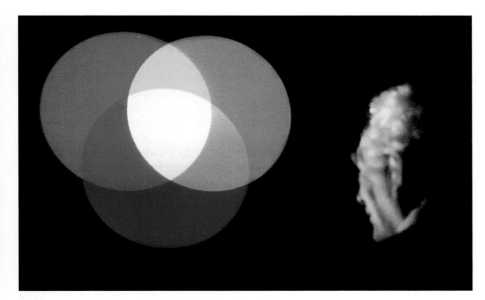

Picture 3 White light can be made from just three colours.

Where all three beams overlap you can see that the *light is white*. The three colours that do this are called the **primary colours**.

At other places, just two colours overlap. They combine to form other colours:

- Red and green combine to make **yellow**.
- Red and blue combine to make **magenta**.
- Green and blue combine to make **cyan**.

These 'double' colours are called the **secondary colours**. You get these effects when the three primary colours are balanced so that they are equally effective. By using different brightnesses you can create all the colours of the rainbow, and many other colours that go to make up the everyday world.

Colour television uses this property of primary colours. In the TV screen there are just three kinds of paints which glow when electrons hit them **(phosphors)**. The phosphors glow red, green or blue. The screen contains thousands of small 'picture elements' (pixels) each containing a set of the three phosphors. By making these glow at different brightnesses we can get the whole range of colours that we see on a TV screen. Colour films and colour printing work in much the same way, using just three basic colours.

■ Why is a red book red?

Paints and dyes work by **reflecting** light. When white light shines on a red surface, the dye absorbs all colours except red, which it reflects. If you shine blue light, for example, on the surface it looks dark, because there is no red light present to be reflected. The same happens when you shine green light on to the red surface.

But if you put the red surface in *yellow* light it will look red. This is because yellow light is a mixture of green and red light, as explained above. The red surface absorbs the green light but can reflect the red.

The colour of an object depends not only on its own 'colour' but also on the colour of the light you view it with. The 'white' of artificial light is different from the 'pure' white of sunlight. They contain a slightly different mix of colours. This is why clothes bought in a shop under artificial lighting may look quite different when seen out of doors in sunlight.

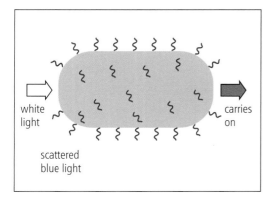

Picture 4 Atmospheric scattering.

■ Why is the sky blue?

The upper atmosphere contains millions of tiny particles, ranging from molecules of various gases to small dust particles, ice crystals, etc. Many of these are good at absorbing photons with the energy that makes them blue light. Then soon after absorbing the blue light they reradiate it. Picture 4 shows how this happens; it is called **scattering**. Thus the blue light from the sunlight passing high above us in the atmosphere is first trapped, then some of it is sent down to Earth. So the sky looks blue.

This effect also explains why sunsets are red or orange. Red light is not absorbed in this way and so carries on through the atmospheric particles. When we look at the setting sun we see this reddish light. Most of the blue light has been absorbed and then sent out sideways (see picture 5).

COLOUR, ENERGY AND WAVELENGTH

Light travels as a wave.The difference between red light and, say, blue light is simply that they have different wavelengths. Red light has a longer wavelength than blue light. The diagram of the electromagnetic spectrum in picture 6 of topic A7 shows this (page 37).

The eye and brain work together when we see light. The effect of light of one wavelength makes us see 'red'; other wavelengths trigger the sensation of green or blue.

One theory of vision says that our eyes work like the TV screens described above. Some cells in the retina at the back of the eye detect the red light. Others detect only blue and a third kind detect green light.

When all three types of cell are triggered we see the light as white. Combinations of cells create different colours in the brain in much the same way as combinations of red, green and blue in the pixels of a TV screen create different colours.

Picture 5 Sunsets are red and yellow because the blue light has been scattered.

Picture 6 shows some of these cells in a human retina.

The triggering effect of light on cells in the eye is caused by the energy carried by the light. The effect can only be explained by using the model of light that says it is made of particles called **photons** (see topic A9). The blue photons carry more energy than the green ones, and the red photons carry the least energy.

Infra-red photons don't carry enough energy to trigger any of the cells. Ultraviolet photons are invisible because they carry too much energy, and actually damage the eye cells. Our eyelids screen this dangerous radiation coming from above. But if it comes up into the eye by reflection from water or snow we can be harmed. Skiers and polar explorers guard against this 'snow blindness' by using goggles whenever the sun shines brightly.

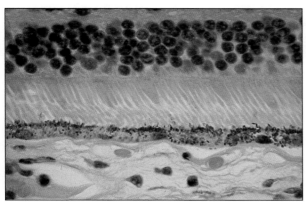

Picture 6 The retina has cells which can detect colour (cones), but most of the rod-shaped cells can't.

Questions

1 Broxton United wear white shirts with blue shorts. Wexley Wanderers wear yellow shirts with black shorts. When they turn out for a floodlit match in the park the referee sends one team back to change their strip. Explain why the referee had to do this. (Hint: There was nothing wrong with the ref's eyesight. They were playing under yellow sodium lamps.)

2 It is said that bees can see ultra-violet light. Design an experiment to test this statement.

3 a Suggest a reason why ordinary electric filament lamps produce a 'white' light that is different from sunlight.

   b Explain why the difference between sunlight and lamp light should affect the colour of clothing.

4 Explain clearly the difference between the **refraction** and the **dispersion** of light by a prism.

5 Fluorescent light tubes bought in England usually give a slightly yellow light. But fluorescent tubes bought in Saudi Arabia give a slightly bluish light. Suggest why they are made with these differences.

6 Yellow is sometimes called 'minus blue'. Explain why.

7 Why do both the human eye and a colour TV camera have just three kinds of colour-sensitive cell?

8 A red rose and a yellow rose are passed through the spectrum from a bright lamp. What colour would each appear to be in:

   a the blue light,
   b the green light,
   c the yellow light,
   d the red light?

Signals from space

The only way we can learn about the universe is from the signals it sends us. For millions of years the only signals from space that humans could detect were carried by light. The ancient astronomers of Egypt, Babylon and Greece observed the Sun, the Moon and the stars. They saw how they changed and plotted their movements through the heavens. They produced the first theories about what the universe was like, as shown in picture 1.

The ancient Romans weren't very interested in astronomy, and when Italy and Western Europe were overrun by 'barbarians' from the steppes of Asia in around 400 AD the old knowledge of astronomy was almost completely lost. But the study of astronomy was carried on by the Arab Muslims who conquered the Middle East and parts of Europe in the years 700 to 1500 AD. If you look at a good sky map you will find that many of the star names are in Arabic.

The telescope was invented in 1610 and over the next two centuries telescopes got bigger and better. Fainter and more distant stars could be seen. Knowledge about the universe increased, but these instruments still used ordinary, visible light.

A breakthrough was to come with the marriage of two old ideas – the **spectrum** of light and the **telescope** – with a new technique: **photography**. But like many scientific discoveries, it was a long time before what had been discovered made any sense.

Newton had explained the 'colours of the rainbow' back in 1666, and had investigated the spectrum of white light (see topic A7). Then in 1802 an English scientist, William Wollaston, noticed that the coloured spectrum of sunlight was crossed with a number of dark lines. He did not know what caused them, and it was 40 years before the mystery was solved.

High technology 1857: the bunsen burner

Robert Bunsen invented the bunsen burner to investigate spectra. He looked at the coloured light given out by elements heated in his clear, colourless gas flame. He discovered that each element had its own spectrum, different from all the others.

Picture 1 The Egyptian universe.

When heated, it gave out light energy in definite wavelengths and in its own pattern. It could be used as a 'fingerprint', to detect the very tiniest traces of any element (see picture 2).

His fellow worker Gustav Kirchhoff made the key connection. The dark lines in the spectrum of sunlight were caused by elements in the Sun that **absorbed** light energy at their own special wavelengths. Immediately, astronomers were able to work out what the Sun was made of! In fact, one *new* element was discovered, up until that time unknown on Earth. It was named helium, after the Greek sun-god Helios.

Photography was discovered in about 1800, and the solar spectrum was first photographed in 1842. Since then, millions of photographs of the spectra of stars, planets, galaxies and comets have been taken. Photographs are needed because some of these objects are very faint. A photograph can collect light for many hours, and so build up its image until it is clear enough to be developed and measured. The details of the spectrum can tell us what elements there are in the star, its temperature,

and even whether it is moving or not.

Then, in 1931, a new radiation was observed coming from outer space: radio waves. This led to the development of radio astronomy, and the discovery of radio stars and galaxies, pulsars and quasars (see topic G6 and picture 3).

Since then, astronomers have been able to use nearly every part of the whole electromagnetic spectrum, from gamma rays at one end to long radio waves at the other (see topic A7). They have found that the pattern of the spectrum of a given element is the same all over the Universe. But they also noticed that the actual wavelengths were sometimes different. This effect was caused by the movement of the star.

The American Edwin Hubble noticed that this difference was greater, the further away the stars or galaxies were. This could only be explained by the theory that these objects were moving away from us. This led to the theory of the expanding universe – and of the Big Bang that started it. The new 'space telescope' is named after this great astronomer.

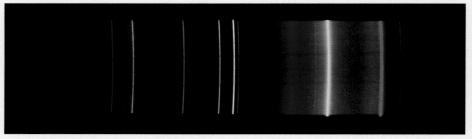

Picture 2 The helium spectrum.

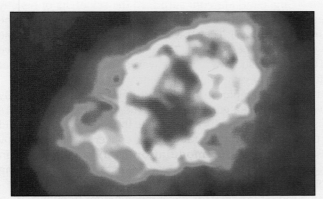

Picture 3 This image was produced using a radio telescope.

Answer the following questions:

1 Suggest why so much early astronomy was done by people living in the desert areas of the Middle East (compared, for example, with people living in Britain).

2 Why are radio telescopes so much bigger (maybe 30 metres or more across) than light telescopes (up to 2 or 3 metres across)?

3 Suggest a reason why it took nearly 200 years for Newton's discovery of the spectrum to be useful in astronomy.

4 Why are light, radio waves and X-rays all thought to be part of the same type of radiation? (Check with topic A7 if you are not sure.)

5 Radio waves don't affect photographic plates. How are these radiations detected and recorded?

Seeing with sound

Modern science uses all kinds of radiation to 'look' at things which are invisible, or to see through materials that light cannot penetrate. X-rays can see through flesh to spot broken bones or faulty hearts or lungs. Even the tiny magnetic fields of hydrogen atoms in our bodies can be used to give us a picture of what is going on deep inside our bodies.

One of the most useful body probes is the *ultrasound scanner*. This produces pictures like the one shown in picture 1, which shows a scan of an unborn baby.

Ordinary sound, which we can hear, has frequencies in the range of 20 Hz to 20 000 Hz. Ultrasound has frequencies well beyond the upper limit that we can hear. It uses sounds at frequencies between 1 and 15

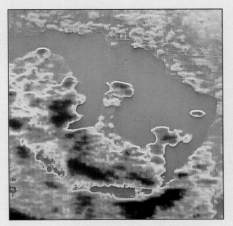

Picture 1 Ultrasound scan of a baby in the womb.

million hertz. This is higher than any animal ear can sense.

At this high frequency, the sound can travel through most materials. But some of it is always reflected back when it goes from one type of material into another. How much of it is sent back depends on the material in the way. In fact it behaves very much as light does in going through materials of slightly different transparency.

Also, the speed at which the ultrasound travels in the material depends on the material it is travelling in. This means that it can be focused. This is done in the same way as glass lenses do for light by using an ultrasound-transparent material with curved surfaces.

The advantage of using sound is that it doesn't harm the living cells, as X-rays may do. But if it is to see fine detail, the sound waves must be very small. They have to be slightly smaller than the small parts (e.g. blood vessels) of the object being looked at (picture 2).

This is the reason for using such very high frequencies. The higher the frequency, the smaller the wavelength. This is because of the wave formula:

$$\text{wavelength} = \frac{\text{speed}}{\text{frequency}}$$

The speed of sound in the human body is about the same as it is in salt water – about 1500 metres per second. If we want to see detail to about 1 mm, the wavelength has to be no more than this length. This means a frequency of 1.5 million hertz (MHz). In hospitals,

ultrasound scanners use frequencies between 1 MHz and 15 MHz.

Answer the following questions:

1 Why can't we hear ultrasound?

2 Doctors prefer to use ultrasound for looking at babies in the mother's womb, even if the images produced aren't quite as clear as they could get using X-rays. Why is ultrasound preferred to X-rays?

3 Use the formula given above to calculate the size of the smallest object you could 'see' using ultrasound at 15 MHz.

4 Bats find their way around at night, and detect their insect prey, using ultrasound at about 50 kHz (50 000 Hz). Suggest why they don't need to use frequencies a lot higher than this, as in ultrasound scanners.

5 Draw a diagram showing what an ultrasound scanner might 'see' if it looked at an orange.

6 Another use for ultrasound is for cleaning things. When ultrasound is beamed at dirty fabrics the particles of dirt fall off the fibres. Suggest why: (a) the particles fall off, (b) this method is used for cleaning very old or very expensive materials.

Picture 2 Long waves miss the fine detail.

Messages through space

Although the world is now criss-crossed with cables carrying all kinds of signals, much of the world's messages are carried by electromagnetic waves through space.

Topic A1 describes how Guglielmo Marconi surprised the scientists of his day be sending a radio message across the Atlantic. Radio waves are part of the electromagnetic spectrum (see topic A7). They travel through space (and air) at the speed of light, 300 000 000 metres per second. The energy they carry can move electrons in a metal and this is the usual way that the waves are detected. But what makes radio waves useful is that they can be used to carry signals.

The first radio signals used a simple on-off code: the Morse code originally designed for telegraph wires carrying a current. But by the early 1920s engineers had discovered how to use electronic circuits to modulate the radio wave. They did this simply by changing the **amplitude** of the radio wave, converting it into a copy of a sound wave. This is called **amplitude modulation (AM),** and is shown in picture 1. The changing amplitude of the radio wave can carry the changing volume and frequency of a sound wave : it is an **analogue** of the sound.

The wave produced in a radio **transmitter** has a much higher frequency than the analogue wave it carries, and is called a **carrier** wave. The sound is changed into a varying electric voltage by a microphone (a transducer) and this is then superimposed on the carrier wave by an electronic circuit. The modulated carrier wave is then amplified and fed to an aerial. This might simply be a long wire. The electrons in the wire follow the changes in voltage of the signal and emit a copy of the signal as an electromagnetic wave that is the actual radio wave in space.

The wave spreads out in all directions. For the signal to be useful it must be taken in by a **receiver**. Picture 2 shows the parts of the transmitter-receiver system.

The energy of the wave is picked up by the aerial, acting as a transducer. Here the varying electromagnetic signal is converted into a varying electrical voltage. This may then be amplified and fed to the next stage. The carrier wave is removed and the audio signal is sent on, amplified and fed into a loudspeaker.

The aerial might pick up many hundreds of different broadcasts, transmitted at different frequencies. A special circuit at the front end of the receiver selects just one frequency to pass on to the next stage. This is called the **tuner**. It is this circuit that is adjusted when you move the tuning knob on a radio. It selects the frequency of the carrier wave.

Picture 1 The radio carrier wave has a high frequency and is modulated in size (amplitude) by the sound wave.

Picture 2 The receiver is much like a transmitter in reverse. But it has the special task of changing the modulated carrier wave into an audible sound.

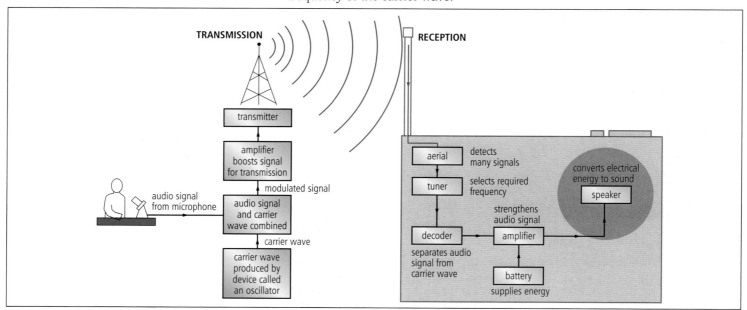

The signal coming from the tuner is a mixture of carrier wave and the audio signal. The **decoder** (or detector) removes the carrier wave. The audio signal is too weak to make a loudspeaker work – but will be strong enough for small headphones. Energy is added to it by the **amplifier**, so that it can make a loudspeaker work. This energy is supplied by the mains or a battery.

■ Frequency modulation : FM

Modern radio uses a much more reliable form of modulation for ordinary radio messages: **frequency modulation (FM)**. Amplitude modulation is susceptible to **noise** – extra signals often caused by such things as nearby electric motors, motor cars etc. These send out amplitude modulated radio-type waves which interfere with the true signal making it distorted. It is also possible for radio waves from other transmitters with a similar transmission frequency to affect the wanted signal. All this is called **radio interference** – not to be confused with the wave superposition effects also called interference (see topic A8 *Light as a wave*).

The carrier wave for FM has to be at a much higher frequency – see picture 4. The audio signal is put into the carrier wave by modulating the frequency instead of the amplitude. This is illustrated in picture 3. Ordinary interference does not affect the audio signal in the carrier wave: they might affect its amplitude but cannot change its frequencies. The result is a much clearer signal with a very low signal-to-noise ratio. FM systems can carry much more information than AM systems – which makes it possible for the signal to be 'doubled' to provide stereo outputs.

Because the carrier wave has such a high frequency (HF) it behaves more like a light wave than the lower frequency waves used for AM broadcasts. It tends to travel in straight lines and does not diffract as much around hills and buildings, so that there may be shadow areas where the signal is weak. This is especially true for the ultra high frequency (UHF) carrier waves used for television. See below for more about this. Because they travel in straight lines they don't follow the curve of the Earth, so have quite a short range. To cover the country FM and TV transmitting aerials have to be placed quite close together, at about 50 km apart. Just one large transmitter might be enough for long wave broadcasts (such as Radio 4 at 198 metres wavelength). See below for more about how the waves travel across the country and in space.

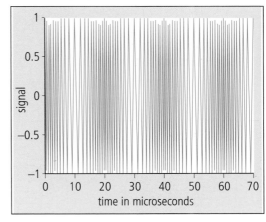

Picture 3 The variations in frequency and amplitude of the audio signal are translated into changes in frequency of the carrier wave.

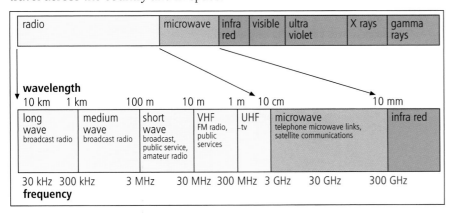

Picture 4 Radio sections of the electromagnetic spectrum.

■ How radio waves travel

In simple theory electromagnetic waves travel in straight lines. Marconi didn't know this, so when he tried to send radio signals from Cornwall to Newfoundland in 1901 better educated scientists expected him to fail. But he didn't, and his success brought him the Nobel Prize in 1909. What neither Marconi or physicists knew at that time is that there is a layer of ionised gases in the upper atmosphere that acts as a mirror for radio waves. Picture 5 shows a possible path that his short wave radio signals took to reach Newfoundland. Radio 'hams' have relied on this reflecting layer, called the **ionosphere**, to send short wave radio around the world ever since.

The ionosphere reflects short waves best, but medium waves can be reflected, especially at night when the ionosphere gets higher and simpler. Waves that can be reflected by the ionosphere are called **sky waves**. Long waves, VHF and UHF waves simply pass through it.

Medium and long wave signals can travel long distances by hugging the ground. This is a complicated effect called **ground** or **surface** transmission. 3 Mhz waves can travel up to 100 km along the Earth's surface this way, while very long waves with a frequency of 1 kHz (very low frequency VLF waves) can travel up to 10 000 km. BBC Radio 4 Long Wave can be picked up as far as the south of France.

VHF, UHF and microwaves are easily obstructed by buildings and hills, and work best when there is a clear line of sight between transmitter aerial and receiver. These waves are sometimes called **space waves**, as they are best thought of as travelling directly through space. Picture 5 shows the three mains ways in which radio waves can travel from transmitter to receiver.

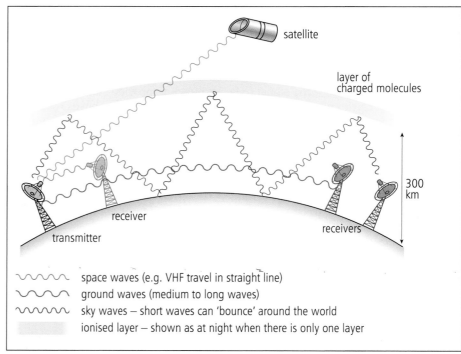

satellite

layer of charged molecules

300 km

receiver

transmitter

receivers

〜〜〜 space waves (e.g. VHF travel in straight line)

〜〜〜 ground waves (medium to long waves)

〜〜〜 sky waves – short waves can 'bounce' around the world

ionised layer – shown as at night when there is only one layer

Picture 5 How radio waves travel. The ionosphere is shown as it is at night, when it collapses to just one main layer of ionised gases.

Picture 6 A dish aerial acts like a concave mirror to focus radio waves.

REFLECTION HELPS RADIO

Short wave radio uses the ionosphere and the surface of the Earth itself as plane (flat) mirrors to help it travel great distances around the Earth. The UHF waves that carry satellite TV broadcasts arrive at the ground as very weak signals. This is because they have travelled a long way and have spread out a great deal. They can be boosted before they get to the aerial by using a curved mirror: a **dish aerial** (picture 7). The mirror is made of plastic with a coating of metallic paint which reflects radio waves. Picture 6 shows how the mirror helps by focusing the waves on to a small aerial. Signals are sent up to communications and TV satellites using large dish aerials. Large radio telescopes picking up even weaker signals from the depths of space use the same principle.

DIFFRACTION HELPS RADIO

Waves can bend around obstacles, as explained in topics A2 and A8. This effect is called **diffraction**. The longer the wave, the easier it is for it to diffract around an object. Light cannot pass around a hill or a building – its wavelength is far too short. But radio waves with wavelengths of tens or hundreds of metres can do so. This means that houses in valleys can still receive most VHF and all short, medium and long wave broadcasts with no problems. Picture 8 shows how this happens. The UHF waves used for TV might present more of a problem, and the aerial might have to be placed on the hill.

But diffraction is also a problem. Even when radio waves are focused by a dish aerial they still spread out because of diffraction. This means that when a signal is sent to a communications satellite far from Earth some energy is lost – most of the signal simply bypasses the satellite (picture 9).

Picture 7   Dish aerials at a ground receiving station.

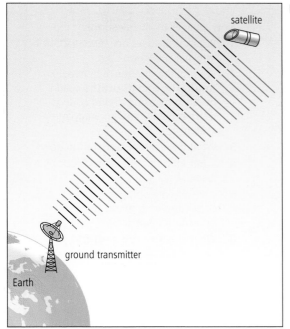

Picture 9   It would be nice if the waves kept to a narrow beam likethis but they spread out due to diffraction like this.

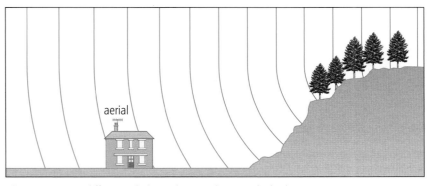

Picture 8   How diffraction helps radio signals to reach shadow areas.

Questions

1   What part of a radio selects the particular programme the listener wants to hear?

2   Mary is sitting in the crowd at a rock concert at Wembley Stadium. Her seat is 200 m from the loudspeakers on the stage. Her brother John is listening to the concert on a radio at home in Edinburgh, over 300 miles away.

   a   Explain why John hears the music before Mary does.

   b   How long does sound take to travel 200 m?

   c   Calculate how far radio waves will travel in the time that the sound takes to reach Mary.

   d   The concert is being broadcast on both medium wave and FM radio. Which of these has the longer wavelength?

   e   Explain why people living in very hilly areas might get better radio reception on medium wave than on FM.
[speed of sound: 340 m/s; speed of radio waves 300 000 000 m/s]

3   Picture 10 shows the display panel on a radio. The pointer on the display is set so that the radio is tuned to receive a medium wave (MW) broadcast from Radio X.

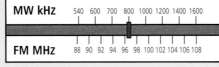

Picture 10

   a   On which frequency does Radio X broadcast?

   b   Calculate the wavelength of the broadcast from Radio X.

4   The Internet uses the telephone system to transmit data. Sometimes the data is sent via satellite. What frequency band is likely to be best for this application?

5   Suggest three sources of radio interference that might exist in your home. Why are these more likely to affect AM broadcasts that FM broadcasts?

6   Describe 2 advantages of FM over AM for transmitting music by radio. Are there any disadvantages to using FM?

Fibre optics

As explained in topic A1, thin glass fibres carrying 'light' signals are much better for carrying information than almost any other medium. The messages are digitally coded (see topic A1, where digital coding is explained).

The 'light' used is normally invisible – it is a form of infra-red radiation. This radiation travels at the same high speed as light, but travels better through glass than visible light does. It is produced by a laser, which gives a very pure form of radiation.

The radiation is coded electronically. When you speak into a telephone the sounds you make are first changed into a varying electric current. This is a copy (analogue) of the sounds you make. An analogue-to-digital converter changes the signal to a set of binary pulses. In turn these are used to modulate the laser beam in the same digital pattern.

At the listener's end the infra-red pulses are changed to an electric signal again. This can be put back into analogue form electronically and used to make the earpiece work.

Optical fibres are very thin, and are made of very pure and transparent glass. Infra-red 'light' is fed in at one end and cannot escape. This is because of **total internal reflection** (see topic A5). A simple fibre works as shown in picture 1. The light bounces off the inside of the fibre. But this produces a distorted signal after the signal has travelled a few kilometres down the fibre. The signal also gets weaker as it travels down the fibre because some of the light is absorbed by the glass. This is called **attenuation**.

A better design uses glass in which the speed of the light changes gradually from the inside out. This means that the light path curves gently as shown in picture 2.

Even so, the signal gets distorted sooner or later. **Repeater stations** are built into the line to reshape and amplify the signals, as shown in picture 3. In a modern telecommunications system using fibre optics the repeater stations can be 40 km apart. This compares with having them just 8 km apart when copper wires are used to carry messages electrically.

Another advantage is that optical fibres can carry many conversations at the same time. This needs quite

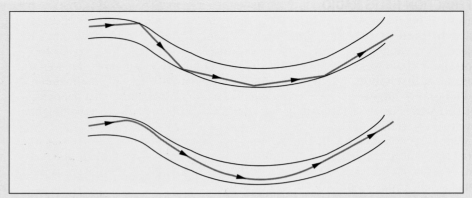

Picture 1 A simple optical fibre (above) **Picture 2** A more sophisicated fibre (below).

complicated electronics, but a typical optical fibre system can allow 11 000 pairs of people to talk to each other simultaneously. The old copper wire system could only carry about 1000 conversations at once.

Optical networks can also carry TV signals and computer data more cheaply and accurately than wire systems can. Thus useful things like home shopping and banking can be much more practicable. But to give everyone an optical fibre correction to their homes is expensive. It isn't cost-effective unless the network is also allowed to carry television programmes.

Now answer these questions.

1 What other uses are there for total internal reflection?

2 What is the difference between **analogue** and **digital**? Explain briefly why using digital code is more reliable than an analogue system.

3 What does a repeater station do?

4 What kind of light is produced by a laser?

5 Give two advantages of fibre optics compared with metal wires as information carriers.

6 What is **infra-red radiation**?

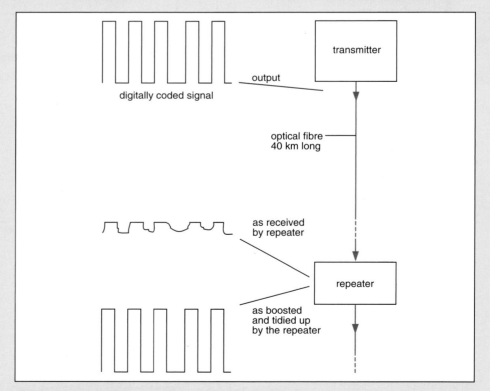

Picture 3 Repeater stations reshape and amplify the signals.

B

Forces and movement

B1

Speed, time, distance

We live in a world of movement – the flight of birds, high-speed trains, Earth satellites, cars and aircraft are all examples.

SPEED

The **speed** of an object is how far it goes in one unit of time. It is measured in units such as metres per second (m/s), or kilometres per hour (km/h). In Britain you will also see the unit 'miles per hour' (mph), but this is not used in scientific measuring.

Table 1 shows the range of speeds of a number of moving things.

Table 1 Comparison of speeds.

Speeds	m/s	km/h
light speed	300 000 000	1 080 000 000
Earth in orbit	29 790	107 244
typical Earth satellite	7 500	27 000
fast jet aircraft	833	3000
Concorde (supersonic jet)	648	2333
average speed of air molecule	500	1800
sound in air	340	1224
Boeing 747 Jumbo Jet	270	970
fastest bird (falcon)	97	350
high-speed train (French TGV)	60	216
motorway speed limit (UK 70 mph)	31	112
town speed limit (UK 30 mph)	13.4	48
Olympic sprinter	10.3	37
average walking speed	1.7	6
average speed of a snail	0.006	0.02

■ Measuring speed

Very many different instruments are used to measure the wide range of speeds shown in the chart. But all of them need to measure just two things: **time** and **distance travelled**.

If you wanted to measure the speed of a sprinter at an athletics track you would measure how long it took the runner to cover the distance of the race. For example, you could use a stop watch, and find that it took the runner 13 seconds to cover a distance of 100 metres. You could calculate the speed (distance covered per second) like this:

$$\text{speed in metres per second} = \frac{\text{distance in metres}}{\text{time in seconds}}$$

$$= \frac{100 \text{ metres}}{13 \text{ seconds}}$$

$$= 7.7 \text{ m/s}$$

Picture 1 Racing against the clock.

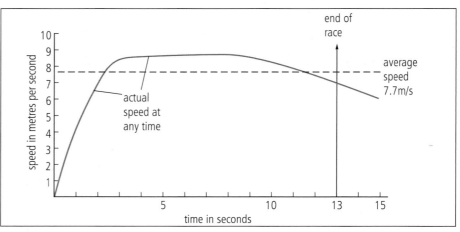

Picture 2 How a runner's speed changes during a race.

Average speed

What we have worked out for the sprinter was the *average* speed over the distance. The runner wouldn't have travelled at this speed steadily for all of the 13 seconds of the race.

A runner starts slowly then accelerates to her fastest speed. She might slow down near the end when her legs get tired. A graph would show this (see picture 2).

In the same way, a car might take four hours to travel a distance of 200 km. Unless it was on a very clear motorway it isn't likely that it would have travelled at the same speed of 50 km/h all the time. It's useful to know the *average* speed of a car on different kinds of roads. When you are planning a journey you can use it to work out how long the journey is likely to take.

We can work out average speeds using a formula:

$$\text{average speed} = \frac{\text{total distance covered}}{\text{time taken for journey}}$$

Written as a formula: $\quad v = \dfrac{s}{t}$

Picture 3 Police can measure the speed of a car using radar.

INSTANTANEOUS SPEED

Sometimes we need to know more about what happens when moving things are changing speed. To do this we need to be able to measure the speed at any given instant. This is not so easy to do. It means that we have to measure the distance an object travels in a very small interval of time, usually much less than a second.

This can be done by using **radar**, as the police are doing in picture 3. The radar 'speed gun' measures the distance the car moves in a time of less than a millionth of a second! A built-in computer works out the result.

In school laboratories a useful device called a ticker-timer does the same job. It uses a time interval of a fiftieth of a second. See activity C for more details of how to use a ticker timer.

Your school lab may also have electronic speed measuring devices using interrupted light beams (see picture 5). All these things might look quite complicated, but all they do is what you do with a stop watch and measuring tape. They measure time and distance covered

Picture 4 Speed, distance and time.

Picture 5 These children are using a computer-assisted speed measuring device.

MOVEMENT FORMULAE

$\text{average speed} = \dfrac{\text{distance covered}}{\text{time taken}} \qquad\qquad v = \dfrac{s}{t}$

$\text{distance covered} = \text{average speed} \times \text{time taken} \qquad s = vt$

$\text{time taken} = \dfrac{\text{distance covered}}{\text{average speed}} \qquad\qquad t = \dfrac{s}{v}$

Working things out

Suppose you wanted to estimate how long it would take to cycle from your home to a holiday area. You might be staying at a camp site or a youth hostel when you get there.

You work out on the map (picture 6) that it is 55 miles away. You now have to decide what your average cycling speed is. A reasonably fit person could cycle at 10 miles an hour on fairly flat roads.

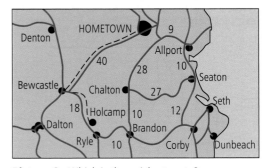

Picture 6 Which is the quickest route?

You would use the formula:

$$\text{time taken} = \frac{\text{distance covered}}{\text{speed}}$$

$$t = \frac{s}{v}$$

$$t = \frac{55}{10} \text{ miles per hour}$$

time needed = 5.5 hours

This is just an estimate, of course. You might decide to stop for a coffee. The route might be hilly. So you'd allow an extra hour or so to make sure.

Car and lorry drivers have to make the same kind of estimates every time they take a new route. Drivers soon learn that the hardest thing to get right is a prediction of the vehicle's average speed.

HOW FAST DO YOU WALK?

People who do a lot of walking need to have a good estimate of their average walking speed. If you go hiking in the countryside, especially in mountains, you have to make calculations very carefully (picture 7). You may be far from roads and shelter, and mistakes could be dangerous. You wouldn't want to find yourself far from shelter as night falls or the weather turns bad.

Experienced hikers use *Naismith's Rule* to help them calculate timings. This says: *allow 1 hour for every 3 miles (5 km) you measure on the map then add 1 hour for every 2000 ft (600 m) you have to climb.*

This rule works for a fit walker, not carrying a lot of equipment. Question 5 asks you to use this rule to work out some walking times.

■ Speed and direction: scalars and vectors

You tell a friend 'I'll meet you at 6 o'clock 500 metres from the clock in the High Street'. The friend will be slightly puzzled. 'In which direction?' he asks. For most purposes the distance of one thing from another is only half the story. It is also important to know the direction of one object from another. The same is true of movements: being able to bowl a cricket ball at 100 km per hour is frighteningly good – but it's useless unless the ball goes towards the wicket. Serving a tennis ball at 120 km an hour is first class – but is a fairly useless skill if the player can't hit it in the right direction.

Information about movements is incomplete unless both distance and direction are given. The combination **distance plus direction** is technically called **displacement**. The combination **speed plus direction** is technically called **velocity**. Distance and speed on their own are called **scalar** quantities. Displacement and velocity are **vector** quantities.

Vectors are drawn as arrows to show both their direction and their value.

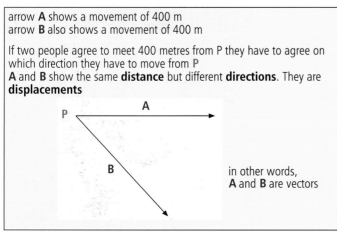

arrow **A** shows a movement of 400 m
arrow **B** also shows a movement of 400 m

If two people agree to meet 400 metres from P they have to agree on which direction they have to move from **P**
A and **B** show the same **distance** but different **directions**. They are **displacements**

in other words,
A and **B** are vectors

Picture 8 Displacement vectors.

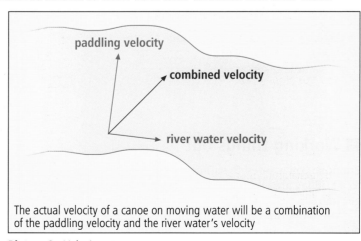

The actual velocity of a canoe on moving water will be a combination of the paddling velocity and the river water's velocity

Picture 9 Velocity vectors.

Picture 7 How fast do you walk?

Activities

A Timing pendulums

The first accurate clocks were based on the principle of the pendulum. A pendulum is a weight on a cord, made to swing from side to side. Does it swing from side to side in a constant time? What decides how long the weight takes to swing from side to side?

Do an investigation to answer these questions. First list the things that might affect the time of swing. Then think of how you can measure the time of swing accurately. Is it good enough to measure just one swing?

This investigation could take a long time if you tried everything yourself. Organise your group into small teams that can investigate different things. Make sure that they all share their results at the end.

B Measuring average speed

For this investigation you will need a stop watch. You will also need some way of measuring the distances involved. Measure the time taken to cover a measured distance and use the formula:

$$\text{average speed} = \frac{\text{distance travelled}}{\text{time taken}}$$

Try some or all of the following measurements:

1 the average speed of a runner,
2 the average speed of a cyclist travelling to school,
3 the average speed of a car passing the school or your home,
4 the average speed of a bird in flight,
5 the average speed of an object falling: (i) from a height of 2 m, (ii) from a height of 5 m,
6 the average speed of flow of a river or stream.

C Using ticker-timers

In a ticker-timer, a length of paper ticker tape is pulled through the timer. It prints a dot on the tape through the timer. It prints a dot on the tape once every fiftieth of a second. It works using electromagnetism and is controlled by the mains ac frequency of 50 hertz. Thus the distance between the dots shows the distance the tape moved in just 1/50 of a second.

Use the timer to investigate one or more of the following:

1 Do you walk at a constant speed?
2 Do objects fall at a constant (steady) speed?
3 How does the speed of the weight at the end of a pendulum change as it swings from side to side?

Hints:

i) Use a fairly short piece of tape (about 1 metre long).
ii) Work with 'ten-space' lengths, not one-space lengths. (Ten spaces represent a fifth of a second, which is usually accurate enough)
iii) You can make your length of tape into a kind of graph showing the motion. Start at the beginning of the tape and count off ten spaces. Call this piece of tape (a 'ten-tick') number 1. Count off the next ten spaces and carry on doing this to the end of the tape, numbering each short piece. Cut the tape into your numbered ten-ticks and set them out on a base line as shown in picture 10.

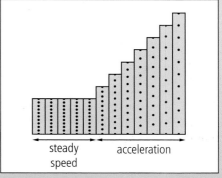

Picture 10

Questions (ICT)

1 Estimating speed

Look at table 1 (page 58) showing the speeds of a number of well-known objects. Use it, and any other information you might have, to make a sensible guess at the likely (average) speeds of the following:

a a cyclist in a long-distance road race,
b a tennis ball during a serve,
c the signal from a TV transmitter,
d a marathon runner,
e the growth of grass.

2 Use the information about speeds on page 58 to estimate the following:

a The time it would take a fast jet aircraft to cross the Atlantic, a distance of 5000 km.
b The time it would take a Jumbo Jet to cover the same distance as in part a.
c How long it would take a falcon to dive from a height of 200 metres on to its prey.
d The distance to the Moon from the Earth if a radar signal takes 2.5 s to make the journey there and back.
e How far an average walker might expect to walk in a time of 5 hours.
f How far away a cliff is if the echo of a handclap is heard 2.4 s after it is made.
g How far the Earth travels in its orbit in a day.

3 Using formulae

Use the formulae given on page 59 to calculate the following:

a The speed of a train that covers 300 km in two hours.
b The speed of a walker who covers 24 km in five hours.
c How far a cyclist would travel in five hours at an average speed of 12 km/h.
d How far a car would travel in eight hours at an average speed of 70 km/h.
e How long it would take a ship to travel a distance of 400 km at an average speed of 25 km/h.
f How long it takes light to travel the distance of 149 600 000 km from the Sun to the Earth, at a speed of 300 000 kilometres per second. Give the answer in minutes and seconds.

4 A student measured the distance of a cyclist from a given point every 2 seconds. The results are shown in the table:

Time/s	0	2	4	6	8	10	12	14
Distance/m	0	10	20	30	40	50	55	60

a Draw a graph of the data, with time along the horizontal axis.

b Describe the shape of the graph.

c Use the numbers in the table to calculate the average speed of the cyclist during (i) the first 4 seconds (ii) between 4 seconds and 10 seconds (iii) between 10 seconds and 14 seconds.

d How does the shape of the graph link with the results of your calculations in part c?

5 Jane, Sally and Salman need to travel from the bridge in the village of Dent (see the map in picture 11) to meet their friends who are staying in Chapel-le-Dale. They plan to travel by the route shown.

a Use the scale of the map (and a piece of cotton, say) to work out how far they have to walk.

b How many feet do they have to climb?

c They are fit and not carrying a load. Use Naismith's Rule (page 60) to work out how long it should take them.

6 A bird flies 500 metres in a straight line from a tree and lands in another tree. A second bird then also flies 500 metres from the same tree to another tree.

a What do you need to know about their flights to tell whether both birds land on the same tree?

b Speed is a scalar quantity. Velocity is a vector quantity. Use the bird example above to explain the difference between a scalar and a vector quantity.

7 The London Eye is a large Ferris wheel on the banks of the Thames. The compartments travel around the rim of the wheel at a constant speed. Explain why they are not moving with constant velocity.

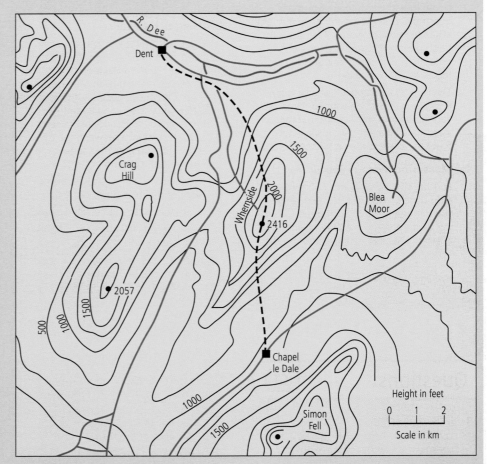

Picture 11

Crashes and bangs

Stopping and starting can be gentle – but what about when they are not? the key idea is momentum.

Picture 1   Hitting a tennis ball.

HITTING THINGS

The photograph in picture 1 shows an old picture of a tennis ball just as it is being hit by the racket. You can see why they change the balls so often, and why rackets have to be made so very strong. The forces on both are very large.

Both the ball and the racket are distorted by the impact. The ball is squashed almost flat, and the racket strings are stretched. This is a good example of one of the basic laws to do with forces and movement.

■ The law of action and reaction

This was first discovered by the great scientist Isaac Newton over 300 years ago. He said that action and reaction are equal and opposite. This means simply that the force exerted on the ball by the racket – the 'action force' is the same in size as the force exerted on the racket by the ball – the 'reaction'. The forces are acting in opposite directions.

■ Twin forces

This law of Newton's is one of those laws of nature that always applies. Another way of looking at it is to assume that forces occur in pairs.

Blow up a balloon and let it go. The balloon rushes forwards and the air in it rushes out backwards. In a rocket or jet the force produced by the engine acts just as much on the vehicle as on the hot gases rushing out at the back (picture 2). This means that the forces involved are equal in size and opposite in direction.

Even when you walk, your foot pushing back on the ground causes a reaction that pushes you forward. When a magnet attracts a piece of iron, there is an equal and opposite force pulling the magnet towards the iron. If you try this you can feel both forces.

■ Collisions

In a collision, forces act for a very short time. The forces are often quite large and the objects that collide run a risk of being damaged. This is what happens in traffic accidents.

In ball games the equipment is designed to avoid damage, although cricketers might not agree! (Picture 3.)

Picture 2   Forces occur in pairs: the upward push on the rocket equals the downward push on the exhaust gases.

But apart from any damage that might happen in a collision, there is also a change in movement. Objects speed up or slow down. Large objects seem to be harder to speed up and slow down than smaller ones. Think of the difference between tennis and table tennis, or between pushing a pram and pushing a car.

It was again Isaac Newton who realised that there are just two things that are important when collisions happen.

According to Newton, these are:

- the **speed** and its **direction**,
- the **masses** of the colliding objects.

In any collision, the more massive the object and the faster it is going the more effect it will have. The combination is a quantity called **momentum. Momentum is mass (m) multiplied by speed in a given direction**. Speed in a given direction is called **velocity (v)**. So

$$momentum = mv.$$

■ Mass

Mass was a very new and strange idea in 1680, and it's not that easy to grasp even now. We can think of it as a measure of how hard it is to make an object move, even when it is perfectly free to do so, like an object in space. The more matter there is in an object, the more mass it has. This idea helps to explain why table tennis bats aren't much use on a tennis court. The property of mass that makes it hard to move is called **inertia**.

FORCE AND MOMENTUM

The effect of a force is to change the momentum of an object. The change is bigger when the force is *larger*, or when the force *acts for a longer time*.

■ So what exactly happens in a collision?

Let's start by thinking about an easy example.

A SIMPLE COLLISION
The simplest collision is when a moving ball collides centre to centre with another, identical ball which is perfectly still ('at rest'). As they make an impact, the forces between them are the same all the time. The moving ball stops dead and the other one moves off with the same speed and in the same direction. In terms of momentum, all the momentum of the first ball has been given to the second one.

■ The law of momentum

Collision experiments produce the result that whenever a collision happens the total momentum of the colliding objects stay the same. The key formula is:

total momentum before collision = total momemtum after collision

Picture 4 shows this. Try it with two coins.

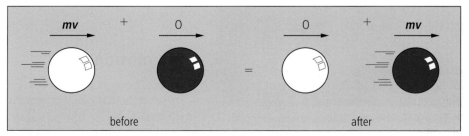

Picture 4 In collisions, momentum stays the same.

Picture 3 This sportsman is prepared to withstand unwanted forces.

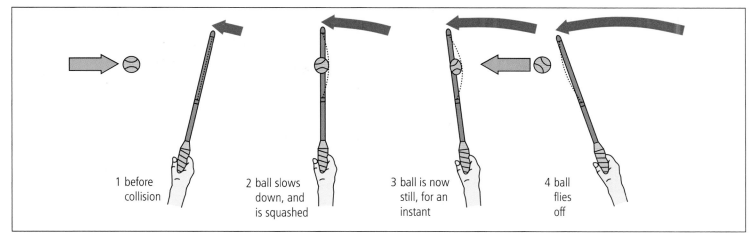

Picture 5 Forces and movement in tennis.

STICKY COLLISIONS

In some collisions the two objects stick together. This might happen when an ice skater picks up his partner when both are moving on the ice. Sometimes a large car or a lorry collides with a smaller car and both vehicles move together. The momentum rules still apply: the separate momenta of the two objects before the collision must add up to the final momentum of the combination. The faster ice skater will slow down and the slower one will gain speed. Exactly what happens depends on their masses. In traffic accidents the police will measure the distance moved by the combined vehicles and can use the data to work out if the vehicles were travelling inside or outside the speed limit. See picture 9.

TRICKY COLLISIONS

Let's consider a slow motion action replay of what happens when a tennis ball is hit by a tennis racket. As the ball touches the strings of the racket the action–reaction forces begin to act. The ball is crushed, and the strings are pushed back. The forces increase and at some stage the ball is stopped, probably when the forces are greatest.

The racket is only slowed down a little. This is because it is so much more massive than the ball, while the force on it is the same as the force on the ball.

But this is only half the story. The forces are still acting, even if they are getting less. The ball regains its normal shape and the strings go back to being straight. The forces are now pushing the ball forward very quickly, faster than the racket in its 'follow through'. So the ball flies away from the racket. The drawings in picture 5 summarise this.

But what has all this to do with real life? Think about safety on the road and other places where collision accidents can happen.

■ Stopping safely

To stop a moving object you have to take away its momentum. The only way to do this is to provide a force. Think of stopping a car. It can be done using a large force over a short time – as in a collision. Or it can be done with a small force over a longer time – by using brakes.

A safe design allows fast-moving objects to give up their momentum slowly. Cars are designed with 'crumple zones'. The front of the car is deliberately made 'softer' than it could be, so that it crumples slowly in a collision. In the same way, playground surfaces should be made of a non-rigid material. Picture 6 shows some ways of doing this. The surface 'gives', so that the falling child takes a little bit longer to stop. The chart in picture 7 shows how far a child can fall on to a number of surfaces without danger to life.

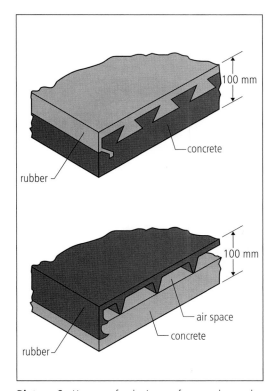

Picture 6 How a safe playing surface can be made.

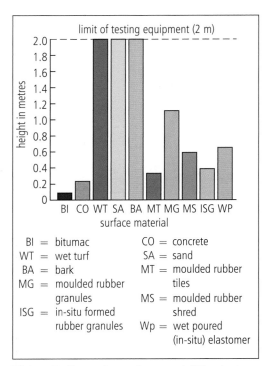

BI = bitumac   CO = concrete
WT = wet turf   SA = sand
BA = bark   MT = moulded rubber
MG = moulded rubber   tiles
     granules   MS = moulded rubber
ISG = in-situ formed   shred
      rubber granules   Wp = wet poured
                         (in-situ) elastomer

Picture 7 How safe are playgrounds? The chart shows how far a child can fall on various surfaces reasonably safely.

Force and change of momentum

The key rule is that:

$$\text{force} \times \text{time} = \text{change of momemtum}$$

For a given momentum change we can have a small force for a long time to get the same effect as a large force for a small time.

Example
A car with a mass of 1000 kg travelling at 30 metres per second (110 km/h) has a momentum of 30 000 kg m/s. To stop it in 5 seconds, using the brakes, needs a force F_{brakes}. We can calculate the force using this rule:

$$F_{brakes} \times 5 = 1000 \times 30$$

giving

$$F_{brakes} = 6000 \text{ newtons}$$

In a collision, the car might stop in a tenth of a second. The force needed is F_{bang}, given by:

$$F_{bang} \times 0.1 = 1000 \times 30$$

so that

$$F_{bang} = 300\ 000 \text{ newtons}$$

This is 50 times bigger than F_{brakes} – the force involved in stopping the same car with the brakes. It will certainly cause damage to the car – and maybe the driver and passengers as well.

Picture 8 Do posters help to save lives?

■ Travel slowly – think quickly

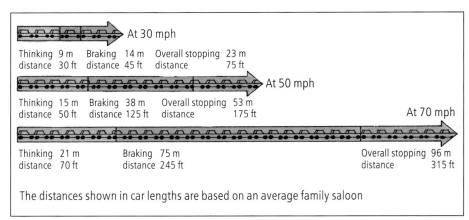

At 30 mph
Thinking distance 9 m / 30 ft   Braking distance 14 m / 45 ft   Overall stopping distance 23 m / 75 ft

At 50 mph
Thinking distance 15 m / 50 ft   Braking distance 38 m / 125 ft   Overall stopping distance 53 m / 175 ft

At 70 mph
Thinking distance 21 m / 70 ft   Braking distance 75 m / 245 ft   Overall stopping distance 96 m / 315 ft

The distances shown in car lengths are based on an average family saloon

Table 1 Official stopping distances.

The chart in table 1 shows the official stopping distances for cars with good tyres and good brakes. It has been worked out by the government's Department of Transport. The faster a car is going, the more momentum it has, so it takes longer to stop. The 'braking distance' is how far the car travels in this time.

The chart also shows the 'thinking distance'. It takes time for a driver to react to an emergency. The thinking distance is how far the car travels before the driver reacts by stepping on the brake pedal.

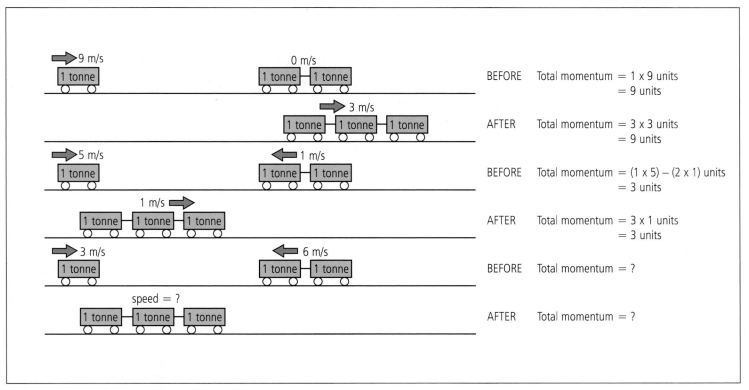

BEFORE	Total momentum	= 1 x 9 units	
		= 9 units	
AFTER	Total momentum	= 3 x 3 units	
		= 9 units	
BEFORE	Total momentum	= (1 x 5) − (2 x 1) units	
		= 3 units	
AFTER	Total momentum	= 3 x 1 units	
		= 3 units	
BEFORE	Total momentum	= ?	
AFTER	Total momentum	= ?	

Picture 9 Momentum stays unchanged in a collision.

SPEED LIMITS

The physics of this topic should help you understand the reasons for speed limits on the road. At high speeds both thinking distance and braking distance are increased. In fact the braking distance is quadrupled for a doubling in speed (picture 8).

Also, the force of a collision is greater at a greater speed, so that more damage is done. In fact, the damage more than doubles when the speed doubles. This is because a bigger force acts for a longer time.

SEAT BELTS

For safety, all people travelling in a car should wear a safety belt. When they are strapped in they are part of the car. This means that they are stopped at the same rate as the car. In a crash they stay with the car, instead of flying through the windscreen.

If the car stops slowly, so do the people in it. The friction force between them and the seat is enough to slow them down. In a crash, or even very sharp braking, they will *carry on moving* unless they are strapped in. In a crash at 100 km/h they will hit the dashboard or windscreen of the car at this very high speed. Very serious injuries are caused in this way (picture 10). This is because the stopping time is so short. Seat belts are designed to increase the stopping time. The belts are made so that they 'give' a little, and the driver and passengers takes a little longer to stop than the car does.

Crumple zones and *air bags* also reduce damage by increasing the stopping time.

The principle is the same when you jump from a height on to soft foam rubber, compared with rigid concrete. You take longer to stop and so the stopping force is less.

Picture 10 Why safety belts and crumple zones are helping to save lives.

■ Explosions

Explosions are what happen in guns and fireworks as well as bombs. It even makes sense to think of rockets as being made to move by a continuous explosion of the rocket fuel. Before the explosion all the parts are still. Think of firing a shell from a gun. The explosion converts energy stored in chemicals into the kinetic energy of moving parts. The law of conservation of momentum says that momentum **does not change**. This means that the shell carries away just the same quantity of momentum as the gun – but in opposite directions (picture 11).

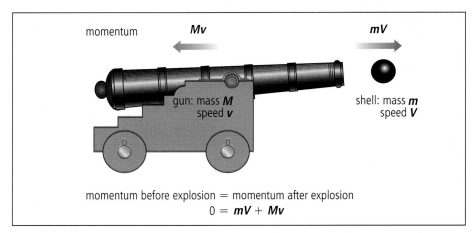

momentum before explosion = momentum after explosion

$$0 = mV + Mv$$

Picture 11 Both shell and gun have the same amount of momentum – but in opposite directions. Why doesn't the gun move as fast as the shell?

Remember that momentum is a vector: the shell has momentum mV while the gun has momentum Mv. V and v must be in exactly opposite directions. As momentum at the start is zero, then after the explosion it is still zero, so

$$mV + Mv = 0$$

This will only work if V is opposite in direction to v, so that one of them carries a minus sign.

Suppose the gun has a mass of 2500 kg and shell a mass of 2.5 kg. The explosion propels the shell at a speed of 800 m/s. As the gun is a thousand times more massive than the shell it will move at just one thousandth the speed of the

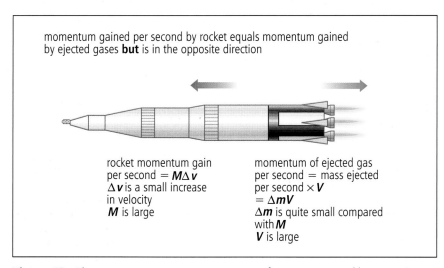

momentum gained per second by rocket equals momentum gained by ejected gases **but** is in the opposite direction

rocket momentum gain per second = $M\Delta v$
Δv is a small increase in velocity
M is large

momentum of ejected gas per second = mass ejected per second × V
= ΔmV
Δm is quite small compared with M
V is large

Picture 12 The waste gases carry away an amount of momentum equal but opposite to that given to the rocket.

shell: 8 m/s. This in fact would be a dangerously high speed for such a massive object – sailors in Nelson's time knew all about this. A modern gun gets rid of this unwanted momentum by using it to push out or compress gases.

Rockets burn a fuel explosively and propel the waste gases out at the back at a very high speed – making a very simple kind of motor. See picture 12. The momentum gained by the high speed mass of gas is equal and opposite to the momentum gained by the much more massive rocket. It gains speed quite slowly as the gases pour out. Rocket engines of this type are used to put satellites into orbit – rather expensively. Most of the rocket's mass on the launch pad is fuel which eventually gets up. The payload is a tiny fraction of the mass of the fuel. In fact most of the fuel on the launch pad is needed to propel the rocket to its final orbital stage.

Questions

1 Predict and try to explain what happens when:
   a a car travelling at 30 mph on an icy road comes to a sharp bend,
   b a cyclist travelling downhill at 40 mph puts on the front brake.

2 Why do heavy container lorries need stronger, more powerful brakes than an ordinary passenger car does?

3 a How do they stop ships (like tankers or liners)?
   b How do they slow aircraft down while they are in the air?
   c How do you slow down, when you are running fast?
   d Why do Jumbo Jet aircraft need longer airport runways than ordinary jets?

4 How does a 'crumple zone' help to protect the passengers in a car?

5 Design an experiment you could do to test a playground surface to see if it was a 'safety surface' or not.

6 Calculate the momentum of the following:
   a a man of mass 70 kg running at 10m/s,
   b a container lorry travelling at maximum speed on a motorway (mass = 30 000 kg; speed 30 m/s),
   c an ocean liner travelling at its cruising speed (mass 50 thousand tonnes (50 000 000 kg), speed 20 m/s).

7 Use your answers to question 6 to answer the following.
   a What would be the force exerted on the runner if he bumped into a tree and stopped in a time of 1/20th second (0.05s)?
   b What would be the braking force needed to stop the container lorry if it stopped in a time of 5 seconds? (This is the braking time assumed in the Highway Code.)
   c What might happen if the lorry had brakes which were, say, ten times as powerful?
   d How long would it take to stop the ocean liner if the stopping force was 1 MN (1 000 000 newtons)?

8 A car designer thought of an idea which he thought would cut down the injuries produced in road accidents. He suggested that cars should be made to a new and very strong design. They would use steel which was very elastic so that the cars would neither break nor crush, but just bounce off each other.
   a What would happen if two cars of this type collided with each other head on?
   b Would this kind of design be a good idea? Explain.

9 Describe what you would expect to happen to the speeds of the moving objects as a result of the following collisions:
   a A small boy running along a corridor bumps into a very large man.
   b A large oil tanker moving at speed collides with a small yacht.
   c Two equal sized cars travelling at 80 km/h in opposite directions collide with each other head on.

10 Give simple explanations of the following, using the ideas of momentum and/or of 'action' and 'reaction'.
   a A moving snooker ball moves another one when it hits it, but doesn't seem to move the table when it hits the side.
   b One way to get off a perfectly smooth surface, such as a sheet of very slippery ice, would be to take off a boot and throw it along the ice.
   c Sprinters use spiked shoes.
   d When a gun fires a shell, the gun 'recoils'.
   e Kicking a football is quite easy, but kicking a stone cannonball of the same size could seriously damage your foot.

11 When a gun is fired the bullet leaves it at a very high speed. It is driven out by the force of expanding gases. This force acts on both the gun and the bullet (by Newton's Law 3). Why doesn't the gun move backwards at the same speed as the bullet goes forward?

12 A railway truck of mass 200 tonnes is moving at a speed of 8 m/s in a shunting yard. It bumps into a group of three similar trucks (total mass 600 tonnes) and sticks to them. At what speed will the four trucks begin to move off together?

13 A spacecraft has a mass of 2000 kg. It switches on its rocket engine for a short time during which it emits 6 kg of hot gas at a speed of 4000 m/s.
   a How much momentum is carried away by the gas?
   b How much momentum is gained by the spacecraft?
   c Show that use of the rocket engine has changed the spacecraft's speed by about 12 m/s.

The mathematics of movement

Physics and mathematics go hand in hand. The great value of physics is that it can use mathematics to make very accurate predictions.

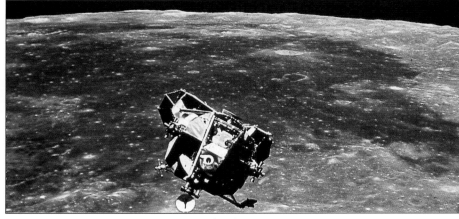

Picture 1 Accurate scientific calculations have enabled us to send capsules and satellites into space – and keep them there.

■ Moving in space

1969. A space craft is orbiting the moon. At exactly the right moment, to the nearest hundredth of a second, the rockets are fired. They produce a very precise force, in exactly the right direction. They are on for a precisely calculated time. The capsule, and the precious human cargo it contains, land safely on the lunar surface.

1840. The planet Uranus, orbiting the Sun moves slowly against the background of the fixed stars. Astronomers plot its path, and calculate exactly where it should be in a week's, a month's, a year's time. Then they notice that it is not quite where it should be. What has gone wrong? Perhaps the laws of physics don't work so far away from Earth? Did they do the sums correctly?

■ A new planet is found

Two astronomers, unknown to each other and working in different countries, have the same idea. Could there be another planet out there in space that no one has seen? The gravity force from the unknown planet could be pulling the planet Uranus out of its plotted path.

One astronomer, Jean Leverrier, is French; the other, John Adams, is English. Unknown to each other, they both work out where the new planet should be. Leverrier sends his predictions to the German astronomers in Berlin, and they spot it in the sky the same night.

PHYSICS AND MATHEMATICS WORKING TOGETHER

John Adams needed four years to make his calculations, using pen and paper. The planet was named Neptune, and was discovered in 1846. The astronauts had their orbits, speeds, forces and times controlled by on-board computers. The calculations were done in thousandths of a second. Picture 3 shows the planet Neptune as it was photographed by the Voyager Space Probe as it flew past in 1989. Although separated in time by over a hundred years, astronomers and astronauts both relied on very accurate mathematical calculations.

Their calculations were based on the same simple rules of physics. These rules were set out by Isaac Newton in the 17th century. They are the laws of gravity (see topic B4), and the laws obeyed by objects moving under the action of forces *(dynamics)*.

The basic mathematics dealing with moving objects is summarised below. You can follow the proofs to help you understand what the formulae mean.

Picture 2 Adams and Leverrier – the discoverers of the planet Neptune.

In this section we use the following symbols for the quantities we measure:

time	*t*	force	*F*
distance	*s*	acceleration and deceleration	*a*
speed at start	*u*	mass	*m*
speed at end	*v*		

■ The equations of movement: speed, distance, acceleration and time

To help you keep track, each formula is numbered.

AVERAGE SPEED

We have already seen in topic B1 that

$$\text{average speed} = \frac{\text{total distance covered}}{\text{total time taken}}$$

Or $\qquad \boldsymbol{v = s/t} \qquad$ (1)

ACCELERATION

Something that speeds up is **accelerating**. If it is increasing its speed steadily we say that it has a steady **acceleration, *a***. For straight line movement, this is defined as **change in speed per second**. To measure acceleration we need to measure not only the change in speed of an object but also the time it takes to change its speed (see picture 4).

That is:

$$\text{acceleration} = \frac{\text{change in speed}}{\text{time taken for change}}$$

Or, acceleration $= \dfrac{\text{speed at end of timing} - \text{speed at start}}{\text{time interval}}$

As a formula: $\qquad \boldsymbol{a = \dfrac{v - u}{t}} \qquad$ (2)

The unit is $\dfrac{\text{metres per second}}{\text{seconds}} \quad$ or $\quad$ m/s²

The formula (2) can be rearranged as $\boldsymbol{v = u + at} \qquad$ (3) $\quad$ (See the Mathsbox.)

Picture 3 The planet Neptune.

Changing the subject of a formula

a stands for acceleration
u stands for speed or velocity at the start of timing
v stands for speed or velocity at the end of timing
t stands for the timing period
s stands for distance

From the definition of acceleration we have

$$a = \frac{v - u}{t}$$

Multiply both sides of the equation by **t** (so keeping things fair):

$$at = \frac{v - u}{t} \times t \qquad \text{these \textit{t}'s cancel each other out}$$

so we get $\qquad \boldsymbol{at = v - u}$

Now add **u** to both sides:
$$u + at = v - u + u$$

The two **u**'s on the right cancel each other out:
So we get $\qquad \boldsymbol{u + at = v}$
Swapping the sides around gives: $\boldsymbol{v = u + at}$
Final speed **v** is now the subject of the formula.

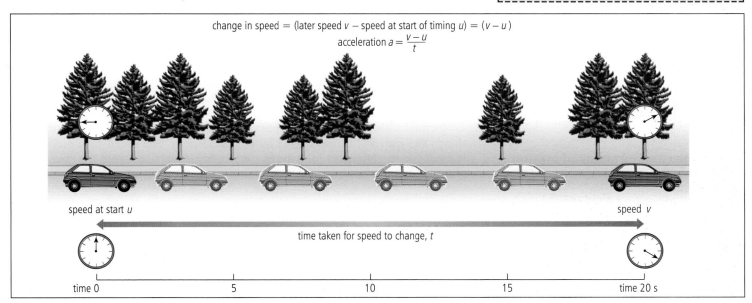

Picture 4 How acceleration is calculated.

■ Picturing motion

One of the best ways for both visualising, analysing and predicting movements is to use graphs. Data from experiments might produce long columns of numbers. These will be hard to read and make sense of. But it is easy to convert the set of measurements into a graph using a spreadsheet. Data can be captured electronically and converted automatically into a graph on a computer screen. You can even draw graphs by hand!

Picture 5 shows the data from an experiment that has been put into a spreadsheet. The data was then used to draw the graph.

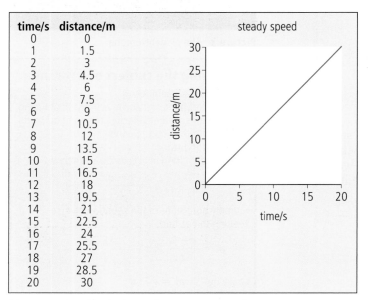

time/s	distance/m
0	0
1	1.5
2	3
3	4.5
4	6
5	7.5
6	9
7	10.5
8	12
9	13.5
10	15
11	16.5
12	18
13	19.5
14	21
15	22.5
16	24
17	25.5
18	27
19	28.5
20	30

Picture 5 Steady speed on a distance–time graph.

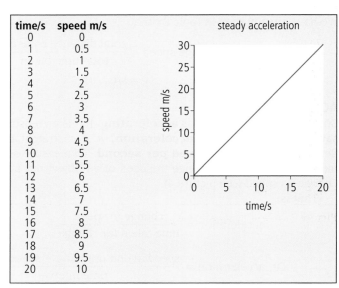

time/s	speed m/s
0	0
1	0.5
2	1
3	1.5
4	2
5	2.5
6	3
7	3.5
8	4
9	4.5
10	5
11	5.5
12	6
13	6.5
14	7
15	7.5
16	8
17	8.5
18	9
19	9.5
20	10

Picture 6 Steady acceleration on a speed–time graph.

In this example the distance increases steadily with time. Every second the object travels 1.5 metres further. In other words, the object is moving at a **steady speed** of 1.5 m/s. Whenever you see a straight line graph of distance plotted against time, the object is moving at a constant speed. When the graph line is curved, the speed is changing.

Picture 6 is a speed-time graph. It is a straight line showing that the speed is increasing steadily with time. This means that the object is moving with a steady (constant) **acceleration**.

The data shows that the object is increasing its speed by 0.5 m/s every second. Its acceleration is 0.5 m/s². Again, a straight line speed-time graph tells us that we have a constant acceleration.

Picture 7 shows a more complicated movement. This is more natural. Real things like cars and runners don't move that steadily. The speed-time graph here is what you might expect for a short car journey. Compare it with the speed-time graph of a runner on page 58.

EQUATIONS OF MOTION

It is often quicker to predict or analyse movements using a set of formulae called the **equations of motion**. These only work when the movement is simple: the objects are moving at constant speed or with constant acceleration. The equations are listed in the Mathsbox.

Equations and formulae of motion

$$\text{average speed} = \frac{\text{distance covered}}{\text{time taken}}$$

$$v = u + at$$

$$s = \tfrac{1}{2}(u + v)t$$

$$v^2 = u^2 + 2as$$

$$s = ut + \tfrac{1}{2}at^2$$

Also: $F = ma$

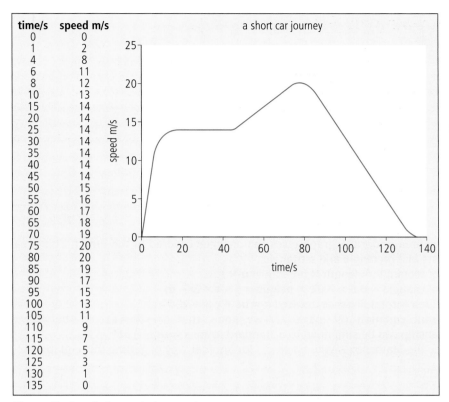

time/s	speed m/s
0	0
1	2
4	8
6	11
8	12
10	13
15	14
20	14
25	14
30	14
35	14
40	14
45	14
50	15
55	16
60	17
65	18
70	19
75	20
80	20
85	19
90	17
95	15
100	13
105	11
110	9
115	7
120	5
125	3
130	1
135	0

Picture 7   A realistic speed–time graph.

■ Finding the distance travelled from a knowledge of speeds and time

The simplest case is when an object is moving at constant speed – or we are given the average speed for a journey. For example, experience tells a driver that on a motorway she can expect to travel at an average speed of 90 km per hour, allowing for some traffic jams here and there. It is easy to work out that she will expect to travel 270 km in 3 hours.

The idea can be written as a formula:

$$\text{distance covered} = \text{average speed} \times \text{time}$$
$$s = vt$$

This idea works of course not only for an expected average speed, but also when the speed is actually constant.

Now look at the top graph (a) in Picture 8. It is a speed-time graph showing a constant speed v. The shaded area is a rectangle of sides representing v and t. Its area is vt – the distance travelled, s. The idea of giving some meaning to the area under a graph is important and useful. It is obvious here that the area under the speed-time graph gives us the distance travelled. In fact this is true whatever the shape of the graph – even the complicated car journey graph of picture 7.

Now look at the bottom graph (b) in picture 8. It shows an ideal case: an object starts off at a speed u then accelerates steadily to speed v. The area under this graph gives us the distance travelled in the time t. Picture 9 shows this for actual numbers: note that the time and distance units must match: we can't mix km/h with m/s.

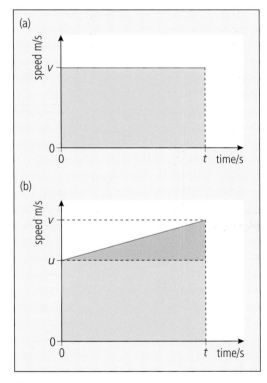

Picture 8

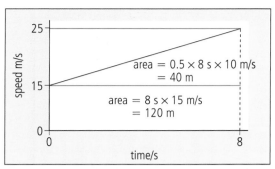

Picture 9 The area under a speed–time graph tells us the distance travelled.

The area under the graph gives the distance covered in the time t. This area consists of a rectangle and a triangle.

Area of rectangle = length $\times$ breadth = $\boldsymbol{u \times t}$

Area of triangle = 0.5 $\times$ base $\times$ height = $\frac{1}{2} \times \boldsymbol{t} \times (\boldsymbol{v - u})$

Total area = total distance covered $\boldsymbol{s = ut + \frac{1}{2}(v - u)t}$

But from equation (2) (page 71) we know that $(\boldsymbol{v - u}) = \boldsymbol{at}$, so the above relationship can be simplified to a standard form: $\boldsymbol{s = ut + \frac{1}{2}at^2}$

See the Mathsbox *Algebraic proofs* for another way of getting this equation.

Algebraic proofs

The equation of motion for distance

This equation lets us predict how far a vehicle will travel, say, in a time t when it starts accelerating from a initial speed $\boldsymbol{u}$.

Look at the motion shown in picture 8(b).

Average speed in the time $\boldsymbol{t}$ is $\dfrac{(\boldsymbol{u + v})}{2}$

Distance covered $\boldsymbol{s}$ is average speed $\times$ time = $\dfrac{(\boldsymbol{u + v})}{2}\boldsymbol{t}$

$\qquad \boldsymbol{s = \frac{1}{2}(u + v)t}$

Remove the brackets: $\boldsymbol{s = \frac{1}{2}ut + \frac{1}{2}vt}$

The idea is to get an equation that doesn't need final speed $\boldsymbol{v}$, but uses the acceleration $\boldsymbol{a}$.

Remember that $\boldsymbol{v = (u + at)}$

Insert this value for $\boldsymbol{v}$

so $\qquad\qquad \boldsymbol{s = \frac{1}{2}ut + \frac{1}{2}vt}$

becomes $\qquad\quad \boldsymbol{s = \frac{1}{2}ut + \frac{1}{2}(u + at)t}$

remove brackets $\quad \boldsymbol{s = \frac{1}{2}ut + \frac{1}{2}ut + \frac{1}{2}at^2}$

and simplify $\qquad \boldsymbol{s = ut + \frac{1}{2}at^2}$

What if we don't know the time....?

Start again with $\boldsymbol{s = \frac{1}{2}(u + v)t}$

Use $\boldsymbol{v = (a + at)}$ again, but make $\boldsymbol{t}$ the subject of the equation:

$\quad \boldsymbol{v = u + at}$ becomes $\boldsymbol{v - u = at}$ becomes $\boldsymbol{t = (v - u)/a}$

Insert this value for $\boldsymbol{t}$

$\qquad \boldsymbol{s = \frac{1}{2}(u + v)t}$

$\qquad \boldsymbol{s = \frac{1}{2}(u + v)(v - u)/a}$

which multiplies out to become $\boldsymbol{s = \frac{1}{2}(v^2 - u^2)/a}$

and can be rearranged (multiply both sides by 2 and by $\boldsymbol{a}$) to become

$\qquad \boldsymbol{2as = v^2 - u^2}$

This is usually written as $\boldsymbol{v^2 = u^2 + 2as}$

This equation can be used to find any one of $\boldsymbol{a}$, $\boldsymbol{u}$, $\boldsymbol{v}$ or $\boldsymbol{s}$ given the other three quantities

Dynamics: momentum, force and acceleration

We have already come across momentum (***mv***) and the idea that it is a combination of force (***F***) and time (***t***) that causes a change in momentum: (see page 64)

$$\boldsymbol{Ft} = \text{change in } (\boldsymbol{mv}) \quad (4)$$

Momentum changes when speed changes, so it makes sense to rewrite (4) like this:

$$\boldsymbol{Ft} = \text{momentum change}$$
$$\boldsymbol{Ft} = (\text{momentum with ending speed}) - (\text{momentum with starting speed})$$
$$\boldsymbol{Ft} = \boldsymbol{mv} - \boldsymbol{mu}$$
$$\boldsymbol{Ft} = \boldsymbol{m}(\boldsymbol{v} - \boldsymbol{u}) \quad (5)$$

Ft is called **impulse**, and the formula put into words says

$$\text{impulse} = \text{change of momentum}$$

We can rearrange formula (4) like this:

$$\boldsymbol{F} = \boldsymbol{m}\frac{(\boldsymbol{v} - \boldsymbol{u})}{\boldsymbol{t}}$$

$$\text{Now } \frac{(\boldsymbol{v} - \boldsymbol{u})}{\boldsymbol{t}}$$

looks familiar. It is what we defined above (2) as **acceleration, *a***. The formula becomes simpler:

$$\boldsymbol{F} = \boldsymbol{ma} \quad (6)$$

In words: ***force = mass × acceleration.***
   This is one of the most important formulae in physics. It is the basis of space flight, astronomy, car performance and indeed any kind of animal and human movement.

THE NEWTON

It is the above formula (6) that is used to define the unit of force used in science and engineering. A **newton** is the size of the force that can give a mass of 1 kilogram an acceleration of 1 m/s².

$$1 \text{ N} = 1 \text{ kg} \times 1 \text{ m/s}^2$$

Newton's Laws of Motion

Newton wrote down three simple laws to describe how and why objects move. They summarise the ideas we have already met.
   Newton 1: An object will keep still or carry on moving at a steady speed in a straight line unless a **force** acts on it.
   Newton 2: The effect of a force on an object free to move is to change its momentum such that force × time equals the momentum change produced.
   Newton 3: Forces are always found in **pairs**, equal in size but acting in opposite directions.
   Newton's Laws are very reliable in everyday life and in astronomy. But in this century we have found that they break down at very high speeds and we have to use Einstein's ideas instead.
   Newton's Laws are very important in physics, and they will be used a lot in the next sections. As you use them you will learn to understand them better.

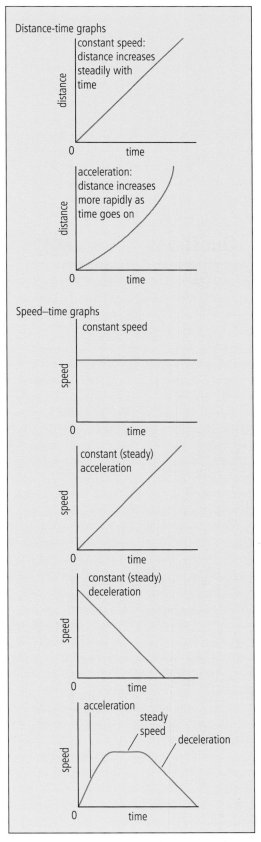

Picture 10 Graphs showing different kinds of movement.

Activity

A Use a library, CD-ROM or encyclopaedia to find out what you can about:

1 the Apollo space flights and Moon landings

2 the discovery of Neptune.

Questions ICT

To answer these questions you may need to use the formulae given in this section or to draw graphs.

1 a A cyclist travelled 25 km in two hours. What was the average speed of the cyclist?

b How far would a car travel in 5 hours at an average speed of 80 km per hour?

c How long would it take an athlete running at an average speed of 5 m/s to cover a distance of 2000 metres?

2 Calculate the following:

a the change in speed produced when a car accelerates at 2m/s^2 for a time of 15 seconds,

b the acceleration required to speed up an aircraft from a speed of 100 m/s to 500 m/s in 40 seconds,

c the speed change produced in a ship when it is decelerated at a rate of 0.2 m/s^2 for 100 seconds,

d how long it would take a car travelling at 30 m/s (about 70 mph) to stop, at a deceleration of 4 m/s^2.

3 Look at Newton's Law 1 (above). It says that any moving object will carry on moving unless a force acts on it. When you hit a snooker ball it moves off at high speed, but it doesn't keep on moving for ever, even on an empty table.

a Why is this? Does this mean that Newton was wrong?

b Is there any object anywhere in the universe that moves at the same speed in a straight line, for ever?

4 Why is it harder to push start a bus than a mini-car?

5 The following measurements were taken on a specially calibrated car speedometer.

time after start in s	speed (in m/s)
0	0
2	3
4	6
6	9
8	12
10	15
12	18
14	20
16	21
18	21
20	21

a Draw a speed/time graph of these results.

b Describe the motion of the car during this 20 second period.

c By how much did the speed change in the first 10 seconds?

d What was the acceleration of the car during the first ten seconds?

e The car had a total mass of 800 kg. What force was needed to produce this acceleration?

f How was this force actually made to act on the car?

6 In the Highway Code it says that a car should be able to brake to a stop from a speed of 14 m/s (about the speed limit in towns) in a distance of 15 m.

a What is its deceleration in m/s^2?

b A typical car has a mass of 1500 kg. What force must the brakes exert to stop it in this distance?

c How long will the car take to stop?

7 Look at picture 11.

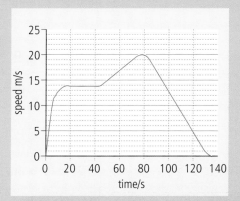

Picture 11 A short car journey

a Describe how the movement of the car changed during the journey.

b Between what times was the car accelerating?

c Between what times was the car decelerating?

d Use the data from the table or from the graph to estimate (i) the rate at which the car began to accelerate (ii) the rate at which the car decelerated as it came to a stop.

8 A car is braked to a stop from a speed of 30 m/s in a time of 6 seconds.

a What is the deceleration of the car?

b The car has a mass of 1090 kg. What average force did the brakes exert on the car?

c The manufacturer claims that the car can accelerate to a speed of 27 m/s in a time of 12 s. What average force must the engine produce to get this result?

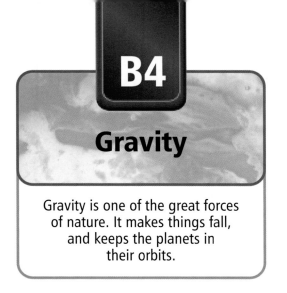

B4

Gravity

Gravity is one of the great forces of nature. It makes things fall, and keeps the planets in their orbits.

GRAVITY IS EVERYWHERE

Everything we do is affected by gravity. Running, jumping, swimming or just standing still, our bodies are affected by the force that pulls us towards the centre of the Earth. We are so used to it that our very bones grow weaker without it. This happens to astronauts who spend a long time in 'free-fall' (see below).

We can't switch gravity off, the way we can switch off an electromagnet. We can't neutralise it, like we can the forces of static electricity. We have to live with the fact that everything on the surface of the Earth is in a strong gravity field.

The design of roads, railways, buildings, aircraft and even the bodies of living things have to take gravity into account. The study of movement under gravity is vital in physics and engineering, as well as in ball games like tennis and football.

THE GRAVITY FORCE FIELD

Every object attracts every other object with a gravity force. The gravity force between you and the person sitting next to you is very small. You attract each other with a force of about a millionth of a newton. You will not notice this.

Gravity forces become important when at least one of the objects is very massive. The earth has a mass of about six million million million million kilograms, so its gravity field is quite strong.

■ The Earth's gravity field

The strength of a gravity field is measured in terms of how much force it exerts on a 1 kilogram mass.

On Earth, the force of gravity on an object of mass 1 kilogram is about 10 newtons – or 9.8 newtons to be more exact. So the strength of the Earth's gravity field, g, is 9.8 N per kg.

If we put a more massive object in the gravity field it will have a bigger gravity force acting on it. A piece of iron with mass 2 kg has twice as much iron in it as a piece of iron with a mass of only 1 kilogram, so it will be pulled towards the Earth with twice the force.

A 2 kg mass feels heavier than a 1 kg mass because it is being pulled down by a force of about 20 N, compared with only about 10 N for the 1 kg mass. The force caused by gravity on a mass is called its **weight**.

We can get a rough measure of weight by just holding the object up. To measure it more accurately we need a newton meter. This is usually a spring balance marked off in newtons.

The weight of an object of mass m – the force F due to gravity on it – is given by the formula $F = mg$.

gravity force (weight) = mass × field strength

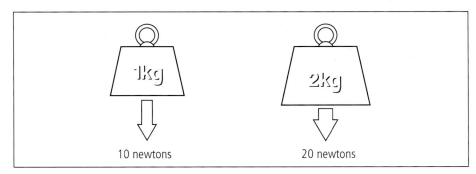

Picture 1 Playing with gravity.

Picture 2 Gravity fields pull harder on a greater mass.

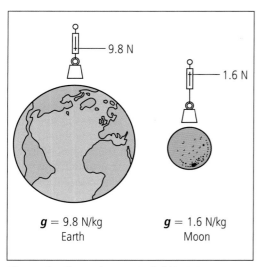

Picture 3 The Earth's gravity field is 6 times stronger than the Moon's.

WHAT DECIDES THE STRENGTH OF A GRAVITY FIELD?

Gravity is a force between two or more objects. The size of this force depends on two things:

- how massive the objects are,
- how far apart they are.

Like all forces, gravity forces occur in pairs: both objects pull equally on each other.

This means that you pull on the Earth with just as much gravity force as the Earth pulls on you. Of course, when you jump off a diving board into a swimming pool you do the moving, not the Earth. This is because the Earth has so much more mass than you have, and so doesn't move so easily.

When we look at objects on Earth, the Earth is so massive that it alone decides the strength of the field. By comparison, a tennis ball, an aeroplane or even a continent is too small to make much difference to the main field.

THE SUN

The Sun is very much larger than the Earth and its field is so strong that it affects the Earth. The Sun is a long way away, but it is the Sun's gravity that makes the Earth travel in an orbit around the Sun. It also helps to make the tides of the sea.

THE MOON

On the Moon, the gravity field is smaller than on the Earth, because the Moon is so much less massive (picture 3). Its field strength is only 1.6 N per kg – about a sixth of that on Earth. So on the Moon you weigh only one-sixth of your weight on Earth.

■ Gravity and distance

But distance also comes into it. The further away you get from a massive object the smaller is the strength of its gravity field (picture 4).

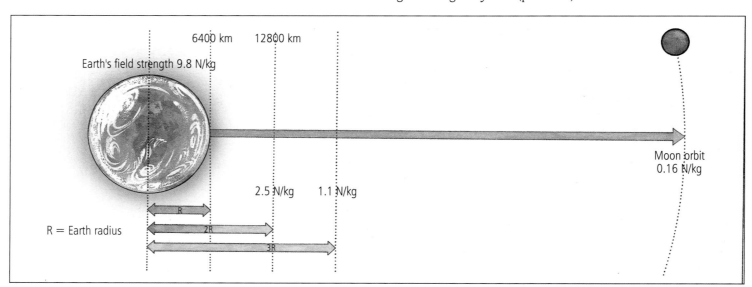

Picture 4 The gravity field grows weaker with distance – doubling the distance cuts the field to a quarter.

If the Earth was compressed to the size of the Moon the gravity field on its surface would be a lot bigger – about 14 times bigger. This is because you would be much closer to the centre of the Earth. You would weigh 14 times as much and need much stronger bones to be able to stand up and move about. Life on Earth would be very different.

■ Black holes

If you could get a very large mass squashed into a very small space indeed it would produce an immensely strong gravity field. We think this is what happens in a **black hole**. The Earth would become a black hole if it was squashed to the size of a table tennis ball. Its gravity field would be so strong that nothing could get away from it – not even light. This is illustrated in picture 5. See topic G6 for more about black holes.

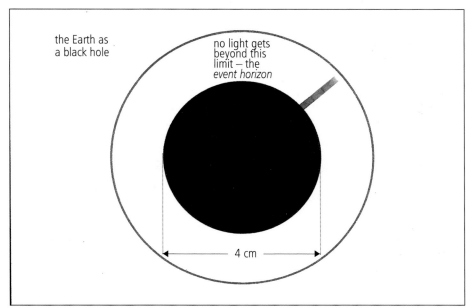

Picture 5   The gravity field of a black hole is so strong that not even light can escape from it. As a black hole, the Earth would collapse to be about 4 cm across.

■ Measuring the strength of the Earth's gravity field

The strength of the Earth's gravity field is defined as the force it exerts on a kilogram of matter. The easy way to measure it would be to use a newton meter as a force measurer and hang a mass of 1 kilogram on it (picture 6). But this would be cheating! The newton meter has been made at a factory and tested for accuracy by seeing if it gave the right reading when a mass was hung on it. It has been marked off on the assumption that the Earth's gravity field at the surface is 9.8 newtons per kilogram.

A better way is to measure the *acceleration of free fall*, **g**. As explained in the next topic (topic B5), the acceleration of free fall is numerically the same as the field strength, i.e. 9.8 m/s^2.

Because its gravity field is so weak the Moon doesn't have an atmosphere. Air has weight, and it is the force of gravity that holds it on the Earth. But there is more to this than just the weight of the air.

Air molecules move very fast – on Earth they move at an average speed of about 500 metres a second. Some molecules move a lot faster than the average, of course. Now to escape from the Earth, they would need to move at the speed of an Earth satellite – over 11 000 metres per second. This is called the escape speed for the Earth. Hardly any molecules move this fast so air stays on Earth.

On the Moon the escape speed is much less, because of its weaker gravity field. It is only 2400 metres per second. The fastest molecules travel faster than this, so any atmosphere on the Moon would gradually leak away.

Picture 6   Measuring the strength of the gravity field.

Activities

A Agreeing about gravity

In this activity the idea is to get the whole class to agree about some statements about gravity. You will be given some paper. Write on it your own personal opinion about the statements below. You have to say whether you agree with them or not. You are not allowed to say 'don't know'!

Next, team up with one other person. Discuss the statements and decide for each one whether you agree or not. You have to argue until you agree with each other!

Then, find another pair of students and do the same, until all four of you agree. Then team up with another four and come to an agreement with them.

Finally, get a fresh sheet of paper and pin it up on the wall with your large group decision on it. Walk around and see what the other groups have decided.

If you all disagree your teacher will probably do something about it! If you all agree and you are wrong, your teacher has some work to do!

Task

Say whether or not you agree with the following statements about gravity.

1 The Earth is not affected by the gravity of the Sun because it is too far away.

2 An astronaut in a spacecraft going around the Earth is not acted on by the Earth's gravity.

3 There is no gravity above the Earth's atmosphere.

4 A heavy stone will fall faster than a light stone.

5 The air is too light to be affected by the Earth's gravity.

B Black holes

Research anything you can find about 'black holes'. Draw a poster explaining what they are.

C Gravity and animals

The pull of gravity on animals depends on their mass. An ant has a mass of, say, 0.1 g, while an adult African elephant has a mass of about 6 tonnes. The largest land animal known is an extinct dinosaur. This was Brachiosaurus, and it had a mass of about 100 tonnes. The largest animal on Earth today is the blue whale, which has a mass of about 130 tonnes. Think about the problems of being very light and very heavy. Work as a group to give answers to the following questions.

1 What problems does an animal have if it is very light?

2 What problems would a very heavy animal have? (Think about leg size, moving fast, falling down…)

3 Why are sea animals able to be so much more massive than land animals?

4 What problems would a human being have on (a) a planet with a very strong gravity field (b) a planet with a very weak gravity field?

Questions

1 Why is the gravity field near the Earth bigger than the field near the Moon?

2 a What is the difference between the mass of an object, and its weight?

 b How far would an object have to be from the Earth (or any other planet, or a star) so that it didn't have any weight?

3 An astronaut on the Moon drops a hammer. It falls to the ground more slowly than it would on Earth. This is because:

 a there is no air pressure on the Moon to push it down,

 b the hammer has less mass on the Moon than it has on Earth,

 c the gravity field of the Moon is weaker than the gravity field on Earth,

 d the force of gravity is always weaker in a vacuum.

4 Use the formula:

 gravity force (weight)
  = mass × field strength

and the data given in the table to calculate the weight of the following:

 a a car of mass 800 kg on Earth,

 b an astronaut of mass 70 kg on the Moon,

 c an astronaut of mass 70 kg on Earth,

 d an apple of mass 0.2 kg on the planet Jupiter,

 e an astronaut of mass 70 kg on the surface of a neutron star.

Place	Gravity field strength, g N/kg
Earth	10
Moon	1.6
Jupiter	26.3
neutron star	2×10^{12}

Use the equations of motion from page 74 to help answer the following questions. Take the acceleration of free fall (due to gravity) as 10 m/s^2.

5 A metal ball is dropped from the top of a tower 25 high.

 a At what speed should it hit the ground? (Ignore friction.)

 b Show by calculation that the ball takes about two and a quarter seconds to reach the ground.

6 A powerful player mis-hits a tennis ball and it goes straight upwards with a starting speed of 26 m/s. Show by calculation that (a) it rises to a height of 34 m (b) it is in the air for just over 5 s.

7 A stone is dropped into a deep well and the splash as it hits the water is heard after 1.8 s. How far down is it to the water level?

A spreadsheet for investigating accelerated motion

	A	B	C	D	E	F	G	H	I	J	K	L	M
1		accelerated motion											
2													
3	data				algorithms								
4	initial speed V1 =		10	m/s	change in speed DV = a × Dt				= $C$5*$C$6				
5	acceleration, a =		2	m/s²	speed = old speed + DV				= B9+$C$5*$C$6				
6	interval, Dt =		0.1	s	change in distance Ds = average speed × Dt				= $C$6*(B9+B10)/2				
7					distance = old distance + Ds				= C9+$C$6*(B9+B10)/2				
8	time	speed	distance										
9	0	10	0										
10	0.1	10.2	1.01										
11	0.2	10.4	2.04										
12	0.3	10.6	3.09										
13	0.4	10.8	4.16										
14	0.5	11	5.25										
15	0.6	11.2	6.36										
16	0.7	11.4	7.49										
17	0.8	11.6	8.64										
18	0.9	11.8	9.81										
19	1	12	11										
20	1.1	12.2	12.21										
21	1.2	12.4	13.44										
22	1.3	12.6	14.69										
23	1.4	12.8	15.96										
24	1.5	13	17.25										
25	1.6	13.2	18.56										
26	1.7	13.4	19.89										
27	1.8	13.6	21.24										
28	1.9	13.8	22.61										

distance–time graph for constant acceleration — distance/m vs time/s

speed — speed m/s vs time/s

Picture 1

Picture 1 shows a print-out of the beginning of a spreadsheet simulation of accelerated motion. You can change the rate of acceleration to see what happens to the speed of an object and how far it travels in a given time. It shows this on graphs.

You may need help with starting with a spreadsheet program. This example was made on Excel, but other programs will work just as well.

Data
These are put in at the start. You can decide the starting speed of the object and its rate of acceleration. The calculations are repeated for small time intervals chosen here to be 0.1 second.

Algorithms
This is the name for the instructions that tell the program what to calculate.

For speed:
First, it repeatedly **adds**, every small time interval Dt, the change in speed during that interval to the speed at the start of the interval. This is done using the equation of motion:

change in speed = acceleration × time of change.

The speed changes in a jerky manner but the time interval is so small that it is hard to notice this.

For distance:
It has to make two calculations to find the total distance travelled.
First it calculates the change in distance for each small time interval: this is called Ds and is

average speed in time interval × time interval

Next it adds this distance to the distance covered by the start of the small time interval:

new distance = old distance + the small change in distance (Ds).

Constructing the spreadsheet
The easiest way to do this is to copy the formulae put into the first two rows in the columns headed time, speed, distance. The first few rows are shown in picture 2. Then you can copy down the formulae in the second row to a time of say 5 seconds. If you don't know how to do this read the program instructions – or ask someone to show you.

	A	B	C
8	time	speed	distance
9	0	=$C$4	0
10	=A9+$C$6	=B9+$C$5*$C$6	=C9+$C$6*(B9+B10)/2
11	=A10+$C$6	=B10+$C$5*$C$6	=C10+$C$6*(B10+B11)/2
12	=A11+$C$6	=B11+$C$5*$C$6	=C11+$C$6*(B11+B12)/2
13	=A12+$C$6	=B12+$C$5*$C$6	=C12+$C$6*(B12+B13)/2
14	=A13+$C$6	=B13+$C$5*$C$6	=C13+$C$6*(B13+B14)/2
15	=A14+$C$6	=B14+$C$5*$C$6	=C14+$C$6*(B14+B15)/2
16	=A15+$C$6	=B15+$C$5*$C$6	=C15+$C$6*(B15+B16)/2
17	=A16+$C$6	=B16+$C$5*$C$6	=C16+$C$6*(B16+B17)/2
18	=A17+$C$6	=B17+$C$5*$C$6	=C17+$C$6*(B17+B18)/2
19	=A18+$C$6	=B18+$C$5*$C$6	=C18+$C$6*(B18+B19)/2
20	=A19+$C$6	=B19+$C$5*$C$6	=C19+$C$6*(B19+B20)/2

Picture 2   Accelerated motion spreadsheet.

Things to try

Change one factor at a time.

1   What happens when you change the value of the initial (starting) speed? Try changing by 10 m/s at a time.

2   What happens when you change the acceleration?

3   Use the graph of distance v time to answer the following.

How far does an object travel in 5 s for:

a   an initial speed of zero and an acceleration of 4 m/s^2?

b   an initial speed of 5 m/s and an acceleration of 4 m/s^2?

c   an initial speed of zero and an acceleration of 8 m/s^2?

d   an initial speed of zero and an acceleration of 12 m/s^2?

e   What is the pattern linking acceleration and distance travelled in a given time?

4   The acceleration of free fall is -9.8 m/s^2. The minus sign is because speed is upwards and acceleration is downwards. We can build in the difference using the sign. Put this value of acceleration into the spreadsheet and answer the following questions. Each time explain how you got your answers from the graph.

a   Find out how far an object will fall in 3 seconds when you just let it go from a tall building.

b   How does the graph let you know the object is travelling downwards?

c   You throw an object up at an initial speed of 20 m/s.
   i   How long does it take to reach the ground?
   ii   How high does it go?

Gravity, movement and energy

All movement on Earth is affected by gravity. This topic deals with the way objects move in a gravity field.

Picture 1(a) shows a ball falling freely towards the Earth. It has been taken using a flashing light that lit the ball every tenth of a second. As you can see, the ball travels a greater and greater distance in each tenth of a second. It is accelerating.

This is because it is being pulled down with a steady force, and this produces a constant acceleration (see topic B3). It is called the **acceleration of free fall**.

Picture 1(b) shows the ball again. This time it has been thrown sideways. But gravity still acts, and the ball is pulled downwards exactly as before. This will happen however fast the ball is thrown sideways.

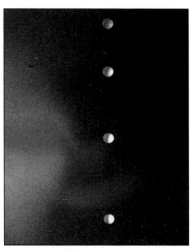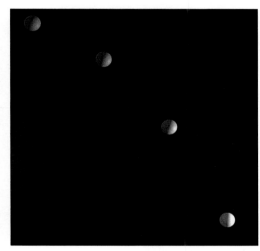

Picture 1   A freely falling object accelerates.

DO HEAVY OBJECTS FALL FASTER THAN LIGHT ONES?

No – but keep on reading.

An object is **heavy**, and feels heavy, because gravity is pulling on it with a large force. This is because a heavy object has more mass than a light object.

But because it has more mass it is harder to accelerate! The extra gravity force on the heavy object exactly compensates for the extra mass. So the acceleration of free fall is exactly the same, whatever the mass of the object – see picture 2. This is shown below mathematically.

Topic B3 has shown that a force causes an acceleration according to the rule

$$\text{force} = \text{mass} \times \text{acceleration}$$

$$\text{or } \boldsymbol{F = ma} \qquad (1)$$

The gravity force on an object in a field of strength $\boldsymbol{g}$ is

$$\text{force} = \text{mass} \times \text{field strength}$$

$$\text{or } \boldsymbol{F = mg} \qquad (2)$$

Putting these two ideas together (1) and (2) tell us that if the accelerating force is gravity, then

$$\boldsymbol{F = ma = mg}$$

and this can only be true if $\boldsymbol{a = g}$.

The size of the acceleration of free fall in a gravity field is equal to the size of the field strength.

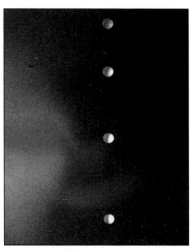

Picture 2   Freely falling objects accelerate at the same rate. The falling ball obeys Newton's Laws of Motion: it is being accelerated by the force of gravity.

1 kg   10 kg

10 N   10 m/s²   10 m/s²

100 N

small mass and small force   larger mass and larger force

result: same acceleration

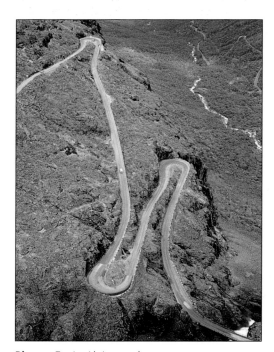

Picture 4 Parachutes greatly increase the force of air resistance.

■ How free is free fall?

There is another force that acts on a falling object, on Earth at least. This is the force of friction caused by the object moving through the air. This force depends on the size and shape of the falling object. People falling from an aeroplane accelerate quite rapidly to a high speed – unless they are using a parachute. The shape of the parachute increases the air friction, so they slow down once the parachute is opened.

But whether they wear a parachute or not the falling people eventually reach a steady speed, when they are not accelerating any more. This happens because the force of air resistance acts on them in the opposite direction to the gravity force – see picture 3.

The force caused by air resistance gets bigger the faster you go. (You can feel this when you travel fast on a bicycle.) When the air resistance becomes equal to the gravity force a falling object stops accelerating. It has reached what is called its **terminal** speed.

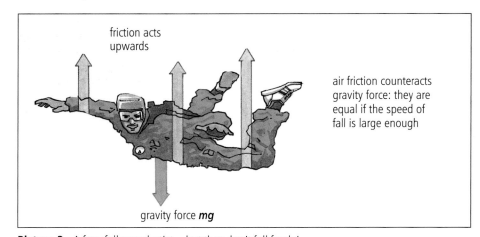

Picture 3 A free-fall parachutist – but they don't fall freely!

BALANCED FORCES

At this terminal speed the forces on the falling object are equal in size but opposite in direction – gravity pulling down, friction acting upwards. We say the forces are **balanced**. The total force is zero, and the object does not accelerate. In accordance with Newton's Laws it carries on moving with a constant speed in a straight line downwards.

WORKING AGAINST GRAVITY

Climbing up a hill is usually hard work, whether we walk or ride a bicycle. We are doing work by using muscular force to lift outselves against the force of gravity. Mountain roads and paths are built in zig-zags to make this job easier (see picture 5).

This makes the way less steep, so that we gain height more slowly, using less force at each step.

We can do this work by using part of the 'energy store' in our bodies, obtained from the food we eat. But not all of the energy is used to lift us uphill against the gravity force. We still have to keep our bodies alive, and doing such hard work makes us feel much hotter. Our bodies are quite good at getting rid of this waste heating energy. But quite a lot of the work we did hasn't been wasted. It has been transferred into a mysterious kind of energy called **gravitational potential energy**.

Picture 5 An Alpine road.

■ Potential energy

This potential energy can be a rather dangerous kind of energy for someone high up on a mountain. You can't see it and you can't feel it. But mountain climbers have more than enough of it to kill themselves, if they don't control it properly.

The reason for this is that this potential energy can be changed to movement energy, which is usually called **kinetic energy**. If you fall off a mountain the gravity force pulls you down and you move faster and faster. The energy that you put into climbing the mountain is being given back to you as you fall!

Energy can't just disappear or appear from nowhere (see topic D5). It makes sense to think of work you do as you go uphill as being stored as hidden or 'potential' energy. This turns into kinetic energy as you fall.

Of course, potential energy does you no harm at all. Neither does the kinetic energy. It is what happens when you hit the ground that causes the damage.

Picture 6 illustrates the kind of energy transfers that happen when we climb up a hill and come down again.

DON'T LET ENERGY KILL YOU!

People coming down from the mountains have to get rid of their potential energy safely, a little bit at a time. Climbers and walkers come down carefully – never running! Cyclists need to keep braking, moving the potential energy safely into the surroundings by heating the wheels and brake blocks. This is much better than storing it as more and more kinetic energy!

(a)

(b)

Picture 6   (a) Climbing a mountain is hot work. The climber warms up the surrounding – but also gains potential energy. (b) If the climber fell, the change of potential energy to kinetic energy would happen much too quickly.

■ Measuring potential energy

Whenever we do work against the force of gravity there will be an increase in potential energy. Lifting a can of beans on to a high shelf gives them extra potential energy. You can't eat this extra energy, but it will give you a nasty bump if the can falls on your head.

Topic D2 explains how energy is measured and how the formula for calculating potential energy is obtained.

The formula is:

$$\text{potential energy} = \textbf{\textit{mgh}}$$

m is the mass of an object, g the strength of the gravity field and h the height through which the object has been lifted, or can fall.

When you lift a can of baked beans on to a shelf a metre above the ground you have given it some extra potential energy. If the can weighs 0.5 kg you increase its potential energy by

$$\textbf{\textit{mgh}} = (0.5 \text{ kg} \times 10 \text{ N/kg} \times 1 \text{ metre})$$
$$= 5 \text{ joules}$$

This is not very much, considering that the beans in the can have over **1 million** joules of 'food energy'!

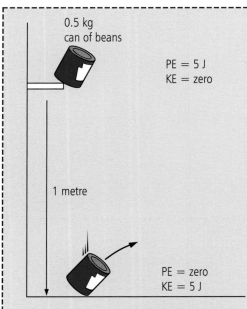

0.5 kg
can of beans

PE = 5 J
KE = zero

1 metre

PE = zero
KE = 5 J

Picture 7 Potential energy changing to kinetic energy.

Potential energy to kinetic energy

The energy in a moving object depends on how massive it is and how fast it is going. It is calculated using the formula:

$$\text{kinetic energy, } E = \tfrac{1}{2}mv^2$$

(m is the mass of the object, v is its speed).

When an object falls freely in a gravity field its potential energy is getting less and its kinetic energy is increasing.

Its loss in potential energy equals its gain in kinetic energy.

So if our can of beans fell off the shelf, its kinetic energy would be 5 joules just before it hit the ground (picture 7). Its potential energy would now be zero.

How fast would it be going just before it hit the ground? We can use these two formulae to work this out:

$$\text{kinetic energy gained} = \text{potential energy lost}$$
$$\tfrac{1}{2}mv^2 = mgh$$

divide both sides by m and multiply by 2

$$v^2 = 2gh$$
$$\text{i.e. } v^2 = 2 \times 10 \times 1$$
$$\text{giving speed } v = \sqrt{20} = 4.5 \text{ m/s}$$

KINETIC ENERGY AND ROAD SAFETY – SPEED KILLS

The formula for kinetic energy tells us that the energy increases as the square of the speed. This means that doubling the speed increases the energy by 2^2. It becomes four times as much.

In a road collision, or in a fall, doubling speed means that four times as much energy is available for causing damage. If the speed is tripled, e.g. from 30 mph to 90 mph, the energy becomes **nine times as much**.

Topic B2 and topic D2 also deal with aspects of kinetic energy.

Activity

A The monkey and the hunter

A hunter sees a monkey hanging by its arms from the branch of a tree (picture 8). He points his gun straight at the monkey's head, and fires off a bullet.

The monkey sees the hunter and lets go of the branch at exactly the same time as the hunter fires the gun. The monkey hopes that when the bullet gets there he will have fallen far enough to escape the bullet.

Does the monkey escape?

Argue about it, then persuade your teacher to set up a 'model experiment' (no need to use a real monkey, or a gun!) to test your prediction.

Picture 8

Questions

Picture 9

1 Which of the drawings in picture 9 gives the best idea of how a ball moves when it is thrown?

2 a Why does a parachute slow down the rate of someone falling from an aircraft?

 b Why does a person falling without a parachute eventually reach a steady speed? (If they fall far enough!)

 c Why do you think airline passengers are never issued with parachutes?

3 In theory all objects fall at the same rate, owing to gravity. So why does a coin fall to the ground faster than a feather?

4 When you throw a ball across a field it eventually comes down to the ground again, however fast you throw it.

 a Draw a sketch showing the path taken by the ball as it goes from your hand to the other side of the field.

 b Draw the forces acting on the ball:
  i just as it leaves your hand,
  ii half way across and
  iii just before it hits the ground.
  Show the forces with labelled arrows and label them with their correct names.

Take $g = 10$ N/kg for these questions

5 The formula
$$s = \tfrac{1}{2} g\, t^2$$
can be used to work out how far an object falls when it is let go and then falls freely. In this formula s is the distance fallen and t is the time it takes to fall that distance.

 a What is g?

 b A girl dropped a coin down a well and timed how long it took before she heard the splash as the coin hit the water. The coin took 2 seconds to reach the water. How far down was the water?

6 Name one situation in each case where gravitational potential energy might be:

 a dangerous,

 b useful.

7 Hydroelectric power stations need lots of water stored in dams. Why are these dams usually high up in the mountains?

8 Explain the difference between potential energy and kinetic energy.

9 Copy the diagram in picture 10. It shows the path of a car as it goes from

A to E. It stops at E. What kind(s) of energy does the car have at each of the points A to E? Write your answers on your diagram.

10 Calculate the change in gravitational potential energy when:

 a a car of mass 500 kg climbs a hill 400 m high,

 b a climber of mass 65 kg climbs a rock face 200 m high,

 c a bird of mass 0.5 kg flies from the ground to a height of 500 m.

11 Do you do any work when you stand still with a 10 kg mass in each hand?

12 A stone of mass 5 kg falls from a cliff 25 metres high to the beach.

 a How much potential energy did it have before it fell? Use the formula: potential energy = mgh.

 b What was happening to this potential energy as the stone fell?

 c How much kinetic energy had the stone gained, just as it was about to hit the beach?

 d Use the formula $E = \tfrac{1}{2} mv^2$ to calculate the speed with which the stone hit the beach.

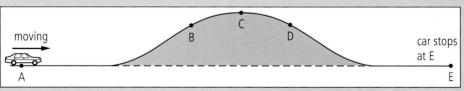

moving

car stops at E

Picture 10

Weighing the Earth

How do scientists know how much the Earth weighs? Strictly speaking, the Earth doesn't weigh anything, of course…

When we 'weigh' something we are really trying to find out what its **mass** is. The mass of an object is a measure of how much matter it contains. **Weight** is a measure of the gravity force on a piece of matter in a gravitational field. As the Earth is in its own gravity field it doesn't make much sense to talk of its 'weight'.

Also, as the Earth is in free fall orbit around the Sun it is 'weightless' even as far as the Sun's gravitational field is concerned.

The laws of gravity were discovered by Sir Isaac Newton (see page 107). He realised that gravity is caused by mass. The bigger the mass, the bigger is the gravity force it can exert. Two masses (of size M and m, say) exert an equal gravity force (F) on each other, given by a formula:

$$F = G\frac{Mm}{r^2}$$

r is their distance apart, in metres. G is a constant, called the **universal constant of gravitation** (see picture 1). This formula could be used to measure the mass of the Earth – M, say – if the other values are known.

Newton could measure the force on a mass m in the Earth's gravity field. In modern units it is well known to be 9.8 newtons for a 1 kilogram mass. He also had a good idea of the radius of the Earth. This had been calculated quite accurately in 1684 by the French astronomer Jean Picard. Its modern value is 64 000 000 metres (6.4×10^6 m).

But at that time no one knew the value of the constant G. Indeed, Newton died before it was measured. So he never knew the mass of the Earth that his theories had made it possible to measure. It is hard to measure G because gravity is such a weak force. The gravity force between you and the person sitting next to you, for example, is about one ten-millionth of your weight.

The first fairly accurate measurement of G was done in 1774, nearly 70 years after Newton's death. It was done by a Scot, Nevil Maskelyne. He used a simple pendulum which he set up near a cone-shaped mountain in Scotland (see picture 2). The mass of the mountain caused a small gravity force which pulled the pendulum sideways. It was a very tiny effect, but he was able to measure it.

He then worked out the volume of the mountain and measured the density of the rocks it was made of. He then calculated the mass of the mountain using the formula:

mass = density × volume

He now had enough data to put into Newton's formula to get a value for G. A modern experiment which measures the force between two gold spheres a small distance apart, gives a value of:

$$G = 6.7 \times 10^{-11} \text{ N m}^2/\text{kg}^2$$

This is the force in newtons between two 1 kg masses a metre apart. It is just 670 billionths of a newton!

The result of such experiments allows us to calculate the mass of the Earth,

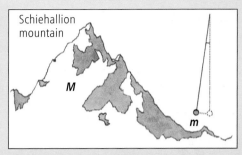

Picture 2 Maskelyne's experiment.

the Sun and the other planets. We also use it to calculate the masses of distant stars and galaxies.

1   'Gravity is a weak force'. Yet it seems to be quite a large force when you lift up a loaded suitcase, or try to cycle up a steep hill. Why is this?

2   Why is it so hard to measure the value of G?

3   A kilogram mass on the Earth's surface has a gravity force of 9.8 newtons on it. The mass of the Earth acts as if it was all at the centre, as far as gravity is concerned. The centre of the Earth is 6 400 000 metres from the surface.

Use a scientific calculator to check that the mass of the Earth is about
$$6 \times 10^{24} \text{ kg}.$$

Use Newton's formula, with the values:

$F = 9.8$ N $m = 1$ kg $r = 6\,400\,000$ m
$G = 6.7 \times 10^{-11}$ Nm^2/kg^2

4   The volume of the Earth is
$$1.1 \times 10^{21} \text{ m}^3$$

a   Use the formula
$$\text{density} = \frac{\text{mass}}{\text{volume}}$$
to calculate the density of the Earth.

b   You should have got an answer of about 5500 kg/m^3 for the density of the Earth. But the density of nearly all the rocks we find on the Earth's surface is about 2500 kg/m^3. How can this be explained? (See topic G1.)

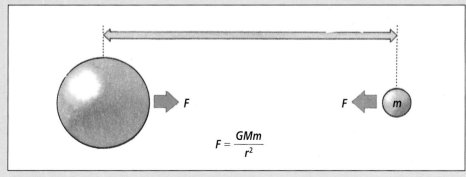

$$F = \frac{GMm}{r^2}$$

Picture 1   The bigger the mass, the bigger the gravity force it exerts.

22nd Century Physics Lesson

Declan logged on to school at the Physics Class site. Half the class were already there, and gradually as the clock ticked around to 9 a.m. the other three students appeared as thumbnails around the screen border. Last as usual, Thomas looked as though he had just got out of bed and Steve as if he'd never been.

Doctor Joan's face appeared and there was a chorus of *good mornings*. Faces disappeared. The title grew on the screen: *Physics in History: Course 225 June 10th 2105.*

Picture 1

Dr Joan: *What you are seeing is a typical road scene from the year 2005, exactly one hundred years ago. It is taken from a helicopter and shows a section of what was called a motorway, in fact the one that circled London, called the M25. You can't see the road, because it is covered with motor cars and lorries (or trucks). A motor car was a small box with a wheel at each corner. A car could carry 4 people, possibly 5 or 6, but you would find that most cars in the photograph only carried one person.*

Amanda: *Where were they all going?*

Dr J: *At that time of day most were going to work. Some might be going out shopping – to buy goods from a large store. But the larger vehicles would be carrying goods. In those days most people went to work – nowadays of course most work comes to people!*

The picture on the screen changed. It showed a section of motorway with a tangled mass of wrecked cars and lorries, some of them on fire. There were ambulances, police and firemen working desperately to pull bodies and people from the wreckage. Declan was shocked by the sight.

Dr J: *This is a traffic accident. It is amazing to think that in those days small cars and large lorries travelled on the same roadway at speeds of up to 110 kilometres per and hour, with no central guidance controls at all! Each vehicle was under the control of individual drivers, who often drove closer together than the distance each would take just to think about stopping – let alone using the brakes to do so. In this example a large lorry had stopped suddenly for some reason, and the following vehicles simply couldn't stop quickly enough to avoid collisions. This is a large 'accident'. Smaller ones took place every day on smaller roads, where the cars and lorries travelled in opposite directions on the same carriageway, with no barriers between them. On these roads most accidents were collisions between vehicles travelling in opposite directions. The collision might happen at combined speeds of 180 kilometres per hour. In towns and cities it was common for cars and lorries to collide with walkers, causing injury and even death. Children were especially vulnerable.*

The picture changed to show an ambulance with siren blaring entering a hospital yard. An injured person was carried inside on a trolley. There were scenes in an ER room, then the sight of a heart monitor changing its signal to show no activity.

Dr J: *In England, in the year 1997, 3600 people were killed on the roads in different types of accident. Another 324 thousand were injured – 43 thousand seriously.*

Declan: *Why did people put up with this? It all seems pretty stupid to me.*

Steve: *I expect people just wanted to get around faster. And you could move freely, wherever you wanted. You didn't have to hang around waiting for a bus or the metro.*

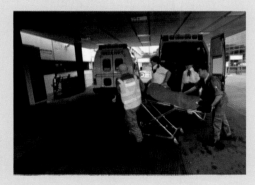

Picture 2

Dr J: *There's something in what you say, Steve. Freedom of movement is nice to have. But here are a few more facts. Back in 1900, transport in London was mostly horse-drawn. But there were so many carriages that the average speed in the city centre was about 6 kilometres an hour – not much more than walking speed. At busy times the traffic came to a halt – it was called a traffic jam. In the year 2000 all transport used the internal combustion engine. A typical horse-drawn carriage had a maximum speed of about 30 km/h; a typical car had a maximum speed of perhaps 140 km/h, but this was limited to 50 km/h in towns. In 2000 the average speed of any vehicle in London was 12 km/h – except for a bicycle, which was faster at 14 km/h. Not very free!*

The screen showed a typical traffic snarl-up in a city, then changed to show clouds of fumes coming from a car exhaust.

Dr J: *The traffic also produced air pollution – another new word for you. It means poisonous or corrosive gases in the atmosphere. It was calculated that in the year 2000 a third of all air pollution from traffic was produced by parents taking their children to school! In total, in 1997 there were 27 million motor vehicles on the roads of Britain – many of them at the same time! Only in the past twenty years has carbon dioxide in the atmosphere stopped increasing.*

Betty: *So when did all this change? How did we get rid of all those cars?*

Dr J: *Well, what do you all think? You should know enough about life in the last century compared with life now to suggest a few answers to Betty's*

questions. *Start with your own lives – and your parents'.*

Robert: *Well, we don't go to school very often. School comes to us! Our physics class meets once a fortnight and we can all walk to meet you at the Learning Club.*

Dr J: *And you go to Big School once every couple of months for two days. You meet your tutors, get careers advice – organise (or reorganise) your social lives. And you can travel there by bike – or take the metro.*

Robert: *I'm looking forward to it! Going to school is real cool!*
Raisa: *And my parents work from home. My dad controls the factory machines with his computer – he just goes in once a week. I don't know anybody whose parents have to travel more than a few kilometres to work.*

Declan: *My mother works for a firm in Brazil! And she can do this from her workstation at the Neighbourhood Office.*

Thomas: *We can buy all we really need for everyday from the Corner Shop. If we want anything special we buy on the Web – and it gets delivered.*

Steve: *So we still need roads and lorries to deliver things to the shops.*

Amanda: *Right – but not very many.*

Dr J: *What you might not know is what decisions were made after the Great Snarl-up of 2025. And then the fuel crisis of 2028. Fuel prices went through the roof. City Mayors banned cars – or made it too expensive for them to enter cities. The development of smart machines and remote control*

– plus webucation – made it acceptable for the Government to step in. The slogans were 'Neighbourhoods rule! Work to the people – not people to work!' It took 40 years but life has changed!

Now try the following questions:

1 At what average speed do you (a) travel to school (b) get to the nearest shop?

2 How far away is the nearest large supermarket or hypermarket to your home?

3 How would your life change if all private cars were banned?

4 Steve seems to approve of having the ability to move around freely in private cars. The other students don't seem worried about it. Do you agree with Steve? Write out notes for a debate in which you support or oppose Steve's point of view.

5 Explain Dr Joan's statements
   a cars were under the control of *individual drivers, who often drove closer together than the distance each would take just to think about stopping – let alone using the brakes to do so*
   b that on an ordinary road cars might *have a combined speed of 180 km/h.*

6 In the wonderful days of 2105, what work might still need to be done by people who had to travel long distances?

7 Suggest some jobs where the use of modern technology should make it unnecessary for the worker to travel more than a few hundred metres.

Is the Earth the centre of the Universe? How far away are we from the Sun? How close to the Moon and the stars? Does the Earth move through space? These questions were hard to answer, but some people thought that they were important – and trying to answer them led, over hundred of years, to the discovery of most of the physics in this book …

The Earth is underneath us, and everything else in the Universe is above us. It seemed obvious therefore, for thousands of years, that the Earth was at the centre of the Universe. People disagreed about the shape of the Earth, but by 2500 years ago the few people who actually worried about things like that had convinced themselves that the Earth was round, like a ball. By 200 BC the Libyan geographer Eratosthenes had measured the Earth's diameter to an accuracy of about 15%.

But the Universe seemed to be a more complicated affair. First of all there are the Sun and the Moon. They rise and set, and the Moon even changes size and shape. Then there are the stars. These rise and set too. It seems to make sense to think of all these objects as somehow spinning around the still Earth. They did so at slightly different rates close to the standard time given by day + night – our modern 24-hour period. Sometimes the Moon got in front of the Sun and eclipsed it. Sometimes the full Moon went dark for an hour or so. This was no surprise, careful study of the paths of the Sun and Moon in the sky allowed astronomers to predict eclipses of the Sun by the Moon and the Moon by the Earth's shadow. So the Moon must be closer to the Earth than the Sun. Stars were eclipsed by both Sun and Moon getting in the way, so they must be further away still.

Sun, Moon and stars followed a fixed and predictable pattern. The pattern changes with time, but even these changes were predictable. For example, Eratosthenes had measured the direction the Earth's axis – the line from North to South poles – made with the plane of the circle that the Sun moved in. This was known to change slowly with time, taking 26 000 years to complete a cycle that brought it back to where it started. But a few stars seemed to play to different rules. Most stars moved through the sky together, fixed in the same patterns called constellations: such as the constellation of the great hunter Orion, or the winged horse Pegasus. The odd stars were quite bright, and wandered through these constellations. The ancient Greeks called them 'wandering stars' – we call them planets from the Greek *planeos* – to wander. There were five of these, important enough to be named after the top Greek gods: Mercury, Venus, Mars, Jupiter and Saturn.

Fitting the wanderers into a pattern was difficult. The end of a long story was a model worked out by the Egyptian-Greek astronomer Ptolemy of Alexandria. He lived from about 90 AD until 170 AD and his model lasted until the 17th century. It was a marvel of complexity that included the movements of the planets, stars, Sun and Moon, and allowed capable mathematicians to predict their future movements with good accuracy – considering that clockwork and accurate timing had not yet been discovered.

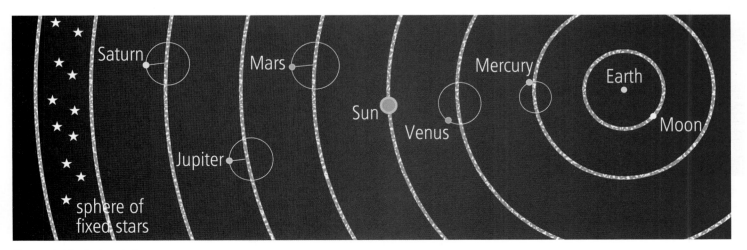

Picture 1 The Ptolemaic System

This splendid building is part of a one-time mosque called the Mezquita in Cordoba, Spain. It was built in the 8th to 10th centuries when the skills and science of Moslem Arabs were far in advance of European contemporaries.

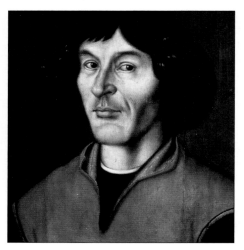

Nicholas Copernicus (1473–1543). Portrait by an anonymous 16th century artist.

Pages from Copernicus's book *De revolutionibus orbium coelestium* (On the revolution of the heavenly spheres) of 1543, with the first diagram showing the Sun at the centre of the Solar System.

Picture 2

The model was based on the Earth at the centre of the Universe, surrounded by spheres ever-increasing in radius, that carried Moon, Sun and stars. These moved in their cycles at the speed that matched with what was observed. Some spheres had to be off centre, the Sun for example seemed to move faster at certain times of the year. He correctly saw that this was because it was nearer the Earth at that time. The main spheres rotated in a period of 24 hours. Planets were fixed to some of these spheres but to allow for their odd movements they had to be placed in smaller spheres that had their centres based on a main sphere. To get it all right Ptolemy needed to use 80 interconnected spheres.

Ptolemy lived at a time when the Western world was run by the Romans. They ruled most of Europe (up to the river Rhine), Britain (up to Hadrian's Wall) and most of the Middle East. But by 500 AD the Roman Empire was collapsing. From north and east came the 'barbarians': Germanic tribes like Saxons, Goths and Vandals. They overran western Europe and took Spain and North Africa. By now the centre of the Roman Empire had moved from Rome to Constantinople (modern Istanbul in Turkey). Libraries were burnt, schools and scholarship became rare. The growth of Christianity in the Empire put more weight on knowing the bible than knowing the works of old pagan astronomers like Ptolemy. Luckily the next invaders and ultimately the destroyers of the Roman Empire had a more civilised approach. These were the Moslem armies from what is now Saudi Arabia. By 700 AD they had conquered most of the Middle East, Egypt and Spain. It took another 800 years before Constantinople fell to their Turkish converts. In the meantime they had become keen on astronomy (amongst other things) and had translated the old books they had found in Egypt into Arabic. This preserved the work of Ptolemy, which was so valued that his astronomy book was called in Arabic the *Almagest*, meaning the *Greatest*.

In turn, the increasingly more educated barbarians in Europe learnt Arabic – and even Greek – and started translating books like the Almagest into the common language of educated westerners: Latin. Twenty years after the fall of Constantinople a boy was born in Poland called Mikel Koppernigk (1473 – 1543). When he became famous he was known as Nicolaus Copernicus. He studied law, mathematics and medicine in Italy, and was influenced by the surge of new interest in everything and the intellectual excitement of what we now call the rebirth of learning – the Renaissance. But he went back to a fairly quiet life as a church administrator in Torun, Poland. In his spare time he applied his mathematics to producing a better model of the Universe than old Ptolemy's. He thought he could make it simpler and easier to use if he put the Sun at the centre of everything, instead of the Earth. He thought of lots of simple observations that seemed to support his idea. His book with the full description of his Sun-centred (heliocentric) model wasn't published until just before he died in 1543. He probably saw a copy for the first time on the very day he died.

Copernicus's ideas were not welcomed: in fact they were ignored for many years. In the first place his model was almost as complicated as Ptolemy's. Neither model was based on what we might see as physics – involving *forces*, say. An idea of gravity and a proper understanding of motion was many years in the future. The idea of a central Sun was possibly acceptable – but how could anyone live on a moving Earth? Anything not nailed down would be left behind! A more technical worry by good astronomers was that if the Earth moved in an orbit around the Sun, then there should be an apparent movement of the stars just as we see when we move our heads to and fro and see the window frame moving against the outside scene. In fact this effect occurs, but was too small to be detected, before the invention of the telescope.

But the most effective – if unscientific objections – were to appear later, and cause the downfall of one of the greatest scientists of all time, Galileo. In the Bible it said that at the battle of Jericho, 'the Sun stood still'. Which meant it must have been moving to start with. God had stopped it in its tracks long enough for Joshua to win his battle. Now Copernicus had 'stopped' the Sun – an idea close to heresy.

■ Wars – and religion

The 16th and 17th centuries saw Western Europe divide into two main religious camps, both Christian. One was the old Catholic version, the other was a new one – Protestantism. Protestants believed in the same God but thought that the Catholic Church, led by the Pope in Rome, was corrupt and the priesthood and their customs put a barrier between the believers and their God. Services were in Latin, and devout Germans, the English, Dutch, Swiss and French wanted services and the Bible to be in their own languages. People believed strongly, and wars broke out as princes and kings took up one side or the other. 'Heretics' on both sides were burnt at the stake. And in 1618 a long war broke out that lasted until 1648 and laid waste to the small German and other states in central Europe. The physicist and astronomer Galileo Galilei, an Italian and so by birth a Catholic, was born in 1564 and died in 1642. His adult life was spent in a time of religious wars that spread over almost all of Europe.

Galileo became famous at several levels. One was amongst the other scientists of his day, with his new ideas and theories backed up with clear mathematics and – what was revolutionary – experiments. His strength was in the topic of motion, and showed that the old Greeks were often wrong, even the great Aristotle. He was the first to realise that falling objects accelerated at a constant rate and measured this acceleration of free fall, g. He explained clearly how cannon balls actually moved – and so became popular with kings and princes, whose armies could make good use of these ideas. He also developed a fairground toy which used two glass lenses to make distant objects seem closer. The telescope had probably been invented many times, but Galileo was smart enough not only to understand how it worked but also to sell the idea – for a good increase in salary – to his then employers, the rich republic of Venice.

Then he became famous with ordinary people. He did this by writing books about physics and astronomy in ordinary language, Italian instead of Latin. He also made them funny and interesting. But this annoyed the scientists whose old-fashioned ideas he was criticising. All was going well for Galileo until he turned his telescope – and his powerful pen – to revive the by now half-forgotten theories of Copernicus.

In 1610 he published a book called the Starry Messenger describing his observations with his improved telescope. This book was the one that made him famous with ordinary people. He had discovered spots on the Sun – up until then a 'perfect' heavenly object. He saw that the planet Venus had phases like the Moon, suggesting that it was in orbit around the Sun rather than Earth. He also saw that one member of the Solar System had smaller objects in orbit around it: he had discovered the moons of Jupiter. This last discovery clinched his belief that Copernicus's theory was right. Not everything in the Universe rotated about the Earth.

Picture 3 Galileo, who challenged Aristotle.

Picture 5 But this is what does happen, as worked out by Galileo.

Picture 4 This is what should happen when a cannon is fired – according to Aristotle.

Picture 6 The title page of Galileo's *Dialogue*.

Against some opposition to his ideas he published another book – but not until 1632. His *Dialogue about the Two Chief World Systems* compared the Copernican with the old Ptolemaic systems. He tried to give a balanced view but it was obvious that he believed that Copernicus was right, and many fellow astronomers agreed. But in almost all scientific controversies traditionalists are hard to convince: why give up a theory that had worked – in detail - for over a thousand years? More seriously, it was decreed that the Copernican theory contradicted the teachings of the Catholic Church. In 1633 Galileo was arrested and interrogated by the Inquisition, a body set up in the 13th century to check on heresy and false teaching. They had a lot of work on their hands in this period of religious division. Galileo was shown one of the main ways of encouraging true confessions in the 17th century: the instruments of torture. He was now 69 years old, and thought it best to agree with the Church and denounce the Copernican theory. He was kept under arrest – but at his own home – until he died nine years later.

History can be thought of a sequence of inevitable accidents. Sooner or later the true picture of the Solar System would have been discovered and accepted: Copernicus and Galileo both lived at a time when people in Western Europe were beginning to question what had been taken for granted for so many centuries. It was also a time of a revolution in communications. When Copernicus was born in 1473 nearly all the books in Europe had been written by hand – 'copyists' had laboured, quill pen in hand, for many months over each book. But by 1445 the German Johann Gutenberg had produced the first *printed* book. Once the page of type had been set in place it was simply a matter of pressing it against sheet after sheet of paper to produce many copies of a book, each one identical to the others. It was inevitable that ideas could spread rapidly from country to country, from brain to brain.

But how exactly the new ideas were put forward, supported or banned depended upon individuals who were bright enough to understand them and brave enough to fight for them, if necessary. Another factor was a growing need for more reliable knowledge about the movements of stars and planets. Columbus 'discovered' America in Copernicus' lifetime (in 1492), although he thought that he had landed in India, annoying many generations of native Americans who have had to live with the name of Indian ever since. Western Europeans became world traders, and wanted a more accurate sense of position on the Earth than Columbus had shown. So new ideas about stars that helped navigation had a ready – even enthusiastic audience.

By the time of Galileo this new means of communication had produced an information explosion as great as the one we are now living in, in the time of the Internet. More and more people learned to read – books were now so much cheaper. Many books were small and could be carried from place to place easily – defeating customs men and attempts to ban books. Even so, it took many years before it became respectable to accept that the Sun was at the centre of the Solar System – and that the Earth did in fact move.

Activity `ICT`

A Finding out about Galileo and Italy

Use a library or the Internet to find out more about what Italy was like at the time of Galileo. Why did people think that his scientific ideas were so important? Why did other people disagree with him so strongly that they would have put him to death?

Questions

1 People said to Galileo: 'The Earth can't be moving! If it did, we would all be left behind! There'd be chaos!' How would you answer these critics, using modern science? Galileo didn't know about gravity. How could you answer these critics without using the idea of gravity pulling down on everything on Earth? (Hint: think of dropping something on a train.)

2 What was the key piece of evidence that Galileo used to prove that it was at least possible that the Earth and planets went round the Sun?

3 'Of course the Sun goes round the Earth! You can see it moving, every day!' How can you explain the apparent movement of the Sun through the sky, from dawn to sunset?

4 Galileo's ideas about the Sun and the Earth were thought at the time to contradict the Bible. The Church in Italy thought that this would confuse ordinary people and make them lose their faith in God. Other scientific ideas such as Darwin's Theory of Evolution might have the same effect.

a Can you think of any modern examples of such 'dangerous' ideas?

b Should such ideas only be learned by people who are intelligent enough not to be confused by them?

Satellites

No engines. No wings.
What keeps satellites up there?

Picture 2   Modern communication satellite.

Picture 1   Sputnik – the first artificial satellite.

■ 'I just don't believe it!'

The first artificial satellite to orbit the Earth was launched in 1957. It was a Russian satellite, named **Sputnik**, shown in picture 1. It had a mass of 84 kg and it moved in an orbit between 217 km and 944 km above the Earth's surface.

The Astronomer Royal at the time didn't believe it! He didn't think that a rocket engine could provide enough energy to lift any object that far above the Earth. Since then many thousands of satellites have been launched, some as big and as heavy as a bus. Picture 2 shows a typical modern Earth satellite.

NEWTON AGAIN

Earth satellites had been predicted by Isaac Newton in 1666. The way he thought of getting them into orbit was not very practical, as he well knew. Picture 3 shows his idea. But we can learn from this how actual satellites do in fact stay in orbit.

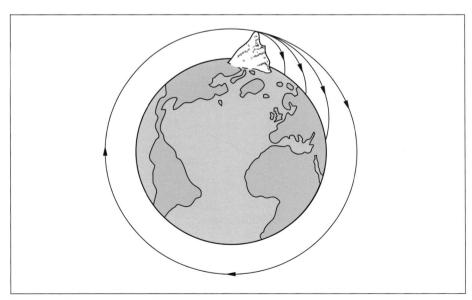

Picture 3   Newton imagined firing a cannon ball from the top of a high mountain. The faster it went, the further the cannon ball would travel before it hit the ground. At a high enough speed, it wouldn't hit the ground at all!.

Any object fired sideways (horizontally) from a tall mountain will not only move sideways but also fall towards the centre of the Earth. It is pulled there by the force of gravity (see topic B4). The faster it is fired the further it will get before reaching the ground. Newton realised that at a certain speed it will never reach the ground, simply because the Earth itself is curved. At this speed the curved path of the falling satellite would exactly match the curve of the Earth.

■ How are satellites launched?

No mountain on Earth is high enough for Newton's method to work. There is no gun powerful enough to fire a satellite at the speed needed to stay in orbit. And if there were, the force needed to accelerate the satellite inside the gun barrel would squash it flat!

Instead a rocket system is used to lift the satellite to the top of an 'invisible mountain'. This is called the **injection point**, and it is at least 200 km high (see picture 5).

Picture 4 shows the rocket system used to launch the American Space Shuttle. Most of what you see of the rocket is simply a hollow tank filled with fuel. Most of this fuel is used to lift itself through the atmosphere. There is just enough spare fuel to accelerate the shuttle sideways when it gets high enough to be put into orbit.

The rocket system has three stages, each with its own engine and fuel supply. The first stage contains the most fuel and has the biggest engine. It lifts itself and the next two stages as high as it can. Then it falls off. Stages two and three take over, in turn, and in their turn are thrown away. The Space Shuttle is left travelling in orbit at the speed required to stop it falling closer to earth (see picture 5)

WHY DO SOME SATELLITES FALL DOWN?

Newton explained why satellites stay up – but they don't stay up for ever. The main reason for this is air friction. The Earth's atmosphere gets thinner and thinner the higher you go, but it never thins away to nothing. Even at a height of 1000 km there is enough air left to cause a drag on a satellite which slows it down. Eventually it is travelling too slowly to stay in orbit. It re-enters the thicker part of the atmosphere where friction becomes so great that the satellite 'burns up'.

The energy transferred from movement energy by this air friction heats up the satellite until it melts and burns away.

Picture 4   The rocket system used to launch the Space Shuttle.

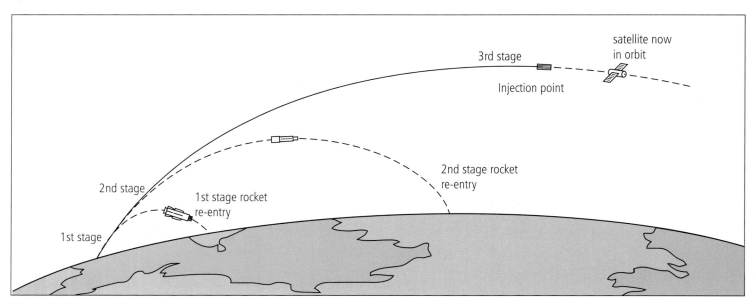

Picture 5   How a satellite is put into orbit.

GEOSTATIONARY ORBITS

Sputnik went around the earth once every 90 minutes. This would have made it useless as a TV satellite. It would be in view at any one place on Earth for only a few minutes in each orbit. The TV aerial would need to be motor-driven to follow it. A neat solution would be to have a satellite which always seems to be in the same place in the sky. This in fact is what is done.

The satellite is put into a very high orbit. It still moves, but its speed is just enough to follow the movement of the spinning Earth (see picture 6). This means that it is always over the same place on Earth.

Physics in Action

This section is about the uses of Earth satellites. How they keep up without falling back to Earth is explained in Section B8.

What are satellites used for?

Most earth satellites are used for military purposes. Powerful governments like to keep an eye on each other! These satellites can monitor radio and other communications signals and see where troops and equipment are kept or moved. They have very good camera systems that can take clear pictures of objects as small as a human being from hundreds of kilometres up in space. They can measure sea levels so accurately that they can tell if there is a submarine hidden underwater by the small disturbance it makes at the water surface.

Where are you?

For civilians the most useful military system is the Global Positioning System (GPS). This was set up by the United States Navy. It uses 24 satellites orbiting at a height of 20 200 kilometres. They orbit the Earth twice a day and send down high frequency signals that can be picked up by a small hand-held receiver. The system is based on the very accurate measurement of the time it takes the signal from a satellite to reach the receiver. A receiver anywhere on Earth can get signals from four satellites at once. The signals tell the receiver where the satellites are and a small computer then works out how far the receiver is from each satellite, using the time it takes for the signal to travel from satellite to receiver. This calculation fixes the position of the receiver on the Earth to an accuracy of ten metres. For this to be so

accurate very precise timing is needed – each satellite carries an 'atomic clock', which uses the oscillation of light waves from a standard atom as a timekeeper. Compare this with the oscillation of a balance wheel in an ordinary clock, or a pendulum in a grandfather clock.

What are you doing?

Some satellites use sensitive cameras to monitor changes on the Earth's surface. For example, the European Union monitors farmers' fields to check that they are growing the crops that they have agreed to grow, or to monitor soil temperature, soil dryness, crop ripeness or diseases. Picture 2 shows a Landsat satellite picture of some farming land. It is a 'false colour' picture made using infra red radiation emitted from the surface. Different crops and soil types emit at slightly different frequencies and so can be shown in different colours by a simple computer program.

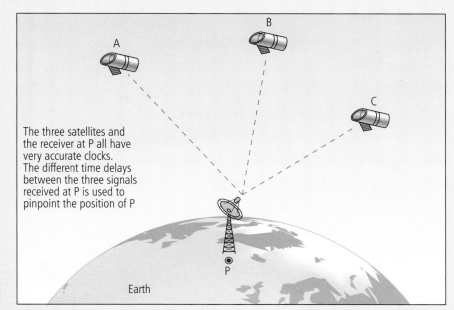

The three satellites and the receiver at P all have very accurate clocks. The different time delays between the three signals received at P is used to pinpoint the position of P

Earth

Picture 1 Signals from Global Positioning Satellites can pin-point a position on the ground to high accuracy.

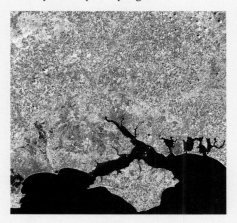

Picture 2 Satellite pictures like this can be made using infra red radiation emitted by the ground and crops. A computer converts the data into 'false colours' that differentiate between different crops, different soil types, etc.

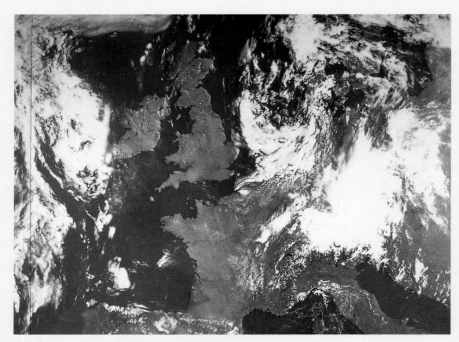

Picture 3 Satellite picture of a depression over Northern Europe.

What about the weather?

No TV weather forecast would be complete without a satellite picture showing where the clouds are, and how they have travelled or grown to be there. Weather satellites use both visible light to show up clouds and rain, and also infra red radiation to monitor the Earth's surface. Infra red radiation (with wavelength just longer than the red of visible light) can pass through clouds and tell us how hot the ground is – the hotter it is the shorter the key infra red wavelength. Britain's weather is critically dependent on the sea temperature in the North Atlantic. Knowing this temperature is very helpful to weather forecasters. Even so, they need large fast computers to make predictions – and they are not always as accurate as we would like.

Weather satellites usually have a polar orbit – they go around the Earth from the North to South poles, taking continuous pictures as they go and sending them down to receivers on the surface. These satellites orbit close to the Earth (between 500 and 1000 km high) and orbit it in about 100 minutes. The Earth spins beneath them so that they eventually cover the whole surface.

The further away a satellite is the longer it takes to complete an orbit. At a distance of 35 890 km the orbital period is 24 hours – exactly the same as the time the Earth takes to spin on its axis. This means that the satellite stays over the same point on the Earth's surface all the time. This orbit is called a

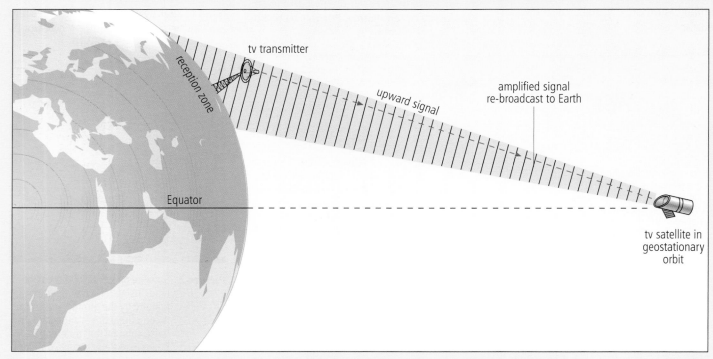

reception zone

tv transmitter

upward signal

amplified signal
re-broadcast to Earth

Equator

tv satellite in geostationary orbit

Picture 4 What TV rebroadcast satellites do.

geostationary orbit. The satellite can monitor the same large area of the Earth all the time. See page 97.

What's going on?

Communications satellites have also transformed our lives. A reporter can set up a small aerial and send film and a commentary from almost any place on Earth to appear – after a few tenths of a second delay – on our TV screens at home. Sporting and other events from all over the world are covered by TV. Many people have subscribed to 'satellite TV' which broadcasts hundred of TV channels from space.

The most useful radio and TV signals beam off into space and don't travel around it. Communication satellites pick up the signals, amplify them and use directional aerials to send them on to their destinations. TV satellites do this as well. The programmes are beamed up from large aerials on Earth, then they are amplified and sent back down again to TV sets over a large area of the Earth's surface.

Communications and TV satellites are generally in geostationary orbits – they can broadcast or rebroadcast over a large area and they are easy to find. They stay in the same place in the sky relative to your home.

Scientific satellites

Passive satellites simply collect radiation emitted naturally by objects in space or on the Earth. This may be emitted because the object is hot and gives out light or infra red rays, or it may simply be reflecting sunlight. The Hubble Space Telescope, Landsat and some other monitoring satellites are passive satellites.

Active satellites send out radiation of their own which is reflected from, say, the clouds or the Earth's surface. The most common radiation used is ***radar,*** which is electromagnetic radiation in the very short wave radio part of the spectrum and is similar to the radiations used to detect and monitor aircraft. The reflected radiation has to travel a long way and needs very sensitive detectors in the satellite to

Picture 5 Satellite view of Russian oilfields seen from space. The River Ob (red) and the city of Surgut (white) can be clearly seen.

make an image. This is the kind of satellite that has to be used to monitor the changing sea level – which it can do to an accuracy of a centimetre or so.

Scientific satellites are used to monitor not only what happens on Earth but also to view the universe at large. Sensitive sensors can measure tiny changes in the Earth's gravity field and so obtain a 'picture' of how the density of the Earth changes from one place to another. This information has been used to find minerals like oil. It has also been used to find the exact shape of the Earth – which is a lot more complicated than a simple sphere. Slight changes in the sea level show where there are ocean currents – maybe with water at different densities and temperatures. The readings can also show what the bottom of the ocean is like.

One of the most famous of all satellites is the Hubble Space Telescope. This orbits at a height of 600 km and contains several telescopes of different sizes to do different jobs. It was put into orbit by the crew of the American Space Shuttle Discovery in April 1990.

It is outside the Earth's atmosphere so allowing very clear pictures to be taken. This means that it can see deeper into space than much bigger telescopes based on Earth.

Scientific satellites have been used to look at special types of astronomical objects, such as those that emit X-rays, gamma rays or infra red rays.

Picture 6 The Hubble Space Telescope.

Energising satellites

Earth satellites need energy to make their circuits work: everything is done electrically. Pictures are taken using the kind of sensors used in digital cameras, which turns them into a stream of digital signals (see page 5). These are then sent as radio waves down to Earth. The energy they need to do this comes from solar panels which absorb the energy in sunlight and use it to make electricity.

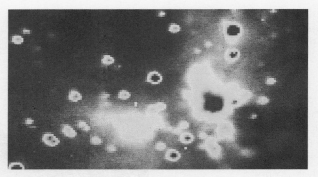

Picture 7 Infra-red image of newborn stars in Orion Molecular Cloud-1

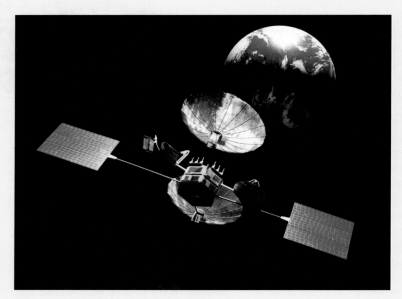

Picture 8 Satellite with solar wings extended.

Activities

A Computing your way into orbit

You might be able to get a computer simulation of satellite launching. If you can, try using different speeds and 'angles of launch' to see what happens.

B Have you ever seen a satellite in orbit?

Some newspapers list the times when important satellites cross overhead at night. Use this information to try and spot a satellite. Explain why you can see it as a shiny spot, although the satellite does not carry any lights of its own.

C Some things to find out

Use a library or any other source of information to answer the following questions.

1 What satellite has travelled furthest from Earth? What task did it have to do?

2 How are messages sent to and from satellites?

3 When did humans first land on the Moon? Do you think it was worth sending them there?

D Space travel

Copy out the following passage about travelling in space, filling in the missing words.

Satellites have not escaped the pull of Earth's _____. This is in fact the force that keeps them in _____ around the Earth. But the astronauts do not feel this force. This is because they are in a state of _____ – _____.

This makes life difficult. The astronauts, and every loose object, will _____ about in the satellite. If astronauts had to be in space for a long time, it would be a good idea to have some artificial _____. This could be obtained by _____ the satellite around its own axis. The faster it _____, the bigger the _____ force they would feel.

The main problem about space travel is that space is so huge that it would take four years to travel to the nearest _____, even if we could travel at the speed of light. At best, spacecraft could travel at about a tenth light speed, so it would take at least _____ years to get there. A return trip would be impossible. Also, think of the supplies they would need. They would have to recycle _____ and _____, and try to grow their own _____. They would also need a good supply of _____ so that they could manoeuvre the spacecraft when they arrived. A starship, with a crew of 16, would need 300 tonnes of consumables, and another 3000 tonnes for the ship itself.

You can read more about the problems of space travel in a science fiction paperback by Robert L Forward, Dragonfly (New English Library, 1985). It's a good read!

Questions

1 Why wouldn't Newton's 'big gun' idea for getting a satellite into orbit work?

2 a Why do many satellites eventually fall back to Earth?

   b Why do we not need to worry about being hit on the head by a satellite when it does fall?

   c Give five uses of Earth satellites.

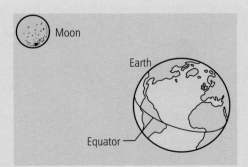

Picture 7

3 Copy the diagrams which show the Earth and the Moon in space (picture 7). On your copy, draw your idea of:

   a the likely orbit of a 'spy satellite',

   b the likely orbit of a TV broadcast satellite,

   c the path that a rocket might take to get into orbit around the Moon.

FORCES AND ORBITS

Satellites stay in orbit because they move under the action of a **central force** (picture 1). This is the force of gravity, which acts towards the centre of the Earth. But there are other things that move in circles.

The same basic rules apply whether it is the movement of wheels, planets orbiting the Sun, or cars going around corners. In topic B3 we looked at what happens when forces are only involved in straight-line movements. The result is an acceleration along the line of action of the force, obeying the rule $F = ma$, or if the force is gravity, $W = mg$ (see page 77).

These rules still apply when the force acts in a different direction to the line of movement of the object. This time the force also causes a change in the **direction** of movement. When a car has to go around a bend in the road it has to change direction. A force is needed to make it do this. The force is produced by changing the angle of the wheels and relying on the **friction** between the tyres and the road to act on the car. No friction – no turn! (See picture 2.)

■ Conkers and fairgrounds

The natural path of an object, free to move, with no force acting on it, is a straight line. To move it off a straight line a force of some kind is needed. When you whirl something around your head on a piece of string it is the inward pull from the string that makes the object move out of its straight path. If you let go of the string it will carry on in the direction in which it was already moving (see picture 3). Not many people believe this – so try it, out in the open where it is safe!

Fairgrounds are great places for scaring people using Newton's Laws applied to circular motion. Picture 4 shows a ride which spins people around at a speed of 80 km/h, then rises up to a vertical position.

The rods holding the seats to the axis of spin have to be very strong! This is because they have to carry the central force that keeps turning the seats, and the people in them, in a circle.

What you *feel* is a force in your back, as picture 5 explains. This is the inward force that keeps you 'in orbit'. The force needed to do this is quite large – about four times your own weight!

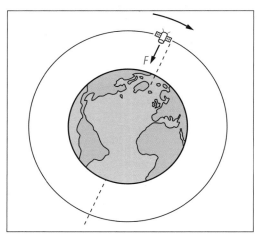

Picture 1 Gravity provides the centripetal force F that keeps a satellite in orbit.

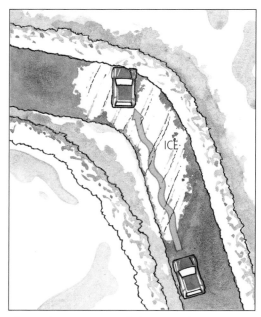

Picture 2 On an icy road, there is no friction to provide the centripetal force, so there will be no turn.

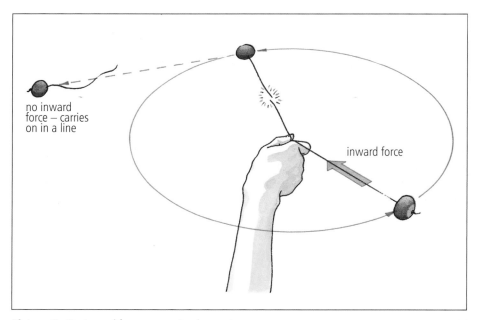

no inward force – carries on in a line

inward force

Picture 3 No inward force, so no circular motion.

Picture 4 Having fun with Newton's Laws.

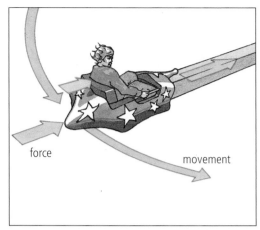

Picture 5 As the ride spins you feel a strong force in your back – the centripetal force that keeps the ride going in a circle.

■ Centripetal force

The name given to the force that keeps an object moving in a circle is **centripetal force**. It acts inwards towards the centre of the circle. Some complicated mathematics shows that the force is given by the formula:

$$F = \frac{mv^2}{r}$$

where m is the mass of the object, v is its orbital speed and r is the radius of the orbit (picture 6).

This formula tells us that the faster the object goes the bigger the centripetal force needed to keep it in orbit. In fact, doubling the speed means increasing the force by a factor of 4. This helps to make fairground rides even more terrifying!

SPIN DRYERS

Spin dryers use this effect to get water out of clothes. As the clothes are spun at high speed, a large force is needed to keep them 'in orbit'. This is provided by the outer wall of the dryer. But the wall has holes in it. Any drop of water next to a hole has nothing to keep it in orbit, so it carries on in a straight line and escapes. Drops of water in the middle of the clothes escape through the holes in the cloth. Eventually they get to the outer, holed wall and escape completely.

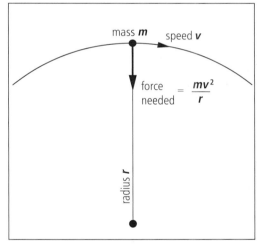

Picture 6 The centripetal force needed to keep an object moving in a circle is $F = \dfrac{mv^2}{r}$

■ Moving in circles

For an Earth satellite the centripetal force F is provided by the gravity pull between the satellite and the Earth. This pull is mg, where m is the mass of the satellite and g is the strength of the Earth's gravity field at that point. See Topic B4.

This force keeps the satellite in orbit distance r from the Earth's *centre* with an orbital speed v.

So we can say $\quad F = mg = \dfrac{mv^2}{r}$

The ms neatly cancel so we have $\quad g = \dfrac{v^2}{r}$.

Close to the Earth g is almost the same (slightly less) than it is at the surface: 9.8 N/kg. The Mathsbox shows you how to calculate a satellite's orbital speed – and how long it takes to complete a circular orbit.

The speed of a weather satellite

A typical weather satellite orbits at a height of 800 km. The Earth's radius is 6400 km, so this means that the satellite is 7200 km or 7 200 000 metres from the centre of the Earth (r). At this height g is 7.8 N/kg, so we have

$$v^2/r = 7.8 \text{ N/kg}$$
$$\text{so } v^2 = 7.8 \times 7\,200\,000$$
$$= 56\,160\,000$$
$$\text{giving } v = 7500 \text{ m/s} \quad \text{or} \quad 7.5 \text{ km/s}$$

The circumference of an orbit is $2\pi r$, so the satellite has to cover a distance of $2 \times 3.142 \times 7200$ km = 45 240 km. It does this at a speed of 7.5 km/s so takes a time of $T = 45\,240$km/7.5 km/s = 6032 s or about 100 minutes.

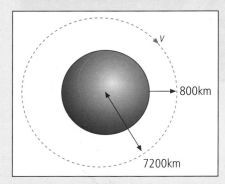

Picture 7

Questions

1. What provides the central (centripetal) force on each of the following objects going in a circle:
   a. the Moon orbiting the Earth,
   b. the Earth orbiting the Sun,
   c. a car going around a circular race track,
   d. the rim of a bicycle wheel,
   e. you, just standing on the Earth's surface?

2. Why is a car going around a corner on an icy road in danger of skidding?

3. If you are confident enough, and suitably dressed, you can whirl a bucket full of water in a vertical circle without losing any water. Explain why the water doesn't fall out when the bucket is whirling upside down.

4. Use the Mathsbox calculation to help you answer the following:

   A satellite is in a circular orbit at a height of 2000 km, where the strength of the Earth's gravity field is 5.7 N/kg. The radius of the Earth is 6400 km.

   a. What is the radius of the orbit in metres?
   b. What is the speed of the satellite in its orbit?
   c. Show that the satellite will orbit the Earth in a time of 2.1 hours.

Picture 1 Time and the stars. Stonehenge and a Maya temple.

■ Humans are very curious

As far as we can tell, human beings have always wondered about the Sun, the Moon and the stars. They have built temples, pyramids and great circles of standing stones. They have lined them up with the main stars, or the rising and setting of the Sun at important times like spring and harvest. They have worshipped the Sun and the Moon, and put their heroes and heroines into the star patterns. They have used them to make clocks and calendars, and to find their way across seas and deserts.

■ Making theories

And from the time of ancient Greeks, over two thousand years ago, they have made theories about what these heavenly objects really are. The Sun is hot, the giver of life, a great ball of fire. The Moon is cold and pale, and just a little dangerous. Stars are tiny sparks, of different colours, in sky patterns that are always the same.

But there are also wandering stars, the planets, which travel through the star patterns, sometimes bright, sometimes pale. Sometimes they disappear altogether, only to return, months later. How can this be explained?

WHAT MAKES A GOOD THEORY GOOD?

It isn't too hard to think up a theory for something. The hard bit is to prove it to other people. One way of doing this is to use the theory to predict what is going to happen.

Astrology is a theory that makes predictions. You can look up 'what the stars foretell' in magazines and newspapers. Do they get it right? Do astrologers always win the lottery?

The job of **astronomy** was also to make some predictions: 'If you follow this star you will get to Damascus'. Or 'If you plant your crops when a certain star is just setting at dawn the crops will grow well'. Astronomy always gave better results than astrology, even if it was less fun. But the next step was to find out *why* the stars moved so regularly, and why the wandering stars (called **planets**) were different. In other words, could you *predict* what the stars and planets were going to do?

To do this people needed a theory about what stars and planets actually were.

■ Why are the stars useful?

Over the many thousands of years that people watched the skies, the patterns of movements became well known (picture 2). Astronomers taught sailors how to use the changing positions of Sun, stars and planets to find their way across seas out of sight of land.

By the 15th century, ships and the skills of navigation became good enough for traders to travel further than they had ever done before. The Arabs and the Chinese sailed across the Indian Ocean and the West Pacific, bringing rich trade to and from the islands of the 'Indies'.

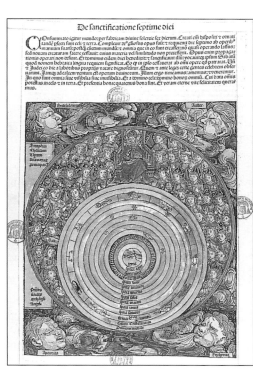

Picture 2 Columbus discovered America, even though he thought that the Earth was at the centre of the Universe.

Picture 3 An old map of the world.

■ The age of discoveries

Then Europeans ventured around the great barrier of Africa to join in this trade. The Portuguese were the first great navigators and the first Europeans to sail around Africa into the Indian Ocean.

Some of these Portuguese sailors were swept off course by wind and current and 'discovered a new land', which we now call Brazil. But they didn't know where they had been, and lost it again (picture 3).

■ Christopher Columbus

It wasn't until the end of the 15th century, in the year 1492, that a good navigator called Christopher Columbus found South America again, or at least the islands where the tribe called the Caribs lived. However, he thought that he had in fact reached India. He called these islands of the Caribs the 'West Indies'. But India was a good 4000 miles further on, across the huge Pacific Ocean.

MONEY IN THE STARS

By the middle of the 16th century great fleets of Spanish galleons were carrying tonnes of gold and silver to the King of Spain. The Spanish investment in Christopher Columbus had paid off handsomely.

All this hope for trade and wealth made the study of astronomy even more valuable. It became more than a hobby or a way of 'seeing your future in the stars'. Kings and emperors employed astronomers to work out more carefully the positions and movements of stars and planets useful for navigation (picture 4).

ISAAC NEWTON (1642–1727)

Isaac Newton was born in 1642, exactly a hundred and fifty years after Columbus bumped into the West Indies. Knowledge of stars and planets had improved in that time, but no one knew what they were, or how and why they moved or stayed still.

Navigation was better, but was still more of an art than a science. Many ships were still lost, their sailors and cargoes never to be seen again.

Picture 4 It was here in Tycho Brahe's observatory in Prague, the Czech Republic, that the astronomer Kepler first proved that the Earth and planets went around the Sun.

The young Isaac Newton was very bright. He was taught at home until he was twelve, when he was sent away from his family farm in Woolsthorp, Lincolnshire, to the local grammar school. He had to learn Latin, Greek and mathematics, but he became well known for the toys and working models he made. He was as good with his hands as with his brain.

At the age of 18 he went to the University of Cambridge, and was made professor of mathematics when he was only 27 (picture 5.)

■ Newton's year of discoveries – 1665

As a young man, before he even got a degree or became a professor, Newton made so many discoveries that we still marvel at him. In 1666 the University was closed down because of the Great Plague and he spent a year at home. It was then, the story goes, that he first thought about the force that made an apple fall off a tree. He thought it might also reach as far as the Moon, and keep it in orbit. In a few months he had worked out his first ideas about the Law of Gravity and his Laws of Motion.

During the next years he had to invent completely new mathematics (the **calculus**) which he needed to prove and check his results (picture 6).

■ All mysteries solved?

The mystery of the solar system was solved. Scientists now knew why and where the planets moved in their orbits (see topic G5). They were able to work out where the planets would be in the future, and when eclipses of planets, Sun and Moon would occur. Sailors could use these calculations to navigate across the widest seas with increasing accuracy.

■ More discoveries

Newton also invented a new kind of telescope, which is still the one most used by astronomers today (picture 7). He investigated the spectrum and produced new theories of light and heat. He became very famous, and his ideas changed the way people thought about the world.

Scientists began to believe that the world – even the whole universe – must be very simple. Everything must obey simple, clear laws of nature – although they hadn't all been discovered yet. Everything, they thought, could then be predicted.

But at the height of his fame, Newton lost interest in science. He left the University and was given the job of looking after the Royal Mint, where the coinage of Britain is made.

It wasn't a very difficult job, and he had plenty of spare time for his new interest in life, which was working out the dates of when things happened in the Old Testament of the Bible. He was made *Sir* Isaac.

Newton had always been very shy and lonely. He had quarrelled with most of the other scientists he knew, and his friends found it very hard to get him to publish the books he had written about his great discoveries. He worried that he might have made mistakes and he did not like to be proved wrong!

EINSTEIN'S NEW UNIVERSE

Albert Einstein (picture 8) was one of the few scientists to become as famous as Newton. At the height of his fame thousands of people would crowd into theatres to hear him explain his theories. He knew that most of them didn't understand a word of what he was saying, so he used to play them a couple of tunes on his violin to make up for it.

Picture 5 Isaac Newton.

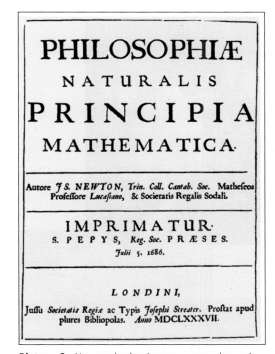

Picture 6 Newton had to invent new mathematics, the calculus, to go with his new physics.

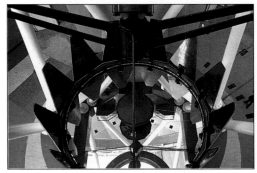

Picture 7 The world's largest single mirror telescope at Zelenchuk, Caucasus, is based on Newton's design.

Picture 8 Albert Einstein, aged 25.

Picture 9 All of these can only be explained by Einstein's work.

TRY HARDER, EINSTEIN!

Like Newton, Einstein was very bright. But he was easily bored.

He was born in Germany (in 1879), and went to school there. He didn't do too well at school at subjects he didn't like, and was unpopular with his teachers. He left school at 15 without proper qualifications and taught himself, while he spent a year hiking and climbing in the mountains of Italy.

Then at 16 he failed the entrance exam to get into the university in Switzerland where he was now living. But he did so well at maths that the professor invited him to join the class anyway. A year later he had swotted up enough of the boring subjects to pass the exam.

But even university was boring – especially the physics lectures! He nearly failed his exams again, and couldn't get a job. After two years he succeeded and became a civil servant, an examiner of inventions for the Swiss Government.

It was a nice easy job, and he was good at it. In his spare time he was a genius. Like Newton, he taught himself because there was no one else who had thought about things as hard as he had.

■ Einstein's year of discoveries – 1905

At the age of 25, still a civil servant, he wrote three scientific papers which changed the world of physics. The ideas that had been worked out by Newton, and by generations of physicists since, had to be looked at in a new light.

Like Newton's great works, they dealt with space and time, light and heat. In one, he showed that light was not only a wave (see topic A7) but also a particle. In another, he produced his first 'Theory of Relativity'. In the third, he worked out from something as simple as the way smoke spreads out, or sugar dissolves in tea, that atoms must really exist. (See Brownian Motion, page 206, and topic A9 *Light as a particle*.)

■ Relativity

Einstein is most famous for his two theories of relativity, which have changed the way we look at the Universe. For Newton, matter was 'mass', the unchangeable cause of gravity. For Einstein, matter can be changed into energy – and back again – in accordance with the formula $E = mc^2$. For Newton, time rolled on at the same rate everywhere. For Einstein, how long something takes to happen depends on how fast you are travelling. At the speed of light, time stands still.

For Newton, gravity was a **force**: for Einstein, it is a **curve** of 4-dimensional space-time.

■ The new universe of modern physics

The universe described by physics has always been hard to understand, and probably always will be. After Einstein, we can't even imagine it, even when we understand it. Newton's ideas made possible the improved navigation of the 18th and 19th centuries. They gave us an understanding of the engineering needed to make and use aircraft, rockets and space satellites. Einstein's ideas have led to our modern world. His theories have given us the engineering underlying nuclear energy – and the nuclear bomb. They have led to the ideas needed for lasers, the understanding of the genetic code, the strange world of sub-atomic particles, the reason why the Sun is hot, why black holes exist, and why the Universe is expanding.

Forces and materials

Squashing, pulling, bending

The way materials react to forces often decides how we use them.

Picture 1 This athlete's vaulting pole has to be strong, light and flexible.

The pole vaulter in picture 1 uses a long glass-fibre pole to pull himself 8 metres above the ground. The pole has to be strong and light. It also has to be bendy – but not too bendy! When he comes down on the other side he relies on the softness of the foam plastic to cushion his fall.

MAKING AND CHOOSING MATERIALS

These materials have been carefully chosen for the job they have to do. They behave in the right way when forces are applied to them. In fact, both of these materials are **synthetic**, which means that they have been made in a factory, and don't occur naturally on Earth.

Modern materials like these are designed and made by materials scientists. They need to know what the materials will be used for. They need to know how much force they must be able to withstand, how 'heavy' (dense) they need to be, and how 'bendy' they must be.

■ Useful materials

Picture 2 shows lots of synthetic materials, as well as some natural ones. Can you tell which are 'natural' and which are synthetic? In some sports grounds even the grass is artificial! The designers and makers of vaulting poles, safety mats – and even the clothes that the athletes wear – have to make a sensible choice of what materials to use.

To help them to design or choose the best materials for a purpose scientists must test them in a standard way. They must also know if changing the size of the object will make any difference. A thinner vaulting pole will be lighter, cheaper and easier to run with, but might break more easily.

■ Plastic and elastic

These words have a special meaning in materials science. They describe what a material does when forces are applied to it. Forces tend to change the shape of an object. If the shape stays changed even when the force is taken away the material is called **plastic**.

Picture 2 Natural and synthetic materials: can you tell which is which?

Mud, Plasticine, clay and putty are good examples of plastic materials.

But if the object returns to its original shape when the force is removed it is called an **elastic** material. Rubber, steel, wood and many other materials behave like this. Both the foam safety mat and the vaulting pole in picture 1 are made of elastic materials.

ARE PLASTICS PLASTIC?

Most of the materials that we call 'plastics' are synthetic materials that *were* plastic at the time they were made. Then they were heated or chemically treated to make them set hard, and they stopped being plastic.

OVER THE LIMIT

Many useful materials are only elastic up to a point. If too much force is applied they will not return to their original shape. Steel is quite elastic, but large forces may bend it out of shape permanently, like a car body that has been in an accident (picture 3). At some stage it stopped being elastic, and became plastic. Metals like copper and lead show this effect more easily, with less force needed.

GLASS

Surprisingly, glass is also elastic. Thin glass fibres can be bent easily. But if too much force is applied glass will not just **deform plastically**, like steel or copper, but shatter. A material like this is said to be **brittle**.

■ Testing for elasticity

The simplest way to test if a material is elastic is put it into a firm support and load it with weights. One way of doing this is shown in picture 4. In a quick test, load it gradually so that the length or shape changes quite a lot, then gradually unload it. If the object returns to its original shape and size it is elastic.

You can check the material more fully by taking measurements as you load and unload it. A graph of the load (or force applied) against the **change in length** it produces shows more clearly how the material responds to forces.

The graphs in picture 5 show how different materials might behave in these tests. The solid line shows what happens as the load is increased. The green line shows what happens when they are gradually unloaded.

Picture 3 Steel is elastic – up to a point!

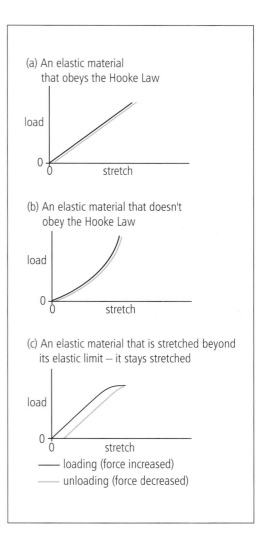

(a) An elastic material that obeys the Hooke Law

(b) An elastic material that doesn't obey the Hooke Law

(c) An elastic material that is stretched beyond its elastic limit – it stays stretched

—— loading (force increased)
—— unloading (force decreased)

Picture 5 Graphs can show how different materials stretch differently.

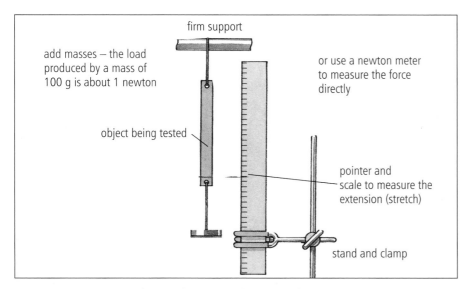

firm support

add masses – the load produced by a mass of 100 g is about 1 newton

object being tested

or use a newton meter to measure the force directly

pointer and scale to measure the extension (stretch)

stand and clamp

Picture 4 Testing to see if material or objects obey the Hooke Law.

■ The Hooke Law

When objects are stretched or compressed they change their shape. For some elastic materials a steady change in force produces a steady change in shape. These materials are said to obey a 'law' first discovered in the 17th century by the English scientist Robert Hooke (1635 – 1703). The simplest way to show this is to think of the change in the length of a material in the form of a rod or string, as in picture 4. The change of length or extension of the object is measured as the object is loaded. The readings are then checked as it is unloaded. If the plot of extension against load produces a straight line as in picture 5 (a) the material obeys the Hooke Law. A similar straight-line graph would be obtained for the material if it were to be squashed rather then stretched, and **compression** plotted against load.

■ Using elasticity to measure forces

Objects that obey the Hooke Law are used in making a spring balance or a newton meter. The marks on its scale show the extension or compression produced by a force. Because the spring inside obeys the Hooke Law the length changes can be marked as **force** changes. Picture 6 shows an example of a force measurer that uses the Hooke Law.

Picture 6 This force measurer relies on the Hooke Law.

Questions

1 Sort the following materials into two groups:

a elastic, b plastic:

steel, glass, wood, clay, Plasticine, cotton, mud, putty, cardboard, foam, plastic, polythene.

2 Use the information given in this topic, plus any ideas you already have, to answer the following questions.

a Why is a pole used by a pole vaulter made of a material which is 'bendy, but not too bendy'?

b Why are most springs made of metal?

c Both steel and foam rubber obey the Hooke Law. Why are the safety mats in the gym made of foam rubber, not steel?

3 Explain as clearly as you can what the following words mean:

a elastic,

b plastic,

c brittle,

d flexible.

4 Which of the graphs in picture 7 of extension plotted against load would you expect to match the following materials:

a rubber,　　　b copper wire,

c a piece of string,　d plasticine.

5 Look at picture 2. Write down the names of the synthetic materials you can identify (e.g. glass).

6 Look at a biscuit.

a Use the words you have learned in this topic to describe its properties as a material.

b Biscuits come in a variety of different packagings (see picture 8). How do the mechanical properties of the biscuit decide what kind of packaging the biscuit manufacturers need to use?

Picture 8

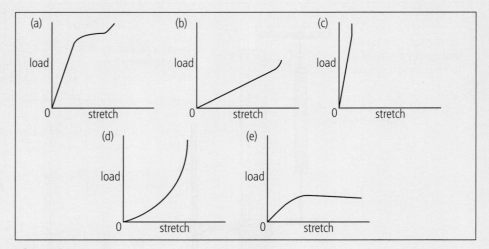

Picture 7

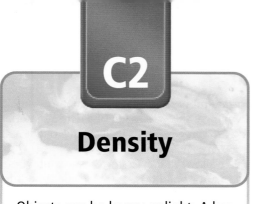

Density

Objects can be heavy or light. A key factor is their density – how much a given volume of a material weighs.

Both the lorries in picture 1 are carrying the same **load**, but one is a load of wood and the other a load of steel. The lorry with the steel looks almost empty, and it would be easy to put a lot more on it. But to do this would be illegal – and dangerous. The result would be too much force on the wheels and axles of the lorry. If both lorries are loaded to their full legal limits then they are carrying the same load – in other words the steel weighs as much as the wood.

The difference between the two materials is that steel is **denser** than wood. 20 tonnes of steel take up far less space than 20 tonnes of wood (picture 2).

Picture 1 Both of these lorries are carrying the same weight.

■ Measuring density

Density means how much matter there is in a given space. In other words, density is **mass per unit volume**.

As a formula:

$$\text{density} = \frac{\text{mass}}{\text{volume}} \quad \text{or} \quad d = \frac{m}{v}$$

Steel has a density of 7700 kilograms per cubic metre; wood is much less dense, even a 'heavy wood' like oak has a density of only 720 kg/m³. We can rearrange the formula and use it to calculate how much space (volume) 20 tonnes (20 000 kg) of oak would take up:

$$\text{volume} = \frac{\text{mass}}{\text{density}}$$

$$= \frac{20\,000 \text{ tonnes}}{720 \text{ tonnes/m}^3}$$

$$= 27.8 \text{ m}^3$$

Use the formula to check that 20 tonnes of steel would only take up 2.6 m³.

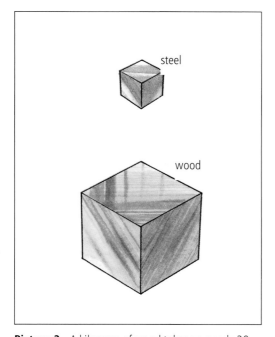

Picture 2 A kilogram of wood takes up nearly 20 times as much space as a kilogram of steel.

Picture 3 An airplane under construction showing the open framework.

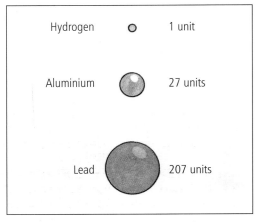

Hydrogen	○	1 unit
Aluminium		27 units
Lead		207 units

Picture 4 Atoms of different elements have very different masses.

■ Why is density important?

The density of a material is a very important property. Think of a structure – like a building, a bridge or the skeleton of an animal. If it was made of a dense material it would have the problem of supporting its own weight, as well as any load it had to carry. This might be difficult to do.

Bones have a hollow structure which allows them to be mostly 'empty', so combining lightness with strength. Modern buildings are also designed to combine lightness with strength, using modern low-density materials.

Aircraft have to be strong, but as light as possible. They are built on an open framework, as shown in picture 3. This framework is made from special mixtures of metals (alloys). Scientists called metallurgists have had to develop new strong alloys with very low densities, such as duralumin (aluminium and copper) and magnesium alloys.

■ Why are some materials denser than others?

The basic reason for some chemical elements being denser than others is that their atoms have more mass (picture 4). An atom of lead is nearly eight times more massive than an atom of aluminium.

But lead is in fact only about four times denser than aluminium. This is because the density of a material is also decided by how crowded together its atoms are. The atoms are 'packed' differently in lead from how they are in aluminium.

■ Floating and sinking

The density of a material decides whether it will sink or float. Materials denser than water will sink in it. Less dense materials will float.

The same rule applies to any fluid – helium and hydrogen balloons float in air because these gases are less dense than air. Carbon dioxide balloons fall, sinking through the air.

Of course, you can make a dense material float by giving it a hollow shape. This means that it contains air, and so the average density of the object is less than the density of water.

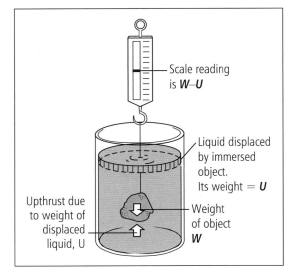

Picture 5 An object seems to weigh less in water.

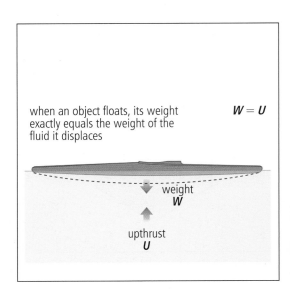

Picture 6 The flotation principle.

Table 1 Densities of everyday materials.

Material	Density in kg per m³
uranium	19 050
lead	11 350
copper	9840
iron	7870
steel (high tensile	7800
aluminium	2700
wood (oak)	720
wood (balsa)	200
glass	2500
rubber	2500
bone	1100
Perspex	1200
polythene (high density)	960
concrete	2200
brick	1700
breeze block	1400
Earth's crust (average)	2500
mercury	13 550
water (at 4 °C)	1000
water (at 20 °C)	998
sea water	1010 – 1050
milk	1030
alcohol	792
lubricating oil	900 – 920
air (at 0 °C and 1 atmosphere pressure)	1.3

Activities

A Physical properties of materials

There are many possible reasons why a designer chooses to use a particular material to make something with. This topic is about just some of the physical properties of materials.

1 List some other properties that you think might be important.

2 Choose any object that you can see and touch that is made of more than one material. Write down what it is made of and say why you think the designer has chosen those materials.

B Finding out about densities

Use a library or a reference book to find out:

1 What is the densest element?

2 what is the least dense element?

3 What is the densest timber?

4 Birds' bones are less dense than, say, human bones. How is this achieved?

C Floating and sinking

1 Use table 1 above and a reference book to find the densities of the following materials: oak, copper, lead, brick, balsa, candle wax.

2 Sort these materials into two groups, those that sink in water (a), and those that float (b).

3 The density of water is 1000 kg/m³. Polypropylene is a plastic with a density of 900 kg/m³. Will it float or sink in water?

4 Alcohol has a density of 800 kg/m³. Will polypropylene float in alcohol?

5 Ice floats with about 90% of its volume under water. Make a reasonable guess at the density of ice.

Questions

1 Make an estimate of how much of the material in your classroom is synthetic ('man-made') compared to the amount that is 'natural' (like wood or stone). Choose one the synthetic materials and give one reason (other than cost) why it might have been selected for its purpose.

2 Using your own experience, put the following materials in order of density, the most dense material first:

oak, expanded polystyrene, lead, glass, the human body, water.

3 Wood is a lot less dense than steel, but most ships are made of steel. How can a steel ship float?

4 Copy out and complete the table by calculating the missing values. You will need to use the formula

$$\text{volume} = \frac{\text{mass}}{\text{density}}$$

5 Describe how you might measure the density of the following:

a a metal cube,

b oil,

c a piece of rock with no definite shape,

d air.

Material	Mass	Volume	Density
copper	200 g	24.4 cm³	
aluminium		400 cm³	2.7 g/cm³
lead		0.5 cm³	11 350 kg/m³
brick	2000 kg	1.2 m³	
steel	2000 kg		7700 kg/m³
wood	2000 kg		600 kg/m³
concrete		4.5 m³	2200 kg/m³

Eureka!

The ancient Greeks were quite broadminded. But the sight of a naked man running through the streets shouting 'I've found it! I've found it!' caused a few heads to turn and probably collected a swarm of children calling out rude words.

The naked man was called Archimedes. He was already famous as a scientist, and he had just solved a physics problem! He had discovered what we now call Archimedes' Principle. The local king had asked him to check whether a new crown was made of pure gold or a cheaper mix of gold and silver.

The answer came to him in the bath. It was based on the fact that when you get in to a bath the water level rises. Everybody knows this! But Archimedes suddenly realised that the volume of water the body pushes aside must equal the volume of the body.

This breakthrough would allow him to measure the volume of the crown. By weighing it he could work out its density (see page 114). If the crown's density was the same as the density of pure gold the king would be happy. If not, a goldsmith was going to be in serious trouble.

Archimedes went on to work out that an object will appear to lose weight in water. When an object is put into water the water level rises. This creates an extra pressure in the water which squeezes the object and tends to push it upwards. Think of grabbing hold of a piece of soap in the bath. This upward push, or upthrust, makes an object appear to weigh less in water than it did in air (picture 5). The weight loss is equal to the weight of the water displaced. This effect occurs in any substance that can flow (i.e. any fluid). So it applies to gases as well as liquids.

Archimedes' Principle: *when an object is wholly or partly immersed in a fluid it will experience an upward force (upthrust) equal to the weight of fluid it displaces.*

An object floats when the upthrust from the fluid is equal to the weight of the object (picture 6).

Suppose a piece of rock weighs 8 N in air and appears to weigh 5 N in water. The weight of water it displaces is thus 3 N. Archimedes realised that it displaces its own volume of water, so he could say

$$\frac{\text{weight of rock}}{\text{weight of same volume of water}}$$
$$= 8/3 = 2.7$$

Thus the density of the rock must be 2.7 times the density of water (the relative density of the rock). The density of water is 1000 kg/m^3, so the rock must have a density of 2700 kg/m^3.

As a general rule

relative density = weight in air/apparent loss of weight in water

Try these questions.

1   Design and carry out an experiment to check Archimedes' ideas.

2   A reel of copper wire weighs 250 g in air. When it is lowered into water it seems to weigh just 222 g. Use these results to calculate the density of copper.

3   Archimedes' rule only works if water has a density of 1 g per cubic centimetre. Why is this?

Keeping in balance

Forces not only move things in straight lines, they also make them rotate – or try to.

Turning forces

Picture 1 shows a small crane on the back of a lorry. It is used for loading heavy objects on and off the lorry. The driver has to be very sure that the load isn't going to pull the lorry over.

Picture 1 What decides whether the lorry can lift the load safely?

Several things will decide whether the lorry will be tipped over or not. One is the weight being lifted – the *force* involved. Another is the **distance** between the load and where the truck can pivot. The load force has a turning effect on the system. This turning effect is technically (and rather confusingly) called a **moment**.

But in picture 2 there is another turning effect involved: the moment of the lorry's weight and it's distance from the pivot. If the turning effect due to the lorry is greater than the turning effect due to the load the driver has nothing to worry about!

Balancing the turning forces: keeping in equilibrium

Picture 3 shows an ideal case of a light beam with two weights hanging from it. The weights tend to turn the beam in opposite directions; clockwise and anticlockwise. The beam will balance, turning neither clockwise nor anticlockwise, if the turning effects or moments of the weights are equal. This is known as the **Law of Moments**, and was first discovered in the 3rd century BC by the Greek scientist Archimedes.

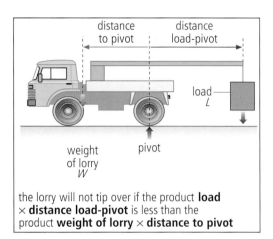

the lorry will not tip over if the product **load × distance load-pivot** is less than the product **weight of lorry × distance to pivot**

Picture 2 The turning effect or moment of the force is decided by the combination of the size of the force and its distance from the pivot point.

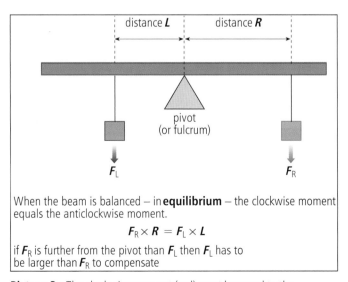

When the beam is balanced – in **equilibrium** – the clockwise moment equals the anticlockwise moment.

$$F_R \times R = F_L \times L$$

if F_R is further from the pivot than F_L then F_L has to be larger than F_R to compensate

Picture 3 The clockwise moment (red) must be equal to the anticlockwise moment (blue) when the beam is in balance.

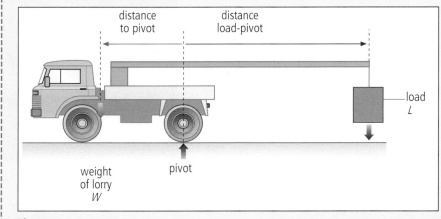

Example of balancing moments

The right hand force due to the weight **R** is 40 N, and produces a clockwise moment. The left hand force **L** is 60 N and produces an anticlockwise moment. For the beam to be in balance the opposite moments must be equal. If **R** is 30 cm from the pivot then its moment is 1200 N cm. This means that the anticlockwise moment must also be 1200 N cm, so **L** must be 20 cm from the pivot.

distance to pivot

distance load–pivot

load **L**

weight of lorry **W**

pivot

Picture 4

STABILITY

An object that is stationary when acted upon by turning forces is said to be in **equilibrium**. In everyday life we tend to take for granted the fact that most things are in equilibrium. But designers have usually taken a lot of care to make sure that turning forces are either perfectly balanced – or that the effect of possible external turning forces aren't great enough to make the object tip over. Objects are made to be as **stable** as possible.

Picture 5 shows part of a high-speed train. It is designed not only to move along at speeds of up to 250 km per hour but also to stay upright and on the track as it goes around bends. It has to be strong enough to withstand the stresses and strains of high-speed motion.

But just as importantly, the train is designed to be as safe as possible in an accident. In a typical accident the passenger sections might leave the track completely. The danger is that the section overturns as it rides over rough ground. If it does the passengers may be injured as the compartment frame collapses or telescopes. Picture 6 shows the internal structure of the passenger section. It is designed for both **stability** and **strength**. Many everyday objects are designed with the same aims, from teacups and jugs to bridges and the towers that carry television transmitter aerials.

■ Stability and centre of mass

A stable object is one that doesn't fall over easily when something bumps into it. Think of bumping into a laboratory stool (fairly unstable!) compared with bumping into a kitchen chair at home (fairly stable). Picture 7 shows three simple shapes and it is easy to tell which is the most stable and which is the least stable.

The basic physical reason for greater or lesser stability is to do with the position of what is called the **centre of mass** of an object. This is the point where the force of gravity acting on the object appears to act. In a metre stick the centre of mass is in the middle, and you can support the stick by balancing it there on your finger.

Picture 5   A high-speed train is designed to be very stable.

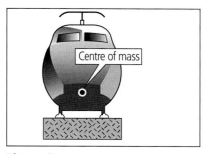

Picture 6

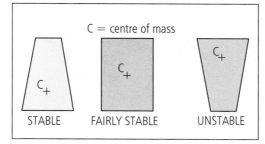

C = centre of mass

STABLE   FAIRLY STABLE   UNSTABLE

Picture 7   The lower the centre of mass, the more stable the object.

The centre of mass of a snooker cue is nearer the thick end so you can support it with one finger at that point, as shown in picture 9.

You could *calculate* the position of the centre of mass of a metre stick or plank of wood by using the **Law of Moments** (see page 117). The moment (turning effect of a force) of gravity pulling down on the left half of the stick is exactly balanced by an equal turning effect pulling down on the right half. But calculation is hard to do when the shapes are more complicated – as in a bridge, a ship or an aircraft. But it is often possible to guess the position of the centre of mass of a sheet with a symmetrical shape, such as a rectangle or a circle.

Centre of mass relates to stability in the following way: *when an object is tilted so that the centre of mass goes over its base, the object will topple.* Picture 10 illustrates this, and shows the difference between a shape with high stability and a shape with low stability.

But the shape is only one factor. An object with a possibly unstable shape can be made more stable by making the bottom parts heavier, e.g. by making them thicker or by using a denser material. This is what is done in the high-speed train, a double-decker bus and a glass tumbler, for example.

Finding the centre of mass of a thin sheet

(also called a lamina)

Hang the flat sheet of material by one point near its edge. Hang a plumb line (a thin string with a weight on the end) from the same point. Both must swing freely. Keep both sheet and line still and use a marker pen to draw a line showing where the plumb line goes across the sheet.

Then hang the sheet from another point near its edge and repeat the procedure. Where the two lines cross is the centre of mass. Check accuracy by drawing a third line from a third point.

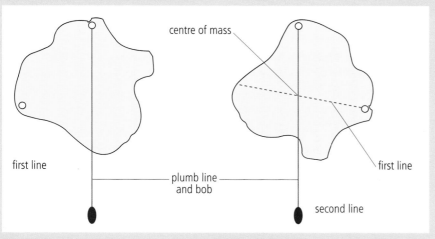

centre of mass

first line

plumb line and bob

first line

second line

Picture 8   Finding the centre of mass of a thin irregular sheet.

Picture 9 The centre of mass of a snooker cue.

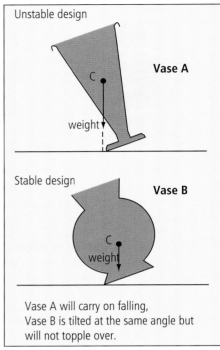

Unstable design

Vase A

weight

Stable design

Vase B

C
weight

Vase A will carry on falling,
Vase B is tilted at the same angle but
will not topple over.

Picture 10

Picture 11 Where would you expect its centre of mass
to be? Is there a good reason for this?

Questions

1 a Sketch a cross-section of an oil
tanker (viewed from one end).
Mark in where you think the
centre of mass would be when the
ship is (i) fully loaded (ii) empty.

b Suggest why an oil tanker is
usually loaded with water (as
ballast) when it has delivered its
load of oil.

2 An aircraft is kept up by a force
called *lift*, which is caused by air
flowing over its wings. It is pulled
down by the force of gravity, acting
through its centre of mass. Why is it
a good idea that aircraft are built so
that the lift force also acts through
the centre of mass?

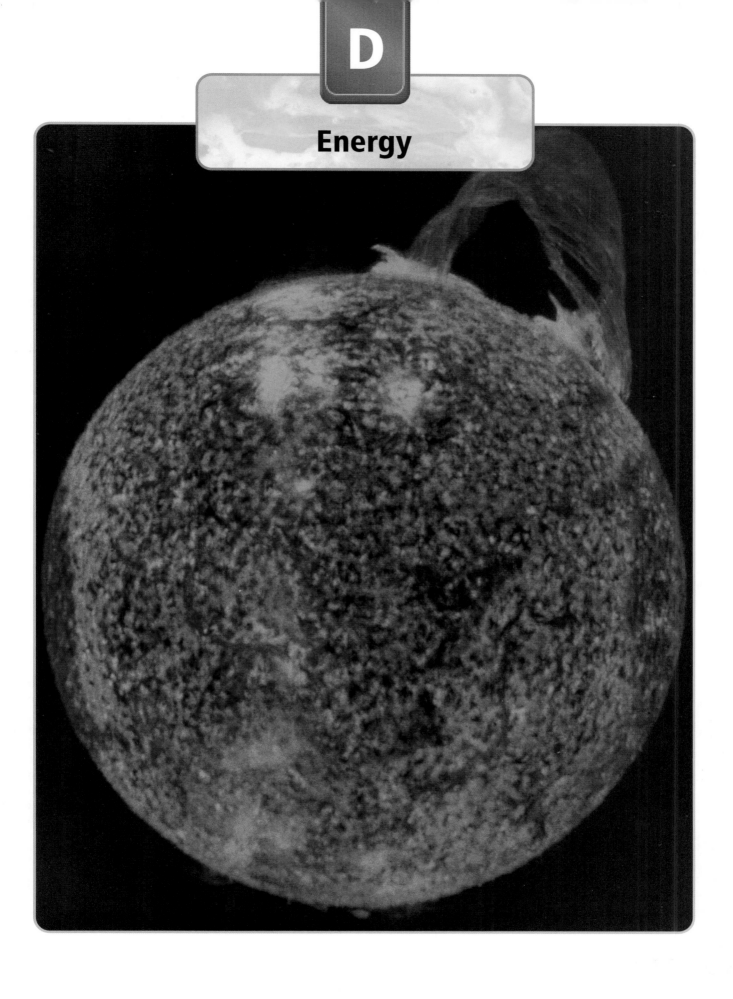

D

Energy

D1

Where does energy come from?

All life on Earth needs energy; we can control it, but cannot create it. Are we using it wisely? Is the world going to run out of energy?

We use energy to make things work. We use it to cook with, and the food we eat is our personal supply of energy. Without this energy, we would die in a matter of weeks. Long before then, we would begin to feel ill and very weak.

This topic is about where the energy we use actually comes from. We usually take it for granted. Just press the switch and electrical machines start to work, or the heating comes on. We stop at a garage and fill up with petrol; someone comes and delivers oil, coal or coke to our homes. The gas supply is always there when we want it.

The pie chart (picture 1) shows where we use energy. Most of it is fairly evenly shared out between home, industry and moving things about. A smaller amount is used for what are called 'services', which means things like schools, hospitals, town halls, shops, etc (commercial and other).

■ How much energy do you use?

One way or another every person in this country uses, each year, the energy that could be got from burning 3.5 tonnes of oil. North Americans use more than twice as much, and the average for the world is 1.5 tonnes per person. Topic D2 is about measuring energy, and it shows you how to measure the amount of energy you use, per day.

■ Changing energy to suit our needs

Of course, the energy you use is not all supplied from oil. One of the great things about energy is that it can be changed into various 'forms', and can be moved about in so many different ways. What is really happening is that the energy is being transferred from one 'system' to another.

A system can be something quite simple, like a spinning wheel. It can also be something very complicated, like a human cell or a power station. Let's take a look at how the energy you get from an electric fire actually got there. It took a longer time than you might think!

MOVING ALONG THE ENERGY TRAIL

Think of sitting in front of an electric fire. The energy has moved along quite a long trail before it reached you.

■ The start of the trail – the Sun

The Sun is millions of kilometres away, and the energy from the fire that warms you started just there, millions of years ago. Nuclear fusion (see topic F5) makes the Sun very hot (picture 2). This makes the sun send out energy as various kinds of **radiation** (see topic A7). A very small fraction of this gets to the Earth and keeps the Earth warm.

Some of the radiation energy, visible light, is used by plants to make the chemicals they need to grow through a process called **photosynthesis**. In photosynthesis, the simple molecules of carbon dioxide and water are turned into new, more complicated molecules of sugar and starches. These are **carbohydrates**.

■ Forming fossil fuels

Over millions of years, the carbohydrates in ancient plants have been converted to fossil fuels: oil, coal and natural gas.

Fossil fuels contain many different chemical compounds, but the most important ones are **hydrocarbons**.

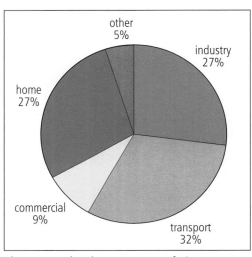

Picture 1   What do we use energy for?

Picture 2   Nuclear fusion changes mass to energy.

■ Energy from fossil fuels

Fossil fuels are now our major source of energy. The energy is released by combustion with oxygen. The waste products are oxides, mostly of carbon (carbon dioxide) and hydrogen (hydrogen oxide – water). This is the reverse of the process which formed the hydrocarbons in plants, by which solar energy was used to convert carbon dioxide and water into sugars with the release of oxygen into the atmosphere.

The main hydrocarbon fossil fuels are: coal, crude oil and gas. Crude oil is a mixture of oils from which useful fuels such as diesel, petrol and paraffin can be extracted. Gas is mainly methane, one of the simplest hydrocarbons.

THE FUEL–OXYGEN SYSTEM

The hydrocarbon chemicals in fossil fuels can only release their energy when they change into other chemicals. The most common way is by combustion (burning). They combine with oxygen and heat up their surroundings, producing the waste gases steam and carbon dioxide. The energy cycle has brought us back to where it started all those millions of years ago, as shown in picture 3.

■ From coal to electric fire

Most of our electricity is generated in power stations that burn coal (see topic E10). As it flows through the resistance wire in the bars of our electric fire, it delivers energy and the wire glows red hot. It is not as hot as the Sun, but it gives out energy in the same way, as radiation. Our skins absorb this radiation, warming up as they do so. It has been a long trail from the Sun to the electric fire, and picture 4 sums up the changes.

THE PROBLEM WITH FOSSIL FUELS

The main problem with fossil fuels is that we are using them up far more quickly than they were made. For example, by the year 2050 there may be no more oil left. Britain's North Sea oil wells will be pumped dry by the time you are settling down to raise a family, but coal will last longer because there is much more of it. Picture 5 tells you how long we expect the reserves of fossil fuels to last. They could last longer, or be used up sooner. This depends how sensibly we use them.

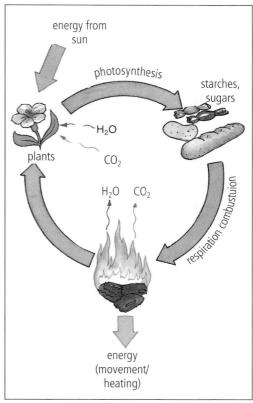

Picture 3 Water and carbon dioxide are recycled in the Earth–Sun energy system.

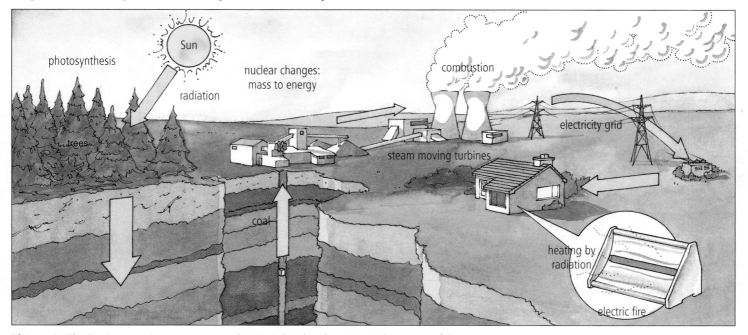

Picture 4 The Sun is our main energy source – but it might take a long time to become useful.

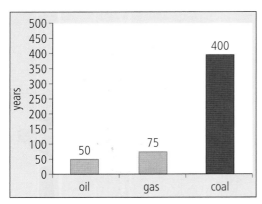

Picture 5 These are estimates of how long world supplies of fossil fuels will last – if we go on using them at the present rate.

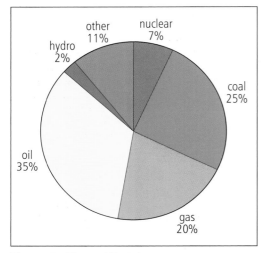

Picture 6 The world's main energy sources.

Picture 7 Most people on Earth use wood as their main fuel.

A great deal of the energy we obtain is wasted because we don't manage it sensibly – see topic D5.

We might also begin to make use of alternative sources of energy. These could be renewable sources such as wind, sun, tides and waves. We can make use of the energy of 'biomass' – from plants and from animal wastes. These sources of energy are dealt with in topic E10. We might also make more use of nuclear energy – see topic F5.

■ Energy supplies

Most of the energy that we use on Earth comes from fossil fuels – at present this is almost 90% of the total. The pie chart in picture 6 shows the main sources of energy that the people of the world use. But it does not show all of it. It shows only the 'artificial' energy that we buy in the form of fuels and electricity.

The chart does not show the energy that we get 'free', for example, the energy coming from the Sun.

All the crops on Earth rely on this solar energy to keep them warm enough to grow, and to give the light they need to photosynthesise. It warms up sea and land, and keeps people warm in summer, so that they don't need to buy so much fuel. We should remember that for most of human history, energy from the Sun was the only energy we were able to use.

Neither does the chart show the energy used by millions of people all over the world that they collect for themselves. It might surprise you to learn that most people on Earth rely on **wood** for their heating and cooking. These people live in Africa, and much of Asia (picture 7). The advantage of wood is that it is a **renewable** energy source – provided people keep on planting trees to replace the ones they cut down for fuel.

WHAT IS ENERGY?

We can usually recognise energy when we come across it, but it is hard to say what it is. The simplest way to describe it is to say what it can do. The main things that it can do are:

- **work**, by means of applying forces to move things,
- **heat**, making things get hotter, melt, boil or evaporate.

Energy is not a 'stuff', like air or atoms, or even like electric charge. It is to do with the way things are arranged.

When an elastic band is stretched, the molecules are rearranged. The forces beween them can pull the rubber back to its original shape. When you stretch the band you have done some work – by applying a force and moving it. When the band goes back it can apply a force – perhaps to a stone in a catapult. It does work on the stone. Each time the force is applied to move something it does work – and energy is transferred to another system.

■ Potential energy

A stretched elastic band looks innocent enough. If you had never seen or used one you wouldn't guess what might happen if it was let go. But it is able to give energy – dangerously – to a stone (picture 8). We use a special term to describe the energy 'hidden' in the stretched elastic band. We call it **potential energy**.

A stone at the top of a cliff can fall and do some damage. Water in a dam high in the mountains can flow downhill and make a hydroelectric power station produce electricity. These are another two examples of potential energy. This time it is due to the way 'things are arranged' in a gravity field. We call it **gravitational potential energy**. Gravitational energy is dealt with further in topic B5.

Kinetic energy

It takes **work** to make something move. Things will only start to move if a force acts on them, like gravity, or the force of a stretched piece of rubber. Work is a way of transferring energy, and the moving object picks up the energy from whatever system provides the force. The energy it carries can be used to do more work. Because we make so much use of moving objects we have a special name for the energy they carry. It is called **kinetic energy**. (See page 127.)

ARE WE USING TOO MUCH ENERGY?

Fifty years ago most people travelled long distances by bus or train. Now we tend to go by car. Then, people washed clothes by hand, instead of using a washing machine. Men shaved with razor blades fitted into a holder, instead of using an electric razor. Not many people had central heating. They just wore more clothes in winter!

We now expect to find fruit and vegetables in the shops at all times of the year, not just in their 'natural season'. This is because we can freeze them and keep them for years, if necessary.

All this makes life a lot more comfortable, but it does take a lot of energy. There was a time when people were very worried that the world was 'running out of energy'. There was an 'energy crisis'. The price of energy went up. Oil, coal and electricity cost more. This made people try to use less energy.

In the 1990s energy has become slightly cheaper. In the UK we have been able to use gas and oil from the North Sea. People have become more careless in their energy use. Now, the problem that is worrying people is the *polluting effect* of energy use. Burning fuels produce carbon dioxide, which increases the greenhouse effect. They often give off gases which make rain more acid.

Do we need to use as much energy as we do? Do North Americans need to use twice as much energy as Britons? What changes would there be in your life if you had to cut your personal energy use by half? And what will happen when everybody in the world is able to use energy at the rate that Western countries do?

Of course, fossil fuels will not last for ever. British oil and gas will run out by early next century. Would it be wise to make it last longer by using it more carefully?

Topic D5 tells you more about energy, and in particular about the laws of energy that allow us to control it. Knowing more about what energy is should help us use it more wisely.

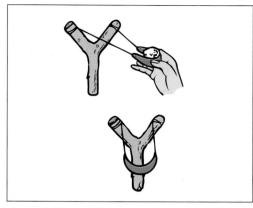

Picture 8 The stretched elastic stores potential energy, then gives it to the stone as kinetic energy.

Activities

A Where does your energy come from?

Make a list of the ways in which energy gets into your home. Find out from your parents which source of energy costs you the most per month. It is likely that the one that costs you the most is the kind that you use most. Try making a pie chart of your results.

B The geography of energy

Use a geography book or atlas to find out where the main sources of energy are in the United Kingdom. Explain why some parts of the country are (a) sources of coal, (b) good for making hydroelectricity, (c) used as the sites for nuclear power stations.

Questions

1   Where does the energy we use come from? Name three of the main energy sources used in this country.

2   Why are coal and oil called 'fossil fuels'? Name one other fossil fuel.

3   Name three devices (or things) that can store energy so that it can be used later. Describe how one of them works.

4   a   What is the energy source most commonly used in transportation (moving people and goods about)?

   b   Suggest two ways in which the UK could cut down on the amount of energy it uses for transportation. For each way, write a sentence or two explaining whether or not you think people would readily accept your suggestion.

5   Think about the energy involved when you ride a bicycle up a hill. Write down an 'energy trail' (as in picture 4) showing the various systems the energy goes through. Start with the energy in the food you ate before you rode the bike.

Make a guess as to where all the original energy has gone by the time you are standing on the top of the hill.

6   Think through a typical day, from getting up in the morning to going to bed at night. Make a list of as many as possible of the energy-using things you have used during the day, and say what energy source it tapped. One kind is given for you to start with.

Device	Source
1 bedside lamp	electrical power station

Measuring energy

Wherever energy comes from we can measure it in the same unit – the joule.

Picture 1 Using energy.

NUTRITION INFORMATION		
Typical composition by weight		
	per 100 g	per 45 g serving
Energy	1410 kJ 330 kcal	635 kJ 150 kcal
Protein	9.8 g	4.4 g
Carbohydrate	72.8 g	32.8 g
Fat	2.1 g	1.0 g
Dietary Fibre	10.5 g	4.7 g

Picture 2 Breakfast energy!

■ Look at the packet

Energy is measured in **joules**. Picture 2 shows the label on a packet of cereal. Amongst other things it tells you that when you eat one serving (45 g) it could supply 635 kJ (635 000 joules) of energy. This is a lot of joules – more than half a million! It is roughly the same as the amount of movement energy you would gain if you fell off a cliff 1000 metres high. It is twenty times the energy carried by a high-velocity rifle bullet.

■ How much energy do you need to live?

The average 16-year-old girl needs to take in 9 million joules of energy a day. Boys of the same age need about 12 million joules a day.

12 million joules is about enough to lift a 60 kg person a height of 20 km. Mount Everest is less than 9 km high! Obviously you do more with your energy intake than just **move**.

So what do you actually do with all this energy? We need energy to keep us moving about – our muscles are doing work. But we use nearly as much when we are asleep. It seems that just keeping alive takes a lot of energy!

■ Working

One way that scientists measure energy is by seeing how much work it can do. This is quite simple, and is dealt with in topic B5, where we look at energy and force in a gravity field. Forces do work when they move something. First we need to measure the size of the force (in newtons). Then we measure the distance (in metres) that the object moves in the direction the force is acting.

Then we can calculate:

$$\text{Energy used} = \text{work done}$$
$$= \text{force} \times \text{distance moved in the direction of the force}$$
$$E \text{ joules} = F \text{ newtons} \times d \text{ metres}$$

Suppose it takes a force of 25 N to move a saw when you cut a piece of wood, and you move it 0.2 metre each time. Then one cutting movement needs 25 N × 0.2 m = 5 J of energy. If it takes 20 sawcuts to get through the wood, you need to supply 100 J (picture 3).

■ James Joule – heating with energy

James Joule lived over 150 years ago. He was one of the first scientists to do experiments which actually measured how much energy was needed to *heat* something.

It seems obvious now that it takes energy to make things hot – just think of the electricity and gas bills. But in those days scientists thought that heating was done by a mysterious gas that seeped in and out of things to make them hot or cold.

James Joule did experiments to show that when you do work, by moving a paddle wheel against the friction of water in a container, the water gets hot (picture 4). More importantly, he showed that the more work he did the hotter the water got. He was *doing work* to *heat a body*.

We now know that energy can appear in all kinds of different ways, doing different jobs. We have also discovered the strange fact that we can only use the energy when *something changes*.

■ Energy and change

Norway gets most of its electrical energy from hydroelectric power stations. In Britain we get most of ours from power stations which run off coal and gas. In both cases, changes have to occur before we get the electricity we need.

In Norway, water stored in dams high in the mountains has to run downhill. The water has to *change its position* in a gravity field (picture 5). In an ordinary power station, coal or oil has to be burned. This is a *chemical change*, in which hydrocarbon molecules combine with oxygen in the air.

In both examples there are other changes as well. The falling water loses potential energy *(mgh)* and does work to drive the turbines. In a coal-fired power station the chemical reaction heats up water, which turns to steam. The steam applies force to turbines, and they do work in turning the generators.

■ Systems

A useful idea is to think of the energy as being in a **system**. The water in a reservoir is able to do work because of the pull of gravity on it. This pull is caused by the Earth, so it makes sense to think of the *water–Earth system* as having the energy. The water wouldn't be much use on its own.

In a coal-fired power station the fuel will only heat water if it burns. This needs oxygen. So here we have a *fuel–oxygen system*. When we use energy we are always moving it from one system to another – or to several others. But there is a very important law of physics that says that the total quantity of energy always stays the same. The trouble is that most of the time it doesn't all go from the starting system to the one we want it to go to! See topic D5 for more about the laws of energy.

A JOULE IS A JOULE IS A JOULE

We can measure energy using a lot of different techniques once we realise that moving energy from one system to another doesn't alter the fact that it is still **energy**. We can lift a can of beans up on to a shelf in all sorts of ways. But whatever source the energy comes from, it always takes the same amount of work to do the lifting. So the same quantity of energy has to be transferred, whether it is done by an electric robot, a conveyer belt or a human being.

Similarly, it takes a standard quantity of energy to warm a kilogram of water by 1°C. This is the principle behind the ways of measuring energy described below.

■ How to measure energy

This is a useful reference section: use it when you need to measure energy for an investigation or when dealing with energy in another topic.

1 **Doing work.** You need to measure the force (**F** in newtons) involved and the distance (**d** in metres) moved. Then use the formula:

$$\text{work done} = \text{energy } \textbf{\textit{E}} \text{ transferred} = \text{force} \times \text{distance}$$
$$\text{or } \textbf{\textit{E}} = \textbf{\textit{Fd}}.$$

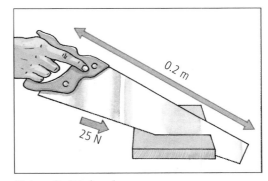

Picture 3 Work and energy.

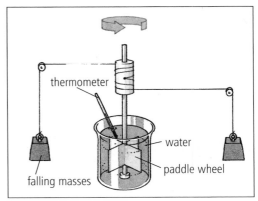

Picture 4 Joule's Paddle Wheel Apparatus showed that 'heat is a form of energy'.

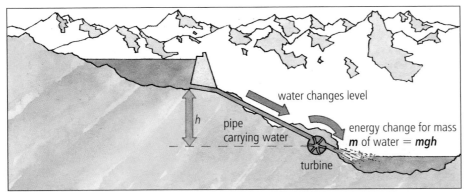

Picture 5 Energy transfers in a hydroelectric power station.

Proof of the formula for Kinetic Energy

A force **F** is acting on a mass **m**. The mass is accelerated and it gains kinetic energy. This energy comes from the work done by the force as it moves the mass.

speed = 0   **s**   speed here = **v**

F Force **F** moves the mass a distance **s** **F**

The mass has accelerated to speed **v**.
Acceleration is **a**.

Use Newton's Laws: $\textbf{\textit{F}} = \textbf{\textit{ma}}$
Work done by force is force x distance moved = $\textbf{\textit{Fs}}$.

Combine these: work done = $\textbf{\textit{mas}}$

This becomes the kinetic energy gained, and equals it.

Now use the equation of motion (page xx) linking speed gained and distance: $\textbf{\textit{v}}^2 = 2\textbf{\textit{as}}$

This gives by rearranging: $\textbf{\textit{as}} = \frac{1}{2}\textbf{\textit{v}}^2$

So now $\textbf{\textit{mas}}$ can be rewritten as $\textbf{\textit{m}} \times \frac{1}{2}\textbf{\textit{v}}^2$, or $\frac{1}{2}\textbf{\textit{mv}}^2$

This is the formula for kinetic energy of a mass **m** moving with speed **v**.

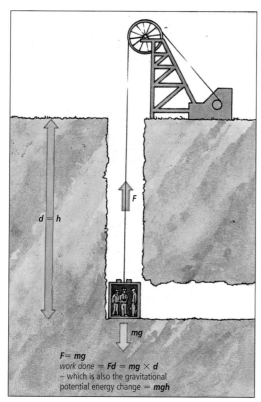

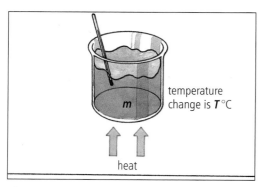

Picture 6 Doing work against gravity: $E = Fd$

Picture 7 Heating water: $E = msT$.

2 **Measuring potential energy.** When you do work against the force of gravity you always increase the potential energy of the object being moved. If it has a mass m it will have a gravity force on it of mg. This is its **weight**. When you move it a through a height h you do work and transfer energy to the object as potential energy. As above we can calculate this as:

$$\text{work done} = \text{force} \times \text{distance}$$
$$\text{or energy transferred as potential energy, } E = mgh$$

3 **Using temperature measurements.** You need to measure the mass (m in kg) of material being heated and the temperature change (T in °C, produced. Then look up in tables the amount of energy (s) needed to heat 1 kg of the material through each Celsius degree. This is the **specific heat capacity**, s. In the case of water, $s = 4200$ J/kg °C. Finally, you can use the formula:

$$E = msT$$

to find the energy E transferred by heating.

4 **Using electrical measurements.** The work done by an electrical current to a device is measured by using the formula:

$$E = VIt$$

(V is voltage, I is current in amps, t is time in seconds; see picture 8 and topic E6).

5 **Kinetic energy.** The energy, E, possessed by a moving object is calculated using the formula $E = \frac{1}{2}mv^2$, where m is the mass of the object in kilograms and v is its speed in metres per second.

6 **Power.** The power transferred is the rate of transferring energy, so

$$\text{power} = \frac{\text{work done}}{\text{time taken}}$$

So power $= VI$ or Fv where v is speed (distance/time).

■ Power and energy

Power is a measure of the rate at which we can do work (page 126). Power is measured in **joules per second**, called **watts**.

$$\text{power} = \frac{\text{work done}}{\text{time taken}}$$

$$\text{(watts)} = \frac{\text{(joules)}}{\text{(seconds)}}$$

A more powerful engine can do work more quickly than a less powerful one. Practical devices have powers of several thousand watts, so we tend to use the unit **kilowatt (1 kW = 1000 watts)**. Power also measures the rate of energy transfer: a 2 kW heater heats up water twice as quickly as a 1 kW heater.

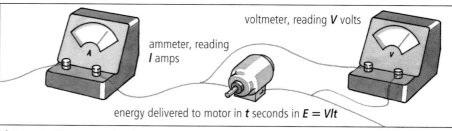

Picture 8 Measuring electrical energy.

Questions

1 a Rub your hands together quickly. Describe any energy changes that you notice.

   b How does your body use muscles to keep itself warm without moving your arms and legs?

2 It takes a force of 30 newtons to push a box along the floor. How much work do you do when you move it 5 metres?

3 How much energy is released in a 12 V electric lamp when a current of 0.5 A flows in it for 1 minute?

4 A kilogram of copper needs 400 J to raise its temperature by 1°C. How many joules would it take to:

   a warm 5 kg of copper by 1°C?

   b warm 6 kg of copper by 20 °C?

5 Mount Everest is 8848 metres above sea level.

   a Calculate how much energy it would take to lift someone weighing 600 N straight up through this height.

   b In fact, a climber would use much more energy than you have calculated in (a) to climb Mount Everest. Give at least three reasons for this.

6 Design an experiment to find out one of the following.

   Say what you would need to measure and give an idea of how it might be done.

   a How much energy can you get by burning 1 kg of wood?

   b How much energy does a gerbil need in a day?

   c How much energy does the Sun deliver on a square metre of ground per minute on a sunny day?

   d How much energy does it take to do the washing up?

7 How much does the temperature of a 2 kg mass of water rise when it is given 21 kJ of heating energy? Use the fact that it takes 4.2 kJ to warm 1 kg of water by 1°C.

8 A rock weighs 2 kg and is just on the edge of a cliff 12 m above the beach.

   a What is the potential energy of the rock? (Assume $g = 10$ N/kg.)

   b The rock falls off the cliff. How much kinetic energy will it have just before it hits the beach?

   c Use a calculator to work out the speed of the rock just before it hits the beach. How much will air resistance affect the speed of the rock?

9 A loaded lift needs a force of 6000 N to move it upwards at a steady rate.

   a How much work does the force do when the lift moves 25 m upwards?

   b If the time it takes to do this is 12 s, show that the power needed is 12.5 kW.

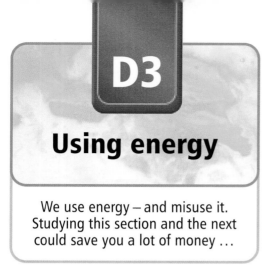

Using energy

We use energy – and misuse it. Studying this section and the next could save you a lot of money …

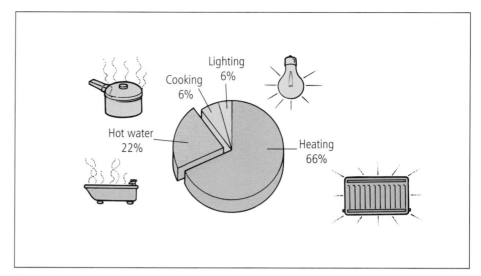

Picture 1   How we use energy in the home.

THE COSTS OF ENERGY

Energy is expensive. You have to pay for producing it. You have to pay for moving it to where you want to use it. Getting fossil fuels out of the ground is expensive. 'Human fuel' – food – is even more expensive to produce.

But there are other costs when we use energy. We get most of our energy from fossil fuels. The unwanted by-products are carbon dioxide and some other gases which cause pollution in one way or another. We are only now waking up to the fact that the bills for the greenhouse effect and acid rain and other kinds of pollution have still to come in.

This section deals with the way we use energy in the home, and how we might save money by using less, and wasting less. Look at the pie chart in picture 1. It shows what we use energy for at home.

■ Home heating

Most of the energy we use at home is used to keep ourselves and our surroundings warm. Nearly all of this heating energy comes from the combustion of fossil fuels, such as coal, oil or gas. We can use the fuels directly or indirectly (see table 1).

Electricity is not a fuel: it is just a very good way of moving energy from one place to another. But the energy it carries is produced in power stations and most of these use fossil fuels.

HEATING COSTS

Table 2 shows how much it costs to provide heating using different sources of energy. The most expensive is 'daytime' electricity. Prices will change, of course. This may be due to inflation and changes in world production of oil, for example. But the prices tend to stay much the same in comparison with each other.

Energy is measured in joules. One joule is a very small quantity of energy. It is about how much you would use to lift this book from a chair to a table. It usually takes a lot of energy to heat things up. For example, to boil a kettle holding 1 kg of water needs about a third of a million joules (0.33 MJ). If this energy were used in working intead of heating, it could raise the kilogram of water higher than the top of Mount Everest! Heating things uses up a lot of energy, and it's by far the biggest part of your household energy use. A 1-bar electric fire is rated at 1 kilowatt (see below). This fire delivers a thousand joules *every second*. In an hour it would deliver 3 600 000 joules (3.6 MJ). This amount of energy is also called a **kilowatt-hour**.

Table 1   Direct and indirect use of fuels.

Directly
coal, oil or gas   in fires, stoves, room heaters, central heating systems
Indirectly
electricity   in fires, convector heaters, storage heaters

Table 2   Costs of producing energy.

Energy source	Cost of producing	
	Yearly cost for typical house/£	1 megajoule p
solid fuel/coal	360	0.02
oil	250	0.015
gas	270	0.016
bottled gas (propane)	455	0.027
electricity		
– daytime	1200	2
– night-time	350	0.75

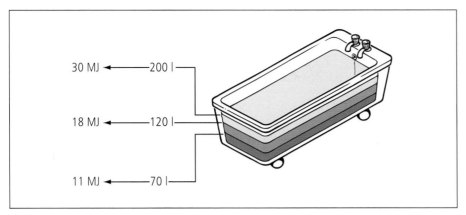

30 MJ ◄ ─── 200 l ─┐

18 MJ ◄ ─── 120 l ─┤

11 MJ ◄ ─── 70 l ─┘

Picture 2   The energy needed to have a bath.

Cleaning, washing and bathing

How much does it cost to have a bath? This depends on how hot you like it, and how much water you use. A standard bath, just about as full as you can have it without it spilling, will take 200 litres of water (picture 2). A litre of water has a mass of 1 kg, so you would use 200 kg of water. Tap water is at an average temperature of 10 °C in winter, a hot bath is about 45 °C.

We can use the formula $E = msT$ (see topic D2) to calculate how much heating energy this needs:

$$\text{energy needed, } E = 200 \text{ kg} \times 4200 \text{ J/kg °C} \times 35 \text{ °C}$$
$$= 29.4 \text{ MJ}$$

You can use the data in table 2 to work out how much this would cost using different energy sources. Using the most expensive, electricity, it would cost about 50p. It should be cheaper to take a shower – activity B asks you to estimate how much taking a shower costs (picture 3).

Table 3 shows how much energy is needed for different cleaning tasks.

Table 3   Energy needed for cleaning tasks.

Washing up (using typical quantities of water)		
in a sink (8 litres)	2 MJ (very hot)	1.3 MJ (hot)
in a plastic bowl (5 litres)	1.3 MJ (very hot)	0.8 MJ (hot)
Washing machine (for clothes)		
using 17 litres of water	heating	5 MJ
	pump, motor	1 MJ
Vacuum cleaning		
for 1 hour		3.6 MJ

Picture 3   Taking a shower.

Cooking

Cooking means heating food to a temperature high enough to change the tough fibres of meat and vegetables into a softer form that we can digest. It also kills any bacteria that might be in the food. Cooking takes time, to make sure that the changes, which are in fact chemical reactions, take place.

The higher the temperature the quicker the changes take place. Frying foods is quicker than boiling them. Frying and roasting temperatures are high, from 150 to 240 °C, compared with the boiling water temperature of 100 °C. Salt water boils at a higher temperature than pure water, but only by a degree or two.

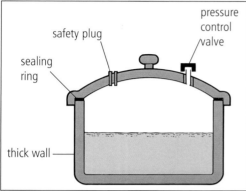

Picture 4　Pressure cookers save energy. How?

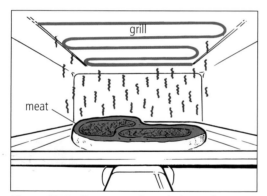

Picture 5　Radiant energy from the hot grill is absorbed in the surface of the food.

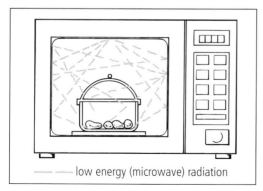

low energy (microwave) radiation

Picture 6　Low energy microwave radiation can pass through glass and plastic and carry heat energy deep into food, where it is absorbed easily by water and fat.

PRESSURE COOKING

Water under pressure needs an even higher temperature before it boils. This effect is used in pressure cookers (picture 4). In these cookers, water is kept boiling very gently (just *simmering*) at about 105 °C. Even this small rise in temperature reduces cooking times by over a half, thus saving quite a lot of energy.

COOKING WITH RADIATION

You do this every time you grill some food. A grill is simply a piece of metal, heated by gas or electricity. Red hot metal gives out not only energy we can see (as red light) but also energy radiation that is invisible – infra-red radiation (see topic A7). In fact, most of the radiant energy in a grill is carried by the infra-red radiation (picture 5). This is absorbed by molecules in the food and the food gets hot, so getting cooked.

Microwaves are like infra-red radiation, but the energy is carried by longer waves (picture 6). These waves interact with the electrically charged parts of water molecules in food, moving them about and so giving them energy. This extra movement is heat energy and the water gets hotter. Microwaves travel deeper into the food than infra red, so that the food is cooked on the inside as well as the outside.

In a grill – and with frying and boiling – the energy has to travel in from the surface. This is slow. We can try to speed it up, by making the fat or the grill hotter. But if we do, the outside may burn while the inside is still raw. Another advantage of microwave cooking is that the microwave radiation is not trapped by glass or plastic. It just affects the food material, and particularly the water in it. This saves energy because only the food is heated up, not the food container.

■ Lighting

Good lighting is important. We all spend a great part of our lives under 'artificial' light, and poor lighting causes eyestrain and headaches. Well designed lighting also makes places pleasant to work and live in. The physics of lighting involves:

● how light is produced
● the colour and colour balance of light
● how light is reflected or absorbed by objects
● the energy costs and efficiency of lighting.

Topics A5 and A10 deal with these ideas.

TRANSFERRING ENERGY THERMALLY

Modern life is based on our ability to make use of a wide variety of energy sources. Most of the energy we use is for heating things – in cooking and keeping warm. Also, when we use energy to make things work we find that much of the energy we put in ends up making things hot. For example, the energy from petrol finally ends up making brake blocks hot. When we run we get hot. To control the heating and cooling we move energy **thermally**. When thermal transfers occur things are *heated* or *cooled*, or a substance *evaporates, freezes, boils* or *melts*. The words in italics name *thermal processes*, and are described fully below.

■ Conduction

A hot object can lose energy by transferring it through another substance which touches it. A hot flame will heat the end of a metal rod, and before long the other end of the rod gets hot too: energy has moved along the rod by **conduction**. Metals are all good thermal conductors. If you hold the end of a piece of wood in the flame it will burn, but the end you are holding will stay cool for a long time. Wood is able to conduct energy, but is not as good at this as a metal is. Wood is such a poor conductor it may be called an **insulator**.

Conduction works because when a substance is heated its particles gain energy. In a gas or a liquid they move around more quickly, thus gaining kinetic energy. In a

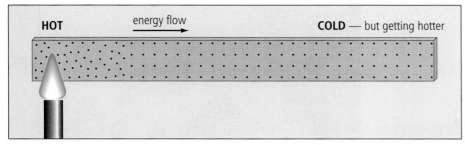

Picture 7 Conduction in a metal rod.

solid the particles vibrate more, gaining a mixture of potential and kinetic energy. This is just like a mass bouncing up and down on the end of a spring. We notice the extra energy as a rise in **temperature**. When one end of a solid is heated the extra vibrations at the hot end affect neighbouring particles, which vibrate more. In turn they affect their neighbours and before long we find that the far end of the solid is getting hot too. Conduction is a vital process in cooking, for example. This is one reason why pots and pans are usually made of metal.

■ Convection

When a gas or liquid is heated the extra movement of its particles makes them spread out more. This means the fluid gets less dense. As the heated fluid is usually surrounded by cooler, denser fluid it floats upwards, carrying its extra energy with it. 'Hot air rises'. The warmed fluid is replaced by cooler fluid, which is then heated and floats away. The hot object is continually losing energy and so cooling by this process called **convection**. The flow of fluid is called a **convection current**.

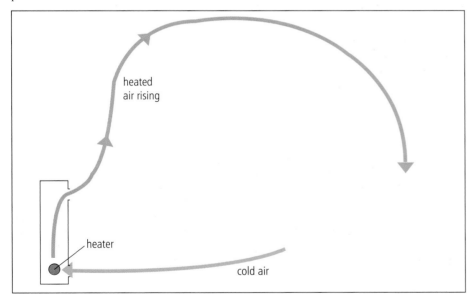

Picture 8 Convection currents in a room.

■ Radiation

All objects radiate electromagnetic radiation (see topic A7). A hot object radiates more energy than its cooler surroundings, so it loses energy and cools down. Most of the energy is radiated in the waveband called **infra-red**. This consists of electromagnetic waves just longer than light, just off the red end of the visible spectrum. We can feel these rays with nerve cells in the skin – particularly those in the back of the hand.

Picture 9 Elephants need to keep cool ...

Picture 10 Mice need to keep warm.

■ Controlling thermal loss – or why elephants have big ears

Energy loss by convection and radiation is greater when the area of the hot surface is greater. An elephant is the largest land animal and generates a great deal of waste energy from its metabolism. Biologists know that the larger the animal the smaller its surface area is compared with its mass. Elephants are in danger from overheating; mice are more likely to freeze to death. An elephant uses its ears as coolers by making its blood flow through the large ear flaps. The large area increases radiation and allows more convection as more air can be heated by contact. Mice keep warm by huddling together to reduce the surface area exposed to cold air.

RADIATORS – GOOD AND BAD

Domestic radiators are designed to have large surface areas for their volume (picture 11). This allows better convection as more air can be heated as it flows over them. They are not good radiators – partly because of their shape but also because they are usually painted white. White and shiny surfaces are not good at radiating infra-red; the best kind of surface for this is a rough black one.

Objects can be heated by absorbing infra-red radiation. This is how cooking grills and toasters work. Again, black and rough surfaces are better than white or shiny surfaces at absorbing infra-red radiation. It doesn't take long for overtoasted bread to catch fire once it gets blackened.

INSULATORS

When we want to stop hot objects cooling down we surround them with insulators. Many plastics are good insulators, as are paper, wool, fur and fat – which have important biological uses! Air is a very good insulator, but when it is heated it tends to float away in a convection current. This can be stopped by trapping the air – in pockets between fibres (rocksil, glass fibre, wool, fur, expanded polystyrene) or in layers as in double glazed windows. The trapped air gets warm but does not conduct much energy through it. In cold weather it is better to wear several layers of thin clothes than one thick layer. Picture 12 shows some common insulating materials.

Picture 13 shows various ways in which thermal transfer of energy may be reduced in the home.

Picture 11 Radiators are not designed to radiate!

1. Cavity wall insulation: fills the space between double walls with a better insulator than air. Payback time, 5 years.

2. Loft insulation: covers the floor of the roof space. Warm air rises, so this is a good place to stop energy escaping. Payback time, 1–2 years.

3. Double glazing: puts a layer of air between windowpanes. Air is a better insulator than glass. Payback time – very long – too expensive to be worthwhile.

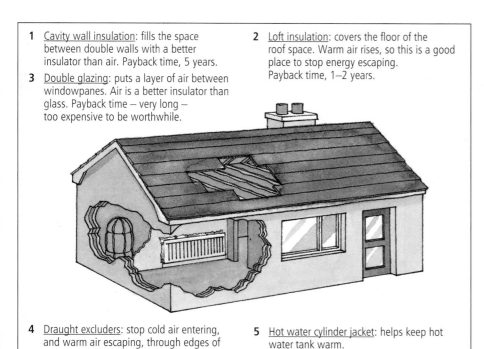

4. Draught excluders: stop cold air entering, and warm air escaping, through edges of doors and windows. Payback time, 2–4 years.

5. Hot water cylinder jacket: helps keep hot water tank warm. Payback time, less than one year.

6. Radiator foil: a shiny material fitted behind radiators on outside walls stops energy escaping as it reflects radiation back into the room. Payback time, 1–2 years.

Picture 13 How to save energy at home.

Picture 12 Wool and rocksil are good insulators for two reasons.

■ Making things hotter

The energy required to make a kilogram of any material hotter by 1°C is called its **specific heat capacity**. Different materials have different values of specific heat capacity: it takes less energy to heat a kilogram of copper by 1°C than it does to heat a kilogram of water by 1°C. See table 4.

Water has a very large specific heat capacity. Hot water is a useful energy store: when the sea is warmed by the summer sun it keeps warm well into the winter. Britain has a mild winter climate because it is an island. The Gulf Stream helps too: it is a flow of sea water heated in the tropics that is still quite warm after it has flowed across the Atlantic as far as Scotland and Norway.

CHANGING STATE

Cooks in a hurry sometimes think that they can cook potatoes faster by turning up the gas or electricity under the boiling water. But all that happens is that the water boils away faster. It doesn't get any hotter and the potatoes take just as long to cook.

When the water is heated the energy we put in makes its molecules move faster. Its molecules are gaining kinetic energy. Some molecules will move faster than others and are able to escape from the surface – they **evaporate**. When the water is hot enough a kind of rapid internal evaporation takes place. The faster molecules gather together in bubbles, usually at certain points at the bottom of the container. More molecules get into the bubbles which swell and rise to the surface. We say that the water is **boiling** (picture 14). Molecules of water are moving from being part of a liquid to being part of a gas: the water is gradually **changing state**.

Table 4

Substance	Specific heat capacity (J/kg °C)
copper	380
aluminium	886
iron	500
lead	127
glass	600
water	4200

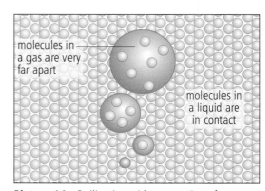

Picture 14 Boiling is rapid evaporation of molecules into bubbles inside the liquid.

When it reaches its boiling point of 100 °C the energy going into it is being used to change its state, not raise its temperature. The energy needed to do this is called **latent heat. Specific latent heat** is the energy transferred when a kilogram of a substance changes state. It always takes more energy to change the state of a substance than to heat it by one Celsius degree. For example, it takes 4.2 kJ to heat a kilogram of water through 1°C, but 334 kJ to melt a kilogram of ice and 2.26 MJ to boil a kilogram of water. The temperature changes of ice as it is steadily heated are shown in picture 15.

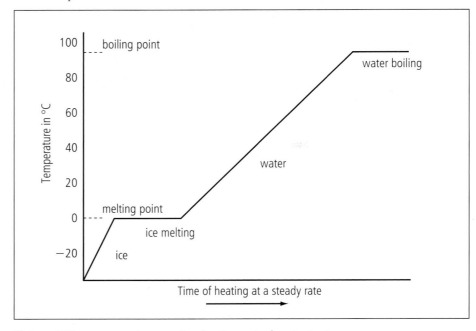

Picture 15 Temperature changes when heating water from ice to steam.

CALCULATING THERMAL ENERGY CHANGES

We can calculate the energy required to heat a substance that doesn't change state by using the formula:

$$E = msT$$

where E is the energy supplied in joules, m the mass in kilograms, s the specific heat capacity of the substance and T the rise in temperature. s has the units J/kg °C (or J/kg K).

The energy required to change the state of a mass m of a substance already at the melting or boiling temperature is given by $E = mL$ where L is the specific latent heat.

Refrigerators rely on the high specific latent heat of the refrigerant liquid. Liquids boil more easily under a low pressure. In a refrigerator the liquid is made to flow into a chamber at a lower pressure. The liquid boils and takes energy from its surroundings to do so. The surroundings cool. The vapour is then pumped into long tubes outside the refrigerator where it is compressed by a pump and liquefies. (See pictures 4 and 5 on page 145.) The condensing vapour releases its latent heat to the surroundings. You can see the tubes at the back of the refrigerator in picture 4 (page 145) – they get quite hot when the refrigerator is working hard.

Activities

A Energy and you

What energy do you use at home during a day? Keep a diary for one day and note down what energy-using devices you use, and how long you use them for. Don't forget to add in your share of the family energy use, for cooking, watching TV etc. Make a list like this:

Device   time used (hours)
         power rating (kilowatts)
         energy used (time × power rating)

Hints.

1   Don't worry about accuracy too much. A rough idea is all you need.

2   Electrical devices have a label on them giving the power rating. If it is in watts, divide the number by 1000 to get kilowatts.

CARE: Don't check appliances while they are switched on or while they are still hot.

3   You may have to make reasonable guesses about non-electrical devices; ask for help from your teacher if you need to.

B Take a shower!

The calculation on page 131 tells you how much it costs to take a bath. Is showering cheaper? How much energy does it use? To find out you will need to measure:

1   How much water the shower gives per minute.

2   How long you take to shower.

3   How much hotter the shower makes the cold water (the temperature rise).

(Note: it takes 4.2 kJ to heat 1 kg of water by just 1°C.)

C Who left that light on?

1   Count up how many electric lights you have in your home or the school science department. What (on average) is their wattage? (This is written on the bulb.) How many watts are used when they are all switched on at the same time?

2   How many watts is a typical electric heater rated at? (If you have one, look at its label to find out.) Write a comment about the energy cost of heating compared with the energy cost of lighting.

D

Plan an experiment to measure either (a) the specific latent heat of melting of ice or (b) the specific latent heat of vaporisation of water.

Questions

1   Put the following energy users into an ordered list, biggest users first: vacuum cleaner, electric kettle, torch bulb, electric cooker oven, room lamp, central heating system, microwave cooker.

    If you find this difficult, the table on page 180 of topic E6 may help you.

2   Electrical energy costs 6p a 'unit'. An electric fire uses 2 units of electrical energy an hour. How much does it cost to use the fire for 6 hours a day, 7 days a week?

3   We spend a lot of money heating our homes in the winter. This energy comes into the home in coal, oil, gas or electricity. Where does energy go to in the end?

4   The pie chart in picture 1 on page 122 shows what we use energy for. Can you think of any other uses of energy that are not shown? Suggest why they don't appear in the chart.

5   Useful energy devices change one kind of energy into another, or move it from one place to another. What kind of energy changes or moves are involved in the following?

    a   An electric drill.

    b   A TV set.

    c   Using a hand saw to cut through a piece of wood.

    d   Using a telephone.

6   A full bath of water might need 30 MJ of energy to get the water to a nice comfortable temperature. Use table 2 to check that this would cost about 50p using electricity to heat the water. How much would it cost if the water was heated by an oil burner?

7   When you get out of an open-air swimming pool on a warm but windy day you quickly feel cold. Explain this 'wind-chill' effect.

8   On a hot day the land warms up more quickly than the sea.

    a   Suggest why this happens.

    b   As a result of this, we get sea breezes – cool winds that blow in off the sea. Suggest why these breezes occur.

9   Calculate how much energy is needed to heat a bath of water from 20 °C to 50 °C. The bath needs 300 kg of water, which has a specific heat capacity of 4.2 kJ per kg °C.

10 a   How much energy would be needed to boil away the bathful of water of question 9 (starting at 20 °C)?

    b   How much energy would the water release to the surroundings if it cooled from 20 °C and then froze?

Machines

Human muscles are weak.
We can increase their effect by
using machines …

MAKING WORK EASIER

Every kitchen and workshop contains tools or implements that make it easier for us to do a job of work. Most of them are used to increase the size of a force. Opening a tin is easy – with a tin opener.

Bottle openers, screwdrivers, scissors – even door handles – are all examples of 'force multipliers': devices which 'multiply forces' (picture 1).

Some machines are very complicated. Just look at a car engine. Even a bicycle has more to it than you might think.

But all these machines are made up of a very few quite simple ones. Some of these are levers, pulleys and sloping planes.

Picture 1　Household machines.

■ Levers

Picture 2 shows a small child lifting a larger one – by using a seesaw. The large weight is being moved by a smaller one, using the **lever principle**.

When you pull on one end of a pivoted bar it will turn around the pivot. Both children on the seesaw are producing a turning effect. When they are exactly in balance each of them is applying the same size turning effect, but obviously in opposite directions. The turning effect (or **moment**) of their weights is given by multiplying the force by the distance they are from the pivot. Picture 3 shows what we mean by this.

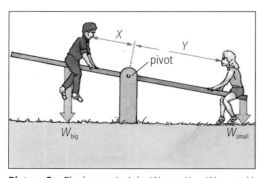

Picture 3　The lever principle: $W_{big} \times X = W_{small} \times Y$.

Picture 2　See-saws are fun.

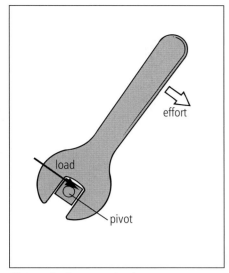

Picture 4 A spanner is a lever.

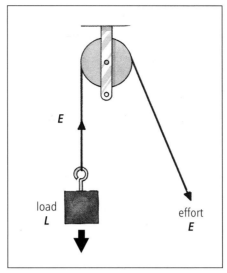

Picture 5 With just one pulley, effort **E** just balances load **L**.

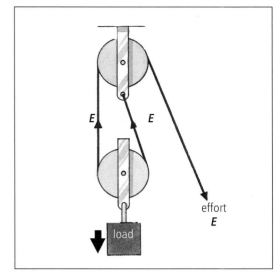

Picture 6 With two pulleys, the effort **E** can be about twice as effective.

A spanner is a simple machine based on this lever principle. The pivot is now the centre of the nut being turned (picture 4). The **effort** force is applied near the end of the handle. The force that is being 'overcome' is called the **load**. In the case of the spanner it is the friction force in the nut being turned.

When the spanner is just turning the nut the lever principle says that:

effort × effort distance = load × load distance

There are very many examples of levers in everyday life. Many of them are 'hidden' as part of more complicated-looking machines. Try counting how many levers there are on a bicycle.

Pulleys

A single pulley is really a kind of moving, circular lever, as shown in picture 5. The wheel is pivoted and so keeps on turning as the load is pulled up. But a single pulley doesn't increase the applied force, because the pivot is exactly in the centre. Pulleys become useful as force multipliers when more than one of them is used.

Picture 6 is a simple two-pulley system. One string goes from the load around both pulleys to where the effort is applied. The load can be nearly twice as large as the effort. This can be explained by the fact that the 'force in the string' is the same all through it. It is E, the effort. The load is supported by a double string, so the upward force is 2 × E. This is only exactly true if there is no friction in the system. If there is, some of the effort force has to overcome friction, so less is left to lift the load.

Sloping planes

These are the largest machines you will ever see. The principle was used by the Ancient Britons to build Stonehenge, and by the Egyptians to build the Pyramids.

Both had the task of lifting very large, heavy stones. They did it by building sloping roads or mounds of earth and sliding them up on wooden rollers (picture 7). The force needed to roll something up a slope is much less than the gravity force acting straight down on it.

The less steep the slope the smaller the force you need. Mountain roads are built in a zig-zag to make their steepness less. Other examples of slopes used as force multipliers are: wedges, knife blades, screws and bolts (picture 8).

Picture 7 A slope is also a machine.

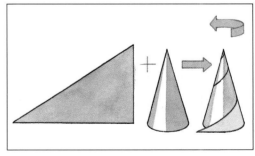

Picture 8 A slope 'fitted' to a cone becomes a screw.

■ Something for nothing?

The use of machines to multiply forces seems to be against the basic law of energy – see topic D5. Are we really getting something for nothing?

The answer, unfortunately, is no. The energy we put into any machine is always at least equal to, and usually greater than, the energy we get out of it. The simple reason for this is that in every single one of the machines dealt with in this topic, *the effort moves further than the load*.

The energy supplied is equal to the work done by the effort. This is measured by 'applied force × distance moved in the direction of the applied force' (see topic D2). The work done by the effort is likely to be greater than the useful energy obtained by moving the load. At best it will be the same. There is no such thing as a machine which does more work that we put into it!

EFFICIENCY

When you use a machine you usually get less work out than you put in. This is because, for example, you have to lift pieces of rope or pulleys which are not part of the 'payload'. You also have to do work against the forces of friction. Thus we talk about the **efficiency** of a machine, defined as a percentage.

efficiency = (useful work done/energy supplied to the machine) × 100%

There is more about efficiency on page 146.

HYDRAULICS

Some of the most useful machinery we have uses the principles of **hydraulics**. Instead of using solid materials to transfer energy and forces, hydraulic systems use liquids. They work because of the way a liquid can transfer a pressure. Imagine a rubber bag full of water. When you squash it in one place the extra pressure you exert acts everywhere – if there is a leak in the bag, water will squirt out. It doesn't make any difference where the hole is. In fact the extra pressure in a pressurised liquid not only acts everywhere but is the same everywhere.

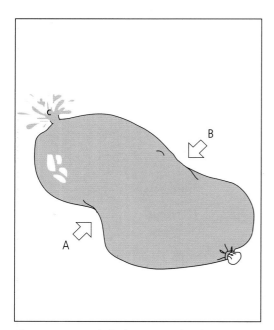

Picture 9 Squash the bag at A and B, the water squirts out at C.

Picture 10 Many large machines use hydraulics.

This principle is used in many machines: in aircraft to move the wing edges and control flight, in car brakes, in large earth-moving machines to lift very heavy loads, in garages to lift cars, in factories to squash and stamp metals.

Hydraulics relies on the simple fact that *pressure = force/area*. You can produce a large pressure by using quite a small force – provided it acts over a very small area. It is the difference between sitting on a chair and sitting on a pin! Soft snow can bear your weight if you spread it over a larger area by using skis or snowshoes.

Picture 12 shows the principles as they are used in a hydraulic car lift. A worker exerts quite a small force at a small piston, which produces a pressure in the hydraulic fluid. Suppose the force exerted is 50 N and it acts over an area of 50 square centimetres – which is 5×10^{-3} m^2.

$$\text{pressure } P \text{ in fluid is } P = F / A = 50 / (5 \times 10^{-3}) = 10\,000 \text{ N m}^{-2}$$

The fluid is usually a special oil. The car is placed on a platform above a piston which has a large area in contact with the oil. Suppose this area is 2 square metres. The pressure acts over all this area and we can calculate that since

$$pressure = force / area$$

then *force = pressure* $\times$ *area* = 10 000 $\times$ 2 = 20 000 N.

This force would hold up a 2 tonne vehicle. The force caused like this, by a pressure, is called a **thrust**.

The pressure is the same all through the fluid, i.e.

$$pressure = E / \text{area } A = L / \text{area } B$$

where, as in picture 12, the effort force is E and the load lifted is L.

Thus the hydraulic car lift has a load to effort ratio $L/E = B/A$. All hydraulic systems rely on having piston surfaces of different areas, A and B. The smaller A is compared to B, the larger the output force that can be produced for a given effort force.

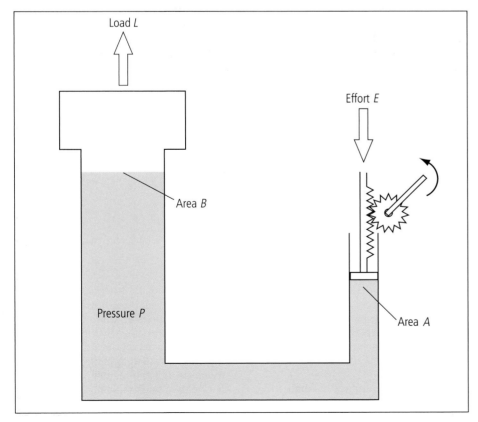

Picture 12

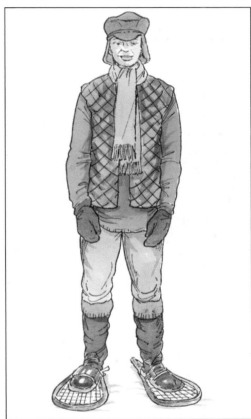

Picture 11 The same force exerts a large or small pressure – depending on the area over which it acts.

Questions

1 Name ten simple machines that you might find in your home or in the laboratory.

2 Why are machines useful?

Describe one machine and explain how it works.

Why can't you 'get more work out of it' than you put in?

3 Put the following useful things into two headed columns 'machines' and 'non-machines':

a bucket, a knife, an egg whisk, a screwdriver, a door handle, a bookshelf, a spanner, a light switch, a spade, a pen-top.

For one example in each column, give your reasons for putting it there.

4 Name or describe five different levers you could find as part of a bicycle.

5 Picture 13 shows two wheels fixed on the same axle. The large wheel A has a radius of 50 cm, the smaller one B a radius of 10 cm.

a What happens to wheel B when A turns around once?

b What happens to the bucket on the rope wrapped around B?

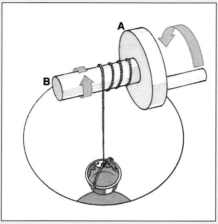

Picture 13 A wheel-and-axle is still useful for getting water from a well.

c Would this device make it easier to lift the bucket of water?

d This is an old-fashioned kind of machine for lifting water out of a well. Can you think of any modern device that uses the same idea?

6 Estimate (a) your weight in newtons (b) the area of your left foot in square metres. Use these estimates to calculate the pressure you exert on the ground.

7 In a hydraulic ram the area of the effort piston is 4 cm² (4×10^{-4} m²) and the area of the load-carrying pistons is 1 m². What force is applied at the load piston when a force of 500 N is applied at the effort piston?

8 Look at a selection of tools and kitchen utensils. Which of them are machines? Draw two that are and explain how they work, based on the principles of the four basic machines described in this topic.

Analysing machines

Machine	1 effort (N)	2 load (N)	3 distance moved (in metres) by *effort*	4 by *load*
1 3-pulley block	20	56	6	2
2 6-pulley block	10	52	12	2
3 Sail-lifter on yacht (wheel-and-axle)	25	120	10	2
4 Bolt cutter	30	270	0.1	0.01
5 Rotary cheese grater	14	2	2.4	0.6

Here is some data about different types of machine. It tells you how much effort is needed to lift or move a given load. It also tells you how far the effort force moves for a typical movement of the load. Use this information to answer the questions below. You will need graph paper to answer some of them.

1 In each machine, the effort force has to move quite a lot further than the load. Considering the design of any one machine, explain why this is. (Two of the machines are illustrated in the picture.)

2 Each machine 'multiplies' a small effort force into a larger load force.

Use the values in the first two columns to calculate how good each machine is at doing this, by dividing the load by the effort. The result is called the mechanical advantage of the machine. Put the results in a list headed 'mechanical advantage'.

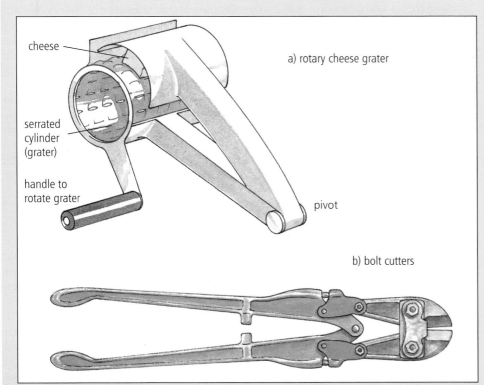

cheese

a) rotary cheese grater

serrated cylinder (grater)

handle to rotate grater

pivot

b) bolt cutters

Picture 1 How are these machines adapted to their different jobs?

3 Use the data in columns 3 and 4 to calculate, for each machine, how far the effort has to move compared with the load. Do this by dividing 'distance moved by effort' by 'distance moved by load'. The result for each machine is a number that engineers call its velocity ratio. Put the results you obtain into a list headed 'velocity ratio'.

4 Look at the values of mechanical advantage (MA) and velocity ratio (VR) you have worked out. It is suggested that there might be a connection between how effective a machine is at moving a load (its MA) and how far the effort has to move compared with the load (its VR).

a Is there any relationship (or pattern) between mechanical advantage and velocity ratio for these five machines? Make a rough guess at what it might be and write it down.

b Now plot the values against each other on a set of graph axes – mechanical advantage up, velocity ratio along.

c Draw the 'best straight line' through these plotted points. Does this confirm your prediction in (a)?

Saving and wasting – the laws of energy

Energy cannot be created, and it cannot be destroyed. But it can be wasted.

Picture 1 Working against gravity.

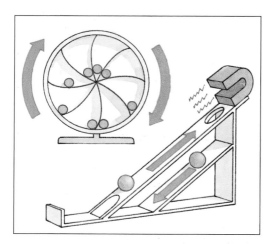

Picture 2 Perpetual motion machines. Will they work?

Whenever we use energy we are moving it from one system to another. The first three topics in this section give many examples of this **transfer** of energy. We are using the energy to **do work**. When you lift a weight you are transferring energy from your body system (sugar and oxygen in the blood) to do work against the force of gravity. If the weight is large you know that you are doing work! (See picture 1.) After you have lifted it the weight is higher above the ground and so has more **gravitational potential energy**. (See topics B5 and D1.)

There are very many other examples of energy transfers like this. The fact that energy can move from one system to another is the basis of life on earth. It is the basis of all movement, and of all the industries that we rely on in the modern world.

In studying energy changes scientists have discovered the laws which describe how energy behaves. They are called the **Laws of Thermodynamics**, and this topic is about the two most important of these.

■ The First Law – you can't win

This law is very simple. It says that whenever any changes take place there is just as much energy at the end as there was in the beginning. Like many of the most important ideas in science, it is impossible to prove this! But the law has been tested, time and time again.

Very careful measurements in all kinds of experiments have shown that in every single case **energy has been neither lost nor created**. Of course, one day someone might do a test in which energy is lost or created, and this would disprove the law.

This first law is the law of the **conservation of energy**. Many people have tried to disprove this law, and all of them have failed. It would be so nice to be able to create energy from 'nothing'. Life on Earth would be very convenient if someone could design an engine or a machine which gave out more energy than you put into it.

Picture 2 shows two designs for such a machine. Look at them. Can you see how they are supposed to work? Can you see why they won't work?

What the law means in practice is that with any machine or engine the best we can do is get out as much energy as we put into it. But even this is optimistic. For real machines we always get less energy out than we put in. This is because of the *Second Law*.

■ The Second Law – you always lose!

Whenever we use energy to do a job of work some of the energy we put in seems to escape. It just doesn't go where we want it to.

When you lift a weight you give it some potential energy. But this is less than the energy produced in your muscles by the chemical reaction (respiration) between sugar and oxygen. Some of that energy goes to make your muscles warmer (see picture 3).

When you do a lot of work you have to sweat a lot to get rid of this 'waste energy'. It ends up warming your surroundings. The molecules in the air move a little faster as a result. They gain some kinetic energy.

The Second Law simply says that when work is done there is always some energy that will somehow escape and spread itself out. It usually ends up as 'heat', which in basic energy terms means that millions upon millions of molecules move a little faster. In other words the surroundings get warmer. At the end of a round trip by car a lot of fuel might have been used. It has gone to heat the air!

CAN WE GET THIS 'WASTE' ENERGY BACK?

Yes – we *can* get this energy back. There is no law of physics that stops us. All we have to do is slow down all those molecules and do some useful work with the energy they lose. Or we could concentrate the energy in one place to warm something up. For example, we could put this energy into water in a central heating system.

The problem is, how can we concentrate this spread-out energy in one place? It is not easy to do, particularly if the energy has spread out a long way over millions of different particles.

MAKING SPREAD-OUT ENERGY CONCENTRATED

If you have a refrigerator at home this is exactly what it is doing. It is taking movement energy from the molecules of the foods inside it. They cool down as a result, so that the food stays fresh longer. The energy they lose is given to the air. You can check this effect for yourself. At the back of the refrigerator you will find a set of tubes which feel warm because of the energy that the food has lost (picture 4).

But this energy is still wasted. After all, we don't normally buy refrigerators to use as house-warmers. But what if we used the same idea, say, to take energy *out of the surroundings* and feed it into our homes? This is simply using a 'refrigerator' in reverse! Such heaters do exist, and they are called **heat pumps**. They take energy out of the air or the ground instead of out of food, and 'pump' it *into* the house to warm it.

Picture 5 shows a commercial heat pump. It is used in large buildings. These need ventilating, which means that warmed, smelly air has to be taken out of the building. This has to be replaced by fresh air – which is cold in winter. One end of the heat pump is placed in the warm 'exhaust air' and takes the heat energy out of it. This energy is pumped to the cold air coming into the building, so that it is 'prewarmed'. This cuts down the heating bills.

SOMETHING FOR NOTHING?

But this effect doesn't happen all by itself. Refrigerators and heat pumps contain a liquid which has to be pumped around the system. The pumps are usually driven by an electric motor and this needs energy to run it. When all the energy sums are done we find that we still get less energy out than goes in, and that *overall* the energy still gets more spread out!

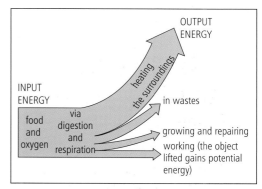

Picture 3 What the body does with the energy it gets – only a small amount can be used to do work.

Picture 4 In a fridge the energy taken out of the cooling food warms the air.

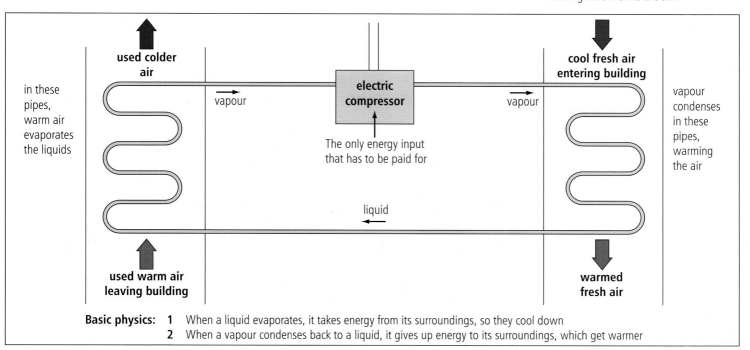

Basic physics: 1 When a liquid evaporates, it takes energy from its surroundings, so they cool down
2 When a vapour condenses back to a liquid, it gives up energy to its surroundings, which get warmer

Picture 5 How a heat pump works.

■ Efficiency

Being *efficient* means being effective at doing a job. The **efficiency** of a machine or engine measures how good it is, in terms of how much of the energy put into it is used where you want it. Efficiency is measured by how much useful energy you get out compared with what is put in. It usually converted to a percentage:

$$\text{efficiency} = \frac{\text{useful energy output}}{\text{energy input}} \times 100\%$$

Table 1 shows the typical efficiency of some energy devices. Some of them, like engines and some machines, use energy from a fuel system to do work. Cars, bicycles, electric drills and trains do this. Other devices are used to make energy more 'usable'. They might do this by taking energy from a fuel–oxygen system and putting it into an electrical system. This is what power stations do. Electricity is very useful because it makes it so easy to move energy from one place to another.

Table 1 Typical efficiency of energy devices.

	Engines and machines producing movement or doing work %	Energy 'movers' %
Train: diesel engine	36	
Car: petrol engine	15	
Train: steam engine	15	
Train: electric motor	90	
Car gears		93
Bicycle		90
Car jack		15
Electric power station	35	
Transformer (electrical)		97
Human muscle	40	

Gears and *transmission systems* in cars, trains and bicycles are the mechanical versions of electric transmission. They carry energy from one part of a **mechanical** system to another. They also allow the force that eventually does the work to be made small or large, according to what is needed.

■ Useful laws

The laws of energy were discovered in the 19th century. They were also very useful in helping to design engines. It was scientists' understanding of these laws that helped improve steam engines and led to the development of car engines (internal combustion engines).

SOME PUZZLING QUESTIONS – AND A SURPRISING ANSWER!

But there were very important questions about energy that these laws couldn't explain. Two of these questions were to do with the Sun and the Earth. We know that the Sun is sending out huge quantities of energy. It has been doing this for thousands of millions of years. What is not so well-known is the fact that the Earth is also giving out energy. This energy is seeping up from the centre of the Earth, causing volcanoes and earthquakes, warming the atmosphere and, eventually, being lost to space. *Where does this energy actually come from? Why does the Sun keep on shining? If the Earth is losing so much heat, why doesn't it cool down?*

The answer to these questions was given by the physicist Albert Einstein. He was able to prove that **matter** – the stuff that makes ordinary atoms and molecules – can be converted to energy such as in electromagnetic radiations. The Sun keeps on shining by actually losing mass – at the rate of four million tonnes a second.

Most people have heard of Einstein's famous equation that calculates the amount of energy E that can be obtained by destroying a quantity of matter, m:

$$E = mc^2$$

where c is the speed of light.

This discovery meant that scientists had to think again about the First Law, the Law of Conservation of Energy. *It would only work if mass was thought of as a kind of energy!* This was a very strange idea. This story continues in topic F5.

Not only must mass be a form of energy, but energy has mass. For example, when an object gets hotter it has extra mass. But in everyday life this mass is too small to be measured.

Questions

1 A car stands in front of the owner's house. It has a full tank of petrol. After a long drive the car comes back and stops in front of the house. The tank is now empty. What has happened to the energy that was stored in the petrol? (There is a very short answer to this question!)

2 The Moon is the main cause of the tides in the sea. Careful measurements show that the Moon is actually slowing down as it goes around the Earth. Use the Law of Conservation of Energy to explain this.

3 A small hoist (pulley system) lifts a load and gives it 3000 J of potential energy. The person who used the hoist supplied it with 5000 J of work. What is the efficiency of the hoist?

4 The efficiency of a type of car jack is 25%. It takes 1000 joules of energy to lift a car high enough to replace a wheel. How much work must be done by the worker who uses the jack?

5 Why do you think engines (petrol, steam) are so much less efficient than gears or bicycles?

6 Picture 6 shows the energy system of a light bulb. It is called a 'Sankey Diagram'. It shows that energy is delivered electrically, and that most of this energy is wasted. Only a small percentage is delivered as useful light. Draw a similar diagram for one of the following:

a Boiling a kettle of water on a gas ring.

b Sawing through a log of wood.

c Just sitting on a chair.

d Winding up an old-fashioned (spring) clock.

7 Some rapid transport systems in cities build the line so that stations are always on a slight hill, higher than the line before it and after it.

Sketch a diagram to illustrate this and use it to explain why this saves energy in using the transport system.

8 Read about—or remind yourself about—the energy flow through an 'ecosystem'. Discuss, and come to an agreement about the following questions:

● What is the source of the energy that all the organisms make use of?

● Where does it all go in the end?

● Which organisms are best (most efficient) at using energy?

● In an ecosystem, materials are often recycled. Is energy recycled?

Write down, briefly, your agreed answers to these questions.

9 A hair dryer is rated at 800 W. It contains a heater and a fan to blow air. In use it needs 50 W to make the fan work.

a How much energy, in joules does the hair dryer use per second?

b How much energy is transferred per second to heating air?

c Calculate the efficiency of the hair dryer as a percentage.

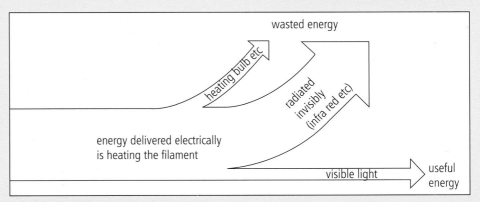

Picture 6 Energy flow in a light bulb.

Energy resources: a summary

Getting and using energy causes problems. In the 21st century energy is cheap, compared with its cost in previous ages. We have a large range of energy resources available to us, especially in those countries which are called 'developed' and are far richer then the average. So what are the problems? What sources of energy are available to us now? Are there any which might come into use in this century?

Table 1 summarises some of the main points about energy sources. There is more detail in various parts of this book

Energy source	Comparative cost	Likely time for being used up	Comments
Coal: the fossilised remains of ancient forests that died millions of years ago	Low	400 years	Fossil fuels are still the most common and widely used energy source. They have been the main factor in the development of the modern world, from a simple animal- and wind-powered economy to the world of cars, trains, aircraft, ships and electricity of today. Problems:
Oil: the fossilised and chemically changed remains of small animals and plants that died millions of years ago	Low – but likely to increase as supplies dwindle	50 years	• Sources are running out (non-renewable) • Pollution: coal especially produces sulphuric acid rain • All produce carbon dioxide which is a main cause of the Greenhouse effect
Natural gas: produced by chemical changes from the remains of small animals and plants that died millions of years ago	Low – but likely to increase as supplies dwindle	60 years	
Sun: provides radiation that lights and heats Earth	Medium	4 billion years	The Sun delivers as much energy to the site of a power station as the station produces from coal, oil etc. Provides the basic energy allowing life on Earth. Solar cells (quite expensive) are able to produce electricity. Useful in remote areas with plenty of sun. Renewable. Non-polluting. Problems: • The energy is too spread out • Most falls where it is least needed (sea, deserts) • Expensive when used to make electricity
Wind: produced by effects of solar radiation	Low	4 billion years	Windmills have provided energy for hundreds of years. Renewable. Non-polluting. Problems: • The energy is too spread out, wind farms need a large area of ground • Unreliable, so needs a storage system which adds to expense and inconvenience • Many people think wind-farms are ugly • Create noise for people living nearby
Tides: caused by gravity force between Earth and the Sun and Moon	Low to medium	4 billion years	A large source of non-polluting energy. Renewable. Problems: • Energy is too spread out • Needs the right geography for it to be harnessed (e.g. estuaries) • Building barrages across estuaries can harm the habitat of birds and other living things.
Rivers and lakes: flowing water can drive turbines to provide hydroelectric power	Low	4 billion years	A reliable and non-polluting source. Water mills have been used for centuries; hydroelectric power is widely used. Renewable. Problems: • Needs the right geography (mountains, plenty of rain) • Artificial lakes take land previously used for farming or forestry

Energy source	Comparative cost	Likely time for being used up	Comments
Waves: sea waves are produced by wind and may carry a lot of energy	Low	4 billion years	Wave energy is natural and non-polluting. Renewable. Problems: • Unreliable because variable • The energy is spread out over large areas
Biological	Low	4 billion years	An alternative use of solar energy. Quick growing plants can be harvested and burnt in power stations. Renewable. Problems: • Needs land that may be better used for food or cash crops • Energy spread out over large area • Burning plants creates pollution and adds to Greenhouse effect
Geothermal: the interior of the Earth is hot, and can be used to heat water	Low to medium	4 billion years	A natural energy source that provides hot water or steam. Could be used more. Renewable. Problems: • Available only in certain places • Technology to exploit it not well developed
Nuclear: fission of large nuclei produces heat to drive turbines	Medium to high	For ever	Cheap to produce and less polluting than fossil fuels. Does not contribute to Greenhouse effect. Fuel source plentiful. Power output easy to control and vary, compared with fuel-powered stations. Widely used in some countries to produce electricity. Problems • It scares people! • High cost of dealing with radioactive waste. • Accidents can be harmful locally and possibly over a wide area (e.g. Chernobyl). • High cost of decommissioning reactors after their natural life span.
Fusion: energy comes from fusing small nuclei into larger ones	Not yet known	For ever	Probably the cheapest, longest lasting and least polluting of all potential energy sources. The 'fuel' used is hydrogen – plentiful in sea water. The product is the harmless gas helium. Problems: • After nearly 50 years of research a working power source has not been made.

Questions

Use the table above and any other source of information to answer the following questions.

1 Why is solar energy more expensive than energy obtained from coal?

2 Give 4 advantages and 4 disadvantages of nuclear fission as an energy source.

3 Summarise the advantages and disadvantages of using the following as energy sources:

(a) tides (b) hydroelectric systems (c) wind generators (d) geothermal sources.

4 What is the basic source of the energy that creates geothermal sources of energy?

5 Discuss or debate the following in small groups. Present your conclusions in a short 1 page report illustrated by charts, diagrams or graphs, as appropriate.

a Nuclear energy should be banned.

b The use of fossil fuels (i.e. by burning them) is environmentally harmful and should be restricted by law or by imposing heavy taxes on non-essential fuel use.

c The government should put more thought, planning and resources into making more efficient use of fossil fuels. For example ……[give your own suggestions, supported by reasoned argument].

E

Electricity and magnetism

Electricity: messenger and worker

The brain, computers, traffic lights, telephones, trains, drills. All these use electricity to make them work.

Picture 1 Electric currents can carry messages.

Picture 2 Electricity is used for controlling light, as well as producing it.

MESSAGES AND MOVING CHARGES

When you pick up a telephone an electric current starts to flow. When you speak into it the microphone in the handset changes the strength of the current to match the sounds you make (see page 18).

When a car comes up to some traffic lights it affects a magnetic sensor in the road. This sends an electric message to a control box to let it know that the car is there. The control box has to decide how and when the lights need to change (picture 2).

When you tread on a drawing pin in bare feet your pain sensors send a message to both brain and muscles so that you react pretty quickly. The message is carried by a moving electric pulse through very long nerve cells.

Electric charges moving through a wire can make it hot: we use this effect in electric kettles and other heaters. Moving charges can interact with a magnetic field to produce forces: we use this effect in electric motors, for example in drills, food mixers, washing machines and electric trains.

■ What is needed for electricity to do its work?

These devices use electricity to carry a message, and for this to work three things are needed:

● electric charge which is free to move,
● energy to move the charge,
● a material that charges can move through – a conductor.

■ Circuits

The examples above are quite complicated devices, using many conductors connected together in complicated ways. But however complicated it may look the basic plan of any electrical device is quite simple: it is a collection of **circuits**. A simple circuit (picture 3) has the energy source (a battery), a switch, some wires and, say, an electric buzzer. The wires are made of a metal which is a good conductor – usually copper.

Luckily, the electric charges are already in the conductor! A metal contains many millions of charged particles that are free to move. These particles are called **electrons**, and all atoms contain them.

For a signal to get to the buzzer, the buzzer has to be connected to the battery by conductors. All the battery does is to provide a *force* to make the electrons move. How it does this is explained later (page 190).

The switch is there to make a gap in the circuit. Air is a very poor conductor – we say it is an *insulator* – so electrons cannot move across the gap. It doesn't matter where the gap is. It is like a blockage on a single road system (picture 4). If cars pile up at the gap, they cause a traffic jam that will tail back to stop cars getting any further. For traffic to flow it has to be able to get into and *out* of the system.

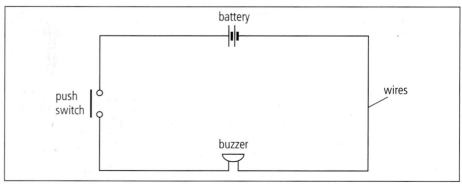

Picture 3 A simple circuit.

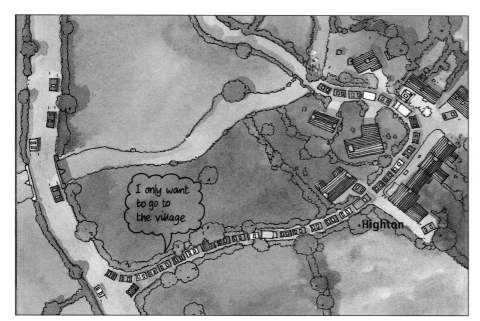

Picture 4 Electricity is like traffic; a gap in a circuit is like a blocked road.

Exactly the same principle applies to electric charges. They need a complete path which runs from one side of the battery to the other. A gap anywhere in the circuit will stop the charge moving. When you close the gap by pressing the switch, the charge starts moving and carries its message to the buzzer, which makes a sound.

■ What can electricity do?

We recognise electricity by its effects. The moving charges in a circuit can:

1 make conductors hot (in lamps, heaters),
2 produce magnetic forces (in electromagnets, motors, loudspeakers),
3 make special chemicals give out light (in LEDs, fluorescent lamps, TV screens),
4 cause chemical changes to take place (in electroplating, charging batteries, etc.).

The first three effects are especially useful in everyday life. Most electrical devices in the home use one or more of these effects (see picture 5). The rest of the topics in this section describe and explain the uses of these effects more fully.

■ Electric charge and electric current

An electric current is a flow of charged particles (see also topic E5). Current is measured in amperes, by an instrument called an ammeter. A small torch bulb may carry a current of 0.2 amperes (0.2 A), a car headlamp bulb may carry 20 times as much (4 A).

The current in a lamp is a flow of electrons. The charge on a single electron is very very small. It takes many millions of moving electrons to carry the charge that flows through an ordinary torch bulb in just one second. This large number is hard to think about and work with, so we need a more sensible unit of charge. Instead, we use **the quantity that moves when a current of 1 ampere flows for one second. This amount of charge is called a** *coulomb* **(or C for short)**.

Obviously, if 1 ampere flows for 2 seconds then 2 coulombs of charge will have moved; if 2 amperes flow for 2 seconds then 4 coulombs will move (picture 6 overleaf).

Charge, current and time are linked as follows:

$$\textbf{charge moved} = \textbf{current} \times \textbf{time}$$

(coulombs) = (amperes × seconds)

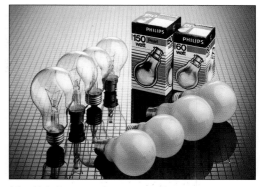

(a) Lighting

(b) Keeping cool

(c) Listening to music

(d) Ironing

(e) Watching television

Picture 5 Electricity can be used for many different jobs.

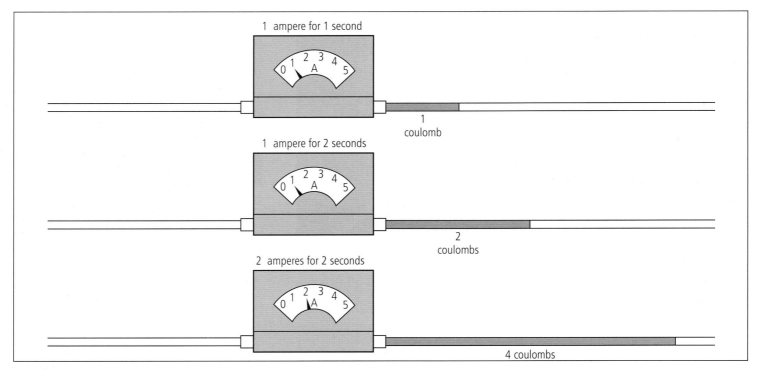

Picture 6 Charge = current × time.

■ Symbols, circuits and formulae

The best way to learn about electricity is by doing experiments and investigations, solving problems, making things work – and talking about them. The activities at the end of the topics will help you to do this. You will meet a lot of new ideas and have to work things out for yourself – with help from your teacher.

Electricity is so useful that it has a language of its own, mostly using circuit diagrams and special symbols to stand for the devices that it uses.

Formulae are used to work out what is happening, or going to happen, in a circuit. All the information that you will need in this section is summarised in table 1 below. Use it when you need to look things up.

Table 1 Symbols and formulae in electricity.
The rest of the topics in this section explain what these words and formulae mean, and how to use them. They are all collected here for you to use when you need to.

Circuit symbols			
cell	—⊣⊢—	capacitor	⊣⊢
battery	—⊣⊢--⊣⊢—	microphone	▭⊏
variable power supply	0 – 12V + dc –	motor	—⊏◯⊐—
lamps	—⊗— ◯—	loudspeaker	▷⊏
resistor	—▭—	transformer	⧙
switches	╱ _	bell	⌂
LED	▷	buzzer	▽
variable resistor	▱	ammeter	—Ⓐ—
voltage divider	▭	voltmeter	—Ⓥ—

Activities

A What uses electricity?

Make a list of as many things as you can see in the room that use electricity.

B What do people think about electricity?

1 (Home activity.) Find ten people and get them to tell you in one sentence what they think electricity is. Write down what they say and tick the statements that you agree with.

2 (Group activity.) Get together with three or four other pupils in your class and look at the thirty or forty statements you have obtained between you.

   Choose the ten most important – or interesting – and write them out on a poster-sized piece of paper for the rest of the class to see.

3 (Class activity.) Decide, as a class, the final ten most important, accurate or interesting statements about electricity that have been produced.

   The result could seriously worry your teacher!

Questions

1 Make lists of:
   a five materials that don't conduct electricity (insulators),
   b materials that do conduct electricity (conductors).

2 What units and instruments are used to measure:
   a current,
   b voltage,
   c resistance?

3 What carries the electric charge through a lamp filament?

4 Electric current in wires is a flow of electrons. Why then don't scientists and electricians measure electric current in 'electrons per second'?

5 Why don't electric charges flow through a conductor unless it is part of a 'complete circuit'?

6 Why are metals usually good conductors of electricity?

7 Use table 1 to help you decide what will happen when the switch is pressed in each of the following circuits (picture 7).

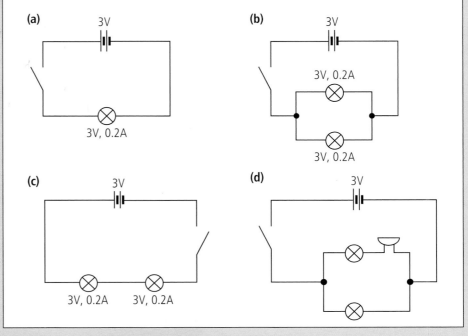

Picture 7

E2

Magnets

Magnetism is a mysterious kind of force. It comes from two sorts of magnets, permanent magnets and electromagnets.

MAGNETS AND MAGNETIC FORCES

Most people play with magnets when they are children. They are useful for finding lost pins – but aren't any good for finding lost coins. These magnets are the kind that keep their 'magnetic power' for a long time, and so are called **permanent magnets**.

Permanent magnets are usually made from special kinds of iron, steel and other alloys. Sometimes the metal particles are baked with clay to make ceramic magnets or mixed with plastic to make flexible magnets. They can attract other things made out of iron or steel. But when you have two magnets together another strange effect can be seen. They can repel each other.

THE MAGNETIC COMPASS

A magnet tied to a piece of thread so that is free to swing will line itself up in a roughly north–south direction. This effect was discovered by the Chinese over a thousand years ago; they soon used it to help them find their way at sea and in unknown territory. This effect is used in the magnetic compass. (See picture 1.)

The mysteries of magnetism began to be solved about 400 years ago, in the time of the first Queen Elizabeth of England. It was a time of great sea voyages, when Western Europeans sailed the world in search of trade, plunder and conquest.

Queen Elizabeth had a doctor called William Gilbert. He experimented with magnets and compasses and produced a theory to explain how compasses worked. He claimed that it must be because the whole Earth is a magnet. The huge Earth-magnet attracts and repels the small compass magnets so that they always line up in the same way (picture 2). On the whole, he had the right idea.

■ Magnetic fields

Magnets can be made in any shape. The simplest shape is a bar magnet. Cover a bar magnet with a sheet of white paper, carefully sprinkle iron filings over the paper and tap it gently with a pencil. You will see the filings forming into a pattern. What has happened is that the small bits of iron have been turned into little magnets and lined up by the forces produced by the big bar magnet.

The pattern shows us the direction of these forces, and gives an idea of how strong they are. It shows what is called the **field** of the magnet.

The iron filings just give a rough idea of the field. You need to use your imagination to draw the field lines sensibly, so that you go from the 'real' iron filings to the imaginary field, as shown in picture 3.

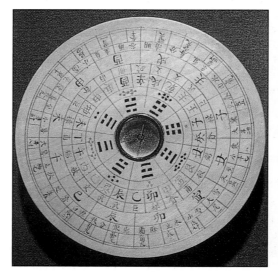

Picture 1 Compasses were invented by the Chinese.

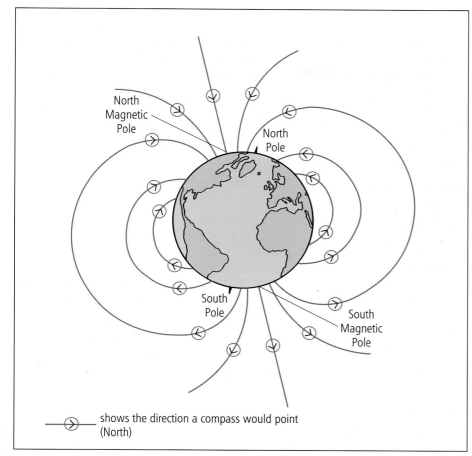

Picture 2 The magnetic field of the Earth.

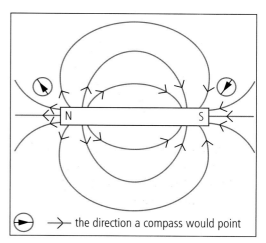

Picture 3 The magnetic field of a bar magnet.

THE EARTH'S MAGNETIC FIELD

The Earth has a magnetic field of its own, but it is quite weak. It is too weak to line iron filings up. But if you set up a thousand compasses all around your school, they would line up to show what the Earth's field is like in your area. It wouldn't look very interesting.

The direction of the field lines is the same as the way a compass would point (to the north). The arrows in picture 3 are in the direction that a small compass needle would point if you put it in the field.

A suspended bar magnet, or a compass needle, lines up so that one end points north, the other south. The end (or 'pole') that points north is called the north-seeking pole, or N-pole. The other end is the south-seeking or S-pole. They show the direction of the field lines (or lines of force) of the Earth's magnetic field.

■ Attraction and repulsion

The rule about magnets is quite simple:

like poles repel; unlike poles attract

This means that N-poles attract S-poles, and vice versa. N-poles repel N-poles and S-poles repel S-poles. This seems to be a basic law of nature; much the same applies to electric charges (see topic E5). The field-patterns of like or unlike poles near each other seem to show this (picture 4). The lines go as directly as they can from N-pole to S-pole, but veer away from each other when like poles are placed close to each other.

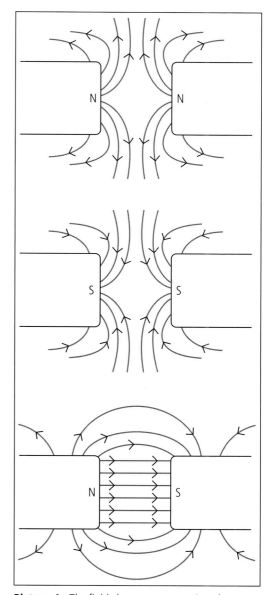

Picture 4 The fields between magnetic poles.

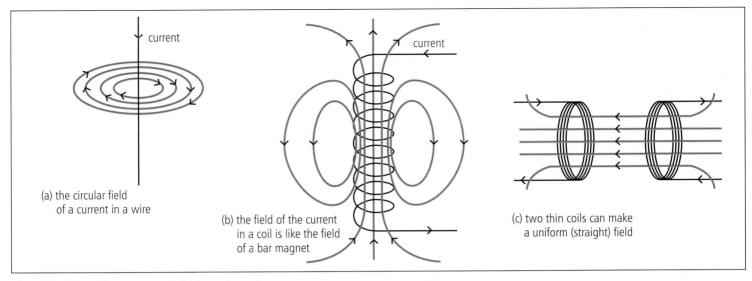

Picture 5 How different magnetic fields can be made.

(a) the circular field
of a current in a wire

(b) the field of the current
in a coil is like the field
of a bar magnet

(c) two thin coils can make
a uniform (straight) field

current

current

ELECTROMAGNETS

Electromagnets are easy to make, and can be very strong. There is a magnetic field around every conductor carrying a current. Picture 5 shows how different kinds of effect can be made by winding the wire in different ways.

An electromagnet can be made to have a field just like the field of a bar magnet. All you have to do is wrap the wire around a pencil to make a coil – see picture 5(b).

The field can be made a lot stronger if the coil is wrapped around a piece of iron. This is because the iron is turned into a magnet, and adds its strength to the field of the coil itself (picture 6).

You can use a small compass or iron filings to investigate the direction of the field near electromagnets.

WHY ELECTROMAGNETS ARE USEFUL

Electromagnets can be switched on and off, so that you can have a magnet only when you want it. Also, by making the current larger or smaller you can make the force field stronger or weaker. Electromagnets are more controllable than permanent magnets. Permanent magnets and electromagnets are used in many everyday devices, and you will meet them again (topics E7, E8 and E10).

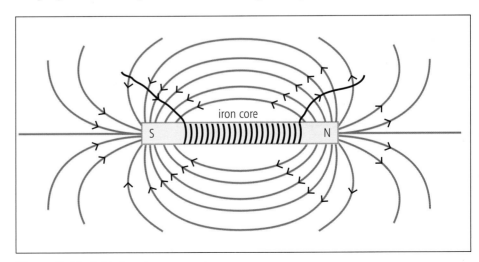

iron core

S

N

Picture 6 The field of an electromagnet.

Activities

A Where do we use magnets?

Look for many places or things in your home where magnets are being used. List all the ones you find. Are they permanent or electromagnets? Draw or describe one use in as much detail as you can.

B Maps and compasses

One of the snags about using a compass to find your way is that it doesn't point exactly north–south.

1 Find out why this is.

2 Use a good compass and a local Ordnance Survey map (1 to 25 000 or 1 to 50 000). Line up the map so that north on the map is aligned with true north on the ground.

3 Identify some local landmarks from the map.

Questions

1 Which of the following objects or materials would be attracted by a magnet?

a a coin,

b glass,

c copper wire,

d wood,

e iron,

f carbon,

g a knife blade.

2 Copy the following arrangements (picture 7) and sketch the field patterns you would expect to find. Mark in the field directions (the way the N-pole of a compass would point) of:

a a bar magnet,

b a long coil of wire carrying a current,

c two N-poles near each other,

d a large N-pole opposite a similar S-pole (e.g. a pair of Magnadur magnets).

3 Explain the following as clearly as you can, using words or diagrams or both.

a What is the 'law of poles' for magnets?

b What is a magnetic field?

c Why does a compass needle line up north–south?

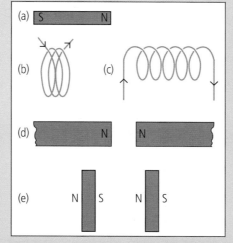

Picture 7

Picture 8

4 a Give two differences between permanent magnets and electromagnets.

b Why aren't electromagnets used in compasses?

c Powerful electromagnets are used in scrapyards and steel works to lift up iron and steel scrap and put it down somewhere else. Why aren't permanent magnets used for this job?

Faraday's legacies

Picture 1 A rare 'action' photograph of Faraday talking with John Daniell. Daniell invented the first reliable electric cell, which was useful in Faraday's electrolysis experiments, some of which can be seen on the table behind them.

Michael Faraday has been called 'the greatest experimentalist of the nineteenth century'. He was just 22 years old when he joined the Royal Institution in 1813 as a kind of secretary cum laboratory assistant to the famous Sir Humphry Davy. These men had things in common apart from excellence at experimental science. Both came from humble backgrounds. Davy's father was a woodcarver and smallholder and he started life as a pharmacist's apprentice. Faraday's father was a blacksmith. Neither had a formal education of the type expected of early nineteenth century 'gentlemen'.

In spite of – or perhaps because of this – they produced highly original work that more than matched the discoveries made by their fellow scientists on the continent of Europe who had all received a university education. Most of these were in fact university professors: for example Oersted at Copenhagen, even Ohm (with some difficulty) a professor at Munich. Ampere became an Inspector-general of all French universities. By contrast the Royal Institution had been set up by the self-taught American adventurer and

Picture 2 Sir Humphry Davy

English spy who called himself Count Rumford. It was this unconventional character who appointed Humphry Davy as the first lecturer in chemistry at the Institution in 1801.

Faraday began by working on Davy's ideas about the effects of an electric current on chemicals. Electric currents were new in the early 1800s. In 1780 the professor of anatomy at Bologna University, Luigi Galvani, had discovered electric effects which he thought came from frog's legs (see page 189). Professor Alessandro Volta of Pavia University however showed that what was happening was not 'animal electricity' of the kind produced by electric eels, say, but was produced by the action of chemicals. At the end of the 18th century Volta produced the first electric 'battery', made from pairs of two different metals separated by a solution such as salt water or a dilute acid. It was this battery that both Davy and Faraday used in their experiments. Using it, Davy studied what came to be called electrolysis and discovered new elements such as potassium, sodium and chlorine.

Picture 3 Faraday's equipment for the transformer effect.

Faraday quantified Davy's work and produced his laws of electrolysis. On top of that he made discoveries that founded the electrical industry: the electric motor, transformer and generator. These devices are described in topics E8 and E10. But how did Faraday think up these devices?

Faraday and Fields

In Faraday's time the accepted theory was that both magnetism and electricity were fluids that somehow managed to squeeze themselves into matter. When Oersted found that an electric current could affect a compass needle it was very difficult to explain using a fluid theory. Did the fluids mix? Or did they fight against each other like oil and water? Faraday said there were no fluids. Both an electric current and a magnet could produce a force that extended into space around them, producing a **force field**. These forces were in fact the same, and the well-known trick in which iron filings made a pattern around a magnet simply showed the field as **lines of force**.

It was hard to show these lines around a current – in those days currents were far too weak to make an effect. But the way a compass needle aligned itself along the lines of force around a wire carrying a current could. The force field here was circular. The field of a current and a magnet could interact – just like two magnets attracting or repelling. He imagined the force field growing as a current was switched on. He imagined a wire cutting through the force field of a magnet. He used these ideas to predict and explain how to make circular motion (the motor effect), how to generate a current in a wire (the dynamo and transformer effects). He even thought that a changing magnetic field might travel through space as vibrations, linking electricity and magnetism with the new ideas that were just becoming respectable about light – that light was a **wave**. Faraday's mathematics was too poor for him to put all this into a respectable physical theory that continental scientists might approve of but his mental models were completely novel and were backed up by experiment. Later in the century a good mathematician, James Clerk Maxwell produced the full theory and showed that light was indeed **electromagnetic** radiation. By the end of the century large cities were lit by electric light generated and transformed using Faraday's principles, the first cars were running on the roads (they were **electric** cars!) and Herz had discovered radio waves.

Michael Faraday in conversation with a politician: "And what is the use of your discoveries, Mr Faraday?"

"I don't know, sir. But I am sure that one day you will tax them."

Picture 4 Faraday's electrolysis globe.

Picture 5 Faraday's first electric motor.

Controlling electricity: current and resistance

To make the best use of electricity, we need to be able to control it. We can also use electricity to control other things.

Picture 1 Sliders move over resistors to control electrical signals in this recording studio.

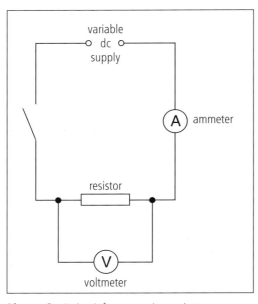

Picture 2 A circuit for measuring resistance.

Picture 3 You can use this triangle to help you rearrange the formula linking resistance, current and voltage.

CONDUCTORS, CARRIERS AND INSULATORS

For electricity to do its work charge has to flow. It flows easily through some materials – they are a good **conductors** of electricity. Metals and solutions of ionic chemicals are good conductors. These materials contain charge carriers that are free to move: metals have free **electrons**, the solutions have free **ions**. An electric cell or battery doesn't provide the charge carriers – they must already be present in the conductor. The battery provides a force which makes the charges move, often called an **electromotive force** (**emf**). As the charges move the force does work (see page 126) and the energy for this is supplied by the cell.

Some substances have no free charges – they cannot carry an electric current and are called **insulators**. Plastics, ceramics, paper and wood are good examples of insulators. Oils and non-ionic solutions are good examples of liquid insulators. Insulators are very useful for keeping charges where we want them to be, such as inside metal wires!

Some materials have a small number of free charges and are both poor conductors and poor insulators. But some materials of this kind are very useful because we can control the number of free charges. These kinds of material are called **semiconductors**: see topic H4 for more about these.

RESISTANCE

Witch a given energy source, such as a battery or a generator, the size of current that flows is decided by the **resistance** of the circuit. All conductors resist the flow of electric charge to some extent, but some are better at it than others. The bigger the resistance of a conductor the harder it is for electric charge to flow through it. For a given voltage applied to it, the current would be less.

It is like water flowing downhill in a river. If the bed of the river is smooth the water can flow easily, and more can get through in a given time. But if the bed of the river is rocky the water can't flow so easily. It will move downhill more slowly, and a lot of energy is wasted – you can hear the noise and see the water being thrown up in the air. We find the same kind of effect in a conductor with a high resistance. It cuts down the flow of charge and energy is released. The conductor gets hot.

■ Resistors

A **resistor** is a special type of conductor made from a high resistance metal or alloy, or perhaps carbon.

A resistor is designed to have a fixed resistance, so that for a fixed voltage exactly the right size of current goes through the circuit.

MEASURING RESISTANCE

Resistance is measured in units called **ohms** (Ω). A 10 ohm resistor would have twice the resistance of a 5 ohm resistor. For a given applied voltage the current in the 10 ohm resistor would be half of that in the 5 ohm resistor.

The size of current is worked out using the formula:

$$\text{current} = \frac{\text{voltage}}{\text{resistance}} \quad \text{or} \quad I = \frac{V}{R}$$

We can switch this formula around to calculate resistance, knowing the current for a given voltage: $R = V/I$

A simple test circuit (picture 2) allows you to measure current and voltage and so calculate the resistance of a resistor.

VARIABLE RESISTORS

Picture 4 shows examples of a very useful type of resistor. By moving a sliding contact, more or less resistance material is put in the way of the current, so making the current smaller or larger. Picture 5 shows how it does this.

These devices can be used in simple circuits to change the size of a current, but they are most often used to control the size of the applied **voltage**.

VOLTAGE

Voltage is not an easy thing to imagine. It measures what the battery or supply actually does, which is to give energy to make charges flow through conductors. We measure the voltage of a supply in terms of how much energy it gives to a **coulomb of charge**. In a lamp circuit the energy would be mostly given to the lamp, heating up its filament.

If a coulomb of charge delivers **6 joules of energy** as it goes around a circuit then the supply voltage is 6 joules per coulomb. We call this **6 volts**.

Another way to look at it is in terms of current and power. This is more practical because the instruments we use measure amps, not coulombs.

The voltage of an energy source such as a battery decides how much **power** a given current can deliver. Power is the rate at which energy is provided, in joules per second or **watts**. See topic D3 for more about power and energy.

A 1 amp current from a 6 V battery can deliver 6 watts (6 joules of energy per second). In comparison, a current of 1 amp from a mains supply at 240 V will deliver 240 watts.

So the voltage of a source tells us how many watts it could provide per ampere of current, according to the formula

$$V = \frac{P}{I} \quad \text{or} \quad \text{volts} = \frac{\text{watts}}{\text{amperes}}$$

You choose the energy source to suit the power you want to use. The mains supply to a house in the UK is 240 V. This means that small currents can be used to run most of the devices we have in our homes. We can see this from the formula, if we rearrange it as $P = VI$. The bigger V is, the smaller I can be to get the same result.

In the USA the mains voltage is 110 V. Their devices need a bigger current if they want the same power. This means they have to be made with lower resistances.

Picture 4   Resistors can be 'variable': you can control both current and voltage by varying the resistance.

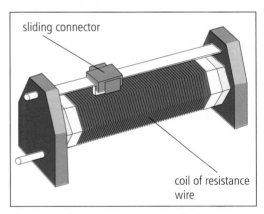

sliding connector

coil of resistance wire

Picture 5   A rheostat – 'flow controller'.

Picture 6   You can use the triangle to help you rearrange the formula linking power, current and voltage

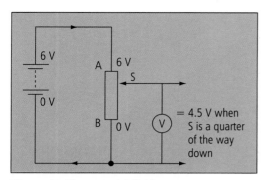

Picture 7 The potential divider.

■ Controlling voltage

When you turn the volume control of a radio or cassette player you are using a variable resistor to control the voltage somewhere in the amplifier circuit. This decides how loud the sound that comes from the loudspeakers will be.

The volume control is a variable resistor. The voltage of the signal being amplified is first of all fed across the whole resistor as shown for a battery in picture 7. By moving the sliding contact you can get all, or just a part, of the voltage fed to the amplifier. The bigger the signal that gets to the amplifier, the louder the sound will be in the loudspeaker. When used like this the variable resistor is called a **voltage divider** or *potential divider*. It divides up the total voltage into smaller amounts.

THE POTENTIAL DIVIDER

Picture 7 shows a circuit which uses a potential divider. AB is a resistor, such as a uniform length of resistance wire, with a sliding contact S. The wire is usually wrapped into a coil. When AB is connected to a voltage supply, such as a battery, current flows through it. The voltage drop across the resistor, from A to B, is the voltage of the battery, say 6 V. S is shown as a quarter of the way between A and B. The voltage between S and B is thus three-quarters of the whole 6 V, which is 4.5 V. Half way down it is 3 V. Thus by sliding S up and down the resistor AB we can get any voltage we like between 0 V and 6 V.

Whenever you turn the knob on a volume control you are likely to be moving a slider along a potential divider, so changing the size of the voltage input to an amplifier.

VARIABLE POWER SUPPLIES

Picture 8 shows a typical low-voltage power supply. Its output can be changed, using a control knob, from 0 to 22 V. The main part of the power supply gives a fixed voltage. The control knob is connected to a variable resistor which changes the output to anything between 0 and the maximum, using a voltage divider.

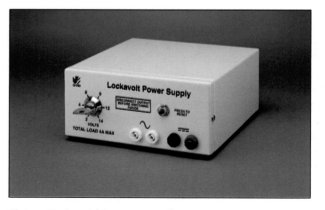

Picture 8 A variable power supply.

MEASURING CURRENT AND VOLTAGE

Current is measured with an **ammeter**, and voltage with a **voltmeter**. Both of these instruments look much the same, and may in fact work on exactly the same principles. This can be confusing, because what they measure is very different. Also, they are placed differently in circuits.

Ammeters tell us how much electric charge is passing though a circuit per second. Remember that 1 ampere is a flow of 1 coulomb of charge per second.

Picture 9 An ammeter will read the current going through it.

Ammeters have to be put directly in the path of the current, so that they can check everything that goes through the circuit (see picture 9).

Voltmeters are trickier. They take a sample of the current in a device or circuit and then *calculate* the voltage that must be across it. They have to keep the 'sampling current' small if they are not to change the circuit too much. This means that they have high resistances and are connected *across* the device being tested (see picture 10).

■ Ohm's Law

For many useful conductors there is a simple rule which connects current, voltage and resistance. If we double the applied voltage, the current is doubled. If we halve the voltage, the current is halved. This effect doesn't work with all conductors, but is true for metals and for carbon, if they don't get too hot.

For most circuits we can use the rule to calculate in advance what will happen when things change.

The rule is: **for a given conductor at a constant temperature the current in it is proportional to the applied voltage**. This is known as **Ohm's Law**.

We can write this as a formula $I = V/R$ where R is *constant*. We can use this formula to make calculations with all values of V for a given conductor. But we have to be careful, because the resistance might change if the conductor gets hot.

WHAT IS A LAW?

Some laws in physics are unbreakable. Gravity always behaves in the same way (see topic B4). Mass–energy cannot be created or destroyed. In every energy change, some always gets less usable. Of course, the Universe is large and can come up with some surprises. But physicists are pretty sure that if any of these laws were broken it would only be because there was a better or stronger law to take its place.

Ohm's Law is not like these. It doesn't say what *must* happen. It just describes how some materials behave. It applies only to metals, ionic solutions and perhaps carbon. There are lots of conductors that don't 'obey' Ohm's Law. This doesn't worry anybody! But if the Law of Conservation of Mass–Energy were broken, the Universe would be a different place!

■ Obeying Ohm's Law – or not!

Ohm's Law applies to metal conductors – but only if they are kept at a constant temperature. Then the current in the metal will be proportional to the applied voltage. This means that a graph of current against voltage will be a straight line (picture 11(a)). But if the current heats a metal conductor it usually becomes more resistive. Current finds it harder to get through as the resistance of the conductor increases. This is what happens in an ordinary filament lamp. The metal filament does obey Ohm's Law – but we can't apply it because the temperature is changing from room temperature to a white hot 2000 °C. So a graph of how current changes with voltage in a filament lamp is as shown in picture 11(b). The curve gets steeper showing that it takes more and more voltage to get a small increase in current.

Some conductors don't obey Ohm's Law at all. This is especially true of semiconductors where the number of particles that actually carry the current can change with circumstances. For example, a light-dependent resistor (see page 301) will have more free electrons to carry current when the light on it is brighter. A semiconductor **diode** is used in electronic circuits because it obeys Ohm's Law in one direction (more or less) but doesn't allow any current at all to pass in the opposite direction. The graph for a diode is shown in picture 11(c).

A **thermistor** gets more conductive when it is heated. As the current in it heats it, so its resistance gets less and so even more current will flow. This effect is shown in picture 11(d).

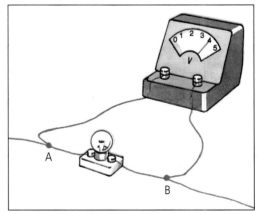

Picture 10 A voltmeter samples some of the flow and 'works out' the voltage between two points (A and B).

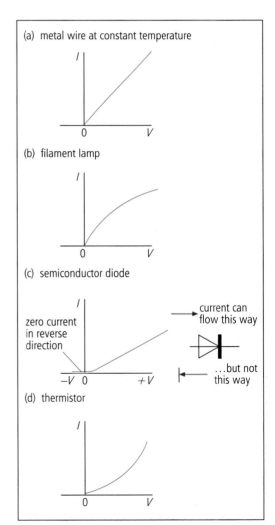

Picture 11 Current v voltage

Activity

A Looking at the label

All electrical devices used in the home must by law have certain information printed on them. Look at some devices and find this information.

1 Copy out what electrical information is given on any one device (e.g. a food mixer, battery, radio, electric razor).

2 Use the information to make the following calculations for any three devices:
   i) the current it takes in normal use,
   ii) its resistance.

You may need to use the formulae given in this topic:

$$R = \frac{V}{I} \quad P = IV \quad \left(\text{or } V = \frac{P}{I}\right)$$

$$\text{or} \quad I = \frac{P}{V}$$

Questions

1 a Name the instruments used to measure current and voltage and draw their circuit symbols.

   b Copy the circuit in picture 12 and label the empty circles with A or V to show which would be ammeters and which voltmeters.

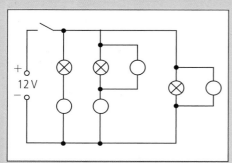

Picture 12

2 You find two wires made of the same metal. One wire is long and thin, the other wire is short and thick. Which do you think would have the bigger resistance?
Give a reason for your answer.

3 People often try to understand about electricity by comparing it with water flowing in a river.

   a In what ways is water in a river like electricity in a wire?

   b In what ways is it different?

   c Can you think of anything else that is like electricity flowing in a wire?

4 Batteries with the same voltage marked on them are sometimes very different in size. Suggest a reason for this.

5 Use the formula $R = V/I$ to work out the resistance of the following devices:
   a a lamp that takes a current of 2 A from a 12 V supply,
   b a lamp that takes a current of 0.5 A from a 12 V supply,
   c an electric toaster that takes a current of 3 A from a 230 V supply,
   d a cake mixer that takes a current of 2.2 A from a 230 V supply.

6 Car headlamps are powered by a 12 V battery or alternator and have a typical resistance of 2.5 ohms. How much current must each lamp take from the supply?

7 Why must ammeters be connected in line (in series) with a device, but voltmeters be connected across it (in parallel)?

8 Draw the circuit you would use to measure the resistance of a torch bulb to be used in a 3 V torch.

9 A resistor used in an electronic circuit must obey Ohm's Law.

   a One such resistor is labelled '20 ohms'. What current would be in it when the following voltages are applied across it: (i) 20 V, (ii) 10 V, (iii) 2 V?

   b Another resistor is labelled '2 kΩ'. What voltage would need to be applied to produce a current of 10 mA in it?

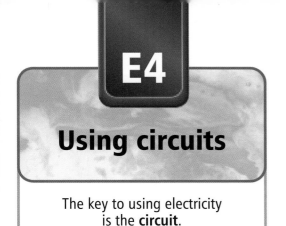

E4

Using circuits

The key to using electricity is the **circuit**.

Picture 1 A Christmas tree. How are the lights controlled?

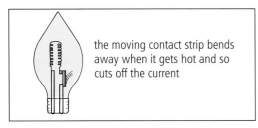

the moving contact strip bends away when it gets hot and so cuts off the current

Picture 2 How a flashing lamp works.

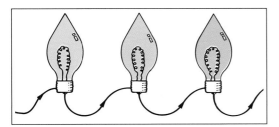

Picture 3 Christmas tree lamps are connected in series. The same current goes through each in turn.

■ How do flashing lights work?

Picture 1 shows a Christmas tree, decorated with coloured lights that can flash on and off. The flashing is controlled by just one bulb that is different from the others. When the filament in it gets hot enough it switches itself off. Then it cools down and switches itself on again (see picture 2). When this control lamp is out all the other lamps go out as well. They only work when the control lamp is on.

Sometimes a lamp in your home stops working and goes out. But this doesn't make all the other lamps go out. Why is this?

■ Series and parallel connections

The Christmas tree lights are connected in a line, one after the other, as shown in picture 3. When a connection is broken in one lamp the charge cannot flow, so all the lamps go out. This way of connecting things in a circuit is called **series** connection.

In a house the lamps in a room are connected in a different way. It would be very annoying if all the lights went out just because one lamp wasn't working. In the home, each lamp is connected separately to the mains supply, as shown in picture 4. Each lamp can have its own switch, and we can have any of the three lamps on, or none of them. This is called **parallel** connection.

WHY DO WE USE PARALLEL CIRCUITS IN THE HOME?

Electrical devices in the home are connected in parallel because we want to control them independently of each other. Each device is connected directly to the mains, so that it gets its proper voltage. Also, we can easily connect other devices into the circuit, without having to 'break it'.

Of course, the more appliances we connect, the more energy we will use, and the more it will cost. This is because when we connect more devices in the circuit in parallel we must take more current from the supply in order to make these extra devices work. This means that the total resistance must get less!

LAMPS IN PARALLEL: MORE MEANS LESS!

We can understand this idea by seeing what happens to the current drawn from the supply when we add more lamps in a parallel circuit. Picture 5 is a standard circuit diagram for 3 lamps connected in parallel to a 12 V supply. Compare this with picture 4 which shows how lamps are connected in a mains supply.

Suppose each low voltage lamp takes 1 A from the supply. When switch 1 is on, lamp A lights and takes 1 A from the supply. Switch 2 adds another lamp – lamp B goes on and another 1 A has to be supplied. Switch 3 adds yet another demand for 1 A. Each time we add a lamp we add another **conductor** which takes more current from the supply.

What has happened to the **resistance** of the circuit? With just one lamp the circuit resistance is R_c, which we can easily calculate:

$$R_c = \frac{V}{I} = \frac{12 \text{ volts}}{1 \text{ ampere}} = 12 \text{ ohms}$$

With the second lamp switched on and a current of 2 A from the supply the resistance R_c becomes 6 ohms.

$$R_c = \frac{V}{I} = \frac{12 \text{ volts}}{2 \text{ amperes}} = 6 \text{ ohms}$$

What would be the circuit resistance if another similar lamp were to be added?

You can work out the answer (4 ohms) in this simple circuit by common sense, but in more complicated circuits you will need to use the formula for resistors in parallel: $1/R_t = 1/R_1 + 1/R_2 + 1/R_3$ etc. This formula is needed when the devices added in parallel have different values of resistance.

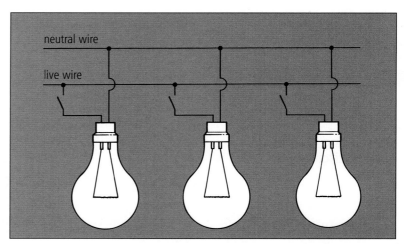

Picture 4 House lights have the lamps connected separately to the mains (i.e. in parallel).

RESISTORS IN SERIES

Picture 6 shows resistors connected in series. If you try this you will find that the more lamps you add the dimmer they get! This is another reason why lamps are usually connected in parallel. The ammeter shows that the current gets less as more lamps are added. This means that the resistance of the circuit has **increased**. When we add resistors in series the total resistance goes up:

$$R = R_1 + R_2 + R_3 \text{ etc.}$$

Picture 7 shows how complicated circuits can get! But all the components you can see in this computer are connected in series and/or in parallel, and the engineers who designed and made it know what current each component has to carry.

RESISTANCE

The resistance of a metal wire depends on four things:

- Its **length** – the longer it is the more resistance it has.
- Its **area of cross-section** – the larger its area of cross-section the less its resistance is.
- The **material** it is made of – gold, silver and copper are better at conducting electricity than iron, for example. Also, we can make metal alloys that are more resistive than even the poorest pure metals. Electric heaters use high-resistance alloys like nichrome and constantan.
- **Temperature** – the resistance of a metal wire increases with temperature.

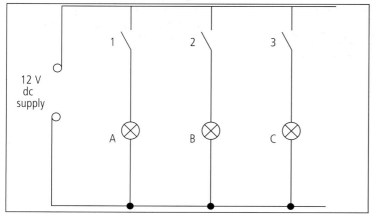

Picture 5

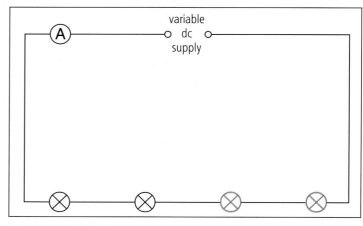

Picture 6 Adding lamps in series.

The above factors are important in designing circuit components. For example, a filament lamp has to have exactly the right resistance, so designers have to choose the right length and thickness of wire once they have chosen the metal out of which the filament is to be made. They also have to allow for the fact that the resistance they measure at room temperature is much less than the resistance when the filament is white hot.

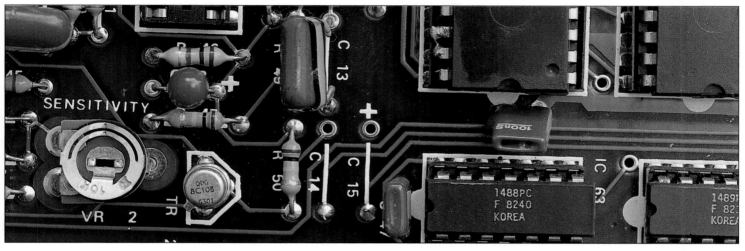

Picture 7   Inside a computer – some circuits are quite complicated!

Questions

1   Draw circuit diagrams showing:
  a   a battery driving two lamps in series with a switch,
  b   a battery driving two lamps in parallel, with a switch for each one.

2   Give two reasons why the lamps at home are connected in parallel rather than in series.

3   Draw circuits showing how you could connect:
  a   a lamp in parallel with a small electric motor, run off a 12 V battery, with a switch that controls both lamp and motor,
  b   a lamp and motor as above, but with each having its own separate switch.

4   Some cars have heated rear windows, with the heater switched on and off by the driver. The makers of the car guard against the driver leaving the window heater on whilst the car is parked overnight.
  a   Why would this be a stupid thing to do? (Try to think of two reasons.)
  b   The simplest way for the car manufacturers to stop this is by making sure that the window heater can't be on unless the ignition switch is also on (the ignition switch has to be on for the engine to work). Draw a simple circuit showing how the two switches are connected.

5   For this question you may need to use the formulae given in the topic for calculating resistances in series and in parallel.

  a   A 6 ohm lamp and a 2 ohm motor are both run from a 6 V battery. They are connected in parallel. How much current is drawn from the battery?
  b   Ten Christmas tree lights are connected in series to the 230 V mains supply. A current of 0.5 A is drawn from the mains. What is the resistance of each lamp?
  c   A 12 V car battery has to supply a heater and a starter motor. They are connected in parallel and have resistances of 12 ohms and 0.5 ohms respectively. What is the effective resistance when both are switched on? What current does the battery have to supply?

What is electricity?

We use 'electricity' every day, but it is more than just a good way of making things work ...

Picture 1 Amber is fossilised tree-sap.

Picture 2 Static electricity is easy to produce.

■ The amber mystery

People have known about electricity for thousands of years. The word electricity comes from the Greek word for amber – *elektron*. Amber is the fossilised sap of pine trees, and is used to make beads and jewellery. It is a shiny, clear, golden material, which may even contain the fossils of insects trapped in it (picture 1).

One snag with amber jewellery is that it seems to get dusty very easily. The ancient Greeks noticed this, and worked out that amber had the mysterious ability to attract small objects to it. This happens when a piece of amber is rubbed by cloth. If you don't happen to own any amber, you can get the same effect by rubbing a plastic pen or comb (picture 2).

The rubbed amber produces a force of attraction which came to be called 'amber force' – or **electricity**. The force was very small, and the effect was completely useless, unlike the forces, say, of magnetism. At least magnets could tell you which way north was. So electricity was forgotten about.

■ The rediscovery of electricity

When electricity did become important it wasn't for good scientific reasons. This renewed interest began just over 200 years ago. At that time 'science' as we know it didn't exist. 'Scientists' called themselves 'natural philosophers'. Some of them were people who were rich and had money and spare time to spend on their hobby, like Robert Boyle who discovered 'Boyle's Law' for gases.

Many earned a living as doctors, like William Gilbert who did experiments on magnets. Galileo (page 93) started off as a doctor of medicine.

Some were clergymen, like Copernicus, who put forward the strange new theory that the Earth went round the Sun, and not vice versa. Some were astronomers or mathematicians, like Isaac Newton.

Some discoveries were made by 'artisans', people who were good with their hands and earned a living making clocks and other instruments. Michael Faraday (see page 160) began life as a bookbinder.

Most of the ones we know about lived in Europe or the British colonies in North America. There were very important discoveries made in China and India, but few of these were heard about in the West.

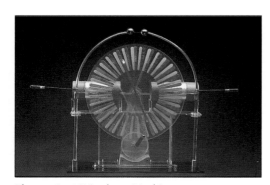

Picture 3 Being charged with electricity is like falling – it doesn't hurt until you touch the Earth!

■ The shocking history of electricity

In the early days the best fun was to be had from 'electrifying' people. Small boys were easily persuaded to be hung up by silken ropes and 'charged' up (picture 3). They were stroked with dry cloths until their hair stood on end. In the dark, you could see sparks leaping from them to anybody standing close by.

Later, machines were invented that used amber-like materials to produce electricity just by turning a handle (picture 4). It was quicker than stroking people with a dry cloth.

Picture 4 A Wimshurst Machine.

Picture 5 Shocking people has always been fun!

The whole thing became so popular that you could earn a living by electrifying people in fairgrounds. People thought that getting charged up was good for the health, and paid money to be strung up and electrified.

In Holland in 1746, Peter van Musschenbroek tried to electrify water in a bottle, and by accident found a new effect. The 'charge' could be stored in a jar. This was the first **capacitor**, and was called a Leiden Jar. This was because he did the experiment in his home town of Leiden.

Now things got more serious – enough charge could be stored to give people a severe shock. The shock could kill small animals and birds, and melt thin wire.

In Paris, 180 of the King's guards were lined up, holding hands, and connected to a charged jar. They all leaped high in the air, at the same instant. The experiment was repeated with 300 Carthusian monks, formed into a line 100 metres long. The results were equally spectacular and even more crowd-pleasing (picture 5). History does not record what the monks thought of it.

Shocks became popular as a cure for gout and rheumatism, and electricity was suddenly all the rage.

■ A theory of electricity

What was going on? What *was* electricity? Where did it come from? Many interested people tried to answer these questions, and it wasn't until the early years of this century that they could be fully answered. But a very good start was made by an American called Benjamin Franklin, who lived from 1706 to 1790 (picture 6).

He started life as a printer's apprentice and then became a successful printer. It was only at the age of forty that he saw some experiments in electricity, and was so fascinated by them that he sold his printing press and spent his whole time experimenting. He was the first man to realise that lightning was a huge electric spark. He flew a kite into thunderclouds, at great risk to his life, to collect charge from them. He learned enough to invent the first lightning conductor, for which he became famous.

Later on he became even more famous as a revolutionary politician when the American colonies rebelled from Britain and became the United States of America.

Picture 6 Benjamin Franklin – rebel, scientist, ambassador and inventor of the lightning conductor.

POSITIVE AND NEGATIVE

Franklin's theory of electricity was simple. He said that every object, even animals and small children, contains electricity. If it has more than its normal share of charge he called it 'plus', if less it was called 'minus'. Since then we have learned that in fact there are two kinds of electric charge, but we still call them 'plus' and 'minus' or **positive** and **negative**.

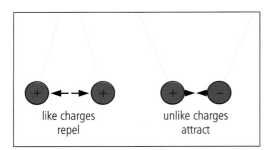

Picture 7   Like charges repel!

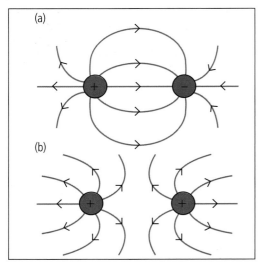

(a)

(b)

Picture 8   Electric field lines.

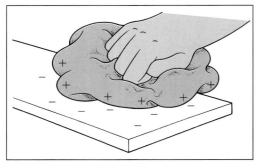

Picture 9   Charging by rubbing. The cloth leaves electrons on the plastic strip. The strip becomes negatively charged and the cloth becomes positive.

Electric forces are caused by the attraction or repulsion between these two kinds of charge (picture 7):

like charges repel, unlike charges attract.

Just as with magnetism and gravity, we imagine there to be an **electric field** near charged objects. We draw field lines (lines of force) with the direction positive to negative (picture 8(a)). This is the direction a positive charge would move under the forces of attraction or repulsion.

In magnetism, we never seem to get N-poles or S-poles on their own. They come together, in opposite pairs. But we can get free electric charges, both positive and negative ones. This is because all matter is made of charged particles which can be separated.

■ Electricity and the atom

All matter is made up of atoms. In turn, atoms are made of a central massive nucleus surrounded by a cloud of very light particles called electrons. The nucleus is positively charged and attracts the cloud of moving electrons because they are negatively charged. The charge on the nucleus is exactly balanced by the charge on the electron cloud. This means that the atoms, and the material they are made of, are normally uncharged. They are **neutral**.

HOW OBJECTS GET CHARGED

Electrons are very small and are easy to move. When a piece of almost any material is rubbed with a cloth electrons are pulled off. Sometimes they go from the cloth onto the material, sometimes they go the other way, depending on the materials (picture 9).

This movement of electrons makes both materials electrically unbalanced. One will gain electrons and it becomes negatively charged. the other loses electrons and becomes positively charged (picture 10).

Moving air can produce the same effect as moving cloth. Cars travelling at speed can have electrons rubbed off them as they pass through the air, and become charged up. Hot air rising on sunny days can become charged, and the charge can be given to water drops in clouds. Sooner or later the clouds have enough charge to cause lightning and thunder (picture 11).

■ How uncharged objects are attracted

A rubbed comb gets charged with electricity. Most materials contain some free electrons that are able to move. A comb you have charged negatively by friction will pick up small pieces of paper, even though the paper is not charged at all. This

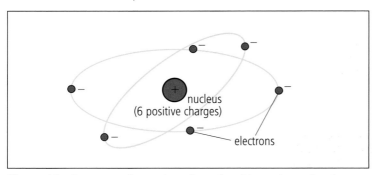

Picture 10   Atoms contain equal numbers of positive and negative charges.

Picture 11   Lightning.

happens because electrons in the paper are pushed away by the negative charge on the comb. The paper nearest the comb is then left with an unbalanced positive charge and so is attracted by the comb – see picture 12.

This effect is called charging by induction: the electrons have been 'induced' to move away from the comb. You can give an object a permanent charge this way if the electrons are allowed to go to earth and then the earth connection is broken – as shown in picture 13.

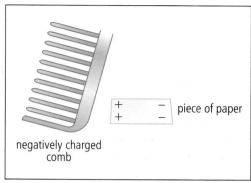

Picture 12 Electrons are pushed away from the comb, which then attracts the positive charge that is left nearer to it than the negatively charged part.

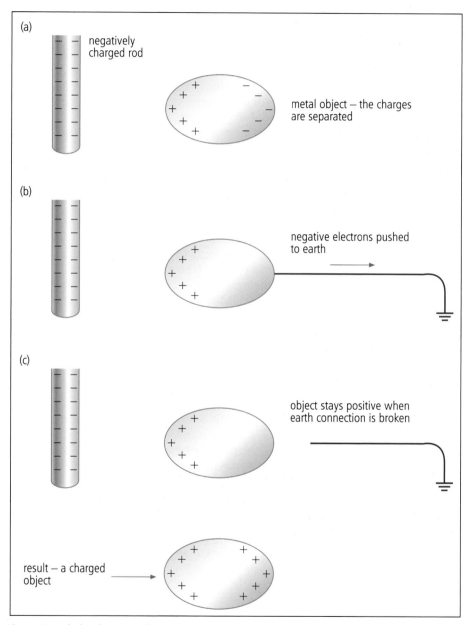

Picture 13   a) The charges in the object are separated by induction. b) the repelled charges (in this case electrons) are allowed to go to earth via a wire, say. c) break the earth connection and the objects is left with a positive charge.

CONDUCTORS AND INSULATORS

Any substance can be electrically charged, but if the material is a conductor the charge might flow away. The most likely place for charge to flow to is the Earth, simply because the Earth is so big that it can hold a huge amount of unbalanced charge without becoming noticeably charged up.

Picture 14 A hair-raising experience.

Human beings are quite good conductors, and for a body to be 'electrified' it has to be kept off the ground by good insulators. Otherwise the charge would flow away to the ground. This is why the children who were charged up in fairgrounds were strung up on silk ropes. Silk was then one of the best insulators known.

Picture 14 shows a girl who has been charged up to about 100 000 volts. The force of repulsion between the like charges on her head and on her hair causes it to flare out. Luckily the electric current is not big enough to give her a dangerous shock. (See topic E7, page 181.)

STATIC ELECTRICITY

When electric charges do not move the effects they produce are called **electrostatic**, and the objects are said to be charged with **static electricity**. Static electricity can be a danger. Small sparks can cause explosions in flammable vapour, such as in the empty holds of oil tankers. Workers and machines have to be properly earthed so that charge doesn't build up.

Ions may also be present in air, as air molecules gain or lose electrons.

■ Electrostatics for printing

Photocopiers are one of the most useful inventions in a modern office. The text or picture to be copied is placed on a glass surface and illuminated by a very bright light. This produces a reverse image of the text which is projected on to a metal plate coated with a light-sensitive material – usually the element selenium. Selenium is a semiconductor (see page 313) and when light falls on it electrons are released and leak away. The result is a plate with positive charges where electrons have leaked away, which arrange themselves as a copy of the reverse pattern of text or image on the original. This plate is then dusted with very fine particles of ink (the **toner**) which are negatively charged. These negative particles are attracted – obeying the laws of electrostatics – to the positive places only and stick there. Then a sheet of paper is pressed against the reversed pattern and picks up a 'right-way-round' pattern on the paper. The paper is then heated just enough to melt the ink particles slightly so that they stick to the paper. The final result is a copy of the original. **Laser printers** work in much the same way, but produce just a small part of a letter, say, at a time.

Ink jet printers work by spraying ink onto paper. Tiny drops of ink are pushed at quite a high speed through very fine nozzles, thinner than a human hair. They leave the ink cartridge through the **printer head** and as they do so they are given an electric charge and are made to pass between two metal plates, very close together. The plates are also charged, one positive the other negative, and provide an electric field to direct the tiny droplets of ink to the right part of the paper to form a very small part of a letter or an image. The electric field can only move the particles up or down. To print horizontally the ink cartridge is moved sideways at just the correct distance to make the complete letter or part of an image. To produce the completed image or page of text the computer printer program (called a 'driver') controls

● when the ink droplet is 'fired' at the paper
● the voltage on the plates or the droplet
● the vertical movement of the paper
● the sideways movement of the cartridge.

Picture 15 shows in principle how an ink jet printer works (not drawn to scale).

CHEMISTRY

Chemistry only happens because atoms and molecules combine together or break apart. This involves making or breaking chemical bonds. The bonds that hold atoms to each other are electric forces. If these forces didn't exist there would be no molecules, no chemical changes, no chemistry and no life on Earth.

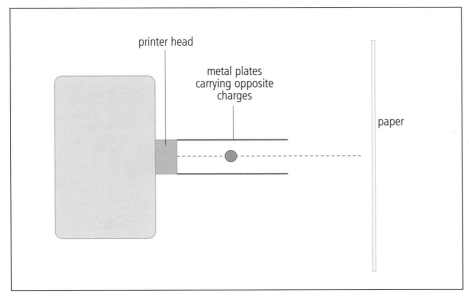

Picture 15 How an ink jet printer works. In some systems the voltage across the plates is varied to control the vertical movement of the ink droplet. In others the plate voltage is constant and different sized charges are given to the droplet.

A metal contains a large number of **free electrons** that are not attached to any particular atom. They are free to move and it is their flow that makes an electric current in a metal. There are so many of them that all metals are good conductors – although some (like gold, silver and copper) are better than others.

Semiconductor materials also contain free electrons, but very much fewer than in metals. Semiconductors are useful because we can control the number of free electrons, and we make use of this in such things as transistors, thermistors and microelectronic devices.

A current of electricity is simply a flow of charged particles. Many chemical compounds split up when they dissolve in water to make charged particles called **ions**. For example, copper sulphate splits up into a *positive* copper ion and a *negative* sulphate ion. Solutions containing ions are called **electrolytes**. Electrolytes are used in metal plating (an example of **electrolysis**) and in batteries.

■ Electrolysis

Many everyday objects are made of a strong but not very attractive metal. It can be made to look better by covering it with a thin film of another metal. Steel is often covered with chromium or even silver, for example. Chromium not only looks better but is less easily corroded than steel or iron, and so helps to preserve the object from rusting. The usual way to cover one metal with a thin coating of another is to **electroplate** it. This is illustrated in picture 16. The object is placed in a solution containing the ions of the metal which is to make the thin layer. It is connected into a circuit to the negative side of the supply – which makes it a **cathode**. The circuit is completed by a rod of the plating metal (e.g. chromium) which is connected to the positive terminal as the **anode**.

The supply drives positive ions to the negative cathode. There they collect electrons and are plated as neutral atoms on to the object at the cathode. More positive ions enter the solution from the anode to keep up the strength of the solution and maintain a conducting circuit.

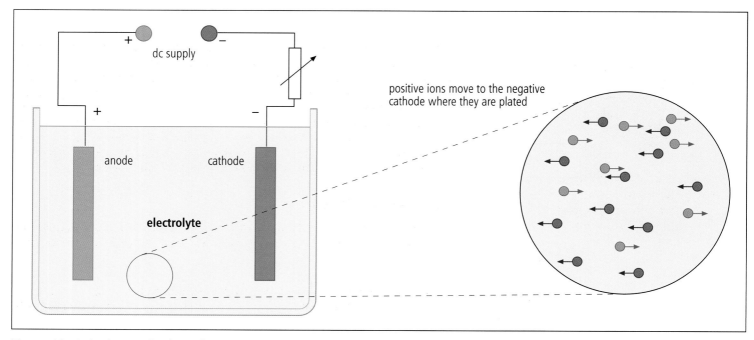

Picture 16   A simple circuit for electroplating an object.

Questions

1 What are the two kinds of electric charge?

2 a What do people mean when they talk about 'static'?

b What happens when an object becomes electrically charged by 'friction'?

c Give two examples of things that become 'accidentally' charged in this way in everyday life.

d Sparks from charged objects can give a shock, or possibly start a fire. For one of the examples you gave in part (b), state
   i) how you could stop the charges building up,
   ii) how you could let the charge get away safely.

3 Explain what the following mean:
a conductor,
b insulator,
c static electricity,
d earthing.

4 Why do you think 'static electricity' wasn't much use in the 17th century? Describe any practical use you know for it nowadays.

5 Why is electricity so important in chemistry? Write a short essay explaining how chemical changes in atoms and molecules involve electric charges.

6 Explain, using diagrams, how a metal sphere can be charged negatively by induction. What role do electrons play in this?

Using electricity: heating and lighting

Electricity is useful because it can carry energy from one place to another and we use it to do many different jobs.

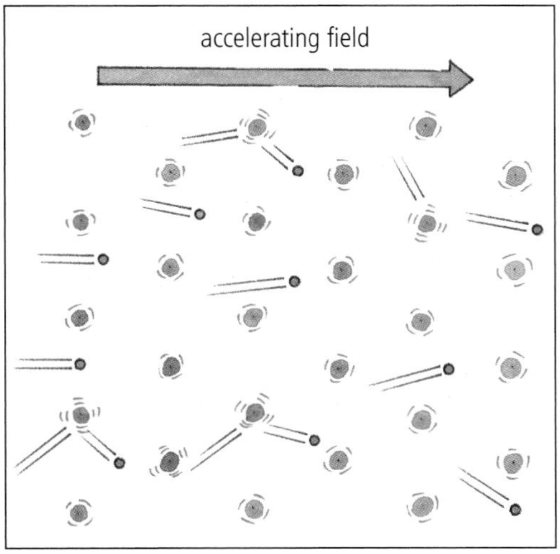

ELECTRIC HEATING

When electrons flow through a conductor they collide with the atoms in the conductor. As they do this they give energy to the atoms. The energy is simply movement energy, transferred from the moving electrons to the atoms. The atoms are fixed, and just vibrate a little more (picture 1). We feel this extra vibration as a rise in temperature – the conductor warms up.

The electrons soon speed up again after the collisions, pushed on by electric forces. These forces are provided by a battery, or a cycle dynamo or the generators in a large power station. Most of the work done by electrical devices in homes and factories uses the energy from fuels burnt in power stations – see page 193.

■ Resistance wires

Electric heaters need special kinds of wire as conductors. The wire in an electric fire element is usually an alloy of different metals. The alloy needs to have the right properties:

- a high resistance,
- a high melting point (to stand the high temperatures produced),
- chemical stability (so that it doesn't burn or corrode at high temperatures in air).

■ Types of heater

Picture 2 shows four types of electric heating device. Only one of them gets to be red hot, with a temperature of 600 to 700 °C. This is the ordinary electric fire, which radiates energy as electromagnetic waves from the hot coil of wire.

An electric kettle has an element which doesn't need to get hotter than about 100 °C, the boiling point of water. If it does, perhaps when the kettle boils dry, an automatic switch cuts off the current.

Picture 1 Electrons give energy to atoms in a conductor by colliding with them.

accelerating field

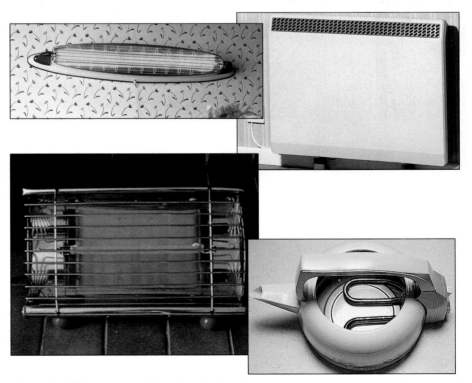

Picture 2 Different ways of using electrical heating.

Picture 3 The parts of an ordinary filament lamp.

Picture 4 Fluorescent tubes being checked.

The night storage heater is very heavy because it is full of special bricks which can store a lot of energy when they get hot. They take a long time to heat up, but take an equally long time to cool down. This is why they are so useful. They release their energy to heat up the room slowly, so that the room is heated over a long period of time. Inside the bricks there is an electric heater, which heats up the bricks at night. Electricity is cheaper at night – see page 200.

Infra-red heaters are another kind of low temperature heater. Unlike ordinary electric fires the hot wire is embedded in a special glass. This means that it can't be touched, and so these heaters are safer for use in bathrooms where the danger of electric shock is greatest.

The glass gets hot, but the heater relies on the fact that radiation energy can get through the glass. It is this **infra-red** radiation that warms up the room and the people in it.

ELECTRIC LIGHTING

There are two main kinds of lighting used in the home. The oldest is the filament lamp (picture 3). This contains a very thin and long piece of wire (the 'filament'). It is made of a metal, tungsten, that can be heated to such a high temperature that it becomes white hot but doesn't melt. At this temperature it would burn in air, so it is kept inside a glass bulb filled with gases that don't react with it, such as argon and nitrogen.

Although it is glowing white hot, and sending out a lot of energy as radiation, most of the energy comes out as invisible (infra-red) radiation. You can feel this if you put your hand near the bulb. In fact, only 2 or 3% of the energy supplied to the lamp is turned into visible radiation (light).

■ Fluorescent lamps

Fluorescent lamps are more efficient. A 40 watt fluorescent lamp produces as much light as a 150 watt filament lamp – and far less heat (picture 4). They work on a completely different principle.

The lamps are filled with a gas (mercury vapour) at low pressure. Electrons flow through the gas and collide with the gas atoms. When collisions take place the mercury gives out invisible (and dangerous) ultra-violet radiation. But don't worry, this radiation doesn't escape from the lamp. It hits a special **phosphor** paint on the inside of the lamp and makes it glow white (picture 5). It is much the same as what happens in a TV tube (see page 201), where high-speed electrons are used to make the phosphors glow different colours.

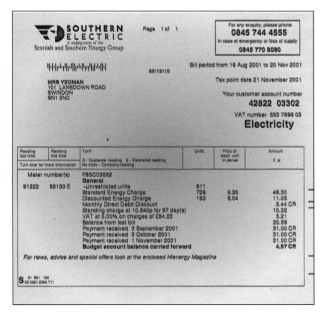

Picture 6 Your electricity bill.

HOW MUCH DOES ELECTRICITY COST?

The electricity boards don't make us pay for 'electricity'! We get that free. What we pay for is the **energy** that is transferred when the electricity runs machines and heaters in our homes.

In science we measure energy in joules, but this is too small a unit to be easily used in everyday life. Of course we could use kilojoules or megajoules, but the electricity boards use a unit of energy called a kilowatt-hour. An electricity bill is shown in picture 6.

The 'units' are in fact kilowatt-hours, and as you can see some cost more than others. The cheap units are the ones used overnight, for putting energy into storage or water heaters. The kilowatt-hour is quite a sensible unit, in practice. It is equivalent to 3.6 megajoules (3 600 000 joules). It is the energy transferred when, for example, you use a 1 kilowatt electric fire for an hour.

POWER RATINGS

The power rating of a device is given in watts or kilowatts. It tells us how much energy the device uses each second. Thus 1 watt is 1 joule of energy per second, a kilowatt is a thousand joules per second. A piece of electrical equipment, like a TV set or a lamp, will usually have its power rating printed on it (picture 7). The power of a device is decided by how much current it takes at its correct operating voltage.

In the home the voltage is kept at 230 V, and the current is then decided by the resistance of the equipment. We can use the formula $I = V/R$ to calculate the current, if we know the value of the resistance.

We can use the formula:

$$\text{power} = \text{voltage} \times \text{current} \quad (\boldsymbol{P = VI})$$

to calculate the power rating if we know current and voltage. We can also use it to calculate the current needed to provide a desired power. Then we can use the first formula to find out what resistance the device needs to have. This is what the manufacturers have to do when they produce the electrical equipment we buy.

Table 1 gives some typical power and current ratings for mains-operated equipment in the home.

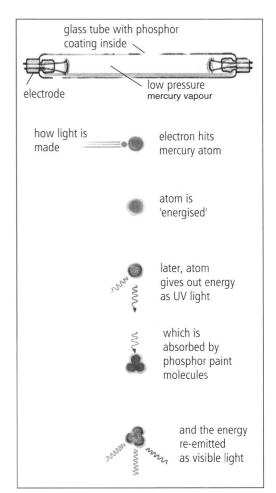

Picture 5 How a fluorescent tube works.

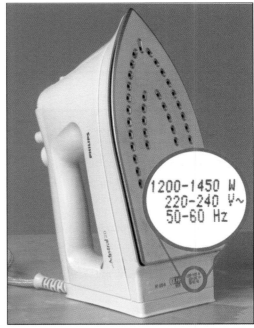

Picture 7 Look for the power rating on your kettle or hair dryer.

Table 1   How much power do appliances use?

Appliance	Power rating (kW)	Voltage (V)	Current (A)	Resistance (Ω)
High power				
storage heater	2.0	230	8.7	26.0
cooker (total)	14.0	230	61.0	0.04
microwave oven	0.65	230	2.8	82.0
3-bar electric fire	3.0	230	13.0	18.0
Medium power				
1-bar electric fire	1.0	230	4.3	53.0
electric kettle	2.0	230	8.7	26.0
hair dryer	1.0	230	4.3	53.0
vacuum cleaner	0.8	230	3.5	66.0
toaster	0.9	230	3.9	59.0
iron	1.0	230	4.3	53.0
drill	0.3	230	1.3	177.0
Low power				
refrigerator	0.12	230	0.5	460.0
lamp	0.06	230	0.3	767.0
hairstyling brush	0.020	230	0.09	2560.0
radio cassette player	0.012	230	0.05	4600.0
calculator	0.005	6	0.08	75.0

Activities

A   How much power do you use?

1   Do this activity at home at 7 p.m. one evening. Find the power of each of the electrical devices that you are using at that time. CARE: Be careful to look at labels on kettles cookers etc., when they are cool and not while they are working. Alternatively, use Table 1. Work out how much total power you are using.

2   Find out how much you have to pay for 1 'unit' (kilowatt-hour) of energy. (If you can't, assume it to be 6p.) Now calculate how much it would cost to run all these devices for 2 hours.

Questions

1   Suggest a reason why electrical energy is cheaper at night.

2   Use the formula:

   power = voltage × current

to work out the power needed to run the following devices:

   a   a 12 V car headlamp that takes 4 A,

   b   a vacuum cleaner motor that takes 3 A from the mains supply at 230 V,

   c   a washing machine heater that takes a current of 11 A from the mains supply at 230 V.

3   Use the formula:

   resistance = voltage/current

to work out the effective resistance of each of the devices in Question 2.

4   Use the data given in table 1 to work out the cost of using some electrical appliances as described below.

Assume the cost per unit (kilowatt-hour) of electrical energy to be 6p.

   a   Using a 3-bar electric fire for 4 hours.

   b   Using a hair dryer for half an hour.

   c   Using a calculator for 10 hours.

   d   Leaving two 100 W electric lights on for 10 hours a day for a week.

   e   Using a microwave oven to cook something for 10 minutes at full power.

5   Copy out the following passage, filling in and underlining the missing words. Choose the words you need from the following list:

current, voltage, thousand, power, energy, resistance, second, hour, cost.

Your electricity bill asks you to pay for the _____ you have used, not the voltage or the _____ supplied. The _____ rating of an electrical appliance tells you how much _____ it uses per _____. The bigger the power rating, the more it will _____ to use. A label on the device that says '1 kW' means that it will use _____ at the rate of _____ joules per second.

Using electricity safely

Electricity can be very dangerous; in fact it is probably the most dangerous thing you let into your home.

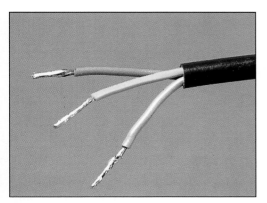

Picture 1 A three-wire cable.

STICK TO THE RULES!

There are very strict rules about how houses should be wired and how electric appliances should be made. This is because electricity can give a strong electric shock which may kill. It can also cause fires. Most of the fires started in homes and buildings are caused by electrical faults. How can we guard against these dangers?

■ The three-wire system

The mains supply uses three wires (picture 1). One pair carries the current 'out and back'. These are the **live** and **neutral** wires. The household supply is **alternating**. The '230 volts' of the mains supply is actually a kind of average of the alternating voltage. Actually, mains voltage swings from +325 volts to -325 volts fifty times a second.

All household devices would work perfectly well with just these two wires, but there is a third wire, the **earth** wire. This is for safety. The three wires are colour-coded, as shown in picture 1.

If an electric appliance is properly made and connected using a three-pin plug (picture 2) it should be impossible for you to get a shock, or for a fire to start, even if something goes wrong.

The earth lead connects the metal case of an appliance to the ground inside or just outside the house. If a fault occurs which would make the case live, electric charge will flow harmlessly into the earth. This stops the charge going through you to earth, or through another part of the appliance which might get too hot (picture 3).

■ Fuses and circuit breakers

The path to earth has a very low resistance, so that as soon as a fault occurs the current that flows is very large. This could be dangerous, because it could make the conductor too hot and start a fire. To guard against this a **fuse** or **circuit breaker** is built into the circuit. Modern wiring systems have both.

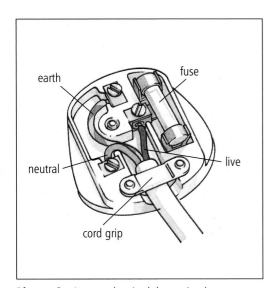

Picture 2 A correctly wired three-pin plug.

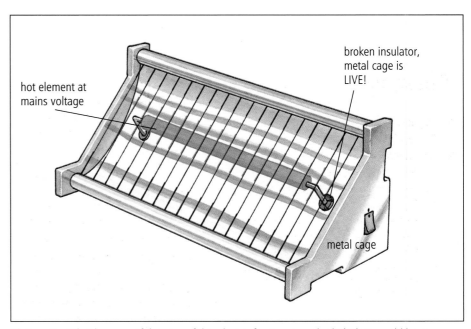

Picture 3 What happens if the case of this electric fire is not earthed? (What would have happened if it was earthed?)

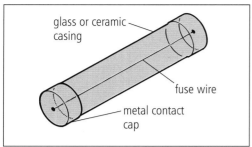

Picture 4 A fuse.

Picture 5 Modern house circuits use a 'leakage' switch for extra safety.

Picture 6 Symbol for double insulation

Picture 7 Water conducts electricity well: wet bodies are at risk. Why are bathroom light switches safer than an ordinary switch?

There is a fuse in each three-pin plug, and many devices have fuses built into them as well. A fuse is simply a short length of wire inside a protective case (picture 4). The wire is made of an alloy with a low melting point. A current larger than its 'rated' value will make the wire hot, and it melts. This breaks the circuit and current stops flowing.

A circuit breaker is usually built into the central distribution board where the mains supply enters the house. It is usually near the fuse box. There are quite small ones that fit into mains sockets so that you can use them to protect you whenever you use especially dangerous equipment. You should use them for electrical devices used out of doors, such as lawn mowers (picture 5).

Circuit breakers use an electromagnetic or electronic device to cut off the current if it gets too large because of a fault, or if current is leaking to earth. They are very sensitive and can detect quite small faults. They work much more quickly than a fuse. They give extra protection because even a small current going through the wrong part of a device can cause overheating, with the risk of fire. An ordinary fuse might not 'blow' under these conditions.

■ Double insulation

Some equipment is 'doubly insulated', so that the live wire cannot reach any outside metal part at all. This means that the equipment does not have to be earthed. Even so, it still needs to be protected by a fuse or circuit breaker in case the lead (cord) is damaged.

■ Electricity and the human body

The human body is quite a good conductor of electricity – once the electricity gets inside it. This is because the human body is largely water, with all kinds of salts dissolved in it.

Luckily, when the skin is dry it is quite resistant to electricity. Also, if you are wearing rubber or plastic soled shoes the charges can't get out easily. So people may touch bare wires at mains voltage and still survive, although they will certainly feel the shock and it's not a lot of fun.

The most dangerous condition to be in is to have a wet skin and bare feet (picture 7). This makes bathrooms very dangerous, electrically, and special care is needed. To start with, all switches in bathrooms have to be operated by 'remote control', using lengths of insulating cord. Heaters with bare wiring are banned. Bathrooms are not the places to watch TV or listen to mains radios! The makers of electric showers have to make sure that the water is kept totally insulated from the mains electricity.

WHAT HAPPENS WHEN YOU GET AN ELECTRIC SHOCK?

The nervous system of the body works by means of electricity. Muscles are controlled by electrical messages from the brain or from nerve sensor cells. When a current enters the body it can override the nerve signals. You lose control of muscles. This means that you might be unable to let go of a live wire, your body might quiver uncontrollably, and you might be unable to speak. This can happen with a current as small as 15 *thousandths* of an ampere.

If the current is larger it could cause burning, due to its heating effect. But the real danger is that the heart stops beating. The heart, like any other muscle, is controlled by electrical nerve pulses. If these are overridden by an electric shock the heart might stop beating, and you will also stop breathing. Death follows in a very short time.

Thus the first aid treatment for electric shock is similar to that for drowning – heart massage and mouth-to-mouth resuscitation. But first-aiders must be careful to switch off the electricity first, otherwise there would be two patients to deal with.

Good advice

The local electricity company produces pamphlets which give very good advice on the safe use of electricity. They can be got free from any showroom. The most common dangers are due to old, frayed wiring, or cuts in new wiring. Everyone should know how to fit a mains plug correctly, and to use the right fuse in it. Appliances should now come with the plug already wired and with the correct fuse fitted.

It is dangerous to 'overload' a circuit. This might be done by connecting high-current appliances (like heaters or even TV sets) to low-current lighting circuits. Instead, they should be connected to the correct 'ring-main' circuit. This is the circuit that has three-pin sockets and the wiring is thick enough to carry the current without overheating. But even this circuit can be overloaded if you use adaptors which allow you to connect too many appliances. Picture 8 shows a selection of dangerous fittings.

Picture 8   Danger! This is a serious fire risk.

Activities

A Danger warning

Make a poster warning either:

1   cooks or

2   children

about one electrical danger they have to guard against.

B Make a safety check

Make a survey of the electrical appliances, wires or fittings in your home that might be a source of danger and need attention. List them and say what needs doing to each.

C Learn to get it right

Practise wiring a three-pin plug. Do this under supervision at school, so that your work can be checked.

D Are you prepared for shocks?

You go into your kitchen. To your horror a member of your family is lying on the floor, still holding an electric iron. You see that the iron has a frayed cable. It is clearly a case of severe electric shock.

What would you do?

If you don't know, find out!

Questions

1   Why are the 3 wires in a household electrical cable colour-coded? What are the colours for:

a   live,

b   neutral,

c   earth?

2   Cartridge fuses (as in picture 4) are normally available as 3 A, 5 A or 13 A.

a   What would probably happen if you used a 3 A fuse in the plug for a 3 kW electric heater?

b   Why is it bad practice to use a 13 A fuse in the plug for a 60 watt desk lamp?

c   What happens when a fuse 'blows'?

d   You buy a second-hand hair dryer, in good condition, but without a plug fitted. The dryer is labelled '230 V, 800 W'. What fuse would you choose to put into the plug? Explain how you worked out your answer.

3   You can get a deadly shock from the 230 V mains, but can be charged up to over 100 000 V by a Van de Graaf machine without danger. Explain these facts.

4   Give four precautions used to cut down the risk of electrical accidents in the home. Write a sentence about each of them, so that a younger person could understand why they are used.

5   a   What is a 'short circuit'?

b   What does 'earthing' mean?

c   Why are many electrical appliances 'earthed'?

d   Why is a short circuit especially dangerous when it happens in a device which isn't earthed?

6   Circuit breakers (page 182) are often used nowadays instead of fuses – especially with appliances that take a large current to make them work.

Why are circuit breakers better than fuses in these cases?

7   Design and sketch a way you could use electromagnetism to switch a current off if it got too big.

8   Most fires in homes and offices are caused by electrical faults. Explain how an electrical fault can start a fire.

A steam iron

Picture 1
A modern iron.

Picture 1 shows a modern steam iron. It is made in three separate parts, or sub-assemblies. Each sub-assembly is made of lots of smaller parts, totalling more than a hundred altogether. The sub-assemblies are:

- the handle,
- the soleplate,
- the thermostat.

The handle sub-assembly

This is made mostly of plastic. It has to be light and be a good insulator for both heat and for electricity. It also houses the terminal block for the electrical connections. It has to be well-designed, both to look good and to make it comfortable to use.

The soleplate sub-assembly

This is made mostly of metal. It has a smooth outer case, particularly underneath, where the metal is in contact with the clothes being ironed. The soleplate has to heat up quite quickly and also allow the energy to transfer from the heating element to where it is useful.

The soleplate contains the heating element, which is a coil of resistance wire that gets hot when an electric current flows through it. It has to be insulated from the main soleplate to avoid electric shocks to the user. This is done by packing the coil in a compressed powder of magnesium oxide (picture 2).

The coil also heats the steam chamber, in which water is boiled to provide steam for making clothes easier to iron. Water is a good conductor of electricity, which is another reason for having the heating coil so well insulated.

The thermostat sub-assembly

This controls the temperature of the ironing surface of the soleplate. It does

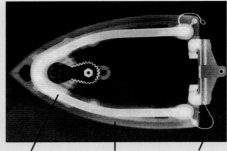

magnesium   mild steel   nickel-chromium
oxide powder casing   wire

Picture 2 Inside a steam iron.

this by switching the current on and off as needed. This means that it has to be made out of very reliable components. In the ordinary life-span of the iron the current will be switched on and off many thousands of times.

Picture 3 shows how the thermostat switch works. It uses a bimetallic strip. This consists of two different metals welded together. One metal expands more than the other when it is heated. Because of this the strip bends when it is heated. Thus when the iron gets hotter than it should be, the contact is broken and the heating coil is switched off. The thermostat control works by moving the contacts nearer together or further apart, so that the contact is broken at the required temperature.

Answer the following questions.

1 a Give three reasons why plastic is used in the handle, rather than metal.

   b Suggest another material that could be used instead of plastic, and suggest a reason why it isn't used.

2 a Why is the heating coil surrounded by an insulator?

   b Plastic could be used instead of magnesium oxide as an insulator around the heating coil. Suggest two reasons why the magnesium oxide might be a better choice.

3 Use the diagram (picture 3) to decide which of the metals used in the bimetallic strip expands the most when heated.

4 a In use the bottom of the iron is surrounded by steam, and it is used over a wide range of temperatures. Suggest what properties the material used to make the base of the plate must have if the steam iron is to be usable for a number of years.

   b The material used for the outside of the soleplate is a *mild steel* plate covered with a smooth coating of *zinc*. The inside of the soleplate is made of cast *aluminium*. Give one reason in each case for the use of these materials (printed in italics).

   c Which part of the steam iron is most likely to break down after many years of use? Give a reason for your answer.

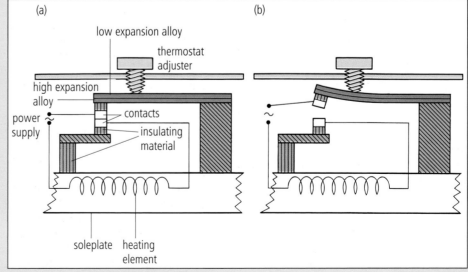

Picture 3 How the thermostat switch works.

Using electricity: motors and dynamos

Electricity currents and magnetism can work together to make things move.

Picture 1 Michael Faraday lecturing to the public.

■ Poor boy makes good!

Two hundred years ago it wasn't easy for a poor boy to get an education, even if he was a genius. Michael Faraday (born in 1791) was the son of a blacksmith. He learned to read and write and do arithmetic but left school at 13 to work as an errand boy for a bookbinder.

At 14 he was promoted to apprentice bookbinder. Keen to learn, he started to read the books that he bound. He was fascinated by the science books, especially the ones about physics and chemistry. He spent some of his small pay on materials and started experimenting at home. He made lots of smells – and an electrical machine.

Later on, he went to lectures put on for the public at a great research laboratory in London called the Royal Institution. He was very interested by four lectures given by a famous scientist called Sir Humphrey Davy, who was the director of the Institution. He made careful notes of what he heard and wrote them out neatly. He used his skills to bind these notes and sent them off to the great man, with a letter asking for a job as a lab assistant.

He was given the job, and at the age of 21 he was able to give up bookbinding for ever. Twelve years later Michael was made Director of the Institution, and had become one of the most famous scientists in the world. Nearly everything you will learn about in this chapter was first discovered by him. The equipment he used can still be seen at the Royal Institution. See page 160 for more about Faraday.

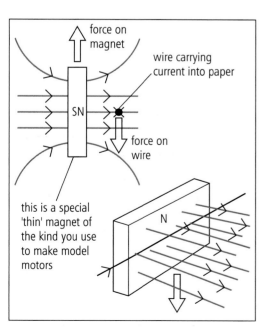

this is a special 'thin' magnet of the kind you use to make model motors

Picture 2 Interaction between a magnet and a wire carrying a current.

■ Electricity and magnetism working together

An electric current produces a magnetic field (see page 158). Put a wire in the field of a magnet and pass a current through it. Both wire and magnet will try to move. There is a force between them caused by the interaction of their magnetic fields (picture 2). This is the **motor effect** which is used in all electric motors, from toy cars to large electric locomotives.

Strangely, the force is exerted at right angles to both the current direction and the magnetic field lines. When you change the direction of the current in the wire, the force on it changes to the opposite direction too. Changing the poles around so that the field is now in the opposite direction also changes the direction of the force on the wire.

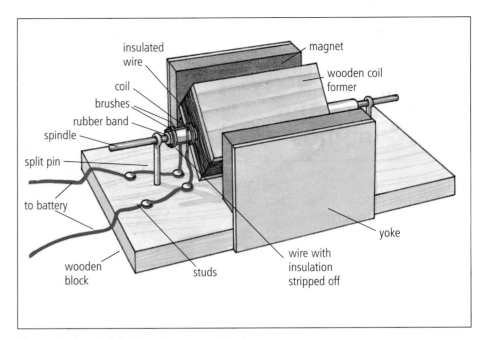

Picture 3 A model electric motor you could make.

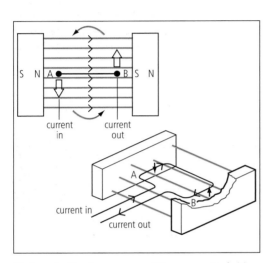

Picture 4 The forces on a coil in a magnetic field make it spin.

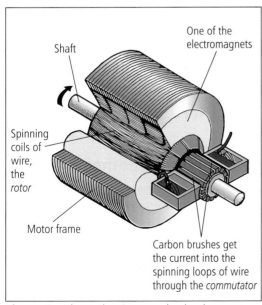

Picture 5 A large electric motor that has been cut open.

You can work out which way the wire will move using Fleming's Left Hand Motor Rule:

Use your left hand: align your **F**irst finger in the direction of the magnetic **F**ield, and your se**C**ond finger in the direction of the electric **C**urrent. Put your thu**M**b at right angles to both fingers – it points in the direction of the **M**otion of the wire.

Check that this works for picture 2.

■ Electric motors

Simple electric motors are scaled up versions of ones you can build yourself from a length of wire and two magnets (picture 3). A model motor uses a special pair of slab magnets that give a straight field between them. The force makes a turning effect that is greatest when the spinning coil is at points A and B (picture 4). The design lets current into the coil only when it is at this position.

SMALL WORKING MOTORS

Picture 5 shows the inside of a small electric motor. A motor like this is used in electric drills or vacuum cleaners. It has a much longer coil than your 'home made' one, and its magnetic field is made larger by wrapping the coil around some soft iron. This turns the coil into an electromagnet (topic E2). It is called an **armature** when it is used like this.

The problem with a spinning electromagnet is to get the electric current into it and out again. This is done by using sliding contacts called **brushes** which just touch the ends of the spinning coil. A real motor has more than one coil with more than one pair of brush contacts. As the motor spins round, one coil after another is brought into action so that the force is almost continuous.

The field is not straight as in the motor that you might make in the school laboratory. It is radial, like the spokes of a wheel. This means that the coils are always at right angles to the field lines and so they always have a strong force on them. In a real motor the magnets producing the field are electromagnets, not permanent ones.

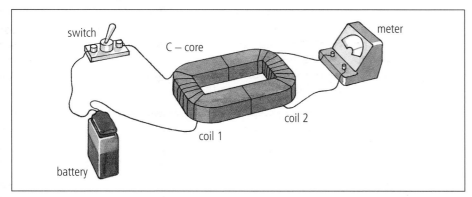

Picture 6 A modern version of Faraday's discovery of induced electricity (the transformer effect).

■ Electricity from magnetism?

Michael Faraday didn't stop at making magnetism and electricity work together to produce movement. He thought that there ought to be a way of using movement and magnetism to produce electricity. It took him seven years to think of a way of doing it, but what he discovered is the scientific basis of the electricity industry – **electromagnetic induction**.

Picture 6 shows a modern version of his experiment. When the current in the first coil is switched on the meter shows a pulse of current in the second coil. Nothing happens when the current in coil 1 is flowing steadily, but another pulse occurs when it is switched off.

If you alter the current in coil 1 steadily, by using a rheostat in the circuit, you get a steady current in coil 2.

All this happens because a voltage is **induced** in coil 2 whenever a current is changed in coil 1. The modern application of this is the **transformer** (picture 7). There is more about transformers in topic E10.

Faraday tried to imagine what must be happening. He had already thought up the idea that magnetic fields could be explained in terms of lines of force. He explained this new effect by imagining that as the current was being switched on and off so were the lines of force of its magnetic field. The voltage in the second coil was made only when the lines grew and died away.

Picture 7 A transformer.

■ A generator

So what would happen if he made the lines of force come and go by a different method, by moving a magnet into and out of a coil? He tried this (picture 8) and it worked. Once more a current was produced. The same thing happened when he kept the magnet still and moved the coil instead.

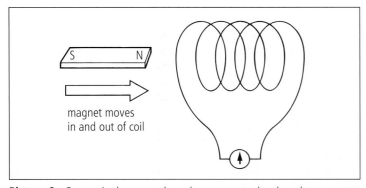

Picture 8 Current is shown on the galvanometer only when the magnet moves in or out of the coil (the dynamo effect).

Picture 9 A bicycle dynamo.

He had invented the first **electric generator**, or **dynamo**. A simple dynamo (picture 9) has the same parts as an electric motor. Both have spinning coils surrounded by magnets. In the motor, putting a current through the coil makes it spin. In a dynamo, making the coil spin produces an electric current. Large dynamos, called generators, are used in power stations to produce the mains supply that we use to run so many things in the home and in industry.

USING ELECTRICITY TO CARRY ENERGY LONG DISTANCES

Most railways now use locomotives driven by electric motors. These are powered by generators which can be many hundreds of kilometres away (picture 10).

The main advantage of electricity is that it is so easy to move it from one place to another. A disadvantage is that it is hard to store. Topic E10, *The electricity industry*, deals with the production and supply of electricity.

Picture 10 Electric locomotive.

Questions

1   Picture 11 shows how you might investigate the force on a wire carrying a current in a magnetic field. What would happen if:

a   the magnets were swapped round, so that the S-pole was on top and the N-pole was on the bottom?

b   the battery connections were then changed so that the current flows in the opposite direction?

c   the current was made bigger?

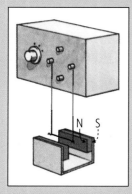

Picture 11 Investigating the motor effect.

2   Name (a) two devices that use an electric motor to move something from one place to another and (b) two devices that use electric motors to do something else.

3   a   Give one place where you would expect to find a transformer being used.

b   What is it being used for?

4   Look at picture 8, which shows a coil connected to a meter, and a magnet. When the magnet is moved slowly towards the coil the meter shows a current as shown.

a   What would happen to the current if the magnet was moved more quickly?

b   What would happen to the current if the magnet was kept still and the coil was moved towards the magnet?

c   What would happen to the current if the magnet was moved, but this time away from the coil?

5   You have made a model electric motor and it works! What could you do to:

a   make it turn faster,

b   make it spin in the opposite direction,

c   make it work as a dynamo?

6   An electric motor is used in a small hoist for lifting goods a height of 5 metres to the second floor of a factory. The motor is rated at 800 W. When it was tested it was found to lift a load weighing 600 N to the second floor in 4 seconds.

a   How much work did the motor do on the load?

b   Show that this hoist is about 94% efficient.

c   Suggest two reasons why the hoist is unlikely ever to be 100% efficient.

Electricity from frogs?

To the ancient scientists all electricity was 'static'. Then by accident, an electric current was discovered ...

■ The first electric current

When electricity was 'rediscovered' 300 years ago (topic E5) it was 'static' electricity. Apart from entertaining people in a shocking way it wasn't much use. But in 1780 an Italian doctor, Luigi Galvani, discovered a way to produce a continuous flow of charge – in fact the first electric **current**. Like many discoveries in science it was a kind of accident.

Galvani was interested in electricity and had all kinds of equipment in his home. The story goes that Galvani was preparing some food for his sick wife, who happened to like to eat frogs' legs. When they were laid out ready for cooking his wife noticed that whenever a spark was produced by a nearby 'electric machine' (see page 170) the frogs' legs twitched.

A MISSED MEAL

She never got to eat the frogs' legs. Galvani started experimenting with them to find out why they twitched. He found that it happened when the leg nerves were stimulated by electric sparks. Then, to his great surprise he found that the legs twitched even when the machine was not working. But this only happened if the ends of the nerves were touched by metals.

He then drew the wrong conclusion. He thought that the electricty came from the frog's leg. It just needed the metals for it to be conducted away. After all, if you can get electric eels (picture 2) why not electric frogs?

■ The first battery

Galvani did his experiment in 1780, and it aroused great interest amongst the electrical hobbyists of the day. But it took another 14 years for the true cause of 'frog electricity' to be explained. This was done by another Italian, Alessandro Volta. He showed that the source of the electric current was not the frog's leg at all. It was caused by the fact that Dr Galvani had used *two different metals, in the presence of salt water*. The frogs' legs had been preserved in salty water. And Dr Galvani had indeed used a zinc dish and steel scalpels, and he had also touched the legs with copper wires.

Picture 1 'You cannot be serious!'

Picture 2 An electric eel.

Picture 3 Dr Galvani experimented with frogs' legs.

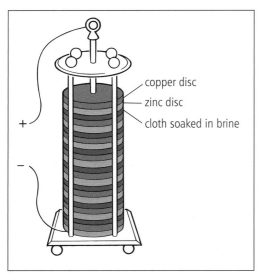

Picture 4 The first battery used zinc, copper and salt water.

copper disc
zinc disc
cloth soaked in brine

+

−

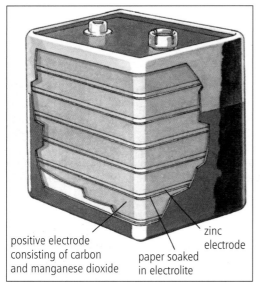

positive electrode consisting of carbon and manganese dioxide

zinc electrode

paper soaked in electrolite

Picture 5 A modern carbon–zinc battery.

Volta used this idea to make the first battery. He made it from alternating pairs of zinc and copper discs separated by cloth soaked in salt water (picture 4). This produced a continuous flow of what he called 'artificial electricity'.

Modern batteries work on the same principle (picture 5). There are many different kinds, but most use a pair of metals with a solution in between. The most common batteries use carbon and zinc separated by a solution (**electrolyte**) of ammonium chloride. Carbon often acts like a metal, electrically. Ordinary torch batteries are of this type.

Other batteries use such metals as nickel, iron, cadmium or mercury.

Galvanometers and **volts** are named after these two Italian scientists who did the early work in making 'artificial' electricity.

CELLS

A pair of electrodes separated by an ionic solution is called an **electric cell**. The solution has to contain ions so that charge can flow between the metal electrodes. A battery is really a collection of more than one cell, although we often use the word for any kind of cell.

■ Electricity and chemistry

The news of this battery soon spread across Europe and it was realised that electricity had a lot to do with chemistry. Michael Faraday's boss Sir Humphrey Davy became famous by using the new 'current' of electricity to break down compounds by what is called **electrolysis**. He discovered new elements like sodium, potassium, calcium and magnesium.

The use of various metals in electric cells led to the idea that metals can be arranged in an **electrochemical series** as shown in table 1. The voltage of a cell is decided by how far apart its metal electrodes are in this series.

Picture 6 shows a variety of batteries in use today.

Table 1 Part of the electrochemical series.

Element	Voltage compared with hydrogen
calcium	−2.76
sodium	−2.71
magnesium	−2.37
zinc	−0.78
cadmium	−0.40
hydrogen	0.00
copper	+0.34
mercury	+0.79

Picture 6 All these batteries rely on the electrochemical series.

Activities ICT

A Fruit electricity

It is possible to get electricity out of a lemon. All you have to do is to stick in two electrodes made of different metals. Design an investigation to see how effective this source of electricity is. Check your plan with your teacher before you carry it out.

Will it work with other fruits? What metals work best? Is this a practical, economic source of electricity?

B Using batteries 1

1 Make a list of everyday devices that use batteries to make them work.

2 For each one, say why batteries are used instead of mains electricity.

3 Find out the cost of a battery and how long it will run one of the devices you have listed.

4 Look at the labelling on the device. Try to find out its power in watts or kilowatts. Calculate the cost of using batteries to run it, per kilowatt-hour. Is it cheaper or dearer than using mains electricity?

(Mains electrical energy costs about 6p per kilowatt-hour.)

C Using batteries 2

Find out the answers to the following questions. You can ask people, read pamphlets, use a library or the Internet.

1 List as many different types of battery as you can (i.e. based on different combinations of chemicals).

2 In what way are car batteries different from ordinary 'torch type' batteries?

3 Many pocket calculators use solar cells. How do solar cells work?

4 What is 'animal electricity'?

D The electrochemical series

Design an experiment to check the order in which elements appear in the electrochemical series. You can use a voltmeter (preferably a digital one) and a solution of dilute acid. Suitable elements include: copper, zinc, nickel, magnesium, aluminium, iron and tin.

Do not carry out your experiment until you have checked it for safety with your teacher.

(Hint: to get reliable results make sure that the samples are clean. Use some emery cloth to scrape off any dirt, grease or layers of oxide.)

Questions

1 Name four metals that are used in making batteries.

2 How could you use four 1.5 V cells to make a 6 V battery? Draw a simple diagram of the arrangement.

3 What do you think happens when a battery 'runs down'?

4 A one-cell battery is labelled 1.5 V. It is used in a device that takes a current of 0.2 A from it. It runs out after 10 hours of continuous use.

   a What power does the battery supply?

   b How much energy does it deliver?

   c How many coulombs of charge does it supply?

   (You will need to use some of the formulae given in table 1, topic E1.)

5 a What are ions?

   b Why does the solution in a battery have to contain ions?

How does it work? An electric bell

The diagram below shows the main parts of an electric bell. Your task is to describe how it works. You can use some clues, which are given here.

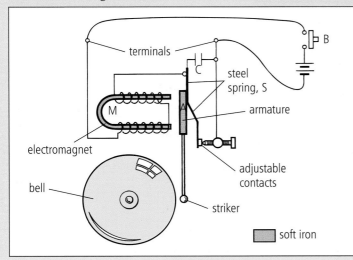

Facts

1 When you press the bell-push (a switch, B), current flows through the circuit that includes the electromagnet.

2 The core of the electromagnet (M) is made of an alloy (e.g. 'soft iron') which is easily magnetised in a magnetic field, but loses its magnetism very quickly when the field disappears.

3 The bell hammer is connected to a piece of springy steel (S), which has another piece of soft iron attached to it (A).

Clues

What happens to the circuit when the electromagnet pulls A towards it?

Then what happens to the electromagnet?

Tasks

1 Now describe as clearly and logically as you can how the bell keeps on ringing as long as you keep your finger on the bell-push.

2 The circuit also contains a capacitor (C). This helps to stop damage that might be caused by high-voltage sparking. Where does this voltage come from?

Seeing further and more clearly

The Hubble Space Telescope was launched in April 1990. It had been designed over a period of 20 years, and will cost $8 billion. It will be effective in space for just 15 years. Picture 1 shows what it looks like in space. The main tube is a Newtonian telescope, with a very large main mirror.

The telescope is designed to see further and more clearly into the depths of space than ever before. The telescope can be used to send its images to one of several detecting instruments in turn. The most spectacular results will probably come from the 'wide-field' camera. This can take large, clear pictures of large objects like nearby galaxies and planets.

It will get its advantages by being outside the Earth's atmosphere. Earthbound telescopes have to look through many kilometres of air. This air makes stars 'twinkle' – which means that their images dance about and aren't clear. Using bigger telescopes just means getting a bigger blur. Also, some radiations are absorbed by the atmosphere, and so never reach the Earth's surface.

Astronomers rarely look through telescopes. The images of stars and galaxies are usually recorded on film. But this method is no good for the Hubble Telescope! Instead, it uses silicon chips.

These chips are very thin layers of semiconductor material. They contain thousands of tiny photon detectors, the pixels. There are a quarter of a million of these to every square centimetre of chip. The photons of light trigger off each pixel when they hit it. They are over a hundred times more sensitive than the best film, so they can detect much fainter images. They are also small enough to make accurate pictures.

They are called charge-coupled devices (CCDs), and picture 2 shows a part of one of them. Four of them are used together in the wide-field camera in the Space Telescope. When photons of light hit a pixel, it releases an electron. This charged particle then moves to form a current. The currents from all the pixels are very carefully aligned to form a signal which can be sent back to Earth. The number of electrons from each pixel tells us how much light hit it. A computer is used to convert the signal current into a picture.

Picture 1   The Hubble Space telescope.

This is just like the way TV works. Indeed, modern TV cameras and digital cameras use CCDs, which means that they are sensitive enough to take pictures in the dark – you can see this in nearly every TV news bulletin.

The image is made on the array of CCDs by the main telescope. They can detect all kinds of radiation – light, UV and even X-rays. The telescope can't focus X-rays – they go straight through it! But light and UV can be focused very accurately. The mirror is curved, and 2 metres in diameter. Its aluminium surface is smoothed to a tenth of a wavelength of light. If it was scaled up to be the size of the USA the biggest bump on it would be just 2 centimetres high. This means it can make best use of the accuracy given by the CCDs.

Now try the following questions.

1   What are the advantages of having a telescope in space, compared with one on Earth?

2   Give a reason why cameras with photographic film would not be much use in the Hubble Telescope.

3   Explain what you understand by the word photon.

4   Why does the mirror surface have to be so smooth?

5   What is the advantage of having the main mirror as large as possible?

6   Give two advantages of using CCDs in this telescope.

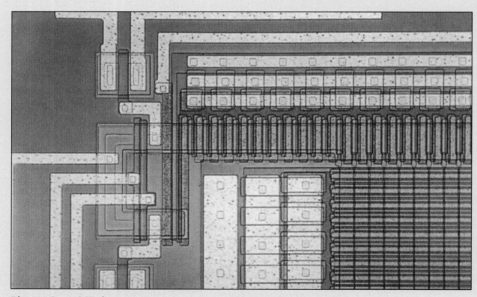

Picture 2   A CCD detector.

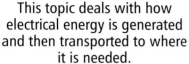

The electricity industry

This topic deals with how electrical energy is generated and then transported to where it is needed.

Picture 1   Drax Power Station near Selby, North Yorkshire.

THE POWER STATION

Picture 1 shows a large power station. You can see the huge stock of coal that will be taken in at one end. At the other end are the pylons holding the wires through which the electricity will be carried away. The diagram (picture 2) shows the main parts of the power station where the energy conversions take place.

■ The energy changes in a power station

Energy is released when coal burns with the oxygen of the air. This energy is used to boil water and then heat the steam to a high temperature. Burning coal also produces large amounts of carbon dioxide which goes into the atmosphere, together with other waste gases such as sulphur dioxide.

The steam is made very hot so that it is at a very high pressure. This means that it can provide very large forces to turn the huge steam turbines. This takes energy from the steam, which cools down, but doesn't become so cool that it condenses back into water.

The spinning turbines (picture 3) are connected to the coils of large generators. These coils carry current and act as large electromagnets. As they spin they induce a high voltage in the fixed coils surrounding them (see page 188 and picture 4). This causes a current which is fed into the **National Grid** system that carries the electricity to wherever it is needed (picture 5).

Picture 3   The turbine generator room of a power station.

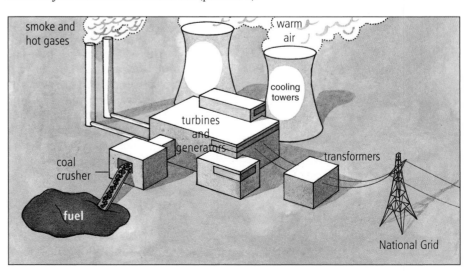

Picture 2   The main parts of a power station.

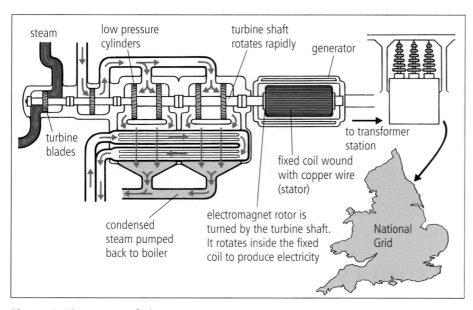

Picture 4 The structure of a large generator.

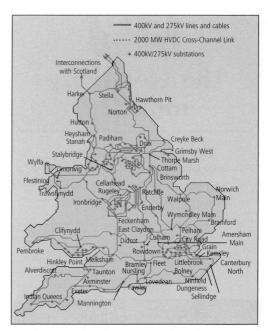

Picture 5 The main power lines of the National Grid.

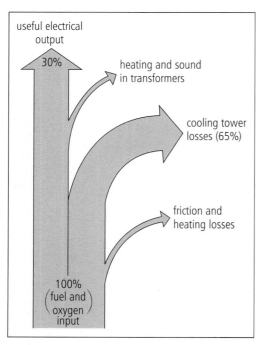

Picture 6 Energy flow in a power station that is 30% efficient.

■ Energy flow in a power station

Picture 6 shows the energy flow through a typical power station. A large power station might be rated at 1000 megawatts. This means that every second it delivers 1000 million joules of energy. This is about the same as the total power output that could be produced by every human being in the United Kingdom working flat out. No modern industrial country could survive on slave labour!

But to produce this energy, fuel equivalent to an energy of 3000 million joules per second has to be supplied. *Two-thirds of the energy input is wasted.*

This means that most power stations powered by fossil fuels can only be 30 to 40% **efficient**.

HOW IS THE ENERGY WASTED?

Some of the waste is 'accidental', because energy leaks out to warm up the air. For example, it moves as hot air from the boiler chimneys, and wiring gets hot.

But most of the waste is *necessary* waste. This is because the turbines can't take all of the energy out of the steam. This leaves lots of steam which is still warm, but cooler than it was when it went in, and too cool to make any turbines work.

This is the reason for the cooling towers. They are used to take energy from the 'used' steam, so condensing it back to water. This energy usually ends up warming a river or the sea.

This waste seems a great pity, but it is a consequence of one of the most ruthless laws of physics. This is the Second Law of Thermodynamics, which says that whenever you try to do something useful with thermal energy some of it always ends up in the wrong place (see topic D5).

In this example, the wasted energy goes into the cooling system and eventually into the surroundings.

CAN WE MAKE BETTER USE OF THIS WASTE ENERGY?

The waste energy can be put to good use. It is stored in warm water. The water is not hot enough to be useful to make electricity – it could not make the steam turbines work. But is quite warm enough to heat homes and other buildings.

In Germany most towns have their own small power stations, and they often pipe the 'waste' hot water to people's homes to keep them centrally heated. These are called **combined heat and power schemes**. They reduce waste and make electricity cheaper.

In the UK most power stations are larger and have been built a long way from towns and cities. This means that using them to produce 'combined heat and power' is not economic.

ALTERNATING CURRENT

The turbines spin the field coils of the generators at high speeds. The wiring is arranged to give **alternating current**. This is done by making the voltage produced by each coil change direction every half-turn. This means that the current changes direction as well. It flows one way for half the time, then in the opposite direction for the next half. This change-over occurs every 1/100 of a second. How this is done is shown in picture 7. Only one coil is drawn, to make the idea clearer.

The rate of spinning and the number of coils is designed to make each coil change (**alternate**) its voltage and current completely 50 times a second.

The speed of movement, the large magnetic field and the large number of turns used mean that the voltage produced is quite high: 25 000 V.

There is a good reason for producing alternating current (a.c.) rather than direct current (d.c.), like a battery produces. It is because it makes it easy to change the voltage of the supply, using transformers. This is explained next.

HOW DO WE GET OUR ELECTRICITY?

The generator produces a large current at an output voltage of 25 000 V, which is extremely dangerous. It could be arranged for this to be 230 V, as used in the home, but this would be very uneconomic. In fact the voltage is made even higher as it leaves the power station. It is raised to 275 000 V or even 400 000 V. The reason for this is the resistance in the cables which take the electricity from the power station to a home or factory.

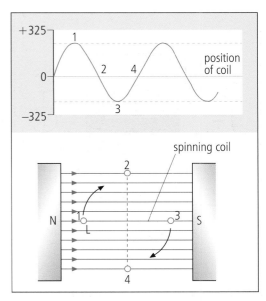

Picture 7 The voltage of the mains supply swings between +325 V and −325 V, 50 times a second
Numbers 1, 2, 3, 4 show where one side (L) of the spinning coil is when it produces the outputs marked 1, 2, 3, and 4 on the graph.

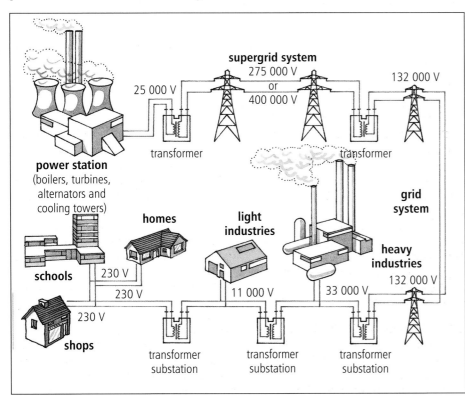

Picture 8 Voltages in the National Grid system.

Picture 9 A power cable.

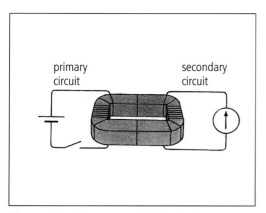

Picture 10 Electromagnetic induction happens when a magnetic field is changing or a conductor cuts through the field.

■ Why is electricity transmitted at very high voltages?

Most people live and work many hundreds of miles from the power stations that produce our electricity. This is because the stations are built near good supplies of fuel and cooling water.

Whenever a current flows in a conductor some power is lost in heating the conductor. Engineers can cut down this energy loss by supplying the current at very high voltages.

The power loss in a conductor is given by $P = VI$, where V is the voltage drop across the conductor. We can change this to give power loss in terms of the current I and the resistance R of the cable. This gives $P = I^2R$ (because $V = IR$). The engineers want the loss in the cable to be as little as possible. They do this by making the resistance (R) of the cable as small as possible. The resistance can be cut down by using very thick cables (see picture 9).

Even so, there will always be some cable resistance, and there comes a point when the cost of making the cable is greater than the value of the energy we are trying to save. The only other thing they can change is the current in the cable. This is done by using very high voltages.

HIGH VOLTAGE, LOW CURRENT

The delivered power is also given by $P = VI$. This time V is the voltage drop at the end where the customer wants to use it. The power is the same for a low current at a high voltage as for a high current at a low voltage. Suppose the customer wants 100 000 W of power to be delivered. This could be done, for example, either by sending 200 A at 500 V or by sending 1 A at 100 000 V.

Now suppose the cable resistance is 2 ohms. The cable loss in the first case (voltage 500 V, current 200 A) is:

$$\text{power loss} = I^2R = 200 \times 200 \times 2 = 80\,000 \text{ watts}$$

This would leave only 20 000 watts for the customer!

In the second case (voltage 100 000 V, current 1 A) we get

$$\text{power loss} = I^2R = 1 \times 1 \times 2 = 2 \text{ watts!}$$

It makes very sound economic sense to send the electric power down the cable at high voltages. But you would not be too happy at having a mains supply at 100 000 volts. This is a very dangerous voltage. This is where transformers come in.

■ What transformers do

Faraday's experiment with two coils (page 187) gives the basic idea of how transformers work. We can switch a current on and off in the primary coil. This produces and then takes away a magnetic field in the iron core (picture 10). The changing field induces a voltage in the secondary coil.

Now, when an alternating current is supplied to the primary coil it also produces a changing field in the iron core. This field changes as the current changes. Just as with the switching experiment this changing field also induces a changing voltage in the secondary coil.

But, if you have investigated transformers, you will know that the voltage in the secondary coil depends also on **how many turns** there are in the coils. If there are more turns in the secondary than in the primary coil, the output voltage is bigger than the input voltage. If there are fewer turns in the secondary than in the primary, the voltage is reduced. Thus we can have **step-up transformers**, which increase the voltage, and **step-down transformers**, which do the opposite (picture 11).

This leads to the transformer rule:

$$\frac{\text{Output voltage}}{\text{Input voltage}} = \frac{\text{secondary turns}}{\text{primary turns}} \quad \text{or} \quad \frac{V_{\text{out}}}{V_{\text{in}}} = \frac{N_{\text{sec}}}{N_{\text{pri}}}$$

step-down transformer
ratio of number of turns 2:1
voltage ratio 2:1

step-up transformer
ratio of number of turns 1:3
voltage ratio 1:3

Picture 11 Step-down and step-up transformers.

■ Transformers and the Grid System

Step-up transformers are used at power stations (pictures 1 and 2) to raise the 25 000 V produced by the generators to the higher voltages which are so efficient for transmitting electricity over long distances. The network of cables carrying current at these very high voltages is called the **National Grid**.

The cables are carried on tall pylons which are easy to spot when you travel about the country. Very many people live in Southern England, and they need a lot of electricity. Some of it comes from as far away as Scotland or France (by undersea cables). The normal Grid supply voltage is 275 000 V, but for moving electricity very long distances the **Supergrid** is used, using a voltage of 400 000 V.

At the customer end, step-down transformers are used. They lower the Grid voltage to the 550 V used in some factories and the 230 V used in the home, in shops, etc.

CLEAN AND EFFICIENT ENERGY?

Devices that are run from electricity are the most efficient of all the ones we use in the home or in industry. Electric motors are about 90% efficient, compared with a petrol engine which may be only 20% efficient. Similarly, electric trains are three times as efficient as diesel engines. An electric fire uses 100% of the energy it receives to heat the room. Coal fires and oil central heating systems lose some energy in hot air and fumes going out of the chimney.

These figures are impressive, but a little misleading. Back at the power station the laws of thermal energy take their inevitable toll (see above). Producing the electricity in the first place is only 30% efficient, which is about the same efficiency as a diesel engine. This loss is there even if we use nuclear energy to power the turbines. The loss is due to the nature of all **thermal engines**, like turbines, that rely on heating to make them work.

Thermal power stations also produce much of the polluting gases, such as suphur oxides and nitrogen oxides, that cause acid rain. This is because coal and oil contain impurities. But what is more, all fuels produce carbon dioxide when they are burnt. It has only recently been realised that this 'harmless' gas may be seriously affecting the environment on a global scale. It is the major gas involved in the 'Greenhouse effect'.

Another problem is that sooner or later, the fossil fuels that we use to run power stations will be used up.

NUCLEAR POWER STATIONS

Nuclear power stations are just about as efficient (or inefficient) as oil or coal-fired power stations. They normally produce little pollution – unless there is an accident, as happened at Chernobyl in 1986. But they do generate radioactive waste, which needs to be stored for perhaps many thousands of years (see topic F5).

ARE THERE OTHER WAYS OF GETTING ELECTRICAL ENERGY?

Electricity is not a *source* of energy. It is a very useful means of *transferring* energy. Power stations and batteries are systems that use sources of energy like the combustion of fuel, nuclear fission and reactions between chemicals to make electric charge move along wires. The moving charges can make things hot (in water heaters etc.) or move things (using electric motors). Most sources of energy are non-renewable. Sooner or later we shall use up all the natural fossil fuels, and possibly even the radioactive elements used in fission reactors. Both sources of energy have environmental effects in that their waste products can cause more or less dangerous pollution. These facts have led to a great interest in non-polluting or renewable energy sources.

Picture 13 A hydroelectric power station.

RENEWABLE ENERGY SOURCES

Taking the very long view there are no such things as renewable energy sources. But what we mean are sources that rely on sunlight, winds, waves, tides, flowing water or biological materials. All these rely on energy from the Sun – and the Sun will eventually die, as even stars do (see topic G5). But our Sun is likely to keep providing this energy for the next 10 billion years or so, which is forever on a human time scale.

The interior of the Earth is hot (see page 252) and can be used as an energy source. Iceland makes use of this **geothermal** energy to provide hot water for space heating in its main towns. This energy is largely due to radioactive decay in rocks which will eventually cease, but the half life of the elements involved is many millions of years.

Hydroelectric power stations provide most of the energy transferred electrically in Norway and they are important also in France. The systems rely on gravitational potential energy as an energy source in mountain areas with enough rainfall or snow melt to provide water that can turn turbines as it flows downhill. The water is recycled by the natural global water cycle, powered by energy from the Sun, that returns lowland and sea water to the mountains.

The kinetic energy of wind is one of the oldest sources of renewable energy. Sails have powered ships for thousands of years. Windmills have been in use since about 600 AD and their use as generators of electricity is becoming more and more popular. They are set up in *wind farms* containing arrays of large windmills: the wind farm in Delabole (Cornwall) contains 10 wind generators each able to produce 400 kW of power when the wind blows at a speed of at least 5 m/s. Wind is an unreliable energy source; it doesn't blow at a steady speed at all times. However, such systems can be used to top up a steady supply available from conventional power stations.

Sea waves also carry a great deal of kinetic energy. As with wind, they are an unreliable source and it is not as easy to collect the energy for useful applications. **Tides** are caused by gravitational forces exerted by the Sun and Moon. This rise and fall of sea water can be tapped as an energy source. The best known tidal power station is at the Rance Estuary in Brittany, France.

Picture 12 A wave powered generator.

Picture 14 Alternative energy sources.

Sunlight and the **infra-red** radiation from the Sun can be used directly to generate electricity or heat water and buildings. Well designed buildings can make best use of the available solar energy and so reduce the need for other energy sources. **Photovoltaic** cells made from semiconductor materials can generate electricity, but at present they are expensive. They are useful in warm sunny climates where heating is not a large drain on energy sources, and particularly in isolated places which would be expensive to connect to a national grid system.

Biomass or biological fuels like wood may be renewable if properly managed. Wood is the main domestic fuel in many tropical countries. Agricultural wastes, like straw and sugar cane stalks, have been considered as an energy supply. Such materials may be fermented to produce an alcohol which can be used to run internal combustion engines. Again, these materials provide energy at too high a cost to compete with fossil fuels at present prices.

CONCENTRATED AND DISPERSED ENERGY SOURCES

The problem with most 'alternative' energy sources as described above is that the energy is spread over a wide area or volume of space. The materials involved have a low *energy density*. Think of the energy in wind compared with the same amount of energy stored in a material like oil – or in uranium. This means that wind farms need more ground area than fossil fuel power stations of the same output. See page 148 for more about energy sources.

CHEAP ELECTRICITY?

Coal-fired power stations can't be switched off easily. The furnaces have to be kept going all the time, because if they cool down they get badly damaged. Thus many power stations are running all the time, both day and night.

At night most people are asleep. Factories are closed down, few trains are running. The demand for electricity is much less than in the daytime.

But the power stations are still burning fuel, even if the turbines are not working at full capacity. It is more economical for the electricity supply industry to sell electrical energy cheaply at night than not to sell it at all. Thus many homes and factories have heaters which are time-switched so that they use only night-time electricity.

Activities

A Somewhere near your house or school there will be a transformer which reduces the voltage of the electricity supply to 230 V. Find the transformer, sketch it and describe it. Write down any official notices that might be on it and explain what they say.

B Ask questions, read pamphlets, look up books in the library, use the Internet to help you answer one or more of the following questions.

1 Where is your nearest power station? What fuel(s) does it use?

2 Why is electricity cheaper at night?

3 In the mountains of North Wales, at Ffestiniog and Dinorwic, there are special kinds of power station called 'pumped-storage' stations. What are these and how do they work?

4 Where in the British Isles would you expect to find:
  a hydroelectric power stations,
  b nuclear power stations,
  c Wind farms.
  What factors decide where such stations are built?

5 How does the electricity industry cope with the problem that much less electricity is used in summer than in winter?

Questions

1 Explain what jobs the following do in a coal-fired power station:
  a generators,
  b cooling towers,
  c step-up transformers.

2 a What is the National Grid?
  b Why are the cables that carry electricity held so far above the ground?
  c Electricity is sent along the National Grid at very high voltages. Why must they be so high?

3 The graph (picture 15) shows the cost per metre of cable of different thickness. It also shows the cost per metre of the power loss in the cable due to resistance heating. Both of these quantities are plotted against cables of different thickness.

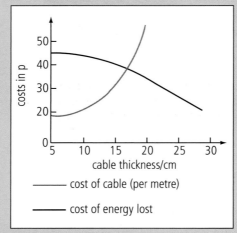

Picture 15

a Why does the cost of lost power go down when the cable gets thicker?

b Why does the cost per metre of cable rise when the cable gets thicker?

c What is the combined cost of cable-plus-power-loss for cables of thickness: (i) 10 cm, (ii) 15 cm?

d From the graph, what is the most economical cable thickness to choose?

e The graph for the cost of the cable rises much more quickly than the power saving cost falls. Suggest a reason for this.

4 a Calculate the current that needs to be taken from a 25 MW power station at a generating voltage of 2500 V.

b What would this current be reduced to if the voltage was stepped up to 400 000 V for the National Supergrid?

c What would be the effect of this reduction in current on power loss in the cables?

So far we have looked at electric charges flowing in wires, liquids or gases. Interesting things happen when we get the charges out on their own, in empty space …

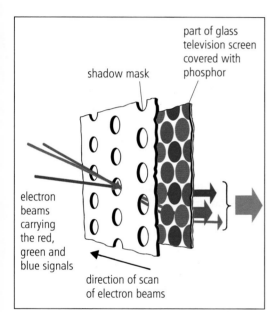

Picture 1 The picture tube screen has more than 300 000 coloured phosphor dots arranged in groups of three on its surface. A metal mask behind the screen has holes which keep each of the three electron beams in line with its own colour dots and away from dots of other colours.

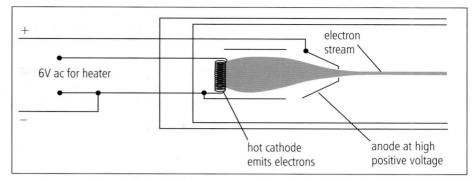

Picture 2 The electron gun in a TV tube.

HIGH SPEED ELECTRONS MAKE PICTURES

A TV tube is mostly empty space. The picture screen is covered on the inside by a **phosphor**. This is a chemical which glows when it is hit by electrons (picture 1). The electrons have to be travelling fast. In a colour tube they need to hit the phosphor at over 15 million metres a second.

■ The electron gun

The electrons are fired from the narrow end of the tube by a device called an **electron gun** (picture 2). The electrons are produced by heating a metal oxide so that it just glows red hot. This is called **thermionic emission**.

This part of the gun is kept negative and is called the **cathode**. The electrons that 'boil off' the cathode are attracted by a metal cylinder which is kept at a very high positive voltage – the **anode**. This produces a force which accelerates them to a very high speed.

The space inside the tube must be completely empty of any gas, otherwise the electrons would collide with the gas molecules. The stream of electrons is focused into a narrow beam which has to be very accurately aimed so that the phosphor screen glows in exactly the right places at exactly the right times to make a picture.

■ Making the picture

The picture is made by **scanning** the electron beam across the screen in a series of lines which are then moved from top to bottom of the screen. There are 625 lines in a screenful, and the screen is completely scanned by the beam 25 times a second (picture 3). If you wave your fingers to and fro in front of your eyes whilst watching TV you can see odd 'gaps'. You don't normally see these gaps because it

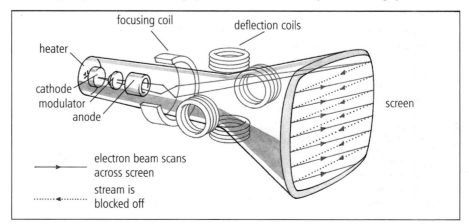

Picture 3 Scanning action. Only a few scans are shown – there are actually 625 in each 'screenful'.

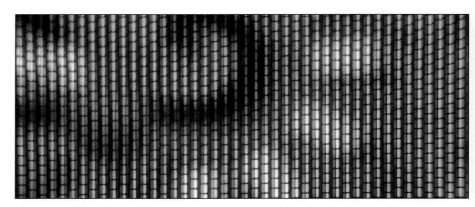

Picture 4 The 'pixels' in a TV screen. A TV picture is made of thousands of these.

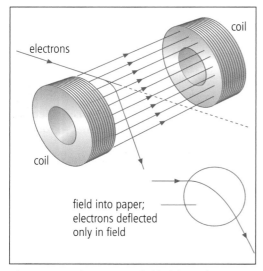

Picture 5 In the magnetic field of the coils, electrons are deflected as shown.

(Labels within Picture 5: coil, electrons, coil, field into paper; electrons deflected only in field)

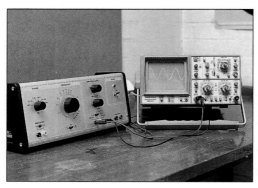

Picture 6 A cathode ray oscilloscope is a very useful instrument.

takes about a twentieth of a second for your eye – brain system to wipe away a picture. The pictures come quicker than that, so one picture merges neatly with the next. Better pictures can be made with more lines in a screen, and the new 'high definition' TV sets use many more lines.

■ Controlling the electrons

The electron beam has to move across the screen very quickly and very accurately. In a colour tube the beam is split into three, so that it can hit three separate picture cells (pixels). The pixels glow red, blue or green (picture 4). These are the primary colours (see page 46). These can be combined to give the illusion of all the colours of the rainbow.

The electrons are directed to the right place by a strong magnetic field. In picture 3 you can see the coils of wire that produce this field. Its strength is controlled by the signal sent out by the TV station and picked up by the TV aerial.

The electron stream is of course just a flow of charge – an electric current. Just like the current in the coils of an electric motor the electron stream can be moved by a magnetic field. The field can direct them to where they have to go to make the picture.

Electrons are the lightest charged objects in the universe, so they change direction very quickly. The magnetic fields have to change very quickly to produce a new picture 25 times a second, but the electrons are light enough to follow the changes.

Picture 5 shows how a stream of electrons is affected by a magnetic field. Just as in a motor, the field has to be at right angles to the electron stream, and the direction of movement is at right angles to both field and current direction.

■ The cathode ray oscilloscope

Another way of changing the direction of a stream of electrons is to make use of electric forces. This is the method used in the measuring and display instrument called a **cathode ray oscilloscope** or CRO (picture 6).

The electron gun in a CRO fires its beam between two pairs of metal plates (picture 7). A positively-charged plate attracts the negatively-charged electrons. The plates are arranged at right angles so that when voltages are applied the electron stream is deflected either up or down or from side to side.

The plates that move the stream vertically are called the **Y-plates**. The **X-plates** move the electrons horizontally. In a CRO the X-plates are used to move the beam steadily across the screen from left to right. This done by a steadily increasing positive voltage applied to the right-hand plate. The steady movement of the beam across the screen is called a **time-base**. It is like the 'time axis' you might draw on a graph. It allows us to see the pattern produced by an effect that is changing with time.

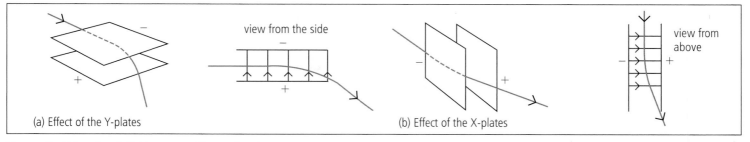

(a) Effect of the Y-plates   view from the side   (b) Effect of the X-plates   view from above

Picture 7   Using electric fields to control beam direction.

The signal to be studied is applied to the Y-plates. For example, if we apply an alternating voltage it makes the beam move up and down. This is because the top plate becomes alternately positive and negative. When this plate is positive the electrons are pulled up. When it is negative they are pushed down.

This up and down movement is very fast, because the mains supply changes direction 50 times a second. If the time-base is switched off we see a straight vertical line. This is because the line is being traced, over and over again, 50 times a second.

But if we use the time-base, set to the correct speed, we see a wavy line which shows us how the voltage is changing with time. This is made visible because the beam is being moved sideways at a steady rate (see picture 8).

■ X-rays

X-rays are yet another example of a scientific discovery made by accident. A German physicist, Wilhelm Konrad Röntgen, was investigating electron streams when he noticed that an unused phosphor screen was glowing. The strange thing was that it was on the other side of the lab. It was much too far away for any 'leakage' of electrons to get to it through the air.

Röntgen brought the screen closer and found that it glowed even brighter. After testing further he proved that the glow wasn't being caused by electrons but by an unknown kind of radiation. Because he didn't know what it was he called them 'X' rays.

Röntgen worked out that the X-rays are produced when a fast stream of electrons hits glass or metal (picture 9).

Then he discovered the most interesting property of X-rays. When he put his hand in the path of the rays he saw that they cast a shadow on the screen. The shadow of his hand was a very strange one. *It showed the bones as well as the flesh* (picture 10).

Within a few weeks of this discovery in 1895, X-rays were being used in hospitals to look for broken bones, swallowed pins, blocked intestines and damaged lungs. But just as with static electricity 200 years earlier, some people

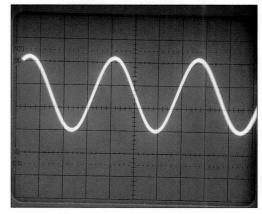

Picture 8   A combination of up and down and sideways movement can draw out a graph.

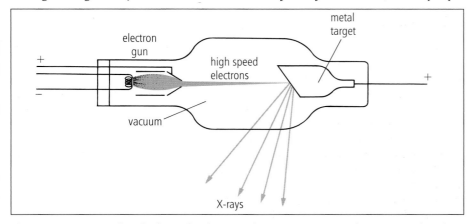

Picture 9   An X-ray tube. The faster the electrons, the more penetrating the X-rays produced.

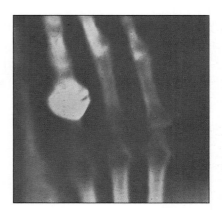

Picture 10   An X-ray shadowgraph of Mrs Röntgen's hand.

Electrons in space   **203**

Picture 11 A modern X-ray machine in use.

went mad about X-rays. They had 'skeleton pictures' taken of themselves and their families. They tried to use them to cure all kinds of diseases.

It took twenty years for doctors to notice that people who used (and misused) X-ray machines tended to get serious cancers. X-rays are invisible, highly energetic electromagnetic waves. These waves interact with matter and ionise atoms. They thus kill the delicate cells of living matter. But they can also alter the cells, making them turn into cancer cells. All ionising radiation, such as that given out by radioactive materials, can do this.

We know now how to manage X-rays so that the 'dose' given to people is as small as possible. Nurses and technicians who operate the machines are well shielded from them (picture 11). X-rays are only used on people when it is medically necessary, after carefully weighing up the balance between harm and benefit.

Activities

A Moving electron streams

Electron streams are used in TV sets and in cathode ray oscilloscopes such as the ones used in your lab. Find out what other devices use electron streams in this kind of way. Write a sentence or two about each device that describes or explains what the device is used for.

B Using a cathode ray oscilloscope

1. Look at the control knobs and switches on the front of the CRO. Find the following: on-off switch, focus, brightness, X shift, Y shift, time-base.

2. Find the spot!
   Switch on the oscilloscope. The most difficult part now follows – find the spot! If you are lucky you will see a spot or line already on the screen. If

not, switch the time-base off (or to EXT X), turn the brightness to the right to give maximum, and use the X SHIFT and Y SHIFT together to try to get a spot of light in the centre of the screen. Use a combination of FOCUS and BRIGHTNESS control to make the spot small, clear but not too bright. If you can't find it ask for help.

3. What does a CRO measure?
   Find the Y INPUT. Use the red connection (it may be marked 'dc' or '+') and connect one 1.5 V cell between it and the **earth connection** (marked '–' or '⏚'). If nothing happens to the spot of light try adjusting the control marked Y GAIN (or 'Y amplitude')

   What happens when you (a) reverse the cell connections, (b) use more than one cell? What does this investigation tell you about what a CRO measures?

4. Using the time-base
   First, remove the batteries you used in part 3 and replace them with an a.c. supply at about 2 or 3 volts. Draw what you see on the screen. Use the X SHIFT to move the spot sideways fairly quickly. Do this once or twice and remember what effect it has. Then find the TIME BASE control and switch it on. Try it at slow, medium and fast. Use the VARIABLE control. The idea is to get a clear, fixed trace of the a.c. supply on the screen (see picture 8).

5. Try 'looking at' the dc output of the supply. How is it different from the d.c. from a battery that you looked at in 3?

6. If you have time, connect a microphone to the CRO and talk, whistle, play music or sing into it. You may need to adjust the TIME BASE and/or the Y GAIN to get a clear trace.

Questions

1. What is a vacuum? Why does a TV tube need to have a good vacuum inside it?

2. Explain briefly how an 'electron gun' works.

3. Draw diagrams to show how electrons would move in the fields given in picture 12 (look at picture 7 to help you).

4. Picture 13 shows a CRO screen with the voltage of a 50 Hz a.c. mains supply displayed on it. Draw diagrams to show what the trace on the screen would be like if: (a) the time-base were to be switched off, (b) the time-base speed were to be halved.

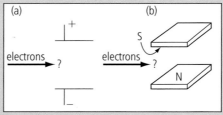

Picture 12

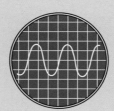

Picture 13

5. Why are X-rays dangerous?

6. X-rays are used in hospitals to look at broken limbs and other parts of the body. Apart from this medical use, what else are X-rays useful for?

Particles

Dr Brown and Dr Einstein

This exercise is about Brownian motion. Before you go any further, you should see Brownian motion for yourself. It was first observed using pollen grains, but you can see it most easily in smoke. You will probably use apparatus like that shown in picture 1. You should see the tiny particles of smoke dancing and jiggling around, as shown in picture 2.

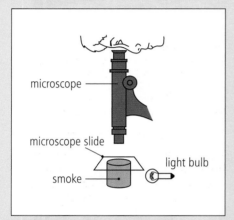

Picture 1 Looking for Brownian motion.

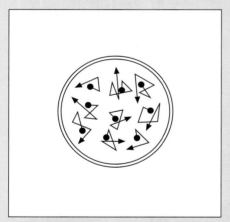

Picture 2 Smoke particles in Brownian motion.

Brown discovers, Einstein explains

In 1827, a Scottish biologist called Robert Brown was studying pollen grains. He used a microscope to examine pollen grains suspended in water. To his surprise, he noticed that the tiny grains were constantly jiggling around in a completely random way.

He explained what he saw by saying that the pollen grains were alive, and moving of their own accord.

In 1905, the great scientist Albert Einstein was 26 years old. In that year he did three pieces of work, all three of them good enough to win a Nobel Prize. There is more about Einstein in topic B9.

One of Einstein's papers gave an explanation of Brownian motion, using the kinetic theory. Einstein suggested that the motion happens because the grains of pollen are bombarded by

Picture 3 Robert Brown discovered Brownian motion.

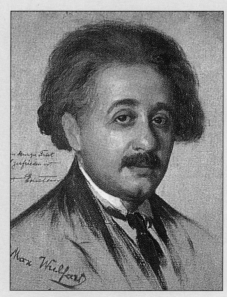

Picture 4 Albert Einstein.

tiny, fast-moving molecules of water. He even worked out how fast the motion should be, and his calculations matched what was actually observed.

At that time there were still some scientists who did not believe that atoms and molecules actually existed. Einstein's work on Brownian motion was a real breakthrough because it convinced even the doubters that atoms and molecules exist.

Imagine Brown met Einstein…
In this exercise you are going to act an imaginary discussion between Robert Brown and Albert Einstein. (Of course, they never actually met because Brown made his discovery over 50 years before Einstein was even born.)

Brown and Einstein would have had different theories about why Brownian motion occurs. Each would have argued for his theory. When scientists disagree on a theory, there is only one thing they can do. They suggest new experiments to test the theory.

Organising the exercise
There are several ways you could organise this exercise. One is to work in groups of four. Two of you will take the part of Brown, and two will be Einstein. The stages are as follows.

Stage 1. Brown speaks for 2 minutes. he describes what he has seen, and explains his theory that the grains move because they are alive.

Stage 2. Einstein speaks for 2 minutes. he describes his theory to explain why the grains move.

Stage 3. Brown speaks for 2 minutes. He gives his reaction to Einstein's theory, and explains why he does not believe it.

Stage 4. Einstein speaks for 2 minutes. he gives his reaction to what Brown has just said.

Stage 5. Brown speaks for 2 minutes. He suggests a new experiment that will test Einstein's theory.

Stage 6. Einstein speaks for 2 minutes. He suggests a new experiment that will test Brown's theory.

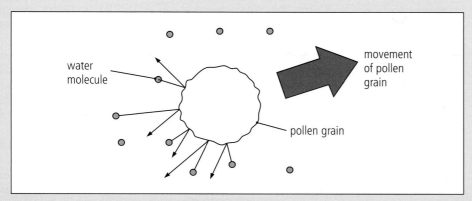

Picture 5 How Einstein explained Brownian motion.

Preparing what you will say
You need to decide how you will present your theory. It would be a good idea to use diagrams. You also need to decide what experiment you will suggest in stage 5 or 6.

These notes may help you.
Brown's theory. Brown believes the grains move because they are alive. After all, pollen is produced by living plants. Being a biologist, he has often seen microscopic organisms jiggling around under the microscope.

Try to get yourself into Brown's way of thinking. The idea of atoms and molecules seems strange to Brown. They are so small that it's impossible to see them, and there is no evidence that they actually exist. In his time, the idea of atoms and molecules was much less well known than it is today.

Einstein's theory. Einstein believes that the grains move because they are being bombarded by fast-moving molecules of water. The pollen grains may look small, but they are far bigger than the invisible molecules of water. Nevertheless, the water molecules move so fast that they can jolt the pollen grains when they collide with them. Picture 5 illustrates the theory.

After you have finished your presentation, discuss how it went.

Were the arguments convincing?

Were the ideas for new experiments good? Would they test the two theories conclusively? What results would you expect from the experiments?

Would Brown's theory have explained Brownian motion in smoke? Would Einstein's theory?

A very good model indeed

A good theory explains, predicts and makes a complicated world easier to understand.

Picture 1 John Dalton

Picture 2 Amedeo Avogadro

We know that matter can change from one state to another. For example liquid water can freeze and turn into solid ice or it can evaporate and turn into an invisible gas. From early times people have wondered about the connection between these states; not just for water but for all kinds of matter.

About 2000 years ago the Greek scientist Democritus reasoned like this: Take a piece of paper (or papyrus in his case!) and cut it in half. Now cut one of the halves in half again and so on. He reasoned that even if you had the finest blade you could not keep on doing this forever. Eventually you would reach something that was indivisible. He called this something an *atom* because *atomon* in Greek means indivisible.

Making a big leap forward Democritus then proposed that everything is made of atoms!

This was the beginning of the Atomic Theory. He thought that the composition of all atoms was the same and that they differed only in shape. At the time there was no real hard experimental evidence to back up his proposals. In fact it took until 1803 and the rather rough and ready work of the English chemist John Dalton before the theory was eventually put on a sounder basis.

Dalton's atomic theory also went further and predicted that different elements were composed of their own kind of atoms each having the same atomic weight. An atom of copper, for example, would have a different weight to an atom of carbon.

Finding the weight of an atom was a bit of a tall order at the time and Dalton had also made a mistake in thinking that all 'particles' are atoms.

A few years later (1811) Amedeo Avogadro realised that some particles are in fact molecules consisting of two or more atoms. We know now that a water molecule is a combination of one oxygen and two hydrogen atoms and that hydrogen gas is a molecule of two hydrogen atoms. Amazingly this breakthrough was ignored for the next 50 years until it was realised that using Avogadro's ideas it was possible to determine atomic and molecular masses.

But all this was *chemistry*: and physicists were very suspicious of these invisible objects that seem to have been invented just to make calculations easier. But they found the ideas useful in a model and in calculations about what happens when gases are compressed and heated. They developed the **kinetic theory of gases** – which turned out to be a very good theory indeed! But many physicists still refused to believe that atoms actually existed – see 'Dr Brown and Dr Einstein'.

THE PARTICLE THEORY OF GASES

■ Early work and basic laws explained

A gas is an awkward substance to handle. It expands to take up the entire shape of the container it is in and it tends to leak away very easily. Clearly the atoms or molecules (the particles) which make up the gas must be in motion.

Further evidence for this incessant chaotic motion is provided by smoke particles in air, which under a microscope can seen to jiggle about in a zigzag way. This effect is called **Brownian Motion.** See page 206 *Dr Brown and Dr Einstein.*

Any good particle theory applied to gases must be able to explain the basic laws that have been deduced from previous ideas or experiments.

■ Varying pressure and volume with temperature constant

Robert Boyle lived in the 17th century and knew practically nothing about the atomic theory. However he was the first to discover a simple law of gases.

He trapped some air in a glass tube with a column of mercury. By adding more mercury he increased the pressure acting on the gas, and its volume decreased. What really pleased him was the fact that this awkwardly chaotic substance gave rise to a very simple pattern linking pressure and volume.

Keeping the temperature constant, he found that if the pressure acting on the gas was doubled then the volume occupied by the gas was halved.

In fact he showed that the pressure of a fixed amount of gas at constant temperature was always in proportion to the *inverse* of its volume.

The results for a modern school experiment using apparatus as shown in picture 3 are shown in table 1. The units of pressure are **pascals** (1 Pa = 1 N/m²).

The simple pattern is stated in **Boyle's Law:**

For a fixed mass of gas kept at a constant temperature, the product *pressure times volume* **is a constant**.

As a formula:

$$P = \frac{\text{constant}}{V} \quad \text{or} \quad PV = \text{constant}$$

Or $P_1 \times V_1 = P_2 \times V_2$ where the volume V_1 changes to the volume V_2 when the pressure of the gas sample changes from P_1 to P_2.

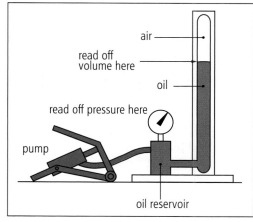

Picture 3   Using modern equipment to investigate how the volume of a gas depends on pressure.

Pressure/kPA	Volume/cm³
100	48
120	40
140	34
160	30
180	26
200	24
220	22
240	20
260	18
280	17
300	16

Table 1   Results obtained using the apparatus in picture 3 to investigate the relationship between **P** and **V** for a gas. The pressure is measured in kilopascals, kPa. Normal atmospheric pressure is 100 kPa.

A reminder about pressure

A weight exerts a force on the ground, but what happens depends not just on the force but on the area as well. Imagine two identical metal blocks put on soft ground.

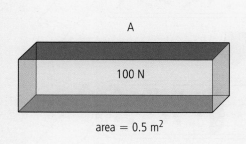

A

100 N

area = 0.5 m²

at A the base has a large area: the weight is supported and will not sink very far, if at all

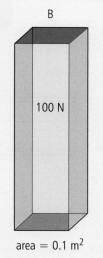

B

100 N

area = 0.1 m²

here at B, the weight is placed on a smaller base area. It is more likely to sink into the ground

Picture 4   Pressure.

At A, the pressure exerted by the weight is smaller than at B. Pressure is defined as

$$\text{Pressure} = \frac{\text{force}}{\text{area}}$$

$$P = \frac{F}{A}$$

Units: newtons per square metre (N/m²) or pascals (Pa)

For the weight at A: pressure = 100 N/0.5 m² = 200 Pa

For the weight at B: pressure = 100 N/0.1 m² = 1000 Pa

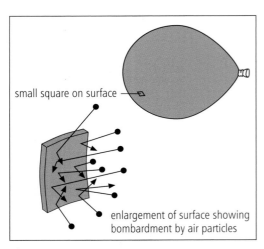

small square on surface

enlargement of surface showing bombardment by air particles

Picture 5 How a gas exerts pressure.

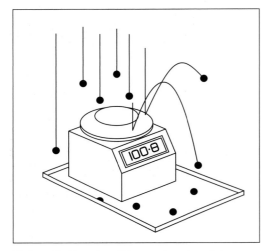

Picture 6 How does this experiment model gas pressure?

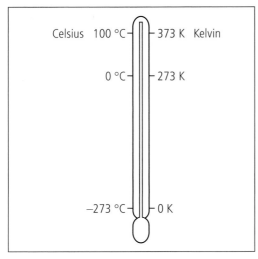

Celsius 100 °C — 373 K Kelvin

0 °C — 273 K

−273 °C — 0 K

Picture 8 The Celsius and Kelvin temperature scales.

Gas pressure can be explained in terms of particles as follows:

- The pressure exerted by a gas is caused by particles (atoms or molecules) that are in constant random motion. They collide with each other and the walls of the container.
- The greater the speed then the greater is the force exerted by the particles on the walls.
- The constant battering by millions of particles adds up to a steady force on each square millimetre, and this is what we call pressure.

This is known as the **Kinetic Theory** (kinetic is from the Greek for moving) Boyle's Law can also be explained in terms of this Kinetic Theory:

- The average speed of the particles depends on the temperature of the gas. Boyle's law says that the temperature and therefore the average speed of the particles must remain constant.
- If you halve the volume of the gas, the same number of particles get pushed into half the space. This means that they hit the walls twice as often and therefore the pressure doubles.

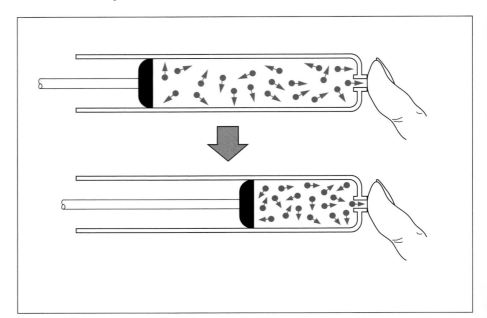

Picture 7 Why the volume of a gas affects its pressure. When the volume is decreased, the particles collide with the walls – and your fingers – more often.

■ Absolute Zero and the Kinetic Theory

The Celsius scale of temperature takes its zero (0 °C) as the freezing point of water. Lower temperatures than this certainly exist! The question is: How low can you get? According to the Kinetic Theory the lower the temperature then the lower is the average speed of the particles. Imagine, then, the temperature at which the particles stop moving altogether. This temperature is the same for all particles and takes a value of −273 °C. This is called **absolute zero** and it is impossible to get any colder than this.

It turns out to be very useful to have a temperature scale whose zero is absolute zero. This scale is called the Kelvin scale or the absolute temperature scale, and its units are kelvins (K) (picture 8).

Kelvins are the same size as degrees on the Celsius scale. To convert a Celsius temperature to a Kelvin temperature you add 273.

Thus 27 °C is (273 + 27) = 300 K.

■ Varying pressure and temperature, with volume constant

According to the Kinetic Theory the pressure of a fixed volume of gas should increase with temperature because the average speed of the particles will also increase. This prediction is certainly true. If a canister of gas is heated a lot its pressure can increase dangerously to point where it may explode (picture 9).

Experiment shows that the pressure of a constant volume of gas is directly proportional to its temperature in kelvins.

As a formula: $P = \text{constant} \times T$

Or $\dfrac{P_1}{T_1} = \dfrac{P_2}{T_2}$ This is called **the Pressure Law**.

The Kinetic Theory explains:

- Keeping the volume constant means that the walls of the container do not move.
- Since the average speed of the particles increases with temperature they hit the walls harder and more often, hence the rise in pressure. (Picture 10.)

THE THREE VARIABLES FOR A GAS

You have probably realised by now that there are three variables for a fixed quantity of gas: pressure (P), volume (V) and absolute temperature (T).

It's best to investigate the variables two at a time, so that you can see how one affects the other without the third interfering. So we keep one of the three variables constant and see what happens when we vary the other two.

So far we have kept the absolute temperature (T) constant for Boyle's Law, and the volume (V) constant for the Pressure Law. We have one more combination left:

■ Varying temperature and volume, with pressure constant

Picture 11 shows the apparatus we can use to see how the volume of a gas depends on the temperature. The pressure stays constant during the experiment, because the tube is open at the top.

The gas being tested is air, trapped in the narrow glass capillary tube. The air is trapped by a small amount of concentrated sulphuric acid. This does two jobs. It dries the air so that water vapour does not interfere with the results. It also serves as an 'index' which moves up and down the scale so you can read off the volume of the air.

You increase the temperature by heating the water, and read it off on the thermometer.

Using this apparatus you can get a series of readings for the volume of the gas at different temperatures, with the pressure constant. You can then plot V against T on a graph like the one in picture 12.

Look at the right-hand part of picture 12 first. You can see that the graph is a straight line. V increases steadily as T increases. In other words, pressure is proportional to temperature. But the graph does not go through the origin: the volume is not zero at zero degrees Celsius.

Now look at the left-hand part. The graph has been extended back (extrapolated) until it reaches the temperature axis. To do this, we have to assume that the gas will behave in the same general way at all temperatures. The volume of the gas gets less and less as the temperature falls. By the time the line meets the temperature axis, the volume of the gas is zero. You can see that this happens at a temperature of −273 degrees Celsius. This is **absolute zero** – zero kelvin.

At absolute zero, the volume of the gas would be zero. As the temperature is increased, the volume increases in proportion to the absolute temperature. If you

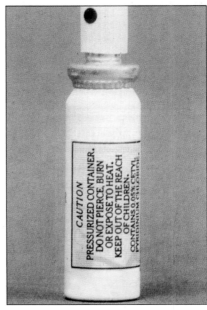

Picture 9   The pressure of a gas can increase spectacularly when it is heated.

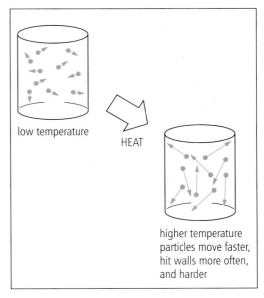

low temperature

HEAT

higher temperature particles move faster, hit walls more often, and harder

Picture 10   Why the pressure of a gas increases when it is heated at constant volume.

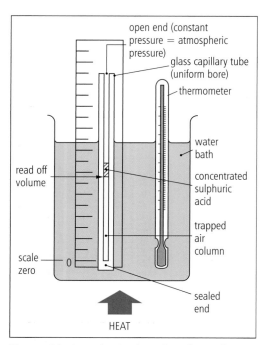

Picture 11 Investigating how the volume of a gas depends on temperature.

double the absolute temperature, the volume doubles. If you halve the absolute temperature, the volume is halved. The volume is proportional to the absolute temperature. This can be written mathematically as

$$V = \text{constant} \times T \quad \text{or} \quad \frac{V_1}{T_1} = \frac{V_2}{T_2}$$

But remember, this assumes that the pressure is kept constant.

This relationship is known as **Charles' Law**, after Jacques Charles, the scientist who first stated the law in 1787. In words, Charles' Law says

> **The volume of a fixed mass of gas is directly proportional to its absolute temperature (on the kelvin scale) if the pressure is kept constant.**

Like Boyle's Law, Charles' Law is not obeyed perfectly by real gases. In particular, real gases turn to liquids before the temperature reaches absolute zero. According to the Kinetic Theory:

- As the temperature increases so does the average speed of the particles and so they begin to hit the walls harder and more often.
- If one of the walls is free to move then the extra force does work and pushes it back thus expanding the gas. It does this so that the pressure inside the gas always equals the outside pressure of the atmosphere
- The gas particles are now hitting the wall harder but they have further to go, so the pressure remains constant

◼ Combining the laws together

We have three equations involving the pressure, volume and absolute temperature of a gas:

$$P_1 \times V_1 = P_2 \times V_2 \qquad \text{(Boyle's Law)}$$

$$\frac{P_1}{T_1} = \frac{P_2}{T_2} \qquad \text{(Pressure Law)}$$

$$\frac{V_1}{T_1} = \frac{V_2}{T_2} \qquad \text{(Charles' Law)}$$

We can combine these into a single equation, called the **gas equation**

$$\frac{P_1 V_1}{T_1} = \frac{P_2 V_2}{T_2} \qquad \text{(the Gas Equation)}$$

Where P_1, V_1, T_1 and P_2, V_2, T_2 are the pressure, volume and temperature in two different situations. Remember that you must always use the absolute temperature, in kelvins.

In practice no real gas obeys the gas equation perfectly. Life's like that!

An imaginary gas, which would obey the law perfectly, is called a **perfect** or **ideal** gas.

MORE EVIDENCE FOR THE KINETIC THEORY

THE SPEED OF SOUND

The Kinetic Theory predicts that the average speed of air molecules at room temperature is about 480 m s^{-1}.

Sound waves moving through the air cause rapid expansion and contraction of the air and this means that the air molecules have to move. Clearly the speed of the sound waves cannot be faster than the speed of the air molecules.

Kinetic theory suggests that the speed of sound in air must be fast but no greater than 480 m s^{-1}.

In fact the speed of sound in air is around 340 m s^{-1} which is about 70% of the average speed of the molecules.

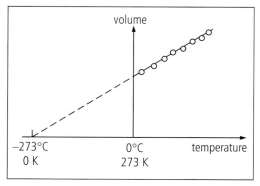

Picture 12 The volume of a gas plotted against its temperature.

NO ATMOSPHERE ON THE MOON

To escape from the gravitational pull of the Moon you must have at least a speed of 2370 m s^{-1}.

Imagine that the Moon had an atmosphere similar to the Earth's at about room temperature. Although the average speed of the molecules may be 480 m s^{-1} a small proportion will have speeds greater than 2370 m s^{-1} and these will escape. The remaining molecules redistribute and again a small proportion (slightly smaller than before) will reach speeds of over 2370 m s^{-1} and so escape.

Over a long period of time nearly all the molecules will be lost into space.

The moon has no active volcanoes to top up any atmosphere with gas and so now we find no atmosphere at all – just a vacuum.

The escape speed for the Earth is a lot greater at 11 200 m s^{-1} and we do have some active volcanoes. Therefore the Earth's atmosphere is fairly stable. Global warming though may have an adverse effect – there will be more molecules reaching the escape speed!

DIFFUSION

Removing the top from a bottle of perfume will allow the molecules in the vapour above the liquid scent to find their way into the surrounding air. Eventually the smell can be detected some distance away, even in perfectly still air.

We can picture the perfume molecules colliding continuously with the air molecules and becoming randomly distributed amongst them. This process is called **diffusion**. (Picture 13.)

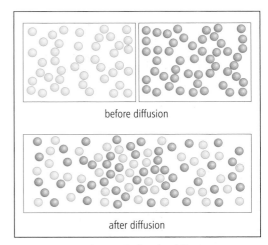
Picture 13 Before and after the diffusion process.

PARTICLES AND THE THREE STATES OF MATTER
■ Solids, Liquids and Gases

GASES

We have seen how the particle model can successfully describe and predict the behaviour of gases. It is possible to extend it to include solids and liquids by introducing attractive forces that act between the particles.

In an ideal gas the particles are free to move around because there are **no** attractive forces acting between them. (The only forces that exist are the collision forces occurring when the particles bash into each other.)

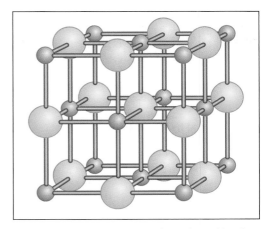
Picture 14 Atoms in a lattice for sodium chloride.

SOLIDS

The extreme situation to this is to be found in solids where the attractive forces (**bonds**) are so strong that the particles are bound together and they can only vibrate about their average position. This is why solids have a definite shape and volume. In crystalline solids, such as quartz or common salt, the bonds only act in certain directions and so determine the structure and appearance of the crystal.

Since the particles are about as close as they can get, solids are incompressible.

LIQUIDS

The bonds between the particles in a liquid are not sufficiently strong enough to prevent them moving around. This is a 'half-way' situation between solids and gases where groups of particles are able to move around each other. This explains why a liquid can adjust and flow into the shape of its container but it cannot expand to fill the entire space as can a gas.

Although the bonds are looser than in a solid the particles are still tightly packed and so liquids are also virtually incompressible.

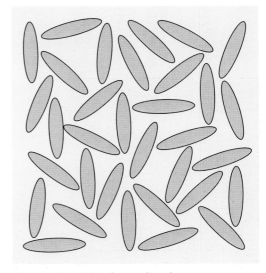
Picture 15 Molecules in a liquid.

Questions

1 An inflated car tyre contains air at constant volume

  a Use the Kinetic Theory to explain why the air inside the tyre exerts pressure on the walls of the tyre.

  b What will happen to the pressure in the tyre on a particularly warm day? Use the Kinetic Theory to explain what happens.

  c Suppose you injected some water into the tyre, so that the air was pushed into half the volume it occupied before. What would happen to the pressure of the air?

2 Look at picture 6 on page 210, then answer these questions.

  a What would you expect to happen to the reading on the balance as the balls are dropped onto it?

  b Explain why this experiment models the way a gas exerts pressure.

  c How would you adapt the experiment to model the effect of increasing temperature on the pressure of a gas?

3 Picture 16 shows a thermometer invented by the great Italian scientist Galileo, (page 93). He used it to measure room temperatures.

  a Explain how the 'thermometer' works.

  b Using equipment available in the school laboratory, how would you calibrate the thermometer so its scale reads temperatures from 10 °C to 30 °C?

  c Give two reasons why this might be a rather inaccurate thermometer.

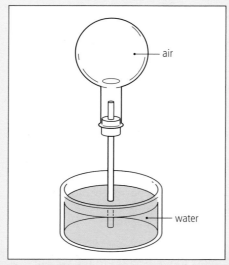

Picture 16 Galileo's thermometer.

4 Use the following steps to show that the results in table 1 obey Boyle's Law.

  a For each set of results, multiply the pressure (*P*) by the volume (*V*). Does *PV* = constant?

  b For each set of results, work out the value of 1/*P*. Now plot a graph of *V* (vertical axis) against 1/*P*. Is *V* proportional to 1/*P*?

  c Use the results to preduct the volume of the gas when the pressure is 400 kPa.

5 A bubble is trapped at the bottom of a lake. The volume of the bubble is 0.5 cm³, and the total pressure at the bottom of the lake is 300 kPa.

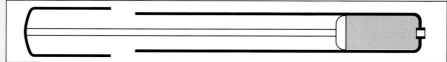

Picture 17

  a The bubble gets dislodged and rises to the surface where the pressure is 100 kPa. What will its new volume be?

  b What assumption have you made in part (a)?

6 Look at the bicycle pump in picture 17. The pump contains 60 cm³ of air at a temperature of 27 °C and a pressure of 100 kPa. Use the gas equation to answer these questions.

  a What will the volume of air become if the handle is pushed in so that the pressure rises to 150 kPa? Assume the temperature does not change.

  b What will the volume of air become if the temperature rises to 87 °C? Assume the handle of the pump is allowed to move freely, so that the pressure does not change.

  c What will the volume become if the pressure increases to 120 kPa and the temperature rises to 47 °C?

7 Liquids exposed to the air will evaporate. Use the theory of particles to explain:

  a Why evaporation occurs.

  b Why evaporation results in a cooling effect.

  c Why a quantity of liquid will evaporate more quickly if it is spread over a flat surface.

8 Ice floats in water. This is an everyday fact, but using your knowledge of particles suggest why this behaviour is really quite *unexpected*!

F2

Strange rays

One of the great discoveries of the 20th century was a new energy source, and it was discovered accidentally!

Picture 1   Henri Becquerel

■ Particles from deep inside the atom

The French scientist Henri Becquerel was interested in those strange minerals that glow in the dark – or **fluoresce**. He detected the weakest glows by using photographic film. In 1896, more by accident than design, he found a mineral that was able to fog a photographic plate even when it was covered with black paper.

The minerals were compounds of uranium, and the effect reminded him of the penetrating properties of X-rays which had only been discovered the year before (see E11 *Electrons in space*). He realised that something very similar to X-rays was penetrating through the paper wrapping and exposing the film. If a small coin was place between the active crystal and the paper wrapping then a 'shadow' of the coin could be seen on the developed photographic plate.

Like most accidental discoveries it took until 1898 and the discovery of other materials with similar properties to uranium for the world to realise the importance of Becquerel's findings. He had in fact discovered radioactivity!

These **radioactive** substances gave out very energetic 'rays' and researchers quickly found out that there were three types of ray. All of them can damage living things, but they are also very useful. When they were first discovered nobody knew exactly what they were. So they simply named them **alpha**, **beta** and **gamma** rays, after the first three letters of the Greek alphabet.

ALPHA, BETA, GAMMA

Table 1 summarises the properties of these rays. It took scientists 20 years after they were first discovered to work out what the radiations actually were, and that they were coming from the **nucleus** of the atom. The structure of the atom is summarised in picture 2.

One property that these radiations possess is their ability to **ionise** atoms and molecules. The radiations knock electrons out of the atoms to turn them into **ions** (picture 3). The atoms and molecules become positively charged. Thus the radiations are called **ionising radiations**.

The reason they are dangerous to life is that they ionise atoms in living cells, which can kill the cells or make them cancerous.

The radiations travel at high speeds, as if they are shot out of the nucleus like a bullet from a gun. What was puzzling to the scientists who first worked with these radiations was where they got the energy from to do this. We now know that it comes from the conversion of matter into energy, and this is explained more fully in topic F5.

Table 1   Nuclear radiations.

Radiation type	What they are	Range in air	Stopped by	Comments
ALPHA	Positively charged. NUCLEI of helium ($^4_2$He)	A few centimetres	A sheet of paper	Because they are so massive and carry a double positive charge they easily affect atoms. They make lots of ions and don't travel far. Alpha emitters are quite safe unless they get into the body.
BETA	Negatively charged. Fast-moving ELECTRONS	A few tens of centimetres	A few millimetres of aluminium	Electrons are small and so can travel further than alpha particles as they don't collide as often. Dangerous but easily stopped.
GAMMA	Uncharged. Very short wavelength ELECTROMAGNETIC WAVES (high-energy photons)	They go on indefinitely	A metre or two of concrete	These are genuine 'rays'. They don't ionise atoms very easily and so travel a long way. They travel at the speed of light. Dangerous because they are hard to shield against.

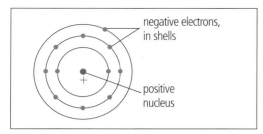

Picture 2 Rutherford's model: a nuclear atom.

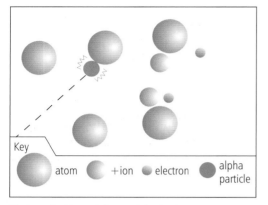

Picture 3 How alpha particles ionise atoms.

Key
atom   +ion   electron   alpha particle

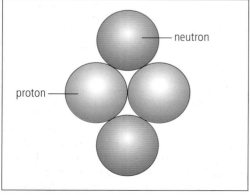

Picture 4 The tracks of alpha particles in a 'cloud chamber'.

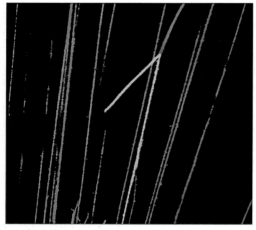

proton — neutron

Picture 6 A helium nucleus.

DETECTING THE RADIATIONS

We detect the rays from atoms using the fact that the rays ionise other atoms. Picture 4 shows the tracks of alpha particles travelling through damp air. The water vapour in the air condenses as droplets on the **ions** made from the air by the alpha particles. This leaves a 'vapour trail' like the ones made by high flying aircraft. This picture was taken as the alpha particles travelled through a special 'cloud chamber'. This contains cool damp air, which is good at making clouds and vapour trails.

Picture 5 shows another detector which makes use of ionisation.

It is a GM tube, or **Geiger–Muller tube**. It contains a gas at a low pressure. The inner wire is at a high voltage. When some ionising radiation goes into the tube it makes ions in the gas. The wire attracts them and so there is a short pulse of current when the ions hit the wire. This is amplified and can be counted by an electronic **pulse counter**. Thus each time a 'ray' gets into the tube it produces a pulse which can be counted.

Geiger counters like this are the most common way of finding out how much radioactivity is present.

ALPHA PARTICLES

Alpha particles are very good at ionising other atoms. This suggests that they carry a lot of energy. This is movement energy (kinetic energy).

But they don't travel very far in air. They barge through the air like a bull in a china shop, hitting lots of air molecules and knocking electrons off them (picture 4). As they do this they lose energy quite rapidly, so they soon slow down.

If we put a piece of paper in the way the alpha particles can't get through it! This is because they hit a lot of atoms in the paper.

Alpha particles are electrically charged, carrying 2 units of positive charge. This is twice as much as the (negative) charge carried by an electron.

Because alpha particles are positively charged they are affected by both electric and magnetic fields. Scientists have worked out exactly what alpha particles are by measuring how strongly they are affected by these fields.

These measurements show that alpha particles are in fact **helium nuclei,** which are four times as heavy as hydrogen nuclei. They have, therefore, an atomic mass of 4. They are made up of two protons (positive particles) and two neutrons, joined very firmly together (picture 6).

BETA PARTICLES

Beta particles do not cause as much ionisation as alpha particles. Also, they travel much further in air before running out of energy. This suggests that they are lighter and smaller than alpha particles. They carry a single unit of negative charge. Measurements using electric and magnetic fields show that they are in fact **high-speed electrons**. An alpha particle is 7333 times as massive as a beta particle.

Because they are so small, beta particles can travel through matter more easily than alpha particles can. But a few millimetres of aluminium will stop them.

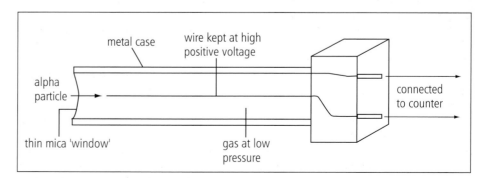

Picture 5 A GM tube. When an alpha particle, for example, enters the tube, it ionises the gas inside. This triggers off a sudden flow of freed electrons to the wire. This registers as a 'count' or a 'click'.

GAMMA RAYS

Gamma rays do not cause much ionisation and they travel quite freely, through air. They carry no charge and so are not at all affected by electric or magnetic fields. This means that they are very **penetrating**. They can travel through thick blocks of concrete, and it takes up to a centimetre or so thickness of a heavy metal like lead to cut down the radiation by a half.

Gamma rays are different from the alpha and beta particles because they have no mass. They travel at the speed of light, and are a type of **electromagnetic radiation**, like light and X-rays. All electromagnetic radiation comes in particle-like chunks called **photons**. Although massless these 'particles' carry units of energy (or quanta) in direct proportion to their frequency. Gamma photons are the most energetic of all those in the electromagnetic spectrum (see topic A7). They carry even more energy than X-rays.

Picture 7 shows how the three kinds of radiation compare in their ability to pass through matter, and what happens to them in an electric field.

■ Absorption and shielding

Ionising radiation interacts with matter. This means that the beam loses energy – usually by losing some of its particles which are absorbed by the substance it travels through. Alpha particles are massive and carry two units of electric charge. They interact easily with matter and even in air can travel only a few centimetres before being completely absorbed. A thin sheet of paper stops them and they turn into harmless helium ions or atoms.

Beta and gamma radiation are more penetrating than alpha radiation: they have a greater **range** in air and other substances. A typical pattern of absorption is shown in the graph (picture 8). Each extra unit of distance takes out the same fraction of the radiation beam. Look at the graph: there is a distance **D** at which the intensity of the radiation is cut to a half. This value of **D** depends on the energy carried by the radiation, the type of radiation and the density of the material. For beta radiation the value of **D** in a low density metal like aluminium might be a few millimetres. For gamma radiation the value of **D** in a heavy metal like lead might be tens of centimetres.

These facts are important for safety in using radioactive materials: users need to be able to calculate how much material is needed for **shielding** people from the harmful effects of the radiation.

■ Half-life

Radiations are given out by decaying atoms. As the atom decays to something else, it 'spits out' the radiation. In a sample of uranium the nuclei don't decay all at once. In fact, only a very tiny fraction of the nuclei in the sample decay each day. It will take four and a half thousand million years for just half of the nuclei in a lump of uranium (U-238) to decay.

On the other hand, it will take only 52 seconds for half of the nuclei in a sample of radon gas (Rn-220) to decay. These times are called **half-lives**, and we can measure them very accurately.

Picture 9(a) shows how the number of undecayed nuclei left in a sample of a radioactive element changes with time. Picture 9(b) shows this in the form of a graph.

The **count rate** is a measure of the number of rays given out per second. As time goes on this count rate will go down, as more and more of the nuclei have decayed. What happens to the nucleus when it decays is dealt with in the next topic.

Your teacher should be able to show you an experiment about how the rate of radioactive decay gets less as time goes on. You should be able to get results to allow you to measure the half-life of a radioactive material. Some sample results are given in question 3 on page 218.

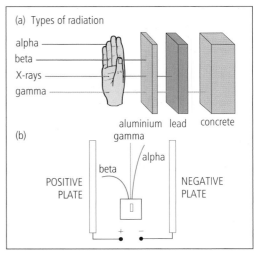

Picture 7 (a) What stops the radiations – or doesn't! (X-rays are shown for a comparison.) (b) What happens to the radiations in an electric field.

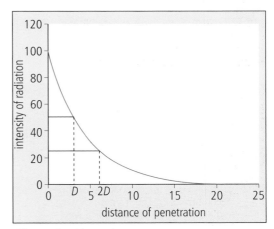

Picture 8 Absorption curve

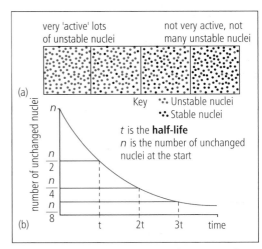

Picture 9 (a) Radioactive decay. The activity of a radioactive substance gets less all the time. This is because the number of unstable, active nuclei gets less. But there is a catch – the new nuclei may also be unstable! (b) A half-life graph.

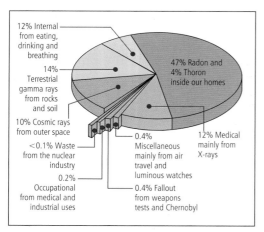

Picture 10 Where background radiation comes from.

Background radiation

Nuclear radiation is all around us. It comes from the rocks and the soil; it comes from plants and even animals. This is because they all contain tiny amounts of radioactive materials that are naturally present on Earth. Some comes from elements made radioactive by radiation from outer space, some from atomic weapons testing thirty or forty years ago. A small amount comes from the operation of nuclear power stations. Also, the nuclear accident in Russia (at Chernobyl) in 1986 produced radioactive 'fall out'.

Picture 10 summarises where this background radiation comes from. It is too low to have a serious effect on health, but it does have some effect. Doctors estimate that background radiation causes 1200 deaths from cancer per year in Britain. Energetic particles can seriously damage your health. It is also likely that this radiation affects the genes in sex cells, so causing slight changes from one generation to the next. This may be one of the main causes of biological **variation**, which is necessary for evolution to occur.

Questions

1 Consider alpha, beta and gamma radiations. Which:
   a travels at the speed of light?
   b causes the most ionisation?
   c has the same mass as an electron?
   d is stopped by a few millimetres of aluminium?
   e is the most massive?

2 Why aren't gamma rays affected by an electric field?

3 Use the figures in the table to work out the half-life of the radioactive isotope (Polonium-218). There's a quick way and a long way – use the quick way!

4 A sample of a radioactive substance was sending out 4000 alpha particles a second at the start of an experiment. Ten minutes later it was sending out 2000 particles per second.
   a What is the half-life of the substance?
   b How long after the start would you expect to measure a count of 500 particles a second?
   c How much activity (in counts per second) would you expect after 10 half-lives?

   d The natural 'background' count of radiation comes from radioactive materials in the ground or in the air. It is about two counts per second in most places. How long would it take for the radiation from the radioactive waste to be just less than this background count?

Time/minutes	0	1	2	3	4	5	6	7
Count rate (counts/second)	260	205	160	129	104	82	64	51

F3

Probing the atom

'The job didn't seem all that important at the time.'

Ernest Marsden

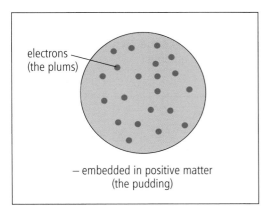

electrons
(the plums)

— embedded in positive matter
(the pudding)

Picture 1 Thomson's 'Plum-pudding model' of the atom.

The atom is a particle and we have seen that some atoms are radioactive (topic F2). Smaller highly energetic particles (alpha, beta and gamma) can be emitted at high speed from these radioactive atoms.

In 1897 Sir J.J. Thomson found that very light, negatively charged particles could be stripped away from atoms. The mass of these particles was found to be more than a thousand times lighter than the mass of the atom itself. All atoms contained these particles which are now called **electrons** (topic E11)

Around the turn of the 20th century the atom had suddenly become a complicated particle. Exactly what was its structure? Sir J.J. Thomson proposed what became know as his 'plum-pudding' model.

He reasoned this way:

'An atom is electrically neutral, so if the light, negative electrons are removed then what is left must be the 'heavy', positive matter'.

He imagined that atoms were made up of uniform spheres of this heavier, positive matter and that the light electrons were embedded within it, rather like currants or plums in a Christmas pudding.

Unfortunately for Thomson, but fortunately for science, his model was shown to be completely *wrong* by the work of the brilliant physicist Ernest Rutherford.

■ The big experiment

Rutherford, Geiger and Marsden devised an experiment in which alpha particles were fired at a thin sheet of gold foil. This had to be done in a vacuum to prevent the air molecules getting in the way and stopping the beam.

Geiger and Marsden collected the data. They used the apparatus sketched in picture 2.

The results showed that:

- Most alpha particles went straight through the gold foil with hardly any deflection.
- Some alpha particles were deflected significantly.
- A few alpha particles were scattered back again towards the source!

Rutherford realised immediately that Thomson's plum-pudding model of the atom could not explain these results because it predicted only slight scattering for most of the alpha particles.

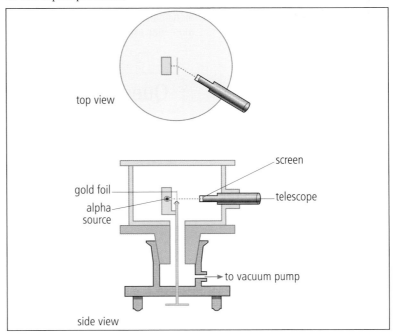

top view

screen

gold foil

alpha
source

telescope

to vacuum pump

side view

Picture 2 The apparatus used by Geiger and Marsden in 1909 to investigate how alpha particles where 'scattered' by thin gold foil.

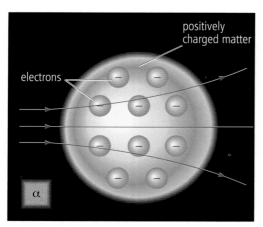

Picture 3 This diagram shows how the alpha particle would scatter according to Thomson's 'plum-pudding' model of the atom.

If the Thomson atom was a correct model there was no way that a big alpha particle travelling at 10 000 km per second could be bounced back by a collection of tiny electrons in a jelly of positive charge. They knew that an alpha particle was about 8000 times as massive as an electron. The time had come for more data: Something in the atom was strong enough to turn an alpha particle back on its tracks.

He reasoned that the atom must be mostly empty space (the electrons being so light that they could be ignored). This was why most alpha particles were not scattered. This being the case the actual scattering agent must be a very small, centrally placed particle that carries all the mass and all the positive charge. i.e. **the nucleus**. There is more about this on page 221.

Rutherford's analysis used the fact that the electrostatic repulsion between the positive alpha particle and the positive nucleus increases as the separation between them decreases. His calculations fitted Geiger and Marsden's data precisely. The nuclear model was here to stay.

Picture 5 represents the structure of the nuclear atom. The nucleus is at the centre. It is tiny, but very dense. The electrons move around outside the nucleus. They move in a random and chaotic way, but to make the picture simpler we've shown them as if they travel in 'orbits' around the nucleus.

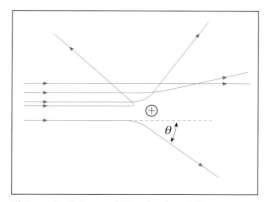

Picture 4 Geiger and Marsden found that some alpha particles were scattered much more than expected.

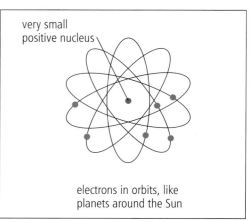

Picture 5 Rutherford's idea – a nuclear atom.

Questions

1 What 2 key quantities does the nucleus of an atom contain?

2 Why were the experimental results of Geiger and Marsden on alpha particle scattering surprising?

3 Explain why Geiger and Marsden's scattering apparatus had to be operated within a vacuum.

4 Suggest why gold was a good metal for Geiger and Marsden to use in their scattering investigation, compared with a metal like lithium, say.

The birth of nuclear physics

Ernest Rutherford was a very bright young man from a large and poor family who managed in 1895 to win a scholarship from his native New Zealand to further his studies in England – at Cambridge University. He worked as the very first research student of Professor Joseph John Thomson, the man who discovered the electron. These were exciting times and the beginning of what was soon called atomic physics – and then nuclear physics.

Rutherford didn't stay long at Cambridge; at the ripe old age of 27 he was appointed a professor of physics at McGill University in Montreal, Canada. He used the skills he had learned at Cambridge to set a series of very ingenious experiments, using simple apparatus, to investigate the radiations that came from Becquerel's radioactive substances (see topic F2). He identified three different kinds. He did not know what they were, except that some were more penetrating than others, or could make air more conducting. He left the question open, and just named them alpha, beta and gamma rays.

In 1907 Rutherford returned to Britain to work as Professor of Physics at Manchester University. By this time he had identified alpha rays as particles identical to charged helium ions. It was also known that beta radiation was also a stream of particles – electrons. At Manchester he found a very competent research physicist called Hans Geiger, then 25 years old, who had also gained his expertise by studying how electricity passed through gases. With Rutherford he invented a new way of detecting – and counting – individual particles in radioactive emissions. This used a very fine wire charged to a high voltage. When some radiation came near it ionised the air and the high voltage caused a spark to jump. This method is still used in the spark counter – and was the basis of the much improved version that came to be called the Geiger-Muller counter. They were both typical experimental physicists, full of bright ideas for making clever apparatus from glass, sealing wax and bits of copper wire. And Rutherford had thought of another way of detecting alpha particles: a glass screen painted with a fluorescent chemical. When an alpha particle hit the screen there was tiny flash of light. Early in 1909 Rutherford decided to ask Geiger to investigate something that had been on his mind for some time. When Rutherford entered the lab he found Geiger working with a cheerful 20-year old called Ernest Marsden. He turned towards him and said: *'See if you can get some effect of alpha particles directly reflected from a metal surface'*

'The job didn't seem all that important at the time' Marsden remembered later.

'I don't think he expected any such result, but it was one of those 'hunches' that perhaps some effect might be observed.'

A week later Marsden had some results: alpha particles were reflected by a metal surface. When he stopped to think about it, Rutherford was surprised by this. In one of his last lectures he was to say **'It was quite the most incredible event that has ever happened to me in my life. It was almost as incredible as if you fired a 15-inch shell at a piece of tissue paper and it came back and hit you!'**

Picture 1 Hans Geiger.

Picture 2 Ernest Marsden.

The nucleus and radioactivity

Most of the atoms we meet in everyday life are not radioactive. This means that their nuclei are **stable**. So why do some nuclei break up?

Picture 1 James Chadwick discovered the neutron in 1932.

■ More and more particles

The nuclear model of the atom proposed by Ernest Rutherford in 1911 was a giant leap forward. Calculations showed that the diameter of the nucleus was at least 10,000 times smaller than the diameter of the atom. Amazingly this tiny object carried all the positive charge and 99.9% of the mass!

The question of 'What is the nucleus made of' was immediately posed. Rutherford considered the simplest and lightest atom of hydrogen and by 1920 he was convinced that its nucleus was a fundamental particle that was also present in all other nuclei. He called this particle a **proton**. Back in 1899 Rutherford has discovered and named the **alpha particle** and it soon became clear that the nucleus of a helium atom was identical to an alpha particle.

Since the alpha particle has 2 units of positive charge it must contain 2 protons, the problem was that the mass of an alpha particle was about 4 times the mass of a proton.

Therefore something else must be present in nuclei bigger than hydrogen which is electrically neutral and carries the extra mass.

However, it took until 1932 before the English physicist James Chadwick managed to discover the **neutron**. This was the missing link in the nuclear model.

■ Numbering atoms

The numbers of protons, neutrons and electrons in an atom decide its properties. As far as chemists are concerned, the most important thing is the number of *electrons*. Because they are on the outside, the electrons decide how a particular atom behaves in a chemical reaction. In the next two topics we will look more closely at the way the electrons are arranged.

The number of electrons in an atom is equal to its number of protons, and this is called the **atomic number**, symbol **Z**. Each element has its own unique atomic number. For example, the simplest atom, hydrogen, has just one proton and one electron, so $Z = 1$. The largest naturally-occurring atom, uranium, has $Z = 92$: in other words, it has 92 protons and 92 electrons.

If you split an atom in two, you get two new atoms. They have different atomic numbers from the original atom, *so they are new elements.* For example, when a uranium atom splits, you get one fragment with 56 protons and another with 36. These are barium ($Z = 56$) and krypton ($Z = 36$).

If you look at a copy of the Periodic Table, you will see that the elements are arranged in order of increasing atomic number.

■ But what about the neutrons?

ISOTOPES

Neutrons don't have any electrical charge, so they don't have to be balanced out by a particle with an opposite charge. This means you can add neutrons to an atom without altering its number of protons or electrons. So an element can have

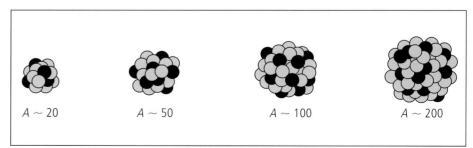

$A \sim 20$ $A \sim 50$ $A \sim 100$ $A \sim 200$

Picture 2 As nuclei contain more and more protons and neutrons they become progressively larger. The mass number, A, increases.

different 'versions' of its atoms. Each version has the same numbers of protons and electrons as all the other versions, but a different number of neutrons. These different versions, or **isotopes**, vary in mass, but they are all atoms of the same element.

> **Isotopes are atoms of a particular element with the same number of protons and electrons but different numbers of neutrons.**

Let's look at an example – the simplest example of all, in fact. Picture 5 shows two isotopes of hydrogen. Both of them have one proton and one electron, so they both have the same chemical properties. But the second isotope has one neutron as well as the one proton in its nucleus. This makes the atom almost twice as heavy. In fact this isotope is sometimes called 'heavy hydrogen'. It is also known as deuterium.

Although it's heavier, deuterium has the same chemical properties as hydrogen. It reacts the same way, and it forms the same kind of compound. For example, 'heavy water' contains deuterium in place of hydrogen. It has the same chemical properties as ordinary water, and you wouldn't notice any difference if you drank it. It's just a little denser.

> **Isotopes of an element have the same chemical properties. They differ in a few physical properties such as density.**

MASS NUMBER

To make it easy to tell isotopes apart, each atom is given a mass number as well as its atomic number.

> **The mass number (symbol A) is the number of neutrons plus the number of protons.**

The protons and neutrons give the atom most of its mass, because electrons weigh very little. So the mass number tells you the relative mass of the atom.

The mass number of ordinary hydrogen atoms is 1, and the mass number of 'heavy hydrogen' is 2. Picture 6 illustrates this idea for another element. It also shows how the symbol of an element can be written with the atomic number and mass number included.

Table 1 sums up the difference between atomic number and mass number.

Table 1   Atomic number and mass number.

Atomic number, Z	Mass number, A
• Z = number of protons = number of electrons	• A = number of protons + number of neutrons
• Fixed for a particular element	• Varies depending on which isotope of the element it is

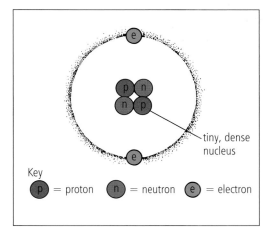

Picture 3   The blue glow from this underwater nuclear reaction is caused by the charged particles it is emitting. Neutrons make excellent 'bullets' for splitting the atom.

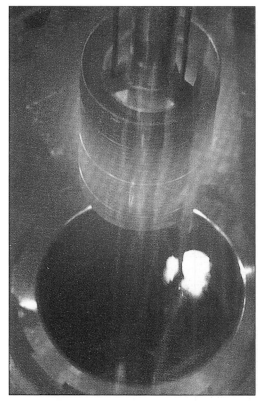

Key
p = proton   n = neutron   e = electron

Picture 4   The structure of the atom. The atom shown here is helium.

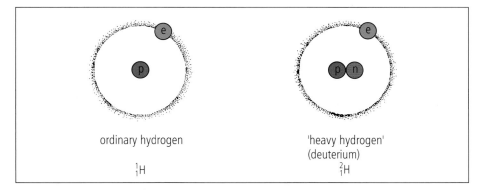

ordinary hydrogen
$^{1}_{1}H$

'heavy hydrogen' (deuterium)
$^{2}_{1}H$

Picture 5   Two isotopes of hydrogen.

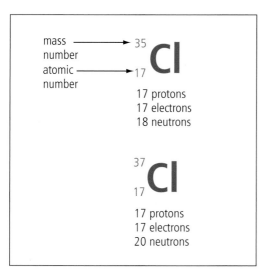

Picture 6 The atomic number and the mass number of chlorine isotopes.

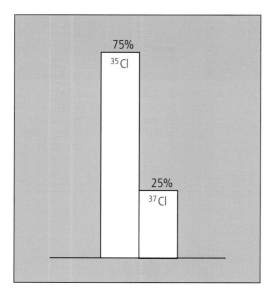

Picture 7 The abundance of the two isotopes in natural chlorine.

If we know the atomic number and mass number of an atom, we can work out the number of protons, neutrons and electrons it must contain. For example, uranium has several isotopes. The isotope that is used in nuclear reactors is uranium-235, or $^{235}_{92}U$. Like all uranium atoms, it has an atomic number of 92, so it must have 92 protons and 92 electrons. It has a mass number of 235, which means its number of protons and neutrons together is 235. So its number of neutrons must be $(235 - 92) = 143$.

ISOTOPES EVERYWHERE

How do we know the mass of atoms? They are much too small to weigh directly. Fortunately, a clever invention called the mass spectrometer makes it possible to find the mass of atoms indirectly.

The mass spectrometer shows that most elements have more than one isotope, and some have as many as 20. Not all of these isotopes are stable. Some are radioactive, and decay into other isotopes by giving out ionising radiations.

■ Relative atomic mass

The relative atomic mass of an element is the mass of its atoms relative to atoms of other elements.

But which atoms are we talking about? Most elements have more than one isotope, and different isotopes have different masses. Relative atomic mass is actually an *average* mass for all the different isotopes. It is adjusted (weighted) to take account of the proportions of the different isotopes. If a particular isotope is present in larger amounts, it makes a bigger contribution to the average.

For example, chlorine has two stable isotopes. In natural chlorine, 75% of the atoms have mass number 35, and 25% have mass number 37 (picture 7). In other words, for every 100 atoms, 75 have mass 35 and 25 have mass 37. The weighted average of these mass numbers is:

$$\frac{75 \times 35 + 25 \times 37}{100} = 35.5$$

This is the relative atomic mass of chlorine. Check this result!

WHAT CAUSES RADIOACTIVITY?

Radioactivity is caused by a change that happens in the nucleus of an atom. Now, about 5 billion years after the Solar System began to form, nearly all the natural radioactivity on Earth stems from just three naturally occurring radioactive elements. These are uranium, thorium and actinium. They all happen to be 'heavy elements' – each with a nucleus containing hundreds of nucleons (protons and neutrons). We can still find them on Earth because they have such a low probability of decaying. This means that they have long half-lives, and so have not had time to decay away completely since the Earth was formed:

Uranium-238	4.5 billion years
Thorium-232	14 billion years
Actinium-235	0.72 billion years

These rather special radioactive elements decay into a new element by emitting either an alpha particle or a beta particle. The new element has a different mass or charge – or both – to the parent element. See below (page 229) for more about these changes. The new nucleus may still be unstable and can get rid of some internal energy by emitting a gamma ray without any further change to its mass or charge.

■ The electric force versus the strong force

The accepted reason why such heavy nuclei are radioactive is that they are simply too big to be stable. Inside the nucleus of uranium-238 for example there are 92 protons and 146 neutrons. The protons are electrically charged (positive) and very close together. They exert strong forces of repulsion on each other – as do all protons in nuclei. The only reason that nuclei can hold themselves together is because there is another, even stronger force, between all the nucleons inside the nucleus. This is, not surprisingly, called the **strong force**. It is a hundred times stronger than the electric force of repulsion trying to blow the nucleus apart. Unfortunately, the strong force has a very short range – about 10^{-15} metre. Nuclei are 10^{-14} m across – ten times larger. The protons that happen to be at the edge of a large nucleus are at risk of falling off. When they do they move away in one of the most stable nuclear arrangements you can get: a combination of 2 protons and 2 neutrons. This is an alpha particle: it has the same structure as the nucleus of the second most abundant element in the universe, helium ($^4_2$He). Sometimes the heavy nucleus is so unstable that it simply splits into two roughly equal parts: this is **nuclear fission**, the source of energy in nuclear power stations.

The nuclei of lighter unstable elements with a proton number $Z < 83$ lose energy through β-decay.

MAKING ELEMENTS RADIOACTIVE

The chemical identity of an atom is decided firstly by how many protons it has in its nucleus. This decides how many electrons normally surround the nucleus, the charge on the electrons has to balance the charge on the nucleus. Chemical behaviour is decided by interactions between these electrons and the electrons of other atoms. The number of neutrons in the nucleus does not affect its chemical behaviour because they don't alter the charge on the nucleus. But when there are lots of neutrons floating around they can get into a nucleus quite easily – there is no repelling charge to keep them away. The neutrons have to be moving fairly slowly otherwise they might bounce off or pass by too quickly. Once inside they are held by the strong nuclear force: the nucleus has become an **isotope** of the original one.

Making radioactive isotopes is big business. For example they can be used:

- as tracers to monitor industrial waste
- to monitor thickness of paper or metal tyre cord
- to check for flaws in solid objects such as aircraft wings
- in medicine for treatment and diagnosis.

See topic F6 *Radiation and life* for more about how radiations are used.

■ Stable and Unstable nuclei

Most of the atoms we meet in everyday life are not radioactive. This means that their nuclei are **stable**. Picture 8 shows the stable nuclei on a chart that plots the number of neutrons (*N*) against the number of protons (*Z*) in their nuclei. Only the first 80 elements are shown. The straight line is the line that nuclei would have if everything was nice and neat and each nucleus had the same number of neutrons and protons. The first 20 stable nuclei do have roughly equal numbers and follow the straight-line trend, but for the rest they deviate ever upwards from the *N* = *Z* line. This means that the heavier the nucleus the more neutrons seem to be squeezed into it

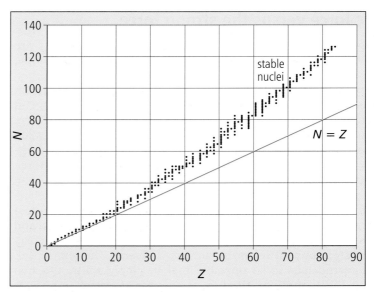

Picture 8 *N–Z* plot for stable nuclei.

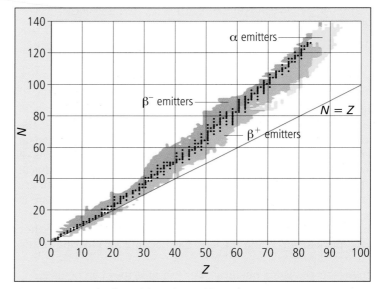

Picture 9 *N–Z* plot for stable and unstable nuclei.

Because they are positively charged the protons repel each other and adding more of them tends to make the nucleus unstable as the protons push apart. Adding uncharged neutrons is not as disturbing and they provide extra nuclear 'glue' by adding extra 'strong force'.

For a nucleus to be stable it must obey one of the following two rules:

For $Z < 20$ $N \cong Z$
For $Z > 20$ $N > Z$

The symbols on the chart (picture 9) show the pattern for both stable and **unstable** nuclei.

- Stable nuclei lie on the stability line which ends when $Z = 83$
- Nuclei above the stability line have too many neutrons to be stable. They decay by emitting a beta$^-$ particle
- Nuclei below the stability line have too few neutrons to be stable. They decay by emitting a beta$^+$ particle
- Unstable, heavy, nuclei with $Z > 83$ decay by emitting alpha particles

BETA PARTICLES

You might be surprised by the fact that there are two types of beta particles, one with negative charge the other with positive charge. In almost all respects they are identical. They have, for example, the same mass and their charges are equal in size.

The **negative beta particle (beta⁻)** is actually a fast electron, ejected from the unstable nucleus. Now an electron has no right to be in a nucleus so where does it come from?

The unstable nucleus in this case has too many neutrons and the extra neutrons will decay by emitting a beta particle. This carries away negative charge from a neutral particle so leaving it positive. The neutron has turned into a proton! This keeps happening until the nucleus reaches the line of stability shown in picture 9.

For unstable nuclei having too many protons (i.e. below the stability line) it is the protons that have to make the change. They emit a **positive beta particle (beta⁺)** which is the **antiparticle** of the electron called a **positron**. (See *The father of antimatter*, page 230.)

A positive charge leaves a positive object: the proton has become a neutron.

Note that in both these kinds of change the nucleus keeps the same mass number because both positron and beta particles have so little mass. But it changes its proton and neutron number: one goes up, the other goes down.

neutron $\longrightarrow$ proton + electron (beta⁻ decay)

proton $\longrightarrow$ neutron + positron (beta⁺ decay)

The smaller nuclei are more predictable. Picture 10 shows a small part of the *N-Z* plot for the lighter elements. Look at carbon, for example. Stable carbon is carbon 12. It has six protons and six neutrons – perfect! High in the atmosphere a nucleus of nitrogen may get hit by a very energetic particle from outer space (a cosmic ray). As a results one of its protons gets changed into a neutron and so nitrogen-14 becomes carbon-14. An isotope of carbon-14 has too many neutrons therefore it decays by beta⁻ emission (a fast electron). A neutron changes to a proton and carbon-14 becomes nitrogen-14 again. This set of reactions is the one used in radioactive dating of carbon-containing materials and is widely used in archaeology.

Other isotopes of carbon can be made artificially. Look at carbon-11. It is unstable because it has too few neutrons. It reaches balance by emitting a beta⁺ particle (a fast positron). A proton has changed to a neutron and carbon-11 becomes boron-11.

These changes are shown in picture 11.

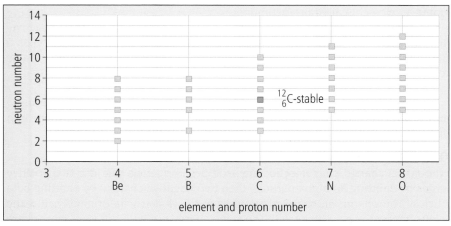

Picture 10   Some lighter isotopes: stable and unstable.

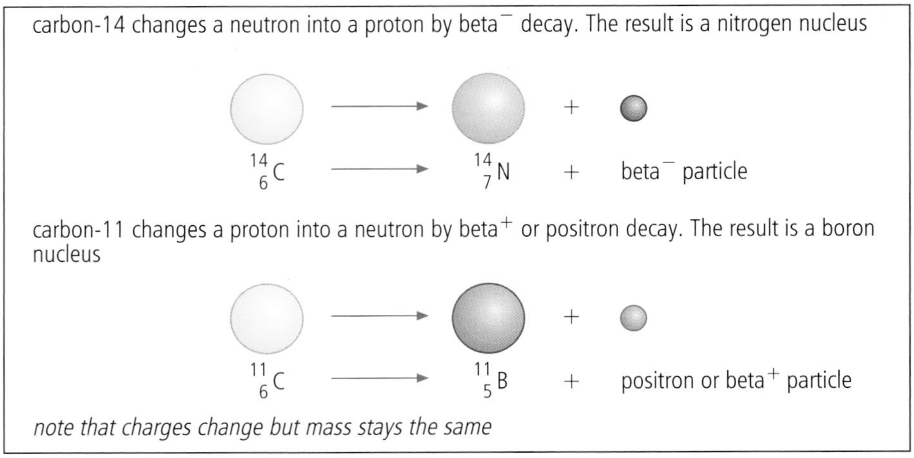

carbon-14 changes a neutron into a proton by beta$^-$ decay. The result is a nitrogen nucleus

$$^{14}_{6}C \longrightarrow ^{14}_{7}N \;+\; \text{beta}^- \text{ particle}$$

carbon-11 changes a proton into a neutron by beta$^+$ or positron decay. The result is a boron nucleus

$$^{11}_{6}C \longrightarrow ^{11}_{5}B \;+\; \text{positron or beta}^+ \text{ particle}$$

note that charges change but mass stays the same

Picture 11   Decay processes for two unstable isotopes of carbon.

■ But things aren't that simple

Unstable nuclei obey some fairly complicated laws of physics. Some reach stability by emitting an alpha particle for example. This is more likely to happen when the unstable nucleus is large, with lots of protons and neutrons. Radium-224 is an example of an alpha emitter. Very massive nuclei might break apart into two smaller nuclei, roughly equal in size. This is **nuclear fission** – which is the process that nuclear reactors use (see topic F5). Some nuclei also become stable by capturing an orbital electron from an inner orbit – a process known as electron capture.

■ The decay chain

The nucleus of uranium-238 is the largest nucleus of any natural element. The '238' refers to the fact that it has 238 particles in it. It contains 92 protons and 146 neutrons.

When uranium-238 decays it sends out an **alpha particle**. An alpha particle has two protons and two neutrons. The nucleus is now lighter (by 4 particles) and has less charge (by 2 units). *This means that it has become the nucleus of a different element.* In fact it has become a nucleus of thorium – thorium-234, but the thorium nucleus is also unstable. One of the neutrons inside the nucleus sends out an electron, as a beta particle, and turns into a proton.

The *mass* of the thorium nucleus stays much the same. After all, it has only lost an electron, which doesn't weigh very much at all. But it has now one more proton. This means that it behaves chemically like a different element. It has become an element called protactinium.

The decay chain doesn't stop there, however. Protactinium is also radioactive. It too decays by sending out a beta particle. This means that it too becomes a different element. Yet more changes have to take place before, finally, a stable nucleus is formed. This will be the element *lead*.

Some of these changes are shown in picture 12.

In many of these changes the nucleus also gets rid of some energy by emitting gamma radiation. This has no mass or charge, so the nucleus does not change into a different one.

ISOTOPES

As the nuclei change, they may become isotopes. A nucleus can lose two positive charges by emitting an alpha particle, then two negative charges by emitting beta particles. The charge on the nucleus is back to what it was originally. But the nucleus has lost mass. Nuclei with the same charge but with different masses are called isotopes.

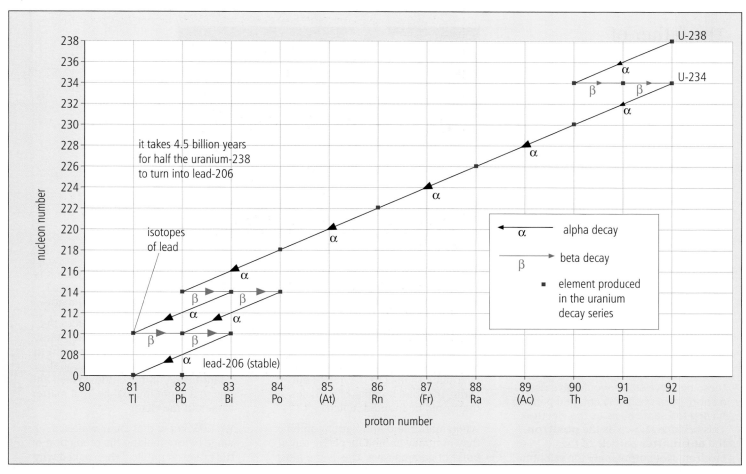

Picture 12   Radioactive decay – how one nucleus changes into another.

■ Why don't nuclei decay all at once?

No one knows the answer to this question. All we know is that some nuclei tend to decay very quickly and others very slowly. Also, no one can predict when any given nucleus will decay. It all seems to be a matter of chance, or 'luck'.

It may seem strange that what happens in such a precise subject as physics depends on 'luck'. But the laws of 'luck' are quite well known. They deal with the **probability** of some event actually occuring. Scientists have known for a long time that many everyday things are decided by the laws of probability as much as by the precise rules of Newton, for example. Many things seem to happen, or to move, in quite a **random** way. Just think of the weather, or the way molecules move in a gas.

But we can still make predictions about gases and about the weather. They might not always be accurate predictions, especially when it comes to weather forecasting. But the 'gas laws' are quite accurate, even though we can't predict how any single molecule in the gas is going to move. The laws are accurate because there are *so many* molecules in any reasonable quantity of gas. The different speeds and energies of the molecules average out to something quite predictable.

In much the same way we can predict quite accurately the 'activity' of a collection of radioactive nuclei. Again, this is because there are so many of them. In just one-hundredth of a gram of uranium, for example, there are 25 billion billion nuclei! We cannot predict what any one nucleus is going to do, but on average we can say quite accurately how many of them will decay in the next hour.

The father of antimatter

Paul Dirac was born in Bristol in 1902, the son of a French teacher. His father was very strict and only bothered to reply if Paul spoke to him in French. Apparently this was a ruse to encourage Paul to become fluent in the language!

The idea backfired because Paul was a stubborn boy and simply refused to speak. For the rest of his life he only spoke if it was absolutely necessary.

Dirac studied electrical engineering at the University of Bristol, but failed to find work, and went on to becomes a graduate student in theoretical physics at Cambridge. It was here that he made a breakthrough whilst applying quantum mechanics to Einstein's special theory of relativity. He found that states of negative energy must exist for electrons and that 'holes' in these negative states would give rise to a short-lived positively charged particle having the same mass as the electron. This became known as the **positron**, the **antimatter** particle of the electron. Not surprisingly the scientific community met Dirac's prediction with great scepticism. However, just one year later in 1932 Carl Anderson in

Picture 1   Paul Dirac (on the left) deep in conversation.

America and Patrick Blackett in England found positrons experimentally and confirmed their existence.

Thus began a hunt for more antimatter. We now know that every particle has its antimatter equivalent. Virtually overnight, thanks to the quiet Paul Dirac, the total number of particles that could be found doubled!

When matter and antimatter combine they mutually annihilate giving out a burst of gamma rays. This is the most powerful release of energy known.

Another way of looking at antimatter is to think of it as real matter travelling backwards in time. Perhaps then it is not so surprising that most of the Universe is composed of real matter.

Very early on in the evolution of the Universe, instants after the Big Bang, matter and antimatter are thought to have been around in almost equal quantities. A titanic battle ensued and, due to a slight imbalance, real matter came out the victor.

We now know that Dirac waited a while before making his prediction of the positron public. When asked why he waited, Dirac replied typically, 'Pure cowardice'.

Activities

A   Nuclear pioneers

Use a library or the Internet to find out about the scientists who investigated radioactivity and the atom in the early years of this century. Find out about Ernest Rutherford, Marie Curie and her husband Pierre. What did they discover? How did they do it? What use have we made of their discoveries? Would it be better if they hadn't made these discoveries?

B   Convincing John Dalton

Explaining an idea to another person is an excellent way of improving your own understanding, as well as theirs.

John Dalton, who produced the Atomic Theory, said 'Thou knowest no man can split the atom'. Imagine he were brought by time travel to the present. Could he be convinced he was wrong?

Work in pairs for this activity. One person will play John Dalton, the other will play themselves trying to persuade him. He would need some convincing, and would be likely to want some proof.

You will need to prepare your cases before you start.

After the activity, discuss how it went. Was 'John Dalton' convinced?

Questions

1 a Why does an atom normally have just as many protons as electrons?

b What happens to an atom when it loses an electron?

c Give an example of what might make an atom lose an electron.

2 What is the difference between a proton and a neutron?

3 In the simple model of an atom, we imagine that electrons go around the nucleus in 'orbits'.

a Explain what an orbit is.

b What might happen if the electrons stopped moving?

4 'The radioactive decay of an atom is a random event.' Make up two other sentences in which the word 'random' is correctly used.

5 a The probability of getting a 'six' in a game of dice is 1 in 6. Why?

b What is the probability of choosing a Queen of Hearts in a card game with a well shuffled pack (52 cards)?

c The probability of a certain type of nucleus decaying in the next 10 seconds is 1 in 5 million. How many would you expect to decay in the next ten seconds in a sample of 100 million nuclei?

6 Give the words that fit in the blanks in the following. The missing words are:

negative, positive, nucleus, isotopes, equal, mass number, atomic number, electrons.

Atoms are made of three kinds of subatomic particles. Protons and neutrons are found in the small central part of the atom, called the ___(a)___. Moving around outside are the ___(b)___. Protons have one unit of ___(c)___ charge, and electrons have an equal ___(d)___ charge. In a neutral atom, the number of protons and electrons is ___(e)___. This number is called the ___(f)___. The number of protons added to the number of neutrons in an atom is called the ___(g)___. Atoms with the same atomic number but different mass numbers are called ___(h)___.

7 An atom of a particular element, contains 13 protons, 14 neutrons and 13 electrons.

a What is its atomic number?

b What is its mass number?

8 Make a copy of table 2. Fill in all the blank spaces.

9 Which of the atoms in table 2 are isotopes of the same element?

10 a All atoms of a particular element have the same atomic number. Explain why.

b Atoms of the same element can have different mass numbers. Explain why.

11 a Bromine, Br, has two isotopes, with mass numbers 79 and 81. Naturally-occurring bromine contains the two isotopes in equal amounts. What is the relative atomic mass of bromine?

b Boron, B, has two stable isotopes, with mass numbers 10 and 11. Naturally-occurring boron contains 20% boron-10 and 80% boron-11. What is the relative atomic mass of boron?

12 Picture 5 shows two isotopes of hydrogen. There is a third isotope, called tritium, which is unstable and radioactive. Tritium atoms contain two neutrons.

a How many: (i) protons, and (ii) electrons do tritium atoms contain?

b What is: (i) the atomic number, and (ii) the mass number of tritium?

13 Copy out and complete the following sentences:

a Nuclei below the stability line have too many ......to be stable a and they decay by emitting ....particles.

b Nuclei above the stability line have too many ......to be stable and they decay by emitting ......particles

c The unstable, heavy ...... with proton number ......than 83 decay by emitting ....particles

d The positron is the antimatter version of the ......

14 A nucleus emits an electron and as a result loses some negative charge.

a What happens to N the neutron number ?

b What happens to Z the proton number?

15 Given that $^{208}_{82}Pb$ is stable. Use a Periodic Table to find the isotope that emits a fast electron.

Table 2

Symbol	Number of protons	Number of neutrons	Number of electrons	Atomic number	Mass number
$^{1}_{1}H$	1	0		1	
$^{2}_{1}H$		1		1	
$^{4}_{2}H$					
C	6	6			12
$^{63}_{29}Cu$	29				
Cu	29	36			
$^{56}_{26}Fe$					
Mg		12	12		

Energy from the nucleus

Nuclear energy powers the movement of continents. We can also use nuclear energy directly – but can we do this safely?

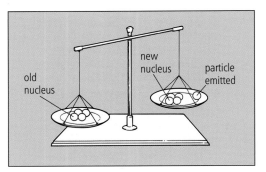

Picture 1 In a radioactive change, the new products weigh less than the original nucleus.

■ 'Moonshine!' says top nuclear scientist

Ernest Rutherford was the physicist who found out what alpha particles were, and who discovered the nucleus of the atom. *There is enough energy in a gram of uranium to send a liner across the Atlantic!* he said in a newpaper interview, 60 years ago. *But the idea that you can actually use it is moonshine. It will take over 4 billion years to get just a half of it out!*

He was thinking of radioactivity, not nuclear power stations. When a natural radioactive substance decays, it gives out energy – but only slowly.

Nowadays we have artificial isotopes that do give out their energy in a shorter time. They are used to power instruments in Earth satellites. They are also used in heart pacemakers.

Even so, the power they can generate is very small and it is very expensive. Nuclear power stations do not rely on 'ordinary radioactivity' to produce energy. But where does the energy come from?

$E = mc^2$

When atoms decay, the energy they release appears as movement energy (kinetic energy) of the high-speed particles they send out. It was Albert Einstein (see topic B9) who came up with the surprising theory that this energy was produced by changing some of the mass of the nucleus into energy. This theory was proved when careful measurements were made. The mass of the emitted particle plus the mass of the nucleus left behind *was less than the mass of the original nucleus* (picture 1).

Energy had appeared. Mass had disappeared. These two facts contradicted the laws of physics as understood in 1905. These laws said that:

● energy could not be lost or created (Law of Conservation of Energy),
● mass could not be made or destroyed (Law of Conservation of Matter).

Einstein would say: *If we say that matter is really a kind of stored energy, then both laws can be correct. In fact, my Theory of Relativity predicts that this should happen. The 'energy value' of any piece of matter is given by my formula $E = mc^2$. No problem.*

The missing mass, m, was converted to kinetic energy, E. The quantity c is the speed of light. This is a very large number – 300 000 000 m/s. It is the *square* of this number which multiplies with the mass to give the value of the energy. This means that it doesn't take much mass to produce a lot of energy.

But the main problem still remained. There was no way to speed up the rate at which ordinary, naturally radioactive materials decayed and produced their energy. The energy was there, but dammed up so well that it could only trickle out at a uselessly small rate.

NUCLEAR FISSION

The breakthrough into 'atomic energy' came in 1938. Physicists working in Berlin proved that some of the unstable uranium nuclei don't just decay by giving out a small particle or some gamma radiation, as described in topic F2. Instead, they split up into two nearly equal parts.

But just as with radioactive changes, mass was lost and converted to energy. What was the more important, *the splitting could be controlled.* Then, in 1939, the Second World War began. It was clear to some physicists that the immense store of energy in a lump of uranium could be released very quickly. The result would be a huge explosion – **a nuclear bomb**.

The bomb was built – it took five years to do this – and two 'atomic bombs' were dropped on Japan by the USA in the summer of 1945. The nuclear age had begun.

The process of splitting nuclei to give energy is called nuclear **fission**. The same process is used in a **nuclear reactor**, but of course it is controlled so that it happens much more slowly than in a bomb. To explain how it works we need to remember what the nucleus of an atom is like.

■ Atomic nuclei

Atoms contain negative electrons moving around a positive core – the nucleus. But a nucleus is not just a blob of positively charged matter. The main parts of a nucleus are the protons and the neutrons (see picture 2). Protons are positively charged and neutrons do not carry an electric charge.

Some nuclei have too many protons and neutrons and tend to be unstable. This causes radioactivity (See topics F2 and F4.) But some very large nuclei may split into two parts, instead of undergoing ordinary radioactive decay.

■ The chain reaction

This splitting is what goes on in a nuclear bomb or reactor. When the nucleus splits in two main parts it also shoots out one or more spare neutrons. These can fly into another nearby nucleus quite easily – and make that nucleus split. In turn, the new neutrons may shoot off into other nuclei and cause them to split.

This builds up into a **chain reaction**, with nucleus after nucleus splitting and triggering off others. Each time a nucleus splits it gives out energy. This process is shown in picture 3. You can compare it to an avalanche on a mountain slope. When someone throws just one stone it can cause them all to cascade down the slope.

The result of an uncontrolled chain reaction is an explosion. This is what happens in a nuclear bomb. In a nuclear reactor the reaction is controlled. The uranium is spread out, as thin rods (**fuel rods**). In between the rods are other rods, made of a material that absorbs neutrons. If all the neutrons are absorbed no further reactions are possible and the reactor stops giving out energy.

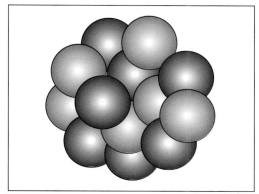

Picture 2 An oxygen nucleus. It has 8 protons and 8 neutrons.

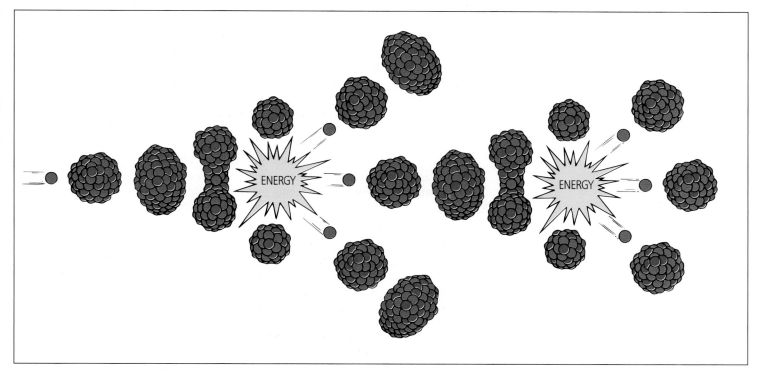

Picture 3 A chain reaction.

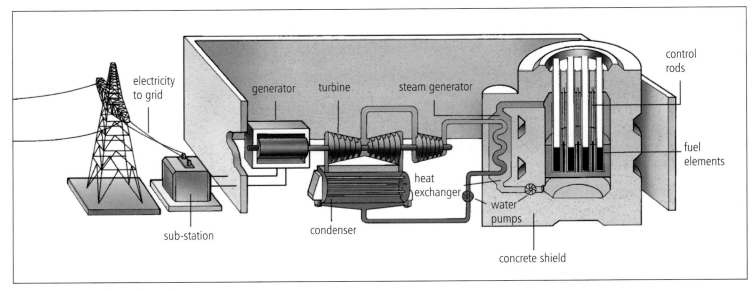

Picture 4 The workings of a nuclear reactor.

In a typical reactor, the absorbing rods (**control rods**) are moved in and out of the fuel rods. This controls the rate of the fission reactions and the amount of energy released. Picture 4 shows the main parts of a nuclear reactor. Other rods (**moderators**) slow down the neutrons so that they are better at causing fission.

The energy released when the nuclei split up heats the fuel rods. The hot 'core' of the reactor then heats water or some other fluid. This hot fluid may become radioactive and has to be kept inside the reactor. The fluid moves to carry its energy to the heat exchanger where it is transferred to boil water. The steam produced drives an ordinary steam turbine.

The turbines turn generators, as in an ordinary coal-fired or gas-fired power station.

NUCLEAR WASTE

When the uranium nuclei in the fuel rods split they form two smaller nuclei. These nuclei are radioactive. Eventually the fuel rods are used up and have to be replaced. The old rods are now very radioactive.

Also, the neutrons that are not used in the fission process are absorbed by control rods and other parts of the reactor. This makes them become radioactive as well.

After anything from 20 to 50 years, the working parts of the reactor are worn out, and have also become highly radioactive. When the reactor is dismantled these materials have somehow to be disposed of. This process is called **decommissioning**. It now seems that this could be very expensive. This means that the total costs of nuclear power are much higher than was thought when the first nuclear power stations were built.

NUCLEAR FUSION

But there is yet another way to get energy from nuclei. The Sun and the stars get their energy from the opposite process to nuclear fission. They use the fact that when light nuclei join together to make heavier ones, energy can be released. Once again, the energy comes from lost mass.

In the Sun, the process involves the nuclei of hydrogen isotopes (protons and deuterons) joining together to form helium nuclei. This process is called nuclear **fusion**.

Could we use fusion to produce energy on Earth? This energy would come from a very cheap material – hydrogen. The process would produce less radioactive waste. Research has been going on for nearly fifty years to produce **controlled fusion**. So far this research has been unsuccessful; the only 'practical' device to have been developed is the hydrogen bomb (picture 5). Although the latest experiments have shown some success, this source of energy is not likely to be available until well into the 21st century.

Picture 5 A hydrogen bomb. So far, we can't control nuclear fusion to give a steady supply of energy.

Activities

A Find out about nuclear power stations

Read all you can about nuclear power stations.

People disagree about whether nuclear power is a good idea or not. Make a list of the points that could be made both for and against using nuclear power to generate electricity. You should consider: *safety, cost per unit of electricity, pollution, convenience of use, storing nuclear waste, the Greenhouse effect*, etc.

Some of the points will be 'scientific', but some may be important but not based on scientific evidence. Mark the ones you think are scientific with a capital S.

B The case for and against nuclear energy

Use a library or the Internet to find out about the following. Make short notes on each one, then combine your thoughts and knowledge into a poster which could be entitled either:

1 Ban the bomb! or

2 Nuclear weapons have kept the free world free!

Topics:

1 The effects of nuclear radiation

2 The hydrogen bomb

3 Hiroshima

4 The end of the 'Cold War'

5 Inter-continental ballistic missile (ICBMs)

6 The nuclear winter

Try to get a good balance of fact and opinion.

Questions

1 Explain briefly why a nuclear chain reaction is like an avalanche of snow or rocks on a steep mountainside.

2 Nuclear 'fuel' – uranium – is quite cheap. Give two reasons why it is still expensive to produce electricity from nuclear power stations.

3 Explain what the *control rods* do in a nuclear reactor.

4 a Describe an atomic nucleus.

   b 'Carbon-14 is an isotope of carbon-12.' Explain what an isotope is, in terms of the difference between these two types of carbon.

5 People argue a great deal about whether nuclear power stations should be built. Give three reasons in each case:

   a in favour of nuclear power,

   b against nuclear power.

6 a Use the formula $E = mc^2$ to calculate how much energy in joules could be obtained from 1 kg of matter if all of it could be turned into energy. The speed of light, c, is 300 000 000 m/s.

   b The total energy we can actually get from 1 kg of uranium is very much less than the answer you should have got for part (a). Why is this?

Radiation and life

Ionising radiations are all around us. Some of it is dangerous, some of it is useful.

Picture 1 Granite outcrops in Dartmoor — granite often contains radioactive elements.

Picture 2 Nuclear waste transporter.

WHY IS RADIOACTIVITY DANGEROUS?

The alpha, beta and gamma radiations from a radioactive material travel at high speeds. Also, alpha and beta particles are electrically charged. When they go into living cells they can kill or damage them. They can do this because they ionise molecules that are vital to life. A large 'dose' of radiation kills so many cells that the effect is like being burned by fire.

Alpha particles are easily stopped. Even a sheet of paper is enough. But beta and gamma radiations can get deep into the body so that cells in internal organs are damaged (see topic F2).

For low levels of radiation you lose just a few cells. This in itself is not dangerous. After all, our bodies contain lots of cells. The danger comes from the fact that the radiation can *change* some of the chemicals we have in cells. These are the complex molecules of DNA and RNA that control how the cell works.

As a result, the cell may go out of control. It grows and divides just as if it was an independent organism that feeds on our bodies. It becomes a group of **cancer cells**.

Also, if sperm or ova cells in the reproductive system are changed, the result could be children with birth defects. They could be born with badly formed or missing limbs, or brain damage.

Table 1 Exposure to radiation in everyday situations.

Type of exposure	Microsievert
1 radiation due to nuclear power stations for a year	10
2 watching television for a year	10
3 wearing a radioactive luminous watch for a year (now not very common)	30
4 having a chest X-ray	200
5 exposure to fall-out in Britain from nuclear bomb testing in 1959	350
6 radiation from a brick house, per year	750
7 working for a month in a uranium mine	1000
8 typical dose received by a member of the general public in a year	1500
9 maximum dose allowed to general public per year	5000
10 maximum dose allowed to workers exposed to radiation per year	50 000

Table 1 shows the radiation doses you might get in different situations, together with the 'allowed doses' for ordinary people and workers in the nuclear industries. They are measured in **microsieverts**, which is a measure of how much energy the radiation delivers to the body.

We cannot escape from ionising radiation. Some comes from outer space, as fast-moving particles. Most rocks contain a tiny amount of some radioactive elements. In many parts of the country radioactive decay produces the radioactive gas **radon**. This seeps into buildings and can be breathed in. The effect of all these sources is to produce the natural **background radiation**.

Granite rocks, which have come from deep inside the Earth, contain more than the average amount of radioactive elements (picture 1). People living in granite areas should make sure that their houses are well ventilated. They should get their homes checked now and again for radon, and if too much is found they should seal their floors.

Biologists believe that background radiation is one of the causes of changes to genes in the reproductive cells of all living things. These changes help to produce **variation** in living things, allowing evolution to take place.

HALF-LIFE AND NUCLEAR WASTE

As explained in topic F5, nuclear reactors produce **nuclear wastes**. Picture 2 shows waste being transported. Radioactive materials are also used in industry, and produce waste. Some of these waste materials have very short half-lives (see topic F2). This means that they give out their radiation very quickly. They are very dangerous – for a short while. But most of the radiation is gone after a few months.

For any radioactive material, after 10 half-lives the material is only a thousandth as active as it was at the start. It has been divided in half ten times. But some radioactive waste materials have half-lives running into hundreds of years. These materials are called low-level waste. Storing these safely is a major problem. This is no way we can speed up the rate at which they decay. Half-lives are fixed and do not change.

■ Storing radioactive waste

Because it is dangerous to humans, low-level radioactive waste has to be stored safely, so that the radiations don't get out. It is stored inside containers made of metal, glass or concrete which absorb the radiations. If low-level waste is to be stored underground, great care will have to be taken to make sure that the containers stay unbroken, perhaps for thousands of years.

Picture 3 shows how radioactive waste might be stored.

These problems of waste disposal have caused many countries, including the UK, to draw back from building a lot of new nuclear power stations. The cost of dismantling the power stations safely and storing the waste seems to make nuclear energy less economic than people once thought.

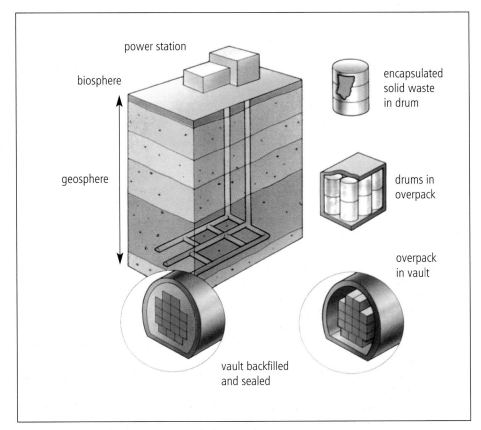

Picture 3   How radioactive waste might be stored.

Radiation in industry

Ionising radiations are used in a wide variety of ways. So what properties decide how useful they can be? Here is a reminder about their key properties. The **range** and **penetration** of the radiations depend on how ionising they are.

- Alpha particles are very ionising and they are easily stopped by a sheet of paper.
- Beta particles are less ionising than alpha and penetrate further but they can be stopped by 3 mm of aluminium.
- Gamma rays are the least ionising and can penetrate large distances into matter. 1 cm thickness of lead will reduce the intensity of a beam of gamma rays by about a half.

By their nature alpha particles have limited use – they are so easily stopped. But a beam of beta particles will have a measurable reduction in intensity when it passes through paper or thin metal. This reduction can be used to monitor the thickness of a strip of metal made by a machine, and the result used to control the machine.

This is an example of **negative feedback.** If the radiation gets weaker than expected it means that the strip is too thick, and the machine is adjusted so that the strip is made thinner.

Picture 5 Beta sources are used to control the thickness of the tyre core metal strip.

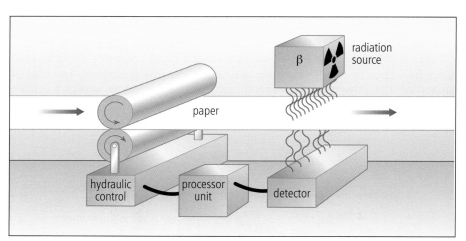

Picture 4 Thickness monitoring using a beta source.

Gamma rays are very useful for sterilising medical equipment since they can easily penetrate through the wrapping and kill any bacteria. The equipment then remains sterilised until the protective wrapping is removed.

Gamma radiation can also be used to sterilise food and improve its shelf life. It does not make the food radioactive but there is some damage inflicted on the molecules resulting in an unpleasant taste. If you owned a food store would you want to sell gamma irradiated food?

Radioactivity in medicine

Radioactive isotopes are also used a lot in medicine. Most large hospitals have a medical physics department that is responsible for all aspects of their use.

- Alpha particles given out by a small amount of plutonium are used to generate electricity in heart pacemakers.
- Special patches can be coated with an alpha emitter and applied to the skin to treat specific disorders.

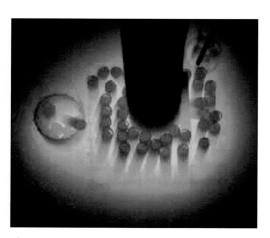

Picture 6 Gamma rays from highly radioactive spent fuel rods are used to sterilise medical products.

- Beta emitters are useful because beta particles are absorbed within a small volume of diseased tissue and the radiation dose can be restricted to this small volume. Such isotopes can be applied to strips or needles, which are then inserted into the patient.
- Gamma radiation can be fired into a patient in order to kill deep seated tumours, but this technique has now been replaced with high-energy X-ray beams instead.

Gamma radiation is most useful for diagnostic imaging. (See *Gamma rays and the body*, page 240.)

■ Working with radiation

We are all exposed to background radiation but people who work with ionising radiations need to keep track of their exposure. They usually wear a Film Badge Dosimeter while they are at work. The film is sensitive to radiation just as ordinary film is sensitive to light. After work the badge is handed in and the film is developed. Picture 7 shows a typical badge that can deal with the different radiations. The amount of blackening behind each window is measured and compared to a known standard.

Film badges are good because they are cheap, easy to wear and give a permanent record of the exposure.

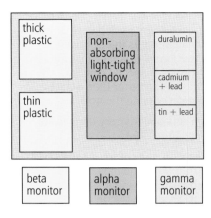

Picture 7 A film badge monitors personal exposure to radiation.

Activities

A Radiactivity all around us

Use a library or the Internet to find out about one of the following uses of radiation. Make notes or a poster so that you can report back to the rest of the class.

1 Smoke detectors.

2 Radioactive tracers in hospitals.

3 Using radioactive materials to check for faults in metal objects.

4 Finding the age of old objects using carbon-14.

5 Using radiation to treat cancer.

B Are you at risk?

Radon gas is radioactive. It can be dangerous if it is allowed to build up in houses or other buildings. Find out what kind of radiation it emits.

Trace a map of the British Isles. Use an atlas to find out which areas are over granite or other igneous rocks. Mark these area on your map. Find out whether your local council has any plans for checking or dealing with radon gas.

Questions

1 You can't escape from ionising radiation on Earth. Name two natural sources of this radiation.

2 Describe briefly two effects of ionising radiation on living things.

3 a What are the three kinds of ionising radiations that are emitted by a radioactive substance?

   b Describe how the human body can be protected from each type.

c From which of the sources of radiation given in table 1 are you personally most likely to be at risk?

4 Why are radioactive substances with a short half-life more active than those with a long half-life?

5 Describe two ways in which radioactive waste (e.g. from hospitals) could be stored safely.

6 Ultra-violet light is also an 'ionising radiation'. What dangers does this present to human beings on Earth? How can these dangers be reduced?

7 List the number of ways in which gamma rays can be used for the benefit of mankind.

8 If radiation is used safely in hospitals why do the medical physics staff need to wear film badges?

9 The radioactive isotope Technetium-99^m has a half-life of six hours. Why is it ideal for use in imaging the human body?

Gamma rays and the body

Radioactive isotopes can be used to 'see inside' the body and the information received helps doctors with diagnosis and possible treatment. Basically a patient is injected with a radioactive liquid which is absorbed by a target organ. A special camera attached to a computer then detects the radiation outside the body.

Although this sounds very dangerous it is actually quite safe!

The isotope that is commonly used is Technetium-99^m (The m stands for metastable – which means almost stable). It decays giving off only gamma rays and it has a half-life of six hours. Gamma rays are not very ionising and easily penetrate through the body to the gamma camera. The six-hour half-life is good because it is time enough for the doctor to take some measurements but it is sufficiently short that the patient will not be radioactive for long.

The clever part is to tag the Technetium-99^m to another molecule so that the resulting complex can collect in the target organ. For example: it is tagged onto a complex phosphate molecule if the doctor wants to check for bone cancer.

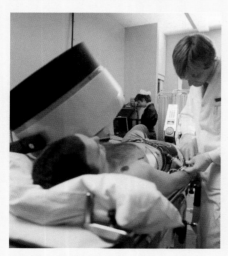

Picture 1   Injection of a radioactive isotope.

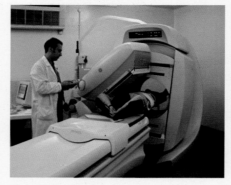

Picture 2   A gamma camera.

Cancer cells in the bone are abnormally active and readily take up the phosphate and the Technetium-99^m along with it. The cancer cells are now radioactive and the 'hot spots' show up on the gamma camera, giving the doctor an idea of the spread of the disease.

The gamma camera contains a special crystal (sodium iodide) that interacts with gamma rays to produce a tiny flash of light. Sets of photomultiplier tubes amplify this and provide electrical signals giving the position and strength of the initial gamma ray. The computer than displays the information as a pixel of appropriate brightness on the monitor screen and a complete picture soon builds up.

Gamma scans also provide real-time information on metabolic processes in the body. For example: if the kidneys are targeted then we can see over a period of time how well a kidney is working or if there are any blockages which prevent it working properly.

Deliberately making the body radioactive may sound crazy but the information gained can save lives!

Picture 3   Hot spots shown in a bone scan.

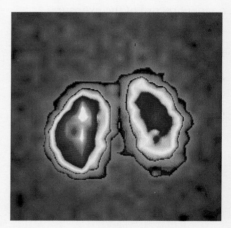

Picture 4   A gamma scan of the kidneys.

F7

Probing the nucleus

*Big fleas have little fleas
upon their backs to bite 'em
Little fleas have lesser fleas
And so on ad infinitum?*

■ Higher and higher energies

Breaking down particles into smaller constituent particles takes energy.

Atoms were probed by energetic alpha particles by Rutherford (see topic F3) and the smaller nucleus was discovered.

Breaking apart the nucleus took even greater energies but eventually by the 1930s the proton and the neutron were found.

The basic technique for discovering elementary particles is simple: Take the particle you want to break apart, hit it as hard as you can with another particle and watch what comes off.

It sounds easy but greater and greater energies are required.

Today physicists use expensive particle accelerators to speed up charged particles (e.g. electrons or protons) to enormous energies, making them collide with stationary targets or beams of particles coming in the opposite direction.

The Stanford Linear Accelerator in California is over 3 km long and the circular synchrotron at Cern near Geneva has a circumference of 27 km.

Picture 1 The Stanford Linear Accelerator, California USA, shown with the circular synchrotron.

Picture 2 The large underground synchrotron at Cern near Geneva.

Picture 3 Delphi: one of the large modern detectors at Cern.

Sophisticated detectors supported by large computers record and process information about the particles given off from the collisions.

New heavy electron-like particles called muons and tauons have been found along with their antiparticles, but the real challenge over the past twenty years has been to probe the inner structures of neutrons and protons.

Quarks

'Three quarks for Muster Mark!' from Finnegans Wake by James Joyce

In 1964 Murray Gell-Mann proposed a theory in which protons and neutrons were made up of three new particles called **quarks.**

There are two quarks from which the nuclei of ordinary matter are composed. These are known as the **up quark** and the **down quark**.

Perhaps the most amazing property about these quarks is that their electrical charge is a fraction of the 'fundamental' electron charge (i.e. they have a charge less than that of the electron).

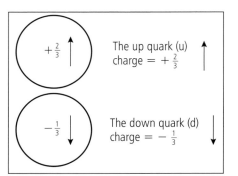

Picture 4

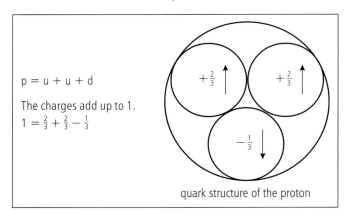

$p = u + u + d$

The charges add up to 1.
$1 = \frac{2}{3} + \frac{2}{3} - \frac{1}{3}$

quark structure of the proton

Picture 5

According to Gell-Mann's theory a proton is made of 2 up quarks and 1 down quark.

The theory also makes life tough for the experimental physicists since it predicts that quarks cannot exist outside of the nucleons. Safe within the proton or neutron the three quarks behave as if they were free, but if we try and move quarks further apart then super strong forces appear which prevent this happening. It's as if they are linked together by loose elastic. Pulling against the elastic starts a force, which gets stronger the more you pull at it. The energy stored in the 'elastic' can even be converted into new quarks!

Despite these difficulties physicists, using giant particle accelerators, have proved that families of quarks and their antiquarks really do exist.

Quarks and beta decay

Knowledge of quarks gives us a deeper insight into the origin of beta decay.

In **beta⁻ decay** a neutron changes into a proton plus an electron

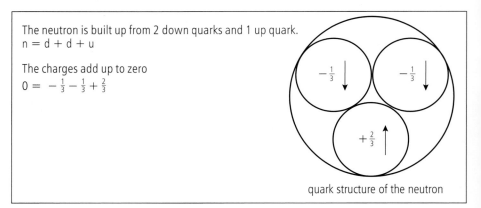

The neutron is built up from 2 down quarks and 1 up quark.
$n = d + d + u$

The charges add up to zero
$0 = -\frac{1}{3} - \frac{1}{3} + \frac{2}{3}$

quark structure of the neutron

Picture 6

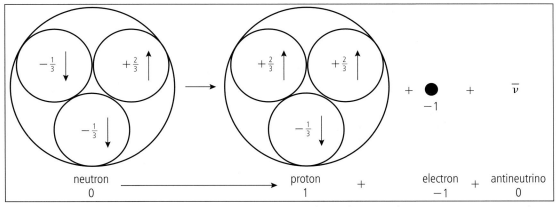

Picture 7 Neutron decay. A down quark changes into an up quark. An electron and an antineutrino are emitted.

Note that the total charge after the decay is the same as it was before. Nature insists that charge is conserved.

The **antineutrino** is a particle with no mass and no charge and therefore it does not upset the charge conservation. However it is also necessary to conserve the total *particle* number. Since we start with one particle on the left-hand side of the equation we must have an antimatter particle on the right-hand side to cancel the extra *particle* number of the electron. In this way the total *particle* number on the right-hand side also adds up to one.

Wolfgang Pauli predicted the existence of antineutrinos and neutrinos in 1930 as a means of explaining the energy variation of beta particles. Amazingly, soon after Pauli's prediction, neutrinos were discovered!

In terms of quarks we can see that one of the down quarks has changed into an up quark and in the process it ejects the electron and the antineutrino. (Picture 8.)

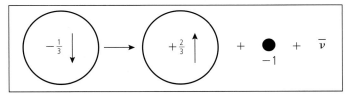

Picture 8

In **beta$^+$ decay** a proton changes into a neutron plus a positron.

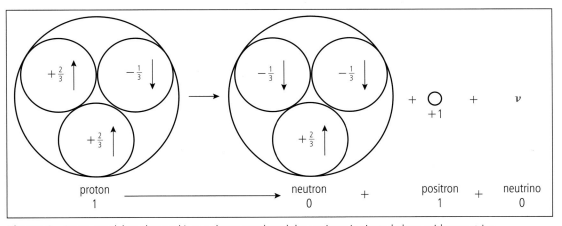

Picture 9 An up quark has changed into a down quark and the positron is ejected along with a neutrino.

Again total charge is conserved.

Note that now a neutrino is emitted thus cancelling the antimatter 'particle' number of the positron.

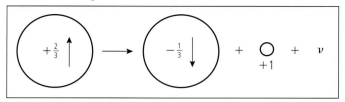

Picture 10

■ Can we carry on creating more and more particles?

Just as Democritus reasoned back in the 5th century BC that small particles stop with atoms; physicists now believe that the building blocks of matter (as we know it today) stop with quarks. The best current theory suggests that quarks are truly fundamental particles.

But there is a problem in that the Universe seems to have a lot of mass missing!

In topic G6 *Galaxies and the Universe* you will learn about the evolution of the Universe and the **Big Bang.** Quarks were formed very soon after space and time began but calculation shows that we should be observing much more matter than there actually is in the Universe. This missing 90% or so of matter seems to be invisible and is known as **dark matter.** Some physicist think that it might be made up of weakly interacting massive particles (WIMPS) – as yet undiscovered. So the search for even more particles goes on!

Questions

1 Explain why protons and neutrons are not fundamental particles

2 Why is it necessary to use high-energy particle accelerators to probe the structure of the nucleons?

3 What other quantity, apart from 'particle' number and charge, is conserved during beta decay?

4 Explain why the force between quarks is radically different to the force between opposite electric charges.

5 Given that quarks have a fraction of the fundamental charge (1) explain why only three quarks can build up a nucleon.

Energy levels: the physics of the very small

When physicists deal with very small particles they have to use a special theory called Quantum Theory because Newton's laws of motion fail to work anymore!

For example if we consider a simple atom of hydrogen where we imagine the electron whizzing in orbit around the proton nucleus.

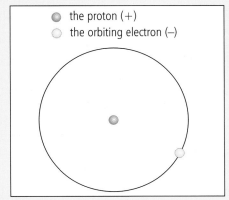

○ the proton (+)
○ the orbiting electron (−)

Picture 1 A simplified picture of a hydrogen atom.

Then according to Newton's second law of motion the electron has centripetal acceleration towards the proton. But according to the laws of electromagnetism this accelerating electron should be continually radiating away energy in the form of electromagnetic radiation. This would result in the electron spiraling into the proton and the hydrogen atom would quickly collapse. So what prevents electrons 'sticking' onto protons?

Clearly this does not happen and so we are forced to admit that Newton's laws breakdown on this small scale.

Picture 2 Niels Bohr quantised the hydrogen atom in 1913.

In 1913 Niels Bohr realised that the orbiting electron only takes discrete values of energy and that there is a lowest energy level below which no electron can drop. For most of the time the electron is to be found on this lowest rung of the energy 'ladder' but if it absorbs just the right amount of energy it jumps up to a higher level.

This excited electron will not stay in a higher level for long and it will soon fall back to a lower level. It may do this in one big jump or alternatively drop down through a succession of levels. Ultimately it will end up back on the lowest energy level.

When an electron drops down from an **excited state** to a lower energy level it loses the energy difference in the form of a particle of electromagnetic radiation called a photon.

$$E_1 - E_0 = \text{energy of the photon}$$

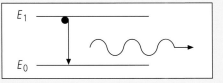

Picture 3

The photon is a quantum particle since it carries away a discrete amount of energy.

The higher the photon energy then the higher is the frequency of the electromagnetic radiation.

Sodium street lights are an example of where the energy difference between the two levels results in a photon of visible yellow light.

The quantum process will also work in reverse:

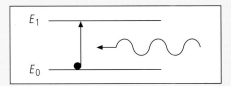

Picture 4

The energy of the incoming photon is absorbed by the electron, which then jumps up to an excited state.

$$\text{energy of the photon} = E_1 - E_0$$

An excited ionised gas will have its own unique set of photon frequencies for both emission and absorption.

Interestingly, astronomers by analysing its absorption spectrum discovered helium gas first in the Sun. Only later was it discovered on Earth.

Since Bohr, the quantum theory has been refined and extended to include all sub-atomic particles including quarks.

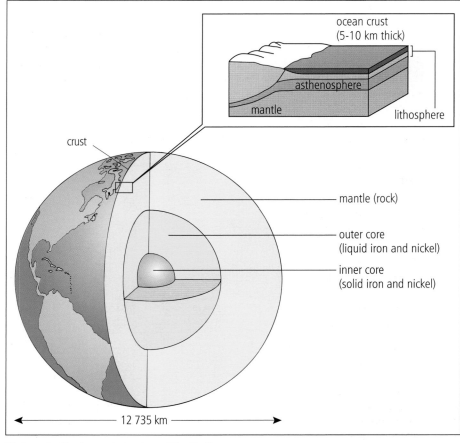

Picture 1 The layered structure of the Earth.

EARTHQUAKE WAVES

The Earth has a layered structure. We live on the topmost layer – the **crust** – which is made of solid rock. Compared to the Earth as a whole, the crust is thinner than the skin on an apple. At most it is 70 km thick. Compare this with the diameter of the Earth, which is about 12 735 km. Yet no-one has been able to drill into the crust for more than 14 km – a mere scratch on the surface. So how have scientists so far been able to discover what lies beneath the crust, to discover the structure of the Earth and what it is made of?

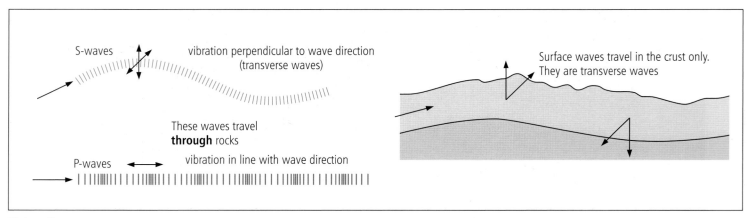

Picture 2

Using earthquake waves

The shock waves from earthquakes are recorded at **seismic stations** all over the world. Seismic stations are places that detect and measure earthquake waves. Their records have provided us with the bulk of the clues about the structure of the Earth. These waves are rather like sound waves – and just as scientists can 'see' what is inside the body with ultrasound, so geologists can 'see' inside the Earth with earthquake waves.

Earthquakes are caused by the movement of rock in the Earth's crust or in the upper part of the mantle. They may occur quite close to the surface or several kilometres below. The nearer an earthquake is to the surface the more damage it is likely to cause. The other main factor is the energy released as the rocks move. The energy is released as shock waves that travel through the rocks. Earthquake damage is caused by the shock waves that reach the part of the Earth's surface closest to the site of the earthquake.

Earthquake waves, called **seismic** waves, are of three types:

- **P-waves** – which are push–pull (longitudinal) waves in which rocks vibrate to-and-fro in the direction of travel of the wave
- **S-waves** – which are sideways (transverse) waves in which the rocks move up and down and/or side to side at right angles to the direction of travel
- **surface waves** – which are more slowly moving waves, consisting of sideways movement of crustal rocks.

Picture 2 shows these three types of wave. Picture 6 shows how they reach a nearby seismic station.

P-waves cause most of the damage to buildings. A tall building can move up and down and still stay in contact with its foundations – think of going up and down in a lift. But a sideways wave can move the foundations more quickly than the building can follow them – think of what happens when you are standing up in a train which suddenly brakes. The building may be torn away from its foundations and collapse.

P and S waves travel large distances through rocks, although they rapidly become weaker with distance and can then only be detected by sensitive instruments called **seismometers**. Seismometers are very simple instruments in principle, consisting of a large mass of metal suspended on springs. When the Earth under a seismograph moves, the heavy mass stays still. A pen attached to the mass traces a wavy line on to a sheet of paper which is of course attached to the quaking Earth. The paper is drawn sideways by a motor so that the sideways motion is drawn out into a wavy line – a *seismogram*. (Pictures 3 and 5.)

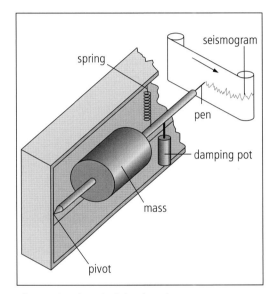

Picture 3 The principle of a seismometer.

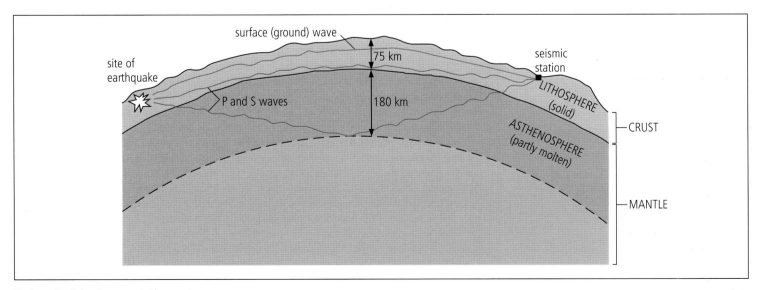

Picture 4 Seismic waves in the crust.

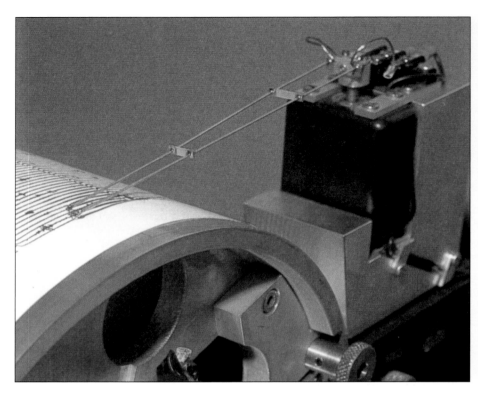

Picture 5 A seismograph in action.

The speed of seismic waves has been measured – and indeed can be predicted from the properties of the ordinary rocks in the Earth's crust. P and S waves travel at different speeds and the difference in their times of arrival can be used to calculate how far away the earthquake occurred. Thus data from a set of seismographs at different places on the surface can be used to work out the exact site of an earthquake – its **focus** (see page 255).

■ Probing deep Earth with seismic waves

The crust of the Earth is made of solid rocks and varies in thickness from 6 km to about 40 km. It is thickest under the continents. The region below the crust is called the **mantle**, which is 2900 km thick with temperatures ranging from 1500 to 3000 K. The crustal rocks are made of compounds of silicon, aluminium and magnesium with small quantities of other elements. The crust and upper layer of the mantle together form the **lithosphere**, which consists of mostly solid interlocking plates (**tectonic** plates) which move around very slowly on the Earth's surface. The lithosphere is up to 100 km thick and in turn rests on the **asthenosphere**, which is partly molten. The lower mantle is a solid but is hot enough to behave as a very viscous liquid. This means that slow convection currents occur in the mantle which provide the forces to move the lithosphere plates across the more liquid asthenosphere, which acts as a lubricant (picture 6). Earthquakes occur as moving plates tear past each other, sometimes moving sideways, sometimes one dipping under the other.

Seismometers are sensitive enough to pick up seismic waves that have travelled from one side of the Earth to the other. Picture 7 shows typical paths for P and S waves. The waves change direction because they are *refracted*, like light waves going from one medium to another. A great deal of careful analysis was needed to identify the depth at which the waves change speed. These depths show where the properties of the rocks change, and that the Earth is indeed made up of layers as shown in picture 1. The calculations from wave speeds tells us what the various layers are made of.

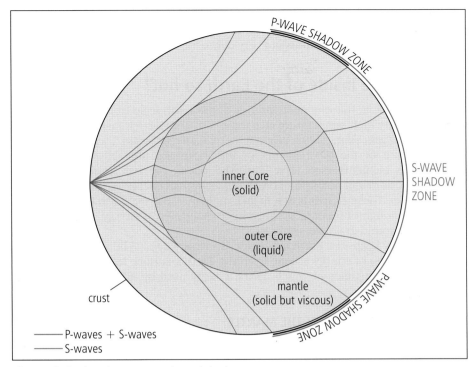

Picture 6 Earthquake waves: paths and shadow zones.

There is a shadow zone for S waves directly opposite the earthquake focus. This suggests that the Earth has a liquid centre. P waves are like sound waves, and can travel through both solids and liquids. But liquids cannot 'bend' – so cannot carry sideways waves. A liquid core would thus stop the S-waves. The temperature in the core is over 6000 K, which is enough to melt iron even at the enormous pressures of over a million times atmospheric pressure. But only the outer core is a liquid. Although the inner core at the very centre of the Earth is hotter than the outer core, pressure increases with depth and the pressure is so great that the iron becomes solid again.

■ Density

Density measurements also give clues about the Earth's interior. The mass of the Earth has been measured using Newton's Law of Gravity (see page 88). We also know its volume so we can calculate that the mean density of the Earth is 5500 kg/m³. However, the density of crustal rocks is on average 2800 kg/m³. The speed of seismic waves depends on the density of the rock they travel through, and the speed measurements show that the mantle has an average density of 4500 kg/m³ and the core density is as high as 10 720 kg/m³. With such a high density the core can only be made of metal. The evidence suggests that it is a mixture of iron and nickel. The mantle is a mixture of compounds, mostly metal oxides and silicates.

EVIDENCE FROM INNER AND OUTER SPACE

■ Lumps of rock

We do have some more direct evidence about what the inside of the Earth is like. Sometimes lumps of rock from deep in the Earth's mantle are found in the lava from volcanoes. Even rocks from space – **meteorites** – give us clues. It is likely that the Earth was formed at the same time as meteorites such as these. (See topic G3.)

The materials of the Earth seem to become denser the deeper you go. So there are light gases in the atmosphere, water in the oceans, relatively light rocks in the crust, dense rocks in the mantle and very dense metals in the core.

■ Why is the inside of the Earth so hot?

One of the reasons that the deep interior of the Earth is so hot is that the Earth formed at a very high temperature (see topic G3). Because the inside is **insulated** by the outer layers some of this original thermal energy is still 'trapped' inside.

Also, some of the 92 elements of the Earth are unstable. They are the **radioactive** elements (see topic F2). The nuclei of such elements (mainly uranium, thorium and potassium) break up, giving out energy as they change into smaller nuclei. These elements are, in fact, quite rare, but the Earth is so large that it contains enough of them to produce huge quantities of energy. Some of these elements are found in crustal rocks.

This energy keeps the Earth hot inside, and every day 2.5 billion billion joules (or 2.5 exajoules) of energy escape from the Earth's surface to help heat the air. This is about four times as much as the energy used by all the people on the Earth.

CONVECTION CURRENTS IN THE MANTLE

Energy flows from the hottest part of the Earth, the core, outwards to the surface. This energy travels in two ways: by **conduction** and by **convection**. Convection is by far the most important as it means that semi-molten material rises and falls in the mantle, creating the effects of plate tectonics described next.

PLATE TECTONICS

As a result of the convection currents in the mantle the Earth's crust has been broken up into large areas called **tectonic plates**. These plates fit together in a spherical jigsaw pattern but move against each other. It is this movement that is the main cause of earthquakes. Picture 9 shows the main tectonic plates and also the places on Earth where earthquakes occur most often. These are also the places which show the most volcanic activity.

The main zones of seismic and volcanic activity are at the plate boundaries or **margins**. Three things may happen at plate margins.

At **constructive** margins two plates are moving apart from each other. Molten rock from the mantle rises up – as a convection current – and cools to form new crust. This is what is happening at the Mid-Atlantic Ridge as the two American plates move away from the European and African plates. The island of Iceland has been made by this process.

At **destructive** margins two plates are moving directly into each other. One of two things might then happen. In some areas **subduction** occurs – one plate is being pushed under the other and as its rocks dive deeper they melt. Thus crustal rock is being destroyed and reconverted to hot molten magma – which may well bubble back up and form volcanoes. This is happening in the 'Ring of Fire' – the ring of volcanoes that surrounds the Pacific Ocean. At other places the colliding plates crumple up against each other forming new mountains. This is what happened when the Indian plate met the Eurasian plate and formed the Himalayan mountains. The Alps, Rocky Mountains and the Andes were formed in the same way.

When plates slide past each other, moving sideways in opposite directions, we have a **conservative** margin. Crust is being neither created or destroyed. The best known example of this kind of margin is on the West Coast of the U.S.A. where part of the North Pacific plate is moving northwards, sliding against the North American plate. Part of California is moving north with it creating the San

Picture 7 The San Andreas Fault.

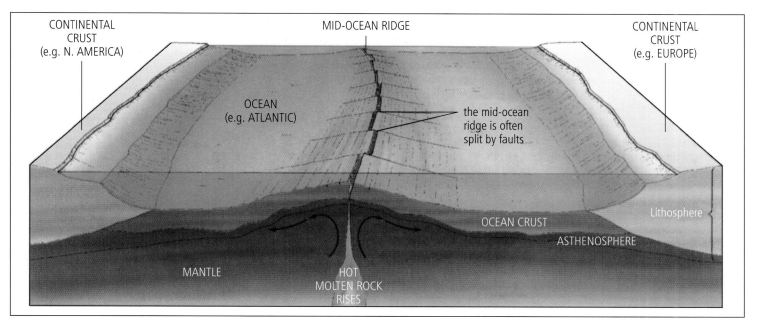

Picture 8 Convection currents and plate motion.

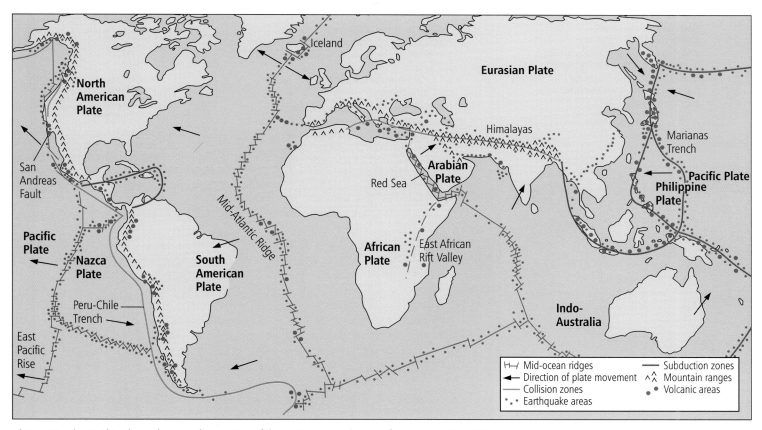

Picture 9 The Earth's plates showing the position of the continents and areas of major seismic activity.

Andreas Fault (picture 7). The movement is not steady. Stress builds up in the rocks on either side of the fault and then they break apart. The result is an earthquake – more or less severe depending on the energy released and the depth of the focus.

Questions

1 No-one has ever been deeper than 14 km into the Earth. How, then, do we seem to know so much about its inside?

2 Waves are either transverse or longitudual. Why are longitudinal-waves likely to cause more earthquake damage than transverse waves?

3 The diameter of the Earth is 12 735 km. P-waves travel through the Earth at an average speed of 5.6 km/s.

a How long does it take P-waves to travel directly across the Earth to a place directly opposite the earthquake site?

b Why can't S-waves travel the same route as the P-waves in (a)?

c A seismic station records the arrival of P-waves at 12.00 noon. S-waves from the earthquake arrive 16 s later. The mean speeds of P and S waves in crustal rocks are 5.6 km/s and 3.6 km/s respectively. Show (i) that the earthquake occurred about 30 s before noon (ii) that the focus was about 160 km from the seismic station.

4 This question is about how simple calculations can tell geologists how far away the site of an earthquake is. The answers are given for each part of this question. Check that they are correct and *show how you did so*!

a P-waves travel at 8 km/s and S-waves at 5 km/s. How far has each travelled after 5 seconds?

b The seismograph at Adamstown, 40 km from the earthquake site, records the arrival of the P wave at precisely 12 noon.
i) how far back are the S-waves at this time?
ii) At what time will the S-wave arrive?

c i) At what time will the seismograph at Berenice, 80 km from the earthquake site, first detect the P-waves? [5 s after 12 noon].
ii) How long will the seismograph at Berenice have to wait for the S-wave to arrive? [they are 30 km behind, so another 6 s]

d Look back at parts (b) and (c). Show that for every second of the time gap between the P- and S-waves at any seismograph station the station is 13.33 km distant from the earthquake site.

e The diagram on page 255 *Seismic ranging of earthquakes* says that for each 3/5th second of time gap the P-waves have travelled 8 km. Explain how this statement fits in with what is said in part (d) above.

5 The diagram shows three seismograph stations, at Concord, Evanstown and Delvin. They are quite close together. The table shows the time of arrival of P- and S-waves at each station.

a Copy the table and complete it. Then use the method illustrated on page 255 to find the site of the earthquake, using a scale drawing

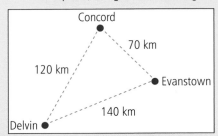

Picture 10

Table 1

Station	Time gap P-S (seconds)	Distance earthquake
Concord	9.0	
Delvin	4.9	
Evanstown	7.5	

b Why must there be at least 3 seismograph stations to identify the earthquake site uniquely?

c The simple method used here would not work too well if the stations were several thousands of kilometres apart. Why?

Seismic ranging of earthquakes

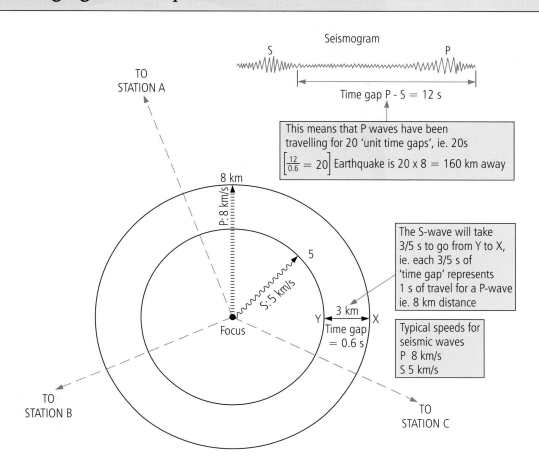

Seismogram

S ‖ P

Time gap P - S = 12 s

This means that P waves have been travelling for 20 'unit time gaps', ie. 20s
$\left[\frac{12}{0.6} = 20\right]$ Earthquake is 20 x 8 = 160 km away

8 km

P: 8 km/s

S: 5 km/s

S

Focus

Y ← 3 km → X
Time gap = 0.6 s

TO STATION A

TO STATION B

TO STATION C

The S-wave will take 3/5 s to go from Y to X, ie. each 3/5 s of 'time gap' represents 1 s of travel for a P-wave ie. 8 km distance

Typical speeds for seismic waves
P 8 km/s
S 5 km/s

P and S waves spread out from the focus of an earthquake. The diagram shows the wave fronts one second after the start of the earthquake: the P wave is 3 km ahead. How far ahead will it be 2 s after the earthquake? What will the 'time gap' between P and S waves be?

DATA from	P-S time gap	Earthquake distance
STATION A	12 s	160
STATION B	9 s	
STATION C	15 s	

Copy and complete the table

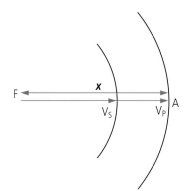

A is distance **x** from earthquake focus F.

Time taken for P wave to reach A

$$t_P = \frac{x}{V_P}$$

For S-wave, time taken

$$t_S = \frac{x}{V_S}$$

Therefore time gap, $T = t_S - t_P = \dfrac{x}{V_S} - \dfrac{x}{V_P}$

ie. $T = x\left[\dfrac{1}{V_S} - \dfrac{1}{V_P}\right]$

Check that this formula gives **x** = 160 km for a time gap **T** = 12 s

Data from 3 seismic stations can pin-point the site of the earthquake

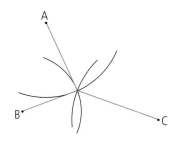

Measuring the Earth

What shape is the Earth?
How big and how old?
This topic explores ways of finding out the answers.

Picture 1 The Earth seen from space.

■ The shape of the Earth

The fact that the Earth is a sphere has been known for thousands of years. Even so, there are still people who don't believe it! Christopher Columbus knew that the Earth was round and sailed west to get around to India, in the East. But his sailors weren't so sure, and were very worried that their ship would fall off the edge of the world.

The simplest evidence for the Earth being a sphere is that we now have photographs of it, taken from space (picture 1). The Ancient Greeks were the first people to realise that the Earth was round. They proved it to themselves by noticing such things as:

- when ships sail away from land you see first the hull disappear, then the masts
- during eclipses of the moon, the *shadow* of the Earth is round.

The shadow of the Earth is cast onto the moon during eclipses. It is always a circle, which it wouldn't be if the Earth were shaped like a flat disc. (See picture 2.)

■ How big is the Earth?

The first reasonably accurate measurement of the radius of the Earth was done by a Greek-Egyptian astronomer, called Eratosthenes. Both Greeks and Egyptians were good at geometry, and in about 200 BC Eratosthenes used it to calculate the size of the Earth.

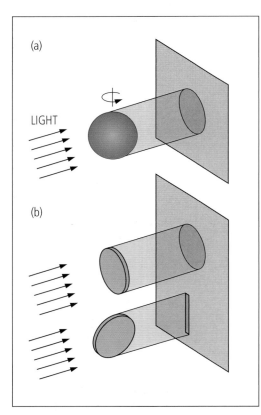

(a)

LIGHT

(b)

Picture 2 (a) The shadow of a spinning sphere is always a circle.
(b) The shadow of a spinning disc is sometimes a circle – sometimes just a thin line!

HOW DID HE DO IT?

It so happened that there was a famous well in southern Egypt at a town called Syene (now called Aswan). The well was famous because on just one day of the year, when you looked down into the well, you could see the reflection of the Sun in the water. This was because the sun was directly overhead. The day it happened was midsummer day, when the Sun is at its most northerly position in the sky.

Eratosthenes realised that if he measured the angle the Sun made with the ground on the same day, further north in Alexandria, he could calculate the circumference of the Earth. The only other information he needed was provided for him by the army, whose soldiers had been trained to march at a steady exact pace. Timing them gave him the distance between the points. Picture 3 explains how he did it.

Astronomers have used much the same method until quite recently, but with more complicated astronomy and more accurate instruments. Nowadays much more accurate measurements can be made using instruments carried by Earth satellites.

■ How old is the Earth?

A bishop once used evidence in the Bible to work out that the Earth was made in the year 4004 BC. But, over the last two centuries, scientists have collected evidence from rocks that suggests that the Earth may be considerably older.

COUNTING THE LAYERS

In some newer rocks it is possible to distinguish lighter and darker layers, laid down in different seasons of the year. So the layers can be counted just like the rings on a tree. Picture 4 shows a rock formed in a Tyneside coal mine during the 1800s. A white mineral, barium sulphate, settled out in a water trough. During working days it was blackened by coal. So, you can see how many days were worked during the week, and count the number of weeks. The rock is artificial, of course. Natural banded rocks like this do occur. But they are very rare and very young compared to the age of the Earth. We couldn't date the whole Earth with them.

■ How we can tell if one rock is older than another

We can use common sense. The positions of different rocks as we see them in the field gives plenty of evidence about the order in which things happened. Look at picture 5. In a pile of sedimentary rocks, the ones at the bottom must be the oldest – sediment is always added to the top.

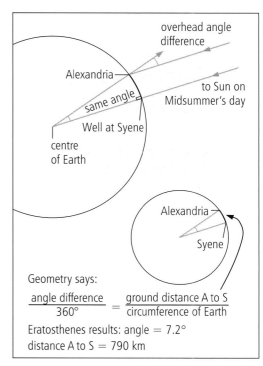

Geometry says:

$$\frac{\text{angle difference}}{360°} = \frac{\text{ground distance A to S}}{\text{circumference of Earth}}$$

Eratosthenes results: angle = 7.2°
distance A to S = 790 km

Picture 3   The actual circumference of the Earth is 40 000 km. How near did Eratosthenes get to this?

Picture 4   The Sunday stone was formed in a Tyneside coal mine in the 1800s.

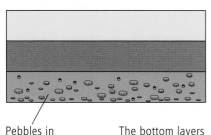

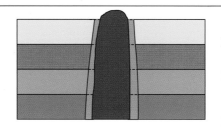

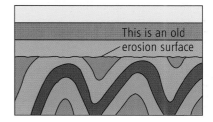

Pebbles in a conglomerate must be older than the rock they're in

The bottom layers of sedimentary rock must be older than the top

The sedimentary rocks must be older than the igneous rocks

This is an old erosion surface

The lower beds were once flat layers. Then they were squashed and folded. The upper layers were later deposited on top

Picture 5   How we can tell the age of rocks by looking at them.

The fragments in any sedimentary rock must be older than the rock itself, so pebbles in a conglomerate are obviously older than the rock that contains them.

An igneous rock must be younger than the rocks into which it has intruded.

If unfolded beds of rock lie on top of folded ones, then the unfolded ones must be a lot younger than the folded one. Think of what must have happened. Sometime after being deposited and turned into solid rock, the older rocks were squashed and folded. Then they were eroded, and then, *after that*, the younger set of rocks was laid down.

■ Using fossils

The remains of living organisms found in the rocks also give information about which rocks are older and which are younger. If we know the time when certain fossils lived, using evidence from one kind of rock, then we can use those fossils to date other rocks that contain the same fossils.

The methods described so far enabled the geologists of the nineteenth century to unravel the story of the Earth. But they could only work out the order in which things happened. They gave names to the various stages and events in the Earth's history (see the time chart page 259). But no-one was able to give reliable dates to these events. It was not until the early part of this century that scientists discovered that **radioactive elements** could be used to date rocks.

■ Radioactive dating

Radioactive elements decay into lighter elements. They decay at a known rate. So, using a special machine called a mass spectrometer, scientists can measure how much of the original radioactive element is left and how much of the new, lighter elements are present. The ratio of the two gives a fairly accurate estimate of the age of the rock. (See topic F2.)

The oldest rock so far found in the world, was found in a remote region of northern Canada and is 3.96 billion years old. It is of sedimentary origin. (Why does this indicate that it couldn't have been the first rock in the Earth's crust?) (Picture 6.)

Radioactive dating has been used to measure the age of meteorites and moonrocks. These measurements suggest that the whole Solar System, Earth, meteorites and the Moon were formed at the same time – 4.6 billion years ago. For the first 4 billion of those years, there was no life as we know it, and people have only been on the Earth for the last 0.003 billion years. We shall learn more about how the Earth was made in topic G3.

Picture 6 Samuel Bowring of Washington University, St Louis, USA, with the oldest rock so far discovered. It is estimated to be 3.96 billion years old.

The history of the Earth: a geological time-chart

Millions of years ago

			Millions of years ago	
CENOZOIC			**0**	Early Egyptian cities, etc
The Earth's climate became colder, resulting in Ice Ages.	**QUATERNARY**	Holocene	**0.01**	
		Pleistocene	**2**	Many Ice Ages Humans migrate over Asia
This is the age of the mammals, but also of insects and flowering plants	**TERTIARY**	Pliocene	**7**	First human beings (Africa)
		Miocene	**26**	India meets Asia, Himalayas form First deer, monkeys, dogs, cat Africa, Europe and Asia collide, Alps form
		Oligocene	**38**	
		Eocene	**54**	
Opening of the North Sea		Palaeocene	**65**	First rodents, elephants, horses Extinction of dinosaurs
MESOZOIC This was the age of the dinosaurs	**CRETACEOUS**		**136**	Final break-up of Pangaea Sea flooded to cover more land Formation of chalk over much of what is now Europe First flowering plants and modern types of insect
The great southern continent of Pangaea broke up, forming most of our modern continents	**JURASSIC**		**190**	Beginning of the Atlantic Ocean First birds and mammals
The Earth's climate was warm and pleasant almost everywhere	**TRIASSIC**		**225**	Many new species Sea levels fall all over the world
PALAEOZOIC	**PERMIAN**		**280**	Rise of the reptiles Formation of Pangaea
At the beginning, most life was in the sea. Plants colonised the land in the Silurian era, followed after a few million years by amphibians. Towards the end of this period the first reptiles appeared, as land animals.	**CARBONIFEROUS**		**355**	Britain at the Equator; coal laid down in many parts of the world. Age of amphibians. First reptiles
	DEVONIAN		**395**	Age of the first amphibians First fish, first flying insects Animal life moves on to the land
	SILURIAN		**440**	Plants move on to the land
	ORDOVICIAN		**500**	} Sea covers many continents Most life in the sea, as shellfish and floating plants
	CAMBRIAN		**570**	
PRECAMBRIAN	**PROTEROZOIC**			First multicellular organism
This covered a huge period of time – over 4000 million years. It began with the formation of the Earth and ended with the first many-celled organisms The first green plants appeared in the sea – and began to put oxygen into the atmosphere			**2500**	
	ARCHAEAN		**4600**	? First free oxygen in atmosphere ? First living organisms – single celled plants and animals 3960 – Age of oldest known rocks Earth cooling down; formation of tectonic plates

TYPES OF ROCK

Picture 7 This front of this bank is made from coarse-grained granite.

The bank in picture 8 is faced with **granite**. Because it's been polished you can see quite easily that it's made up of crystals. The overall speckled effect of grey and white shows that it's made of more than one **mineral**.

The statue in picture 9 is made from **limestone**. You can see the remains of living creatures in it – fragments of sea shell that have become **fossilised**, that is, preserved in rock. It is just possible to see individual grains with the naked eye; they all appear to be made of the same mineral. Parts of the stone look worn or **weathered**.

Many houses are roofed with **slate** (picture 10). Slate has been popular for roofing since the middle of the nineteenth century. It can be split, or **cleaved** very easily into thin sheets. It is usually dark in colour – from purplish grey to green – and it is hard and smooth. You can't see individual grains or crystals in it.

Picture 8 A statue made from Portland stone.

■ Why are rocks so different?

The three rocks in pictures 7 to 10 were formed in three different ways.

Granite is a type of **igneous** rock. Igneous rocks have solidified from molten rock either in volcanoes, or inside the crust.

Limestone is a **sedimentary** rock. These rocks are usually laid down under water as a **sediment**. Sedimentary rocks are made from fragments worn away from older rocks, or from the remains of living organisms.

Slate is a type of **metamorphic** rock. The word **metamorphic** comes from the Greek – *meta* meaning change, and *morphe* meaning shape. These rocks have been changed by heat or pressure, or by a combination of both. They could originally have been either igneous or sedimentary.

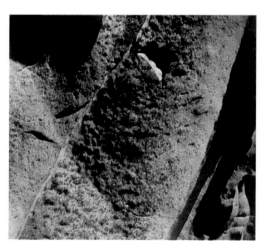

Picture 9 A carving made from Portland stone, showing weathering due to acid rain.

Picture 10 Slate roofs.

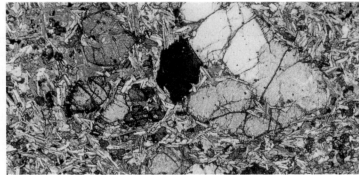

■ Igneous rocks

Igneous rocks are formed when molten rock, called **magma**, cools and solidifies. Nearly all igneous rocks are formed of **crystals**. You can see the crystals in the granite in picture 8. Notice that the crystals are **interlocking**.

Molten rock is less dense than solid rock, and so it tends to rise very slowly towards the surface of the Earth. If the molten magma reaches the Earth's surface and is erupted from a volcano, it is called **lava**. When the lava cools and solidifies it becomes rock. **Basalt**, a smooth black rock, is the most common type of lava (picture 11(a)). There are many less common types of lava, and sometimes volcanoes throw out ash (see topic G2). Rocks formed by eruption from volcanoes are called **extrusive** igneous rocks.

With the naked eye, basalt looks smooth and black. But under the microscope, crystals of several different minerals can be seen. These are different kinds of **silicate** minerals. Picture 11(b) was taken through a special microscope which uses polarised light. This gives some of the minerals bright colours which makes them easier to see.

Sometimes magma contains dissolved gases. When the magma reaches the surface, where the pressure is lower, the gases come out of solution to form gas bubbles. You can see the same effect when you open a bottle of fizzy drink. When the lava cools, the bubbles are preserved in the rock. Pumice is a type of lava with more gas bubbles than rock. If you've used pumice stone in the bath, you'll know it can float.

Very often magma gets trapped inside the crust and never reaches the surface. These rocks are called **intrusive** gaseous rocks. Because the magma is insulated by the surrounding rocks, it takes a very long time to cool – sometimes millions of years.

Granite is probably the most common intrusive igneous rock. It is different from basalt in that it cools very slowly from molten magma deep in the Earth's crust. Because it takes a long time to cool, the crystals are larger. They are easy to see with the naked eye and are much lighter in colour than basalt. (Picture 12.)

Many of the sea cliffs and high moors in Cornwall are made from granite. It has resisted the wearing effect of weather and water for many millions of years.

Picture 12 Granite.

Picture 13 Layers of sedimentary rock. Burton Bradstock, Dorset.

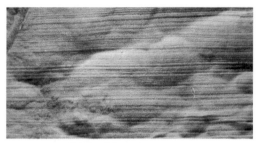

Picture 14   (a) Conglomerate

(b) Sandstone

(c) Mudstone

(d) Shale

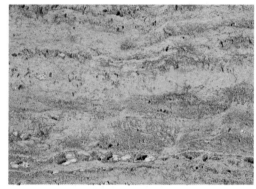

Picture 15   Travertine like this is used on many shop fronts

SEDIMENTARY ROCKS

One way to think of sedimentary rocks is as 'second-hand' rocks. They are made up either of fragments of older rocks or from the remains of living organisms.

Sedimentary rocks often occur in layers, or **beds**. Picture 13 shows the cliffs at Burton Bradstock in Dorset. These cliffs are made of beds of sandstone which were laid down in the seas about 190 million years ago. Moist sedimentary rocks are laid down in the sea, but they may also form in rivers, lakes, and even in deserts.

■ Sedimentary rocks from particles or fragments

Even the hardest rock will start to crumble and weather as thousands of years go by. Fragments of rock fall down hillsides due to gravity, or get washed down by rain. Rivers will carry the fragments down into deltas, lakes, or the sea. Waves beat against cliffs and knock fragments away.

Look again at picture 13. You can see where the cliff has fallen to make a pile of boulders on the beach. The action of the waves will eventually break them up into pebbles and sand. These pebbles and sand could become the sedimentary rocks of the future.

Sedimentary rocks are named according to the size of the fragments that they're made of. A rock made of pebbles is called a **conglomerate** (sometimes called a 'pudding stone' because it looks a bit like an old-fashioned steamed plum pudding). A rock made of sand is called simply a **sandstone**. A rock made of fine mud is usually called a **mudstone**, but if it's flaky and breaks easily into layers, it's called a **shale**. Some of these rocks are shown in picture 14.

Conglomerates and sandstones are made mainly of fragments of the hard, resistant mineral **quartz**. In many cases this will have been weathered from granite. **Quartz** is one of the commonest minerals found in rocks (Quartz comes in many colours, from transparent bright purple (amethyst) to opaque grey or brown flint. This can make it tricky to identify.)

Mudstones and shales are made from clay minerals. These vary in colour from creamy white, to reddish brown, grey, and black. The individual grains are too small to be seen even with a hand lens.

HOW DO SAND PEBBLES AND MUD TURN INTO ROCK?

There are two ways that loose sediment can be turned into rock. First, as more sediment accumulates on top, everything gets squashed and compressed into rock. Second, other minerals sometimes seep between the fragments in the rock, and 'glue' them together. You can see this very clearly in the conglomerate in picture 15. The spaces between the pebbles are filled with brown quartz.

■ Organic sedimentary rocks

Most limestones are made of the shells and skeletons of organisms that lived in the water. Sometimes the shells are so small, or broken up into such small fragments, that you can't see them with the naked eye, or even with a hand lens.

Shells and skeletons are almost always made of calcium carbonate, so limestone is made of calcium carbonate too.

Some limestones are formed chemically when calcium carbonate precipitates out of a solution. The solution of calcium carbonate could be in sea water, in lake water, or in a hot spring. Picture 15 shows a chemical limestone, called **travertine**. It's used as an ornamental stone on the front of most 'Macdonald's' hamburger restaurants.

The limestone in picture 9 is a mixture of a chemical limestone and shells. It was formed, around 100 million years ago, in very warm tropical seas.

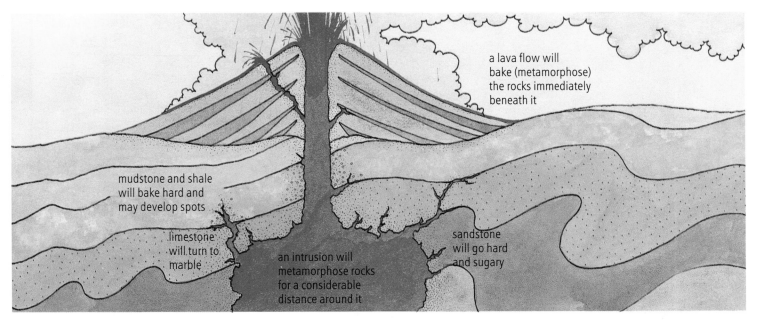

Picture 16 Rocks being formed by contact metamorphism.

Within the image:
- a lava flow will bake (metamorphose) the rocks immediately beneath it
- mudstone and shale will bake hard and may develop spots
- limestone will turn to marble
- an intrusion will metamorphose rocks for a considerable distance around it
- sandstone will go hard and sugary

METAMORPHIC ROCKS

Rocks may be changed or **metamorphosed** in two ways: by heat alone or, more usually by a combination of heat and pressure. New minerals form in the rocks. The texture of the rocks is changed too, and any fossils in sedimentary rocks are obliterated.

■ Heat only

When lava spills out of a volcano onto older rocks, the older rocks get hot, and literally 'cook'. When intrusive igneous rocks get trapped inside the crust they heat the rocks around them. This time the 'cooking' effect is longer and slower, but more pronounced. (See picture 16.)

The heat of the magma tends to make the surrounding rocks harder. The grains in sandstones stick together tightly and form a hard, sugary-looking rock. Limestone changes to a sugary-looking rock too – **marble**. Mudstones and shales turn into hard splintery rocks at high temperatures, but at lower temperatures they develop spots – a sort of geological heat-rash!

■ Heat and pressure

The most common types of metamorphic rock are formed by heat and pressure in the crust at subduction zones or collision zones. (See topic G1 picture 8.)

Slate is one of the commonest rocks formed in this way. It is a metamorphosed mudstone or shale. Slate can be split very easily along **cleavage** planes. The cleavage is caused by the effect of pressure.

Limestone will also turn into marble under the effects of heat and pressure. Most limestone is impure. It is these impurities that form the coloured bands and swirling patterns that make marble so attractive.

■ Rock detective work

Table 1 gives you some clues to help you decide whether a rock is igneous, sedimentary or metamorphic.

Table 1 Clues to rock types

Igneus rocks
- have no fossils
- have an interlocking crystalline structure
- are likely to be hard

Sedimentary rocks
- may have layers (bedding) visible
- will have separate grains (not interlocked)
- may be quite soft (you may be able to rub grains off)
- may have fossils
- if calcium carbonate is present, will fizz with dilute HCl

Metamorphic rocks
- may be able to split along a cleavage
- may be branded or streaked
- may be hard
- may have sparkling mica flakes aligned in streaks or layers
- may have a 'surgery' texture, or be noticeably crystalline
- if marble, will fizz with dilute HCl
- have no fossils

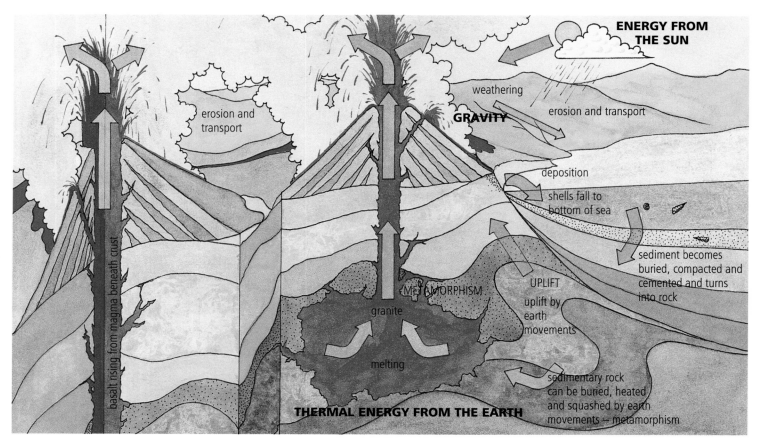

Picture 17   The rock cycle.

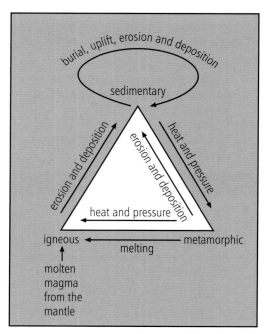

Picture 18   A simplified view of the rock cycle.

THE ROCK CYCLE

We've already seen that older rocks can be worn away to provide fragments to make newer sedimentary rocks. We've seen how rocks can be changed by heat and pressure into metamorphic rocks. In fact if rocks get heated enough (about 600 °C), they can melt to form an igneous magma. So, one kind of rock can be recycled to form another type.

Look at picture 17. If you follow the arrows from the top of the volcano in the foreground, you can see igneous rock being formed from magma, then eroded. The fragments are deposited in the sea as sediment. The sediments harden into rock, and then can be buried and metamorphosed. The metamorphic rock may get so hot as to melt and form magma which will cool to form igneous rock. Then the cycle can start all over again. There are many other ways around the **rock cycle**. A summary of the rock cycle is shown in picture 18.

Questions

1 Why must the pebbles in a rock be older than the rock itself?

2 a Explain what you understand by radioactive half-life.

   b Uranium-238 has a half-life of 4.5 billion years (4.5×10^9 years). By a remarkable coincidence, the Earth is believed to be about 4.5 billion years old. How much of the original uranium-238 is still on Earth, unchanged?

   c Uranium decays, eventually, to a stable form of lead (lead-206). A rock sample was analysed, which showed that the proportion of uranium-238 atoms to lead-206 atoms was 3 to 1.

   i) What fraction of the uranium had decayed?

   ii) Explain why a reasonable estimate of the age of this rock is about 2.25 billion years.

   iii) Would you expect to find a rock in which the ratio of uranium to lead was, say, 1 to 3? Explain your answer.

3 Why is radioactive dating quite accurate for igneous rocks, but is no use for sedimentary rocks?

4 A rock specimen is guessed to be about 100 million years old. Which of the following radioactive elements found in it would be most useful in measuring its age by radioactive dating? Give a reason for your answer.

Element	Half-life
uranium-238	4.5 billion years
radium-226	1620 years
lead-205	50 million years
thorium-230	80 000 years

5 Classify the following igneous, sedimentary or metamorphic rocks: limestone, basalt, slate, conglomerate, marble, sandstone, granite, mudstone, rhyolite, gabbro, shale, serpentine.

6 Picture 19 shows a rock which is used as a facing stone in most high streets. It's called **blue pearl larvikite** and comes from Norway. Is it igneous, sedimentary or metamorphic? Say why you have made your choice.

7 Picture 20 shows a rock from the North Pennines. It fizzes when put in hydrochloric acid. Can you suggest what it might be? Write down as much evidence as you can for your answer.

8 Copy the diagram of the rock cycle picture 17 into your note book. Look at picture 14 – which process in the rock cycle do you see taking place? What evidence can you see that some of the beds of rock in the cliff might be harder than others?

Picture 19

9 Which sort of plate boundaries are likely to produce: (a) basaltic rocks, (b) granitic rocks?

Picture 20

But they didn't believe him – the story of Alfred Wegener

Picture 1 Alfred Wegener

A brand new theory

The trouble with scientists is that the more they know, the harder it is for them to change their minds. Of course, other people are like this as well. But now and again someone comes along and turns the scientists' world on its head. Quite often, the person who does this is an outsider. The world of the geologist – the 'earth-scientist' – was overturned by a weather man.

The biggest change in our understanding of the geology of Earth was made by a man called Alfred Wegener (picture 1). He was born in Berlin, Germany, in 1880 and studied meteorology and astronomy. He worked in universities in Germany and Austria, but he took part in expeditions to Greenland. It was on one of these expeditions that he died, in 1930, twenty years before his ideas became accepted.

It's just a coincidence

If you look at a map of the world (picture 2) you can see that the outline of South America looks as if it would fit quite neatly on to the west coast of Africa. Most geographers and geologists thought that this was just a coincidence. No one could imagine that such huge objects, fixed on the solid Earth, could move sideways for thousands of kilometres. But Wegener had the idea that the continents did move and had been joined together at one time.

There were no known forces big enough to move them. The most that could happen, they thought was that parts of continents might move, very

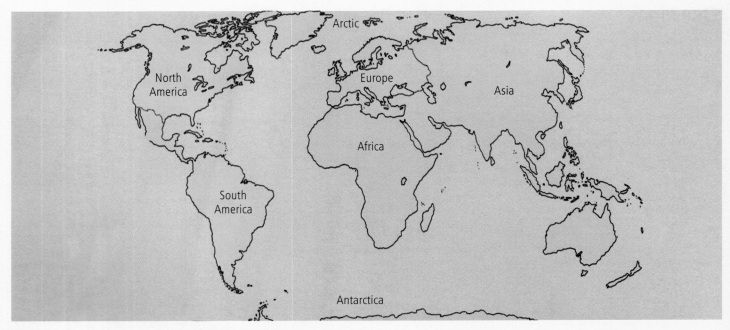

Picture 2 Do the continents fit together?

slowly, up and down to make mountains. The continents were fixed in solid basalt rock, and there seemed no way that they could move.

The arguments

Take a closer look, said Wegener, there's a chain of mountains in South Africa that exactly match a chain in Brazil. They were made at the same time, and have the same rocks.

But it's not an exact match, the experts said.

Look at mountains – like the Himalayas, Wegener pleaded. The rocks are folded so much that they must have been pushed sideways.

Now that is interesting, said the geologists. But the reason, of course is that the Earth is shrinking. It is losing heat, cooling down. Mountains rise, rocks are squeezed because the Earth's surface is getting smaller. No problem. It's just the sort of thing that happens with apples. (Picture 4.)

Wegener pressed on. Why is there coal in Siberia? he asked. Coal is formed from trees, so Siberia must have been closer to the equator at some time. It has drifted north since then.

Well – climates can change, they said.

And maybe trees in cold climates can sometimes grow well enough to form coal.

But look at the animals – and their fossilised ancestors. South American animals are different from African ones. But their fossilised ancestors are almost exactly the same. Their ancestors must have lived on the same continent. And it must have split apart 60 million years ago.

Not at all! There was a thin land bridge connecting Africa with America so that animals could move across. In fact, it must have broken up 60 million years ago. (See picture 5.)

Wegener didn't accept the geologist's arguments. He thought that he was right. He collected together all his reasons and evidence and published them in his book *The Origin of Continents and Oceans* (1920) – see picture 6. But the evidence wasn't powerful enough to prove his case. The world of geologists was against him.

How do new theories get accepted?

This is a typical example of what happens in a scientific revolution. At

Picture 3

Picture 4 Does a drying apple model the Earth?

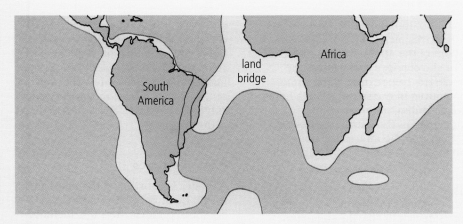

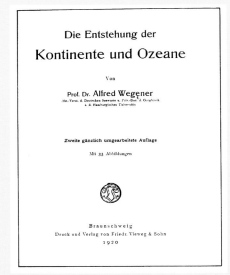

Picture 5 Was there once a land bridge between Africa and America?

Picture 6 The cover of the first edition of Alfred Wegener's book, *The Origin of Continents and Oceans*.

the time, there was no real proof either way. The evidence, as they say, was **circumstantial**. And the man wasn't even a **geologist**. The 'professional' view won the argument.

The moving force

Detectives need to find a motive, a moving force, for a criminal act. What was the moving force that made continents drift?

Wegener didn't know, but just before he died an English geologist put forward a theory for this. Arthur Holmes suggested that they could be moved by convection currents in the hot mantle (see page 252). Direct evidence for this came in the late 1940s. Advanced echo-sounders developed for sub-marine

warfare were now used to map the ocean floors. They charted the underwater landscape.

The oceans, like dry land, had mountains and ridges – and volcanoes. But it doesn't rain under the sea! So the mountains don't get worn down. The Atlantic, in particular, had some strange features. In the middle of the Atlantic is a long line of volcanoes. Some are big enough to reach the surface – in Iceland and the Azores. Either side of this line is a pattern of ridges and hollows. And the pattern is the same each side. See picture 8 in topic G1).

The rocks in each opposite part of the pattern are the same. They are volcanic lava with an overlay of thin sediments from the sea above. It looks exactly as if the bottom of the Atlantic ocean was

being made continuously, on a production line. Like two rolls of cloth rolling up from the central volcanic slit and spreading out sideways. Could the middle of the Atlantic be the very top of one of Arthur Holmes' convection currents? (Picture 8 in topic G1.)

The biggest tape-recording in the world

The final proof that Wegener was right came from a theory in astronomy – which turned out to be wrong. In 1950 Professor Patrick Blackett was

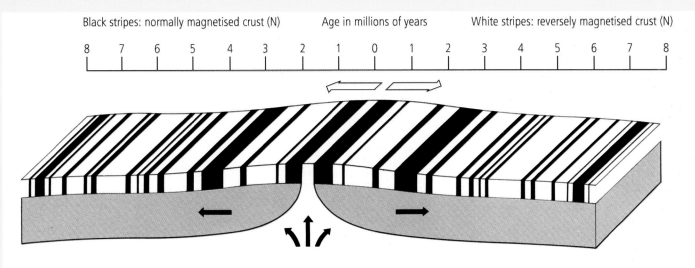

Picture 7 The biggest tape recording in the world.

investigating a theory that would explain why some stars – and planets – had magnetic fields.

He set some of his research students to find ways of measuring the magnetism in rocks. When hot rocks cool down any bits of iron in them become magnetised in line with the Earth's magnetic field (see topic E2). Blackett hoped that their results would give evidence for what the Earth's field was like millions of years ago.

What they discovered was quite unexpected: the Earth's field flips. Very suddenly, every few thousands of years, the North Pole becomes a south pole, and vice versa.

Some years later, in 1963, someone thought of looking at the magnetism of the rocks picked up from the bottom of the Atlantic. The patterns of magnetic changes each side of the middle ridge were exactly the same. The bottom of the sea was like a huge tape recording of the changing magnetism of the Earth over millions of years. But the interesting point was that it was the same record each side of the control ridge.

Imagine that you had a large enough cassette player to play these 'tapes'. Each side would play the same 'tune'. (See picture 7.)

This was the final proof that the rocks, now thousands of kilometres apart, had been formed at the same time. Their magnetism had been fossilized into them as they flowed out of the central volcanic vent into the cold sea. But in the course of many millions of years the new rocks had been pushed further and further away from each other. As they moved they carried the continents of Africa and South America with them.

Plate tectonics

Wegener's theory of 'continental drift' wasn't quite right. The continents do not move on their own. It is the huge 'plates' they are fixed to that move. But Wegener was more right than wrong, and his theories have become the science of plate tectonics. This science, and its importance, is dealt with in topic G1.

Activities

A Putting a case

Divide into groups of about five or six people. Find out a little more about the theories discussed in this topic. Arrange a debate, with Alfred Wegener and Arthur Holmes on one side, and the geologists who opposed them on the other.

Do continents drift? Let the best arguers win!

B Sharp-eyed research

Look at a good map of the world – or a globe. Can you find any other parts of then world that might once have fitted together like Africa and South America?

Questions

1 What do the following scientists study:
   a geologists
   b astronomers
   c meteorologists?

2 What piece of evidence in favour of Wegener's theory do you find most convincing?

3 Make two lists, headed
   A Points for Wegener's theory,
   B Points against Wegener's theory

   Find three facts or arguments to put under each heading.

4 Explain how the research into rock magnetism gave good evidence for the theory of continental movements.

5 Explain what the following are:
   a mountain chain
   b convection currents
   c a magnetic field
   d a land bridge
   e a fossil.

How the Earth was made

No one really knows how the Earth, the Sun and the planets were made. Scientists think that it was probably like this …

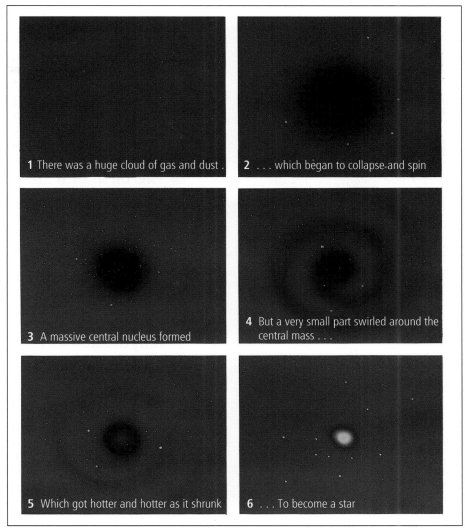

1 There was a huge cloud of gas and dust .

2 … which began to collapse and spin

3 A massive central nucleus formed

4 But a very small part swirled around the central mass . . .

5 Which got hotter and hotter as it shrunk

6 . . . To become a star

Picture 1   The formation of the Sun.

MAKING A SUN

It would have been about five thousand million years ago. On the outer edge of the Milky Way a thin, invisible cloud of gas and dust was collapsing inward, pulled by the force of its own gravity. The gas was mostly hydrogen, but about a fifth of it was helium. These are the two lightest elements, and make up most of the Universe.

As the cloud fell together it began to spin, and the smaller the cloud got the faster it spun (picture 1). When the cloud reached the size of the present Solar System it began to collapse very quickly. It took just twenty years to reach the size of the Earth's orbit.

At this size the molecules of gas were crowded close enough to smash into each other. As the particles fell they lost gravitational potential energy, and the gas got hotter.

■ The first glow

As the centre of the cloud became hotter and hotter it gave out radiation. At first the radiation was invisible infra-red radiation. As the temperature rose the cloud began to glow red. It was almost – but not yet – **a star**.

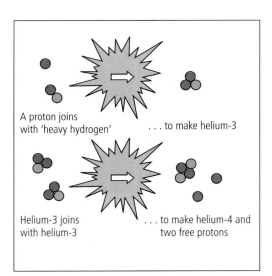

Picture 2 Nuclear fusion: hydrogen is changed to helium.

A proton joins with 'heavy hydrogen' . . . to make helium-3

Helium-3 joins with helium-3 . . . to make helium-4 and two free protons

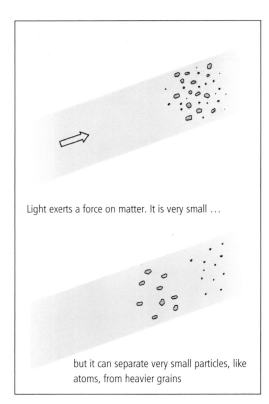

Light exerts a force on matter. It is very small . . .

but it can separate very small particles, like atoms, from heavier grains

Picture 3 Radiation evaporated water and frozen gases, and drove them away from the Sun.

The light did not escape easily from the hot centre. The cloud of hydrogen was not pure. Mixed in with it were particles of other elements, mainly iron, nickel and silicon. There were also compounds: water, methane, silicates. These particles clumped together to make fine dust, or even small 'stones'. The frozen water was mixed with silicates to make lumps of what astronomers call 'dirty ice'. All these stopped most of the visible radiation escaping.

The gas continued to collapse, but much more slowly now that it was so hot. The gas and dust particles were moving very quickly at this temperature. Like any mass of hot gas it was trying to expand. There was a delicate balance between the force of gravity and the tendency of the gas particles to escape.

■ The birth of a star

Time went on. The gravitational energy of the gases falling into the centre of the cloud made it hotter and hotter. It went from being red hot to being white hot. In the hottest part the atoms smashed into each other so hard that their electrons were stripped away, leaving the nuclei of the hydrogen and helium atoms quite bare.

The mixture of electrons and nuclei were squashed together even more under the enormous pressure of the collapsing cloud. They became hotter and hotter, moving and colliding with greater and greater energies.

■ A hydrogen bomb

Fifty million years after the cloud started to collapse the centre of the cloud reached a temperature of 10 million degrees Celsius. The hydrogen nuclei were now moving so fast that they began to stick to each other, producing helium nuclei. This is called **nuclear fusion**.

Now one of Einstein's ideas had come into play, the equation $E = mc^2$. The helium nucleus has less mass than the separate hydrogen nuclei, and the lost mass (**m**) became energy (picture 2).

Nuclear fusion like this is exactly what happens in a hydrogen bomb. The result was a sudden huge release of energy at the centre of the cloud. But the hot centre of the gas cloud did not explode like a bomb – it was far too heavy to be blown apart. It simply kept on working as a giant nuclear reactor, and has been doing so for at least the last five billion years. It had become the star we call the Sun.

■ The force of light

One of the strangest properties of electromagnetic radiation – including ordinary light – is that it can exert a force when it shines on an object. The force that comes from a torch is very, very small – and you are not in danger of being knocked over by just the headlights of a car. But the Sun was now producing so much radiation that it began to have an important effect.

First, infra-red radiation was absorbed by the frozen water and gases, so that they became hot enough to melt and then evaporate. The fog of 'dirt' and ice became clearer. The radiation reached out to exert its pressure on more distant particles. The lighter material was slowly pushed away, leaving behind the heavier rocky and metallic pieces that were to form the inner planets (picture 3).

Radiation pressure pushed away a lot of the dust and gas. The Sun now contained only a small fraction of the original cloud, but it was still an enormous mass. It was enough for its gravity field to hold all the heavy particles and a lot of the gas molecules in orbit. The steady pressure of its radiation carried on the work of pushing the lightest particles into more distant orbits.

Gravity pulled inwards, radiation pushed outwards. The balance between these forces made the lighter material form a doughnut-shaped cloud, which was mostly hydrogen and helium, with ice and some solid grains of rock left from the original gas cloud.

This doughnut was about a thousand million kilometres away from the Sun (picture 4). Between the doughnut and the Sun was a chaotic crowd of grains and pebbles, each in its separate orbit.

MAKING THE PLANETS

Even the smallest particles produce a gravity force, and sooner or later this caused the countless trillions of particles, grains and pebbles to move closer together. When they collided they stuck together.

The larger lumps had a larger gravity field. The bigger they grew the more they were able to attract the smaller particles. Millions of rocky 'planetoids' grew, but in the end the larger ones swept up the smaller ones to make the **planets**.

Most of the particles – nearly three-quarters of them – eventually formed themselves into one very large lump. This was almost big enough to become a second Sun. But its central temperature never became quite as high as the 10 million degrees needed for a hydrogen-bomb explosion. Instead, it settled down to become the largest planet in the Solar System – Jupiter.

Most of what was left became the giant planets beyond Jupiter: Saturn, Uranus and Neptune (see topic G5). These large planets are mostly made of light materials, hydrogen, helium and methane. The heavier materials closer to the Sun formed the **inner planets**: Mercury, Venus, Earth and Mars. Between Mars and Jupiter is a belt of unsuccessful mini-planets which never quite made it – the **asteroids**. The orbits of the asteroids are being disturbed by the gravity field of their huge neighbour, Jupiter. This seems to stop them collecting together into a planet. It also means that some of them may be made to pass very close to Earth.

■ Comets

Far out in space, beyond the orbit of Pluto, there still exists the shell of the gas cloud that formed the Solar System. It contains perhaps 100 billion lumps of rocky ice, up to 8 km across. Now and again something disturbs their slow, distant orbits and one of them is propelled along a very long path towards the Sun. As it enters the Solar System the Sun melts the ice. The pressure of the Sun's radiation and the stream of particles it sends out also affect it. A long streamer of gas, ice and dust is formed. The sunlight reflects off this tail and we see a **comet**. As a comet gets closer to the Sun the gravitational force on it increases – so it goes faster, just as the inner planets move faster than the outer ones.

The most famous comet is **Halley's Comet** (see picture 5). It is a comet that has settled into a fixed orbit. It sweeps in a huge ellipse around the Sun, taking 76 years to complete each orbit. New comets appear quite often, for example, Comet Shoemaker-Levy, which collided with Jupiter in July 1994.

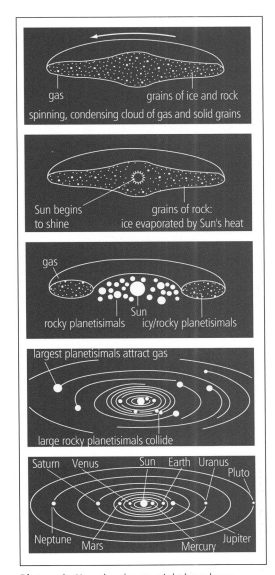

Picture 4 How the planets might have been formed.

Picture 5 Halley's comet.

■ The Earth

The Earth is the largest of the inner, dense planets. Even so, its mass is only 0.3% the mass of Jupiter. It finished being formed about 4.5 billion years ago, according to measurements of the age of the oldest rocks.

The Earth can be called an iron planet. Its core is mostly iron, with some nickel mixed in. It has a very thin layer of lighter materials on top, forming the Earth's crust (see topic G1). It is just the right distance from the Sun for life as we know it to exist. It is not too cold – so water doesn't freeze all the time. It is not too hot, so water doesn't boil.

The Earth's crust is amazingly thin, compared with the size of the Earth, and so is the atmosphere. When you trace the outline of a coin with a pencil to represent the Earth, the thickness of the line would cover both crust and atmosphere. It is this crust, and the thin layer of gases surrounding it, which provide the materials that all life on Earth needs.

The surface of the Earth's crust is changed by the action of wind, water, earthquakes and the mysterious upwellings of new rocks from deeper inside the Earth. The energy to move winds and water on the Earth comes from the Sun.

The energy that produces volcanoes and earthquakes comes from deep inside the Earth.

HOW DO WE KNOW ALL THIS?

The layered structure of the Earth was discovered by the study of earthquake waves. Just as radar waves bounce off different kinds of objects, so the shock waves from earthquakes bounce off the different layers of the Earth. See topic G1 for more details.

RADIOACTIVE DATING

The best evidence for the age of the Earth comes from measurements of the radioactivity of minerals in rocks. This is also explained in topic G1.

Using this and other methods scientists have worked out that the oldest unmelted rock found on Earth is about 4 billion years old. The oldest rocks brought back by the American astronauts from the Moon were 4.5 billion years old. The Earth and Moon were probably formed at the same time, but the Earth is so active geologically that we are unlikely to find the oldest rocks still unchanged.

■ Meteorites

Meteorites are what we call 'shooting stars'. They are bits of dust and rock that enter the Earth's atmosphere from time to time. They travel at high speed and most of them are burnt up by friction before they reach the surface. They are the

Picture 6 The daytime meteorite of 10 August 1972. It weighed 1000 tonnes and could have destroyed a small village.

remains of the original cloud from which the Solar System was formed. Measurements on meteorites that have landed on Earth also give an age of about 4.5 billion years.

The surface of the Moon, and many of the moons of other planets, show the effects of meteorites. In the last stages of the formation of moons and planets meteorites weighing many thousands of tonnes collided with them. They made huge craters. With a good telescope you can see these on the surface of the Moon. They are also shown on picture 4 on page 276 of topic G4.

The oldest parts of the Earth also show large craters, probably formed by huge meteorites. Picture 7 shows Meteor Crater in Arizona. This was made by a meteorite of iron 2000 years ago.

Picture 6 on page 272 shows a meteorite burning up in the Earth's atmosphere on August 10, 1972. It was estimated to have a mass of 1000 tonnes, and its trail was large enough to be seen in daylight. Luckily it burnt out before reaching the ground. The Earth was formed by the collisions of planetoids and meteorites like this. It is in fact still growing, at a rate of 400 tonnes a day. Most of this is due to tiny meteorites which burn up in the atmosphere.

Picture 7 The Barringer Meteor Crater in Arizona. It is over a kilometre wide and 200 metres deep. The largest we know on Earth is 26 km across.

Activities

Picture 8 The Orion Nebula is a huge cloud of dust and gas. New stars were discovered in the Nebula in 1955 that hadn't been there 10 years earlier.

A Looking for stars

The gas clouds which turn into stars are usually invisible, although they can be detected by the radio or infra-red radiation they emit. But a small telescope or pair of binoculars will show you a gas cloud which is glowing brightly with the light of new stars that have just formed. This is the cloud ('nebula') in the constellation of Orion. Picture 8 shows a photograph of this cloud taken with a large telescope, and picture 9 shows where it is.

Use a star map to find Orion. You can get a map from your library, or from the newspapers which publish star maps near the beginning of each month. Use the map to find the Nebula.

B Looking for meteors

Meteors are meteorites that burn up completely in the atmosphere. Most of them are no bigger than grains of sand. They are likely to be the bits that get left behind by comets. Each year the Earth passes through these old comet paths and we get an extra supply of meteors – **meteor showers**.

Try to see some meteors (or 'shooting stars'), during the following periods:

April 12–24: linked with Halley's Comet, best on April 22

July 20–Aug 19: linked with Tuttle's Comet, best on August 11

Oct 11–30: another pass through Halley's trail, best on October 19

Oct 24–Dec 10: linked with Temple's Comet, best on November 13

Dec 5–19: best on December 12

C Catching up

The exploration of the Solar System is still taking place. New theories and evidence are appearing every year. This mostly comes from deep space probes like the Voyager and Galileo spacecraft.

There are plans to send probes, and possibly manned spacecraft, to Mars.

The Hubble Space Telescope is a satellite-based telescope that should revolutionise our understanding of distant galaxies.

Find out all you can about one of these topics and prepare to make a presentation to your class about it.

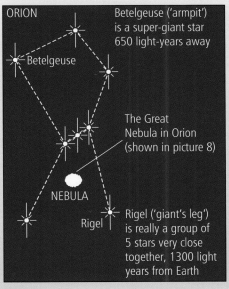

ORION

Betelgeuse ('armpit') is a super-giant star 650 light-years away

Betelgeuse

The Great Nebula in Orion (shown in picture 8)

NEBULA

Rigel

Rigel ('giant's leg') is really a group of 5 stars very close together, 1300 light years from Earth

Picture 9

Questions

1 What are: (a) comets, (b) asteroids, (c) satellites?

2 The Solar System began as a gas cloud. When the gas cloud collapsed it was squashed together by gravity. It got hotter. Give an example from your own experience where squashing a gas makes it hot.

3 Explain why the 'inner planets' are made of denser material than the outer ones.

4 a A million years is a long time. Were you alive a million seconds ago? What were you doing a million minutes ago?

   b A billion is a thousand millions. Where were you a billion seconds ago?

   c What was the world like a billion days ago?

5 How does the Sun get its energy?

6 Explain, using a diagram, why the energy the Earth gets from the Sun is only a tiny fraction of the energy the Sun emits. (Hint: the Earth is 150 million km from the Sun.)

7 Two stars at the same temperature radiate the same amount of energy per square metre of surface. Explain why

   a if one star is twice the radius of the other it will radiate 4 times as much energy in total

   b both stars would look equally bright if the larger star was twice as far away as the smaller star.

8 Compare the life history (evolution) of the Sun with that of a star 20 times as massive.

Planets' atmospheres and life

This question brings together ideas from a number of topics. Table 1 shows what the atmospheres of three planets are like. It also shows what the atmosphere of Earth was probably like, 4 billion years ago. The figures for the gases are fractions of the atmosphere, in percentages.

1 What are the main differences between the atmosphere of young Earth as it was and the Earth now?

2 One gas (very important for life!) has been left off the Earth data. What is it?

3 Where do you think the oxygen on the Earth has come from?

4 What has happened to the carbon dioxide that was in the old Earth's atmosphere?

5 Give two reasons why you would not expect to find life on Venus.

6 Would life be possible on Mars? Give some reasons for your answer.

Table 1

Atmosphere	Venus	Planet — Young Earth	Mars	Earth now
carbon dioxide	98	98	95	0.03
nitrogen	1.9	1.9	1.7	78
oxygen	trace	trace	0.13	21
rare gases	0.1	0.1	2	1
temperature on surface (°C)	477	300	-53	13
surface pressure	90	60	0.064	1

Sky patterns

The stars are fixed in their constellations. We learn about the Solar System by studying the movements of the Sun, the Moon and the planets against the background of the fixed stars.

Picture 1 Orion is one of the easiest constellations to find.

STAR PATTERNS

On a clear starry night you might be able to see five thousand stars, if you have good eyesight. To make sense of them star watchers many years ago arranged them into groups – the **constellations**. Picture 1 shows the constellation called **Orion**. Many of the constellations are named after ancient Greek heroes or heroines. Orion is named after a Greek hero who was a mighty hunter.

You can see Orion from autumn to spring, in the southern sky. If you look at it every hour or so in the winter you will notice that it moves from east to west. You will see other stars rising in the east, like the Sun, and setting in the west.

All the stars follow this same pattern of movement. But if they are high enough in the sky they never rise or set. Instead they circle around a fixed point in the northern sky. (See picture 2.) Close to this point is a star, called the **Pole Star**, or **Polaris**. Picture 3 shows how to find this star by using the two 'pointer' stars in the constellation of the **Plough** (**Ursa Major**).

Picture 2 The Pole star makes a circle around the Celestial Pole. This picture was taken over several hours using a camera pointing at the Pole Star.

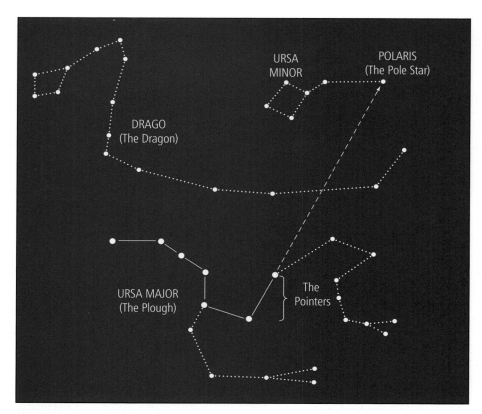

Picture 3 How to find the Pole Star.

Picture 4 The Moon seems to change its shape, 'waxing and waning'.

The Pole Star is directly above the North Pole of the Earth, and so it is very useful in navigation. As you may remember from earlier work, this movement of the stars across the sky is caused by the fact that the Earth is spinning on its axis.

The Earth spins on its axis once every 24 hours, and as we move under the stars they seem to be passing overhead. It is this spinning of the Earth that causes the Sun to rise and set.

THE MOON

The Moon, too, rises and sets. But it also changes shape to give the **phases** of the Moon (picture 4). The rising and setting is because of the spinning of the Earth. Its changing shape is caused by the fact that the Moon actually does move on its own. It is a **satellite** of the Earth. It moves around the Earth in an orbit, taking just over 27 days to complete it.

This is shown in picture 5, which also explains how its shape appears to change. What we see is only the part of the Moon that is in sunlight.

Because it moves on its own, the Moon doesn't keep pace with the stars. If you look at the Moon at the same time every night you will see it in a slightly different part of the sky each night. It seems to slip back against the constellations.

The stars are further away from us than the Moon is. We can tell this because as the Moon moves through the star patterns it cuts them off. We never see stars in front of the Moon.

But the Moon also moves in front of the Sun. When this happens the sunlight is cut off. We then have an **eclipse** of the Sun, or **solar eclipse**. It can only happen when the Moon is 'new', lying directly between us and the Sun.

Sometimes the full Moon gets dark. This happens when the Moon is in the Earth's shadow, so we have an eclipse of the Moon, or **lunar eclipse**. Picture 6 shows how these eclipses are produced.

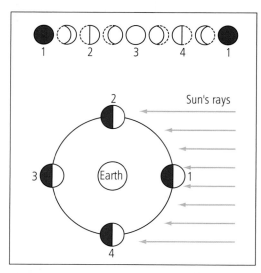

Picture 5 Why the Moon changes its shape: the phases of the Moon.

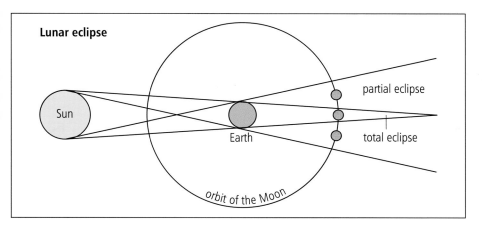

Lunar eclipse

partial eclipse

Sun

Earth

total eclipse

orbit of the Moon

THE PLANETS

The planets look like stars but they are in fact very different. They are much smaller than stars, and do not shine by their own light. We can only see them because they reflect the light of the Sun.

They were first noticed in ancient times. Like the stars, they rise and set. But careful starwatchers picked them out because they also move against the background of the ordinary 'fixed' stars.

The ancient astronomers discovered five of these 'wandering stars'. We still call them by Roman versions of the names given to them by the ancient Greeks, who named them after their gods: Mercury, Venus, Mars, Jupiter and Saturn.

The easiest ones to see are Jupiter, Venus and Mars. Mars and Venus are easy to see because they are the planets closest to Earth. Jupiter is a lot further away but it is the biggest planet of all. We now know that there are three more planets: Uranus, Neptune and Pluto (which was only discovered in 1934).

Uranus and Neptune are visible to the naked eye, but quite hard to find unless you are an experienced observer. Mercury is very close to the Sun and you can see it best just before dawn – if you know exactly when and where to look.

THE ZODIAC

The Sun, Moon and planets all seem to move across the sky through a belt of stars called the **zodiac**. The stars in the zodiac are grouped into 12 constellations – the 'signs of the zodiac'. You will recognise their names because they are often listed as 'birth signs' in newspapers and magazines in their astrology columns.

Don't confuse *astrologers* with *astronomers*. Astronomers observe and measure the positions and properties of stars and they are very accurate. Astrologers claim that they can predict people's future and personality from the positions of the stars and planets. But they get it wrong about as often as they get it right.

Your 'birth sign' is decided by where in the zodiac the Sun was when you were born. If you were born on 12 June, for example, you are a 'Gemini'. At this time the Sun is between us and the constellation of the **Twins (Gemini)**. Picture 8 shows the zodiac and the Sun's position at this time.

THE MILKY WAY

The Milky Way is the part of the sky where stars are most crowded together. It can be seen all through the year. It is a wide band of stars that runs through the constellation of Cassiopeia, which never sets. In the winter it is close to Gemini and Orion, and in summer it is a splendid sight as it crosses the sky from Cygnus to Scorpio.

Look at any part of the Milky Way through a small telescope or pair of binoculars. What to the naked eye looks like a faint whitish blur becomes a mass of stars. Find out more about the Milky Way in topic G6.

Solar eclipse

Partial eclipse zone

Zone of Totality

Sun

Moon Earth

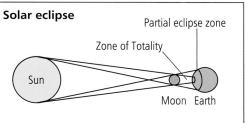

Picture 6 Eclipses of the Sun and the Moon.

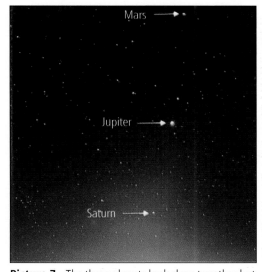

Mars

Jupiter

Saturn

Picture 7 The three planets look close together but Jupiter is much further away from us than Mars.

Questions

1 Give two differences between stars and planets.

2 Explain what the following words mean:
   zodiac, eclipse, orbit, astronomy, astrology, planet, star, lunar, satellite.

3 The Moon goes around the Earth once every 28 days or so. Why don't we get eclipses of the Sun and Moon every month?

4 We don't get eclipses of the Sun when the Moon is a 'half' moon. Explain why not.

5 Your young brother refuses to believe that the Earth is round. 'It looks pretty flat to me', he says.

   What would you say to him, or show him, to prove that the Earth isn't 'flat'?

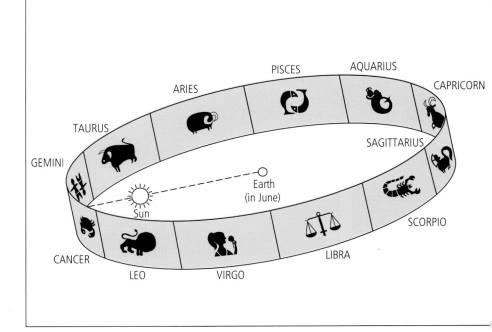

Picture 8 As the Earth goes around the Sun, the Sun appears to move against the background of the stars. The star groups it moves in front of are called the signs of the zodiac.

Activities

A Looking for the constellations

Use a simple star map. These are published every month by some newspapers (The Times, The Guardian, The Daily Telegraph, The Independent) and you should be able to get a

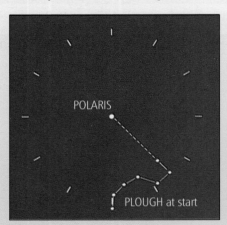

Picture 9 How do the stars move during the night?

photocopy from your library. The best time of the year is when it gets dark fairly early (autumn to spring). Choose a moonless night. Try to find the following constellations: Plough (Great Bear), Cassiopeia, Gemini, Leo, Cygnus, the Pleiades, Orion, Perseus with Andromeda and the Great Square of Pegasus.

B Do the stars move?

Draw or photograph the positions of stars near the Pole Star.

1 Drawing: find the Plough and mark its position on a 'clock diagram' (picture 9) at, say, 7 pm. Mark its position every half hour until 10 pm.

2 Taking a photograph: you need a camera with a 'B' button that lets you keep the shutter open as long as you want. Put the camera on a firm surface pointing at the Pole Star. Open the shutter and leave it open for an hour or so. It is important not to move the camera. Make sure that there aren't any bright lights nearby.

C The moon

1 Use a telescope or a good pair of binoculars to look at the Moon. The best time is when the Moon is between 'half' and 'full'. Can you see the 'mountains'? Draw what you can see as carefully as possible. A good encyclopaedia will have a 'Moon Map' you can use to identify the main features. Try your school library.

2 Draw the shape and position of the Moon (compared with the star patterns) every night for a week – or every other night for a fortnight.

D Looking for planets

Use a newspaper map (see activity A) to find some planets. Draw where they are compared to nearby stars. Do this for a week or two. Comment on what you notice.

E The Milky Way

Use a small telescope or a pair of binoculars to look at the Milky Way. Describe what you see. What does this tell us about what the Milky Way might be?

Stars and planets

The Sun, Earth and planets are part of a pattern in space called the Solar System.

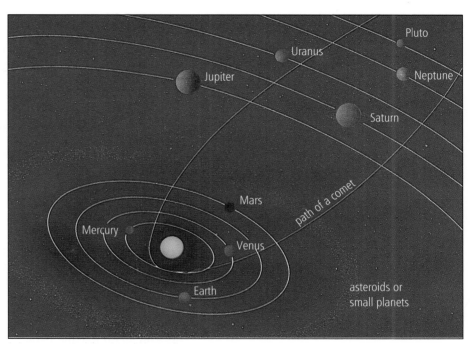

Picture 1 The Solar System. It is not drawn to scale because the outer planets are so far away from the Sun compared with the inner ones.

THE SOLAR SYSTEM

The Sun is the centre of the Solar System. It contains 99.8% of all the mass in the System, and so produces a huge gravity field that holds the planets in their orbits around it (see topic B7). Picture 1 shows the Sun and the planets, viewed from outside the System. The actual masses and distances of the planets from the Sun are given in table 1.

■ The Sun

The Sun is a star. It is quite a small one, as stars go, and it isn't very bright. It is the brightest object in the sky because it is so close to us, compared with other stars. The energy it provides supports all life on Earth. This energy comes from the Sun's own mass, which it uses up at a rate of 4 million tonnes per second.

The Sun emits energy at the rate of 400 000 000 000 000 000 000 000 000 watts (4×10^{26} W). Only a tiny fraction of this energy reaches Earth. Most is radiated into empty space.

Table 1 Planetary data.

	Mass (Earth=1)	Diameter (km)	Density (tonnes per m³)	Surface gravity field (N/kg)	Distance from Sun (10^9 km)	Period 'year'	'Day'
Mercury	0.05	4880	5.4	3.7	58	88d	59d
Venus	0.81	12 112	5.25	8.9	107.5	224d	243d
Earth	1	12 742	5.51	9.8	149.6	365d	23h 56m
Mars	0.11	6790	3.95	3.8	228	687d	24h 37m
Jupiter	318	142 600	1.34	24.9	778	11.9y	9h 50m
Saturn	95	120 200	0.70	10.5	1427	29.5y	10h 14m
Uranus	14.6	49 000	1.27	8.8	2870	84.0y	17h 14m
Neptune	17.2	50 000	1.64	11.2	4497	165y	16h 07m
Pluto system	0.003	2284	2	0.6	5900 (variable)	248y	6.4d

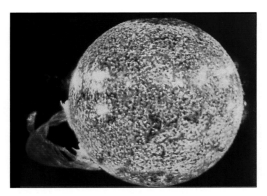

Picture 2 A Sun storm. On the scale of the picture the Earth would be about the size of one of the dark blobs or about half a millimetre across.

Question 6 is about using the Einstein equation $E = mc^2$ to check these amazing figures.

The energy is produced by a process called **nuclear fusion** (see topic F5). The Sun is mostly hydrogen. Hydrogen nuclei in the centre of the Sun are under a huge pressure and at a very high temperature. Some of the hydrogen nuclei collide to form helium nuclei. In doing this they lose a tiny fraction of their mass which is converted to the kinetic energy of the particles that are left.

Picture 2 shows the surface of the Sun. The surface is a gas at a temperature of about 5500 °C, and the picture shows a typical 'Sun storm' in which hot gas is hurled far out into space. These storms reach a peak every 11 years. At times of peak activity the Sun sends out far more ionised particles than usual, which affect our atmosphere and so the weather on Earth.

■ The planets

The planets move in orbit around the Sun. They all move in the same direction, which is anticlockwise when viewed from above. The nearer the planet is to the Sun the faster it moves. The gravitational force from the Sun gets weaker with distance. At the orbit of Neptune the force per kilogram produced by the Sun is about a thousandth of the force per kilogram at the Earth's distance. This force is what keeps the planets in their orbits. It does this by accelerating them towards the Sun along the line joining them, as explained in topic B8 in connection with Earth satellites. The smaller this acceleration the slower the planet will move. So the orbital speed of Mercury is 55 metres per second while Neptune travels at a tenth of that speed, about 5.4 m/s.

Neptune has a larger orbit than Mercury and travels much more slowly. This means that Neptune takes much longer than Mercury to complete its path around the Sun. This orbit time is called the planet's 'year'. A 'year' for Mercury is just over 12 Earth weeks, while Neptune takes 165 Earth years to make one orbit around the Sun.

Mercury is so close to the Sun that its surface is heated up to over 400 °C, which is hot enough to melt tin. It spins on its axis rather slowly, managing to get three spins ('days') for every two orbits ('years') around the sun. It is too small to have an atmosphere.

The next planet out from the Sun is **Venus** (picture 3). it is almost exactly the same size as the Earth and is only a little less massive. You might think it would be a good place to go for a sunshine holiday, but you would be wrong. Its atmosphere is mostly carbon dioxide, so the Greenhouse effect is so great that it is even hotter than Mercury, with a surface temperature of 460 °C.

The atmosphere of Venus is very corrosive, containing hydrogen chloride and hydrogen fluoride. No one has seen the surface of Venus, as it is hidden by clouds of concentrated sulphuric acid and particles of pure sulphur. Also, the atmospheric

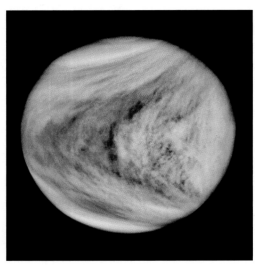

Picture 3 Venus.

	Surface temperature (°C)	Number of moons	Atmosphere
Mercury	350	0	None
Venus	460	0	Thick: carbon dioxide, sulphuric acid
Earth	20	1	Nitrogen, oxygen
Mars	−23	2	Thin: carbon dioxide
Jupiter	−120	16, 1 ring	Hydrogen, helium, ammonia, methane
Saturn	−180	17, plus rings	Hydrogen, helium, ammonia, methane
Uranus	−210	15, plus rings	Hydrogen, helium, ammonia, methane
Neptune	−220	8	Hydrogen, helium, methane
Pluto system	−230	1	None – frozen

pressure is 95 times what it is on Earth, so that a very well-designed space suit would be needed. When the Russian Venus Probe landed by parachute on the surface of Venus in 1972 it managed to survive for only about 30 minutes in these very nasty conditions.

Bypassing planet **Earth**, we next reach the planet **Mars**. At one time it was thought that Mars could support life. Indeed, a nineteenth century astronomer was convinced that the markings he could see on its surface were canals. He was wrong; he might have seen lines of craters or dust blown by the wind and used his very vivid imagination!

But spacecraft sent to Mars have taken photographs which seem to show old river beds. It may be that at one time there was enough surface water on Mars to support life. It also looks as if Mars once had volcanoes (picture 4). This suggests an internal source of energy which might have been able to support some kind of life. Mars even has an atmosphere, but it is much thinner than the Earth's.

In 1976 the American Viking Spacecraft managed to 'soft-land' probes which were able to take pictures of the Martian surface.

These probes also looked for signs of life. They scooped up some Martian soil and tested it to see if carbon dioxide or any other chemical signs of life were present. The first experiment seemed to give a positive result. But when the experiment was repeated many times no more of the chemicals were detected. Scientists now agree that there is no life on Mars.

■ Asteroids

Between Mars and the giant planet Jupiter astronomers have discovered hundreds of stony objects. These range in size from the largest (Ceres) which is just over 700 km in diameter to rocks which are less than a few kilometres across. There are probably thousands of others too small to see. These objects should be called *planetoids* (little planets) rather than **asteroids** (little stars).

The asteroids are mostly clustered in their orbits between Mars and Jupiter. But some of them wander away from this region. They climb high above the plane in which the planets move, or have strange orbits which bring them closer to the Sun even than Earth. It is calculated that one of them, Hermes, might one day pass between Earth and the Moon.

■ The Giant Planets – Jupiter, Saturn, Uranus and Neptune

Beyond the asteroids lies the largest planet, **Jupiter**. It is big enough to hold 1300 Earths. If it was just a little more massive it would turn into a star. As it is, the energy generated as it slowly collapses on itself creates huge storms in its atmosphere. One of these storms, a huge hurricane 48 000 kilometres long by 11 000 wide, has probably existed for thousands of years. This is the famous Great Red Spot, which you can see in picture 5.

At the visible 'surface', Jupiter's gravity field is 2.6 times stronger than Earth's. But what we see is not the planet's real surface, but the top of its atmosphere. This is made of swirling clouds of hydrogen, methane and ammonia. The bands on its surface are huge **jet streams**. Below the atmosphere is a very deep 'sea' of liquid, metallic hydrogen. This covers a comparatively small solid core. The planet's core is very hot. It might be rocky, or even white hot, solid hydrogen.

Like Jupiter, the next three planets are large and have a low density (see table 1). They are also likely to be made mostly of hydrogen and helium.

Saturn is famous for its 'rings', shown in picture 6. These are made of small rocks, pebbles and grains which orbit the planet, all together in the same plane. The Voyager spacecraft discovered that both **Uranus** and **Neptune** have rings as well. They are not so large or as clearly visible as Saturn's.

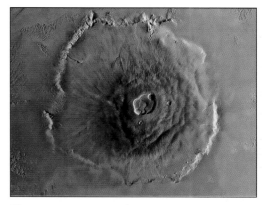
Picture 4 A Martian volcano now extinct.

Picture 5 Jupiter's Great Red Spot.

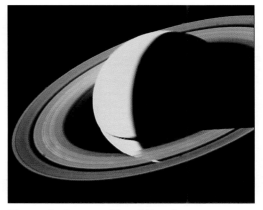
Picture 6 Saturn and its orbiting rings.

All these outer planets have several moons. Some orbit so close to their planet that they are in danger of being pulled apart by its gravity forces. One of the moons of Jupiter, **Io**, is being shaken up so much that it is hot enough inside for volcanoes to exist.

■ The odd one out

Pluto is the furthest known planet of the Solar System. But it isn't always the furthest – it moves in an orbit that cuts inside the orbit of Neptune.

Pluto is small and very hard to see. It was not discovered until 1930, 14 years after its existence had been predicted (just as Neptune had been, because of its effect on the movement of the other outer planets – see topic B3).

It seemed to be a very small planet, probably smaller than Earth. We now know that it is a very strange object indeed. It is a 'double planet', with a moon, Charon, almost as big as itself.

THE LIVES AND DEATHS OF STARS

The Sun is a middle-aged star. It was formed about 5 billion years ago (5×10^9 years) by the process described above (pages 271–2). Will the Sun shine for ever? Or will it eventually run down and cease to exist as the source of energy that supports life on Earth?

The evidence for the likely future of the Sun comes from careful observations of other stars in the sky. The evidence is fitted into the theories of the **astrophysicists** who apply the laws of physics as we know them on Earth to what is seen in the wider universe. The most obvious things that we can see in the stars is that they are:

- **bright** – but some are brighter than others,
- **coloured** – but different stars have different colours.

Picture 7 Stars vary in colour and brightness.

Why some stars are brighter than others

The brightness of a star is called its **magnitude**. One star can look brighter than another for two reasons. The first is that it is larger or hotter than normal stars. Or it could simply be an average star that happens to be quite close to the Earth. The brightest star in the sky is Sirius, the 'Dog Star' in the constellation Canis Major. Sirius is close to the Earth at about 9 light years' distance. It is also hotter than average. If Sirius were twice as far away it would look just a quarter as bright. To compare the brightness of stars astronomers work out how bright they would look at a *standard* distance from Earth. This gives a standard brightness value called the **absolute magnitude** for the star.

Why are stars coloured?

Imagine heating a piece of steel. When it is too hot to touch it doesn't look any different but it emits invisible infra-red radiation (see page 38) which you can feel with your skin. As it gets hotter it begins to glow a dull red. Hotter still, yellow appears and the steel glows with an orange light. Then it becomes white hot. At a high enough temperature the white light is tinged with blue, but the steel will now be melting. All materials show similar colour changes as they are heated, and the colour balance in the radiation they send out is an accurate measure of their temperature.

When a graph is plotted of the absolute magnitudes of stars against their colours an interesting pattern appears. Picture 8 shows this, plotted on a graph called the **Hertzsprung–Russell Diagram**. The colour axis has also been labelled with the corresponding temperature. This is, of course, the surface temperature – stars are much hotter inside. Most stars fit into a broad curving band called the Main Sequence.

Above and to the right of the Main Sequence we find brighter, redder (so cooler) stars. Although these are cool they are bright because they are very large, and are called **Red Giant** stars. The easiest Red Giant to see is Betelgeuse in Orion.

Below and to the left we find dim stars that are quite hot. They are dim because they are small, and are called **White Dwarfs**.

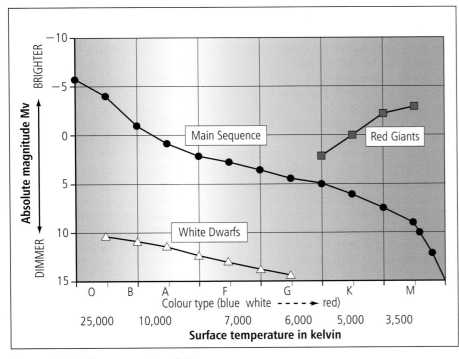

Picture 8   The Hertzsprung–Russell Diagram.

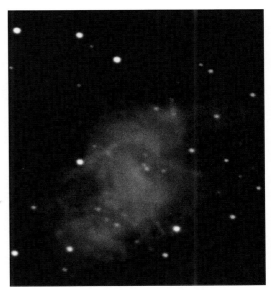

Picture 9   The Crab Nebula is a cloud of hot gas moving away at high speed from a neutron star. It is the remains of a supernova which exploded in 1054, forming a short-lived 'new star' which was bright enough to be seen in daylight.

The life of a star

The Sun is an ordinary type of star, and is firmly in the Main Sequence. It has a surface temperature of about 5800 K and so gives off yellowish white light. Stars that form from much bigger clouds of dust than the Sun started with, collapse to form larger stars – and with much greater pressures and temperatures in the hot core where the nuclear reactions take place. The cores would be larger and more active – making these stars hotter and brighter than the Sun. The hotter the star the more blue the light becomes. Sirius is the brightest star in the sky – mainly because it is one of the closest stars to us. If it was as close as the Sun it would look 23 times as bright as the Sun, with a surface temperature of 10 000 K, and the Earth would be too hot to have life on it. Sirius is also a bigger star – but has a mass only twice as great as the Sun's. A star 40 times the mass of the Sun would have a surface temperature of 40 000 K and be 500 000 times as bright as the Sun.

Table 3   Some facts about Main Sequence stars.

Star name	Type and colour	Surface temperature/K	Luminosity or brightness (Sun = 1)	Mass (Sun = 1)	Radius (Sun = 1)	Lifetime in millions of years
β Centauri	O blue-white	40 000	500 000	40	20	1
Sirius	A blue-white	10 000	23	2	2	80
Procyon	F white	6600	2.5	2.5	1.2	2000
Sun	G yellow-white	5800	1	1	1	10 000
A Centauri B	K orange	4300	0.16	0.8	0.7	20 000
Kapteyn's Star	M dull red	3300	0.008	0.21	0.3	50 000

The larger a star the shorter its life. It is giving out much more energy in proportion to its mass than a smaller, less massive star: Sirius has only twice the Sun's mass but is emitting energy as radiation over 20 times faster. Table 3 shows how stars of different mass are more or less bright and how long they live.

HOW STARS DIE

THE FUTURE OF THE SUN: A RED GIANT THEN A WHITE DWARF

Some stars just fade away, others end in an immense explosion. As time goes on after a star is formed the hydrogen nuclei – protons – in its core are gradually turning into helium nuclei. It is far too hot for electrons to stay with a nucleus to form atoms. The core is hot, at a temperature of over 10 million kelvin. The nuclei move at very high speeds – but they don't get very far because they keep bumping into each other. The nuclear gas is very crowded, with a density 160 times that of water. The high-speed nuclei in the core produce a huge pressure and would fly off into space – except for the fact that the core is surrounded by the huge mass of gas kept there by its own gravitational force. The only things that can escape from the core are photons of light – and neutrinos.

After its life of 5 billion years the core of the Sun has already converted about 60 percent of its mass to helium. As time goes on more and more hydrogen is used up and there will come a time when there simply isn't enough hydrogen left to keep producing energy by converting to helium. This should happened 5 billion years from now. Until then the Sun stays happily in its place on the Main Sequence.

So what happens next? The weight of the Sun outside the core compresses the core and it gets hotter – think of what happens when you pump up a bicycle tire. The Sun will even get brighter. But the compression will bring fresh hydrogen into the outer and now hotter core. This allows more energy to be released, and this in turn will heat up the cooler envelope of gas surrounding the core. The gas envelope – where in fact most of the mass of the Sun is – will expand, taking about

500 million years to do so. As it does so it cools down. The surface of the Sun goes from a hot yellow at about 6000 K to a dull red at 3000 K . The Sun's gases now stretch as far as the Earth's orbit. It has become a **red giant star**. This would mean the end of life on Earth.

Things don't end here. The core of the Sun is now mostly helium, and energy production has stopped. The core carries on collapsing under the force of gravity. It gets hotter as a result and a new energy producing process can start: helium can be converted to carbon by the **triple alpha process.** (See picture 10.)

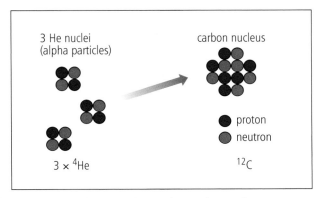

Picture 10 3 alpha particles combine to form carbon.

The triple alpha process acts very quickly. A vast amount of energy is generated as practically all the helium is converted to carbon in just a few minutes: called the **helium flash**. The star explodes, hurling the red envelope far into space. All that is left of the Sun is its core, a very small, white hot star that gradually cools. It has become a white dwarf star. Picture 10 shows such a star inside what remains of its envelope, still glowing with the energy being emitted from the hot white dwarf.

◼ Stars smaller than the Sun

For stars smaller than the Sun the path of evolution is slower. A star three-quarters the mass of the Sun will have a lifetime of about 20 billion years. The Universe is only about 15 billion years old and not many low mass stars have reached the end of their lives yet. If they are massive enough they too will go through the red giant to white dwarf stages. If not they may never get hot enough to trigger nuclear reactions: they become **brown dwarf stars**.

◼ Stars more massive than the Sun

These stars will also go through the red-giant to white-dwarf evolution. But they do so more quickly as their cores get hotter than the Sun's and more energetic nuclear reactions can take place. However after the red giant phase the helium-to-carbon stage takes place more slowly in stars more than twice the mass of the Sun, so there is no sudden 'helium flash' as expected for the Sun. The helium 'burning' to carbon stage may last for millions of years. Very massive stars may go through even more fusion reactions, the core getting hotter then cooler, and the outer envelope growing and shrinking so that the star pulsates, becoming a red giant more than once.

When helium burning is at last over energy production drops and the core again contracts and gets even hotter. The core is now mostly carbon. When it gets hot enough the carbon may combine in various nuclear processes to make heavier elements such as oxygen, sodium and magnesium. This process may also happen extremely quickly – perhaps just a few seconds. The result is a massive explosion: a faint star that nobody has noticed before suddenly becomes **billions** of times brighter: it has become a **supernova**.

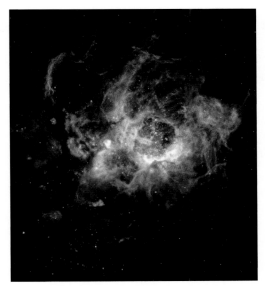

Picture 11 A white dwarf star surrounded by the remnants of the stellar atmosphere that shrouded it when it was a red giant. The Nursery Nebula in the region of nebula NGC 604 in galaxy M33.

A supernova will be as bright as whole galaxy of 10 billion stars. Most of the outer envelope of the star is thrown far into space, ready perhaps to join in making new stars. Particles thrown out from supernova collide with the elements made in the core and produce even heavier elements. This is the only way that these can be made: the carbon, oxygen and phosphorus in our bodies were made in an exploding star.

Supernovas soon cool down – taking just a year or two to do so. What is left behind is that part of the core that was so compressed in the explosion that all its nuclei are converted to neutrons. A core the size of the Earth becomes perhaps just 50 kilometres in diameter. This neutron star is very hot and emits radiation. If it is rotating we detect the radiation as regular pulses of radio waves, just a few milliseconds apart as the star is rotating very quickly. This is the kind of neutron star known as a pulsar ('pulsating star').

Picture 9 shows the object known from its shape as the Crab Nebula. It is the remains of a supernova that was seen by Chinese astronomers on the night of July 4th 1054. At its centre is the pulsar that made it the first supernova remnant to be identified in our galaxy.

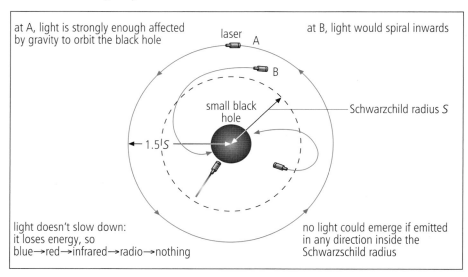

Picture 12 Light and a black hole.

■ Black holes

If the neutron star core of a supernova remnant is greater than 3 times the mass of the Sun the important force becomes gravity. Not even tightly packed neutron stars of this size with a density already of 10^{17} kg/m^3 can withstand the effects of their own weight. All matter is crushed, and the star gets smaller and smaller. The gravity field at its surface becomes so great that nothing can fight its way out against the force of gravity. Not even light. The star has become a **black hole**.

The problem with black holes is that nobody can see them. But astronomers have detected very large objects in the sky that emit very energetic X-rays. They have calculated that these types of X-ray can only come from charged particles accelerated to very high speeds. The most likely cause of such high speeds is that a black hole is pulling into itself the outer envelope of a nearby star. For example, there is an 'X-ray star' in the constellation Cygnus (the Swan) which emits X-rays at a rate 10 000 times the total emission of radiation from the Sun. Very hot objects can give off X-rays, but a hot object emitting all these X-rays would be the brightest object in the night sky, by far.

Activities

A Holidays in space!

Imagine that it is the year 2020 and you are an advertising agent for holidays on the planets. Make up an advertising slogan and:

- draw a poster, or
- produce a TV commercial, or
- write and record a radio commercial

for 'A Holiday on Mars' (or Venus, or Jupiter, or…).

B Exploring the Solar System

Use a library or the Internet to find out what you can about the probes that have been sent out to investigate the planets. Examples are: Venera (to Venus); Mariner (to Mercury and Venus); Pioneer (to Venus); Viking (to Mars); Voyager (to the outer planets).

C Looking for planets

At the beginning of each month some newspapers print star maps which show where the planets are in the sky for that month. You should be able to get one of these maps from school or from a public library. Use it to find some planets. Watch them over a few weeks to track their movements against the background of the fixed stars.

Questions

1 Use table 1 on page 279 to answer the following questions:

  a Which is the most massive planet?

  b Which planet has the greatest gravity field at its surface?

  c Which planet has its 'year' shorter than its 'day'?

  d Which planet has the shortest day?

  e Which planet has the longest day?

2 Why is it hard to get information about:

  a Venus?

  b Pluto?

3 Four planets have much higher densities (around 5 tonnes per cubic metre) than the others (see table 1).

  a Which planets have this higher density?

  b What is the reason for this high density?

c Get a sheet of paper at least 50 cm long and 5 cm wide. Draw a simple scale diagram of the Solar System to a scale of 100 Mm (megametres) to 1 mm. What does the attempt to do this tell you about the high-density and low-density groups of planets?

4 Use the data in table 1 to plot one or more of the following graphs. Put the name of the planet against its point on your graphs. Comment on each graph you draw.

  a Plot the density of the planets against their distance from the Sun.

  b Plot the mass of the planets against their distance from the Sun.

  c Plot the mass of the planets against their density.

  d Plot the orbital period ('year length') of the planets against their distance from the Sun.

  e Plot the surface temperature of the planets against their distance from the Sun.

5 Use the data in table 1 to make bar charts of the following:

  a the sizes (diameters) of the planets,

  b the number of moons of each planet,

  c the day lengths of the planets.

6 The Sun radiates 3.9×10^{26} joules of energy every second. This energy comes from the conversion of its mass into energy, given by the Einstein equation $E = mc^2$. Use this equation to check that to produce this energy output the Sun has to lose 4 million tonnes $(4 \times 10^9\,\text{kg})$ of matter every second.

7 The asteroids are the 'bits' of a planet that was never made. They orbit between Mars and Jupiter. Use the data in table 1, and any other ideas that you have, to answer the following questions.

  a What would such a planet be like?

  b Suggest its 'planetary data' – day length, size, distance from Sun, temperature, etc.

  c Suggest a name for this planet.

G6

Galaxies and the Universe

When you look up at the night sky you are looking across immense distances. You are also looking back into very ancient times.

TIME AND DISTANCE

On September 5th 1977, a space craft was launched from Cape Canaveral, Florida, by the National Aeronautics and Space Administration (NASA). It left Earth at a speed of over 11 kilometres a second. It needed this high speed to escape the pull of Earth's gravity field.

As it climbed away from Earth it slowed down, just as a ball slows down when you throw it up in the air. But after a few minutes the space craft had left the Earth's atmosphere and thrown away the empty shells of its rockets and fuel tanks. Voyager 2 had begun a journey to infinity.

Since 1977 Voyager 2 has been climbing through the gravity field of the Sun. The NASA space engineers have been clever. They have used the gravity fields of the planets to help Voyager 2 on its way. As it gets closer to a planet the space craft speeds up because of the increased gravity pull. Its approach is carefully angled so that the space craft changes direction, swinging around one planet to move off exactly in the right direction to get to the next one. This is shown in picture 1.

Some of the pictures of the planets in topic G5 were taken by Voyager 2.

After exactly 12 years, Voyager 2 shot past Neptune, the last of the giant gas planets in the Solar System. As it leaves the Solar System, it will miss Pluto, the outermost planet, because it is in a different part of the sky.

■ Space travel?

Voyager 2 is now moving into outer space. This is a very empty place. By comparison, the Solar System is crowded with planets, comets, meteorites and asteroids. There are also bits of dust and molecules left over from its formation, ten billion years ago.

■ When will Voyager 2 reach the stars?

When it leaves the Solar System Voyager 2 will be travelling at a speed of about 10 km per second, or 36 thousand kilometres an hour. It will be moving towards the brightest star in the sky, **Sirius**. This is in the constellation of Canis Major which you can find just off the Milky Way, low in the sky below Orion.

Voyager will take nearly 300 000 years to get there. Barring accidents, it will reach Sirius in the year 296036. Sirius is one of the stars closest to the Solar System.

Picture 1 How Voyager 2 used the planets to move out to Neptune.

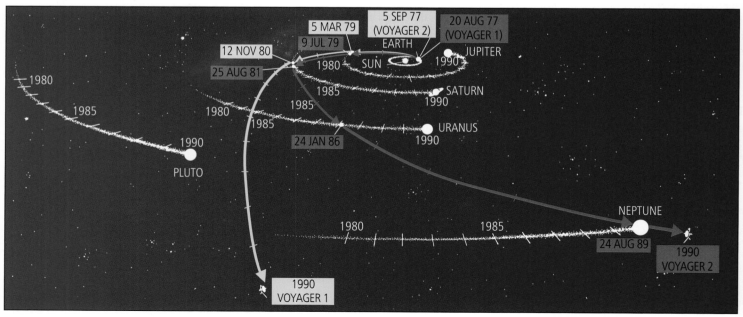

Space travel using rocket engines and space craft as we know them today is possible – but only to nearby planets. Travellers to the nearest stars will not return. If all went well, their descendants would come back, half a million years later.

The signals sent back from the planet Neptune by Voyager 2 took about 4 hours to reach NASA on Earth. They were of course radio signals, travelling at the speed of light. Signals from our nearest star, **Alpha Centauri**, would take 4.3 years to reach Earth. Messages from Sirius will take 9.7 years to arrive.

Light years

The stars are so far away that astronomers measure their distances in terms of how long light or radio waves take to travel from them to Earth. A **light year** is the distance covered by light in one year. As light travels at a speed of 300 000 000 metres per second (3×10^8 m/s) in empty space, this is a very large distance. It is 9.5 thousand million million metres, which we can write as 9 500 000 000 000 000 m, or 9.5×10^{15} m.

Table 1 shows the distances of some well-known stars and galaxies from Earth.

MEASURING THE UNIVERSE

We can use quite simple physics to find out what stars are like and what they are made of. We can measure how far away they are using much the same methods as surveyors use to make maps on Earth. The problem is that the stars are so far away, and the Earth is so small, that the work has to be done very carefully and with great accuracy.

Signals from space

Information about stars comes to us at the speed of light. It is carried by electromagnetic waves (see topic A7), and astronomers now use almost the whole range of radiation, from the very short X-rays to the long radio waves, to find out about stars.

When we look through a telescope our eyes can detect only visible radiation – light. Special photography can record invisible radiations, like X-rays, ultra-violet and infra-red. But most radiations from space are now detected and recorded electronically, and displayed on computer screens.

When it arrives on Earth the radiation from a star is all mixed up together. For it to be useful it has to be split up into a **spectrum**. Picture 3 shows a part of the spectrum of visible light from the Sun. Each dark line running across the spectrum is a clue about what elements the Sun contains.

Picture 2 The 'Red Rectangle' star taken in red light with a CCD camera.

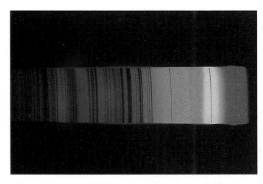

Picture 3 The dark lines in the spectrum of light from the Sun. These lines show what elements are present in the Sun's atmosphere.

Table 1 Distances from Earth of stars and galaxies.

Object	Name	Distance from Earth (light-years)	
star	Alpha Centauri	4.3	Nearest star to Earth
star	Sirius	8.7	The brightest star we can see, the 'dog star' in Canis Major
star	Canopus	196	In Carina, used by air navigators
star	Betelgeuse	650	A red supergiant, the brightest star in Orion
star	Polaris	780	The Pole Star, in Ursa Major
galaxy	M31	2 200 000	The Andromeda galaxy, our nearest galaxy
	M81	10 000 000	In Ursa Major (The Plough)
	M87	42 000 000	The Sombrero Galaxy, in Virgo
clusters of galaxies	Virgo	78 000 000	In the constellation Virgo
	Hydra 3	3 960 000 000	In the constellation Hydra

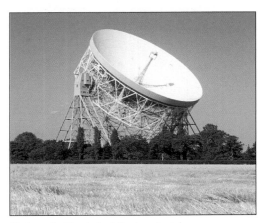

Picture 4 The Jodrell Bank radio telescope. Astronomers now use the whole electromagnetic spectrum to observe the Universe.

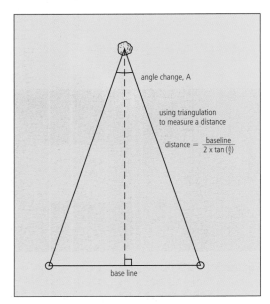

angle change, A

using triangulation to measure a distance

$$distance = \frac{baseline}{2 \times \tan\left(\frac{A}{2}\right)}$$

base line

Picture 5 How triangulation works.

Picture 6 Star field in the Milky Way.

A spectrum is produced when light passes through a **prism**, or through a diffraction grating. Different wavelengths in the radiation are separated out and so they can be photographed and studied.

Light from stars also shows these spectrum lines, and this is how we know what elements a star contains. Astronomers can also work out how hot the star is, by studying its spectrum.

Stars also give out radio waves, which are picked up by huge **radio telescopes** (see picture 4). Radio waves tell us a lot about stars and also about the dark material we find in between the stars.

■ The scale of the universe

Human beings and many other animals are quite good at telling how far away things are. If one object seems to pass in front of another when it moves it must be nearer. This effect can also be seen when you move your head, and one object *appears* to move in front of another. (Just try looking out of the window and moving your head.)

How much the object appears to move gives our brains a good clue as to how far away it is. This effect is called **parallax**, and is used by astronomers to help measure distances of stars using a method called **triangulation**.

Picture 5 shows how triangulation works. Knowing the angles and the length of the baseline, a surveyor can calculate how far away the tree is.

Stars are much further away than trees. So astronomers use the longest baseline they can. This could be the diameter of the Earth, using two telescopes on opposite sides of the Earth. For very distant objects they use the diameter of the Earth's orbit, giving a baseline of 300 million kilometers.

Using this method, astronomers can measure the distances of stars as far away as about 300 light years or so. But this is just a very tiny part of the Universe. There are lots of stars with no measurable parallax which must be even further away.

USING BRIGHTNESS

Some stars are brighter than others. This might be because they really do give out more light energy – or they might look bright because they are closer to us. The star Sirius, for example, is many times brighter than the Sun. But the Sun looks brighter because it is closer to us.

If we know how bright stars really are we can work out how far away they are. This is where the spectrum of starlight comes in again. Stars of different real brightness have different spectra. By looking at the spectrum of a star we can work out its real brightness, and so its distance from Earth.

This method allowed astronomers to take measurements out to nearly all the stars you can see in the night sky. But if you use a telescope you can see far more stars (picture 6). And some of what you see are not stars at all, they are in fact huge groups of stars – called **galaxies**.

■ Galaxies

The nearest galaxy to Earth is in the constellation of Andromeda. You can see it with the naked eye, on a fine summer night. Picture 7 shows it as seen through a large telescope. To begin with astronomers thought that objects like this were clouds of gas – and called them **nebulae**, from the Latin word for a cloud.

We can now see that each speck of light is a star. Astronomers have discovered many thousands of these groups of stars, and we believe that the Universe contains many millions of them.

Edwin Hubble was an American astronomer who was put in charge of a new telescope at Mount Wilson in California. The first thing Hubble did was look at the Andromeda Nebula. He was the first astronomer to see that the 'cloud' was not a cloud of gas, but was made of millions of stars.

Picture 7 The nearest galaxy to Earth – the Great Nebula in Andromeda.

Picture 8 The Virgo cluster of galaxies.

He was amazed to find that the stars in the Andromeda Nebula were further away than any other known object. The Nebula was over two million light years from Earth. He calculated that it contained more than a billion stars.

GALAXIES UPON GALAXIES AS FAR AS THE TELESCOPE CAN SEE

Since then we have discovered many more galaxies. Some are 'quite close', at about the same distance as the Andromeda Nebula. This is our *Local Group* of galaxies: there are 19 of them. Some are quite small, with just a few tens of thousands of stars. Others contain a few thousand million stars, like Andromeda and our own galaxy – the **Milky Way**.

We now know that the Universe is made up of many **groups** or **clusters** of galaxies, separated from each other by huge regions of empty space (picture 8). One of these clusters, in the constellation of Coma Berenices, contains 100 000 galaxies.

THE EXPANDING UNIVERSE

After Andromeda, Edwin Hubble then turned his telescope on other nebulae. He measured them to be even further away.

Hubble also discovered something else. The Universe is expanding. In fact, it is expanding in all directions. He found that every galaxy in the Universe is moving away from every other galaxy. And the further apart they are, the faster they are travelling. It looked like the result of a gigantic explosion that took place billions of years before.

■ The red shift

The evidence for this expansion came from the spectra of the galaxies. But the spectra had all been somehow distorted. The lines did not appear at the same wavelengths as they did in the Sun. They had all shifted towards the red end of the spectrum – the **red shift** (see picture 9.)

To an experienced astrophysicist like Hubble this was not a great surprise. He knew that waves from objects change their wavelengths and frequencies if the object is moving. It is the well-known **Doppler Effect** that you hear when ambulances or police cars move past you with the siren sounding. The effect is used in radar speed traps to measure the speeds of cars.

What was a surprise was the size of the change, and what it told astronomers about the distances of these further galaxies.

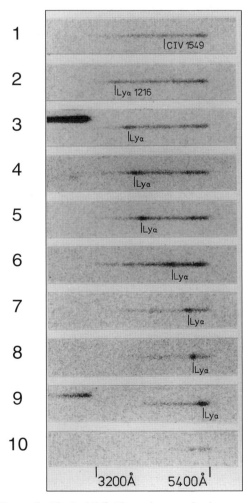

Picture 9 The Red Shift. These photographs show the spectra of very bright 'stars' called quasars. Going from top to bottom (1 to 9), the same spectrum line (Lyα) shifts across. It moves towards the red end of the spectrum – the 'red shift'. Quasars with the largest red shift are thought to be furthest away. The bigger the red shift, the faster they are moving. This fitted in with Hubble's theory of an expanding universe.

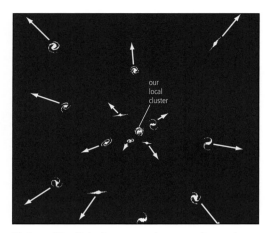

Picture 10 Galaxies are moving away from other galaxies.

The size of the universe

With his new telescope and new techniques Hubble measured the distances of some galaxies that were not too far away. They too showed the red shift. He discovered a simple pattern between red shift and distance. This is illustrated in picture 10. It is known as **Hubble's Law**: *The further the galaxy is from Earth, the bigger is its red shift.*

But what did this mean? The red shift is caused by the galaxy's movement, so what his law really said was:

The further the galaxy is from Earth, the faster it is moving.

But this also means:

The faster it is moving, the further away it must be.

Thus objects with a large red shift must be very far away. This is now how we find the distance away of the most distant objects in the Universe.

Time and the speed of light

The telescopes focused on these distant galaxies are seeing light that left them 9 billion years ago.

We can never find out what they are like now. All the objects in the sky may already have changed! When you look at the Andromeda Nebula you are looking 2.5 million years into the past. Even the sunlight we see has taken 8 minutes to reach us. The night sky is a historical museum of what the Universe was like at any time from 4 years to 9 billion years ago.

The beginning – and the end

Imagine reversing the outward movement of all these distant galaxies. The further they are away the faster they would go back to where the motion started. The fastest galaxies would of course have further to go and it works out that all of them would end up the same place at the same time. It was when astronomers realised this that they thought that as the universe was in fact expanding all of it must have been in one place at one time. Then there was a sudden expansion and everything flew apart. This is the **Big Bang** model of the origin of the Universe that we see today.

It is hard to measure the rate of expansion of the Universe. A reasonable measurement gives the age of the Universe, working backwards as explained above, to be from 12 to 15 billion years.

There is a huge quantity of matter and energy in the Universe. No one knows what it must have been like when it was all compressed into a tiny dot less than 10^{-35} metres across. And we cannot imagine what it was like *before* the Big Bang. But there is overwhelming evidence for what must have happened in the first few seconds and afterwards. Physicists have shown exactly why the Universe contains 75% hydrogen and 25% helium – with just a tiny smidgen of all the other elements. We can detect the last echoes of the radiation that was set free when the universe was just a third of a million years old.

SO WHAT HAPPENS NEXT?

For a very long time – nothing much. In the very very distant future, long after the Earth has been swallowed up by an exploding Sun, one of three things might happen:

1   The Universe will reach a steady state and stop expanding.
2   The Universe will keep on expanding for ever and ever.
3   The Universe will stop expanding and start to fall back in on itself.

These options are illustrated in picture 11.

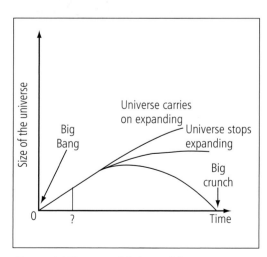

Picture 11 Three possible fates of the Universe.

Gravity will decide which of the above actually happens. The Universe is held together by gravitational forces. These are produced by the combined mass of all the stars, dust and gas in all the galaxies and all the spaces in between them.

If there is not enough of this mass, the Universe will keep on expanding. If there is enough mass, its gravity force will stop the expansion and make the Universe collapse again, perhaps producing another Big Bang.

Activities

A In a different universe

There is a respectable scientific theory that says there may well be many different universes, with different properties. Imagine a Universe in which the speed of light was only 1 metre per second.

As a group activity, work out some of the effects that this would have. For example, on TV broadcasts, on team games, traffic etc.

B Looking things up

Use a good book on astronomy, or an encyclopaedia, to find out what the following astronomical objects are:

1 a black hole,
2 a pulsar,
3 a neutron star,
4 a quasar,
5 a globular cluster,
6 a radio galaxy.

Questions

1 a The speed of light is 300 000 km/s. How long, in kilometres, are the following distances: (i) a light-second, (ii) a light-minute, (iii) a light-day?

   b Why is the 'light-year' a more useful unit for measuring astronomical distances than the metre?

2 Look at table 1, showing the distances of stars from the Earth. Canopus is the second brightest star in the sky, and is just about half as bright as Sirius. Which of these stars has the greater real brightness? Give a reason for your answer.

3 Put the following in order of size, with the smallest first: star, asteroid, galaxy, planet, meteorite.

4 The energy for the expansion of the Universe probably came from the 'Big Bang'. The rate at which the Universe is expanding is getting less. What could be making it slow down?

5 Russia and America are planning to send astronauts to the planet Mars and back. It is the second nearest planet to Earth.

   a What are the problems that they might have to solve so that people could make this journey safely?

   b This expedition will be very expensive, costing perhaps billions of dollars. Is it worth it?

6 Design a space ship that could take people to Sirius (see topic G4).

7 'Space: the final frontier!' How far will humans go?

8 Outline the problems of setting up a permanent human settlement on the Moon. Suggest some solutions to these problems.

Edwin Hubble and the expanding Universe

Edwin Powell Hubble was born in the small town of Marshfield, Missouri in 1889. He was a clever boy and a gifted athlete. He studied mathematics and astronomy at Chicago University then won a Rhodes Scholarship that funded a year at Oxford University. Here he studied law and for a time became a high-school teacher, he was very popular with his students.

He then lost interest in both teaching and practising law and returned to his first love: astronomy. His career was interrupted by his service in the First World War, then he managed to get a job at the Mount Wilson Observatory in California where he was able to use the brand new telescope, a Newtonian telescope with a mirror 100 inches (2.5 m) in diameter – the largest in the world.

Picture 1 The Andromeda Galaxy can be easily seen with a small pair of binoculars. Find the 'Square of Pegasus' (top right). The galaxy is the fuzzy blob above and to the left, in the top centre of the picture. The bright object at lower right is the planet Saturn. See also page 291.

His main interest was the study of cloudy objects in the night sky that had been called 'nebulae' (Latin for *clouds*). The large telescopes being built at the start of the 20th century had showed that these clouds were not all clouds of gas, but clouds of stars. In many of them the *stars* were arranged in spirals.

The big question of the day in 1920 was to do with the size of the Universe. It was realised that the Sun was part of a huge group of stars called the Milky Way or the Galaxy. How big was this? Were the nebulae fairly small and part of this, or were they much bigger and outside it? Edwin Hubble was about to answer these questions and show that the Universe was very much bigger than any astronomer had so far dreamed of.

Henrietta Leavitt

By 1924 Hubble had photographed hundreds of nebulae and confirmed that many of them were made of stars and so could be called galaxies. He classified them into a range of types which seemed to show a progression from vague and formless to well-formed spirals. But this idea has since been shown to be wrong. One night he was studying the largest galaxy to be seen in the sky, the galaxy in the constellation of Andromeda.

Then he made a very important discovery: it contained a variable star. The star was of a type that had first been identified by a Harvard astronomer Henrietta Swan Leavitt. It was a type called a Cepheid variable star. Leavitt had discovered that the brightness of such stars varied in a regular way that was linked to its average brightness. So by measuring the periodic time of its variation you could work out what its real brightness was. Then you could compare this with its apparent brightness, which got less the further away the star was, and so calculate exactly how far away it was. Using this technique Hubble showed

that the Andromeda nebula (see page 291, picture 7) was much further away than any known star, and so was outside our own Milky Way galaxy. This was enough to make him famous – amongst astronomers at least! Up until then most astronomers believed in a 'single galaxy universe' – the Milky Way.

Then he went on to find more Cepheid variables in other nebulae and was able to measure their distances. They were all much further away than even the Andromeda nebula. At a stroke he had proved that the universe was much bigger than anyone so far had thought. This made newspaper headlines. But more was to come. Back in 1912 an astronomer called Vesto Melvin Slipher had studied nebulae too, and his interest was in their movements. Most of the ones he studied showed a red shift in their spectra. He interpreted this as meaning that they were moving away from Earth. Hubble decided to see if there was any connection between the movement of galaxies and their distance from Earth. The rest is history.

Picture 2 A typical spiral galaxy. M74 in the constellation Pisces.

Are we alone?

Is Earth the only place in the whole Universe where life exists? Is there an advanced civilisation out there somewhere trying to make contact with us? Or are there simply dead microbes in Mars?

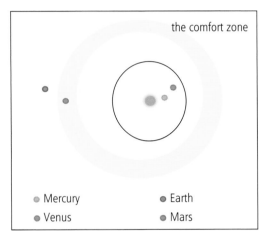

the comfort zone

- Mercury
- Venus
- Earth
- Mars

Picture 1 The shaded area is where a planet has to be in orbit around a Sun-like star for the surface temperature to be suitable for the development of life. It is a very narrow zone: less than 0.95 earth-orbit distance the Greenhouse effect would have turned the Earth into a super-hot Venus. More than 1.05 and all the water would be turned to ice.

The Earth is the only place in the Universe where we know definitely that life exists. But could life exist somewhere else, on a planet or satellite in the Solar System, or on a planet orbiting another star?

Life as we know it is based on compounds of carbon, hydrogen, nitrogen and oxygen: these make up the complicated molecules and structures called carbohydrates. Together with smaller quantities of other elements such as calcium, phosphorus, iron and silicon they make up such essential life chemicals as proteins, haemoglobin, sugars and starches. Apart from hydrogen, all these elements were created inside stars as lighter elements joined together to release the energy that kept the star hot. Elements heavier than iron were made in those spectacular explosions of dying stars called novae and supernovae (see page 285). So we are all made of star stuff – and life could not begin until enough stars had exploded and sent their newly created elements into space, to be recycled into new stars and planets – and possibly life.

One of the essential conditions for the complex compounds needed for life to exist is the existence of water in the liquid state. This means that a planet that has life of our type on its surface has to have a region with temperatures between about 0 °C and 100 °C. This means in turn that a planet has to be situated in a narrow range of distances from its sun. Too far and it will be too cold; too close and it will be too hot. Even so some bacteria have been found in hot springs on Earth at temperatures close to boiling point.

Both Venus and Mars are roughly at the right distance from the Sun for life to be possible. But Venus is just that little bit too hot for water to condense into a liquid. We know now that at one time there were rivers, streams and lakes on Mars, so that life may have developed. There is some evidence for simple life forms (bacteria) found in a meteorite that reached the Antarctic some millions of years ago. This is a piece of Martian rock that got knocked out of its surface by a collision with a much larger meteorite and ended up on Earth. But most experts have decided (in 2001) that these signs of life are fossilised relics of bacteria picked up on Earth.

Jupiter and the large outer planets are too cold for life, but some of their satellites ('moons') have been found to contain liquid water. This water is very cold at −56 °C and deep below the surface. It is kept liquid by the pressure acting on it and heat generated by gravitational tidal forces from Jupiter which keep squeezing the satellite as it rotates in its orbit. It is possible that simple forms of life exist in this water. There is also growing evidence that at one time Mars was a warmer wetter planet – probably with an atmosphere, which has now been lost. Unmanned expeditions are planned in the next few years to try to sample both Mars and some of the moons of Jupiter (Ganymede, Europa and Callisto), in the hope of finding signs of life – or at least fossils of extinct life.

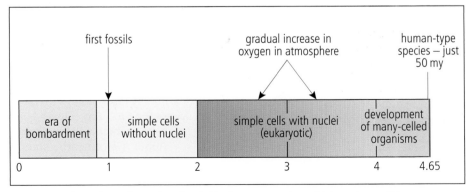

Picture 2 The early Earth was bombarded by large meteorites which made conditions very difficult for life to start. But it took just a short time after bombardment quietened down for simple life to develop – about 50 million years. This is about the same time that it took the human species to develop.

What signs of life might be detected on such expeditions? If no samples can be returned to Earth for analysis, what would the probes be looking for?

Life takes time to evolve into the complicated plants and animals that we find on Earth – let alone intelligent animals such as humans. The Earth is 4.6 billion years old, and life has been on it for nearly 4 billion years. The earliest life were single celled organisms like bacteria, followed by single-celled organisms that had a nucleus. Forms more complex than these have existed for only half a billion years (see picture 2). It is not too hard to imagine how simple living things might get more complex over hundreds of millions of years. The biggest problem about life in the Universe is this: How did life begin? But that's another story …

How many stars have planets?

How likely is it that intelligent life can develop in the universe? The basic need is that a planet orbits a star. How many stars do in fact have planets? We must bear in mind that the universe is about 15 billion years old and is a very large place indeed. The search for planets is a fairly new development, based on some very sensitive detection techniques that are only possible using good computers. The search has been remarkably successful. Practically every month now astronomers are finding stars that do indeed have planets. In the first five years of study over 60 have been discovered (see page 297 for how they do this). So the Sun isn't the only star with a 'solar system'. There are about 100 billion (10^{11}) stars in our own galaxy. There are billions of galaxies each with much the same number of stars. How many of these are nice small stars like the Sun and have nice small planets like Earth at just the right distance away? And have they existed long enough for life to have developed? And has that life become intelligent enough to invent radio? And is that intelligent life also curious enough to send out radio messages to other possible intelligent life in their neighbourhoods? These questions are answered by saying 'probably some'. Page 298 shows how we might estimate the probability of there being advanced extra-terrestrial civilisations that actually send out messages. This estimate is based on a formula proposed by the American astronomer Frank Drake. All we need is to find one message, of course, and that would be the most amazing discovery that humans have ever made.

SETI – the Search for Extra-Terrestrial Intelligent Life

The largest radio-astronomy aerial in the world has been looking for intelligent messages for about 40 years now. It is the Arecibo Radio Telescope built in a large natural bowl in Puerto Rico. The signals it collects are being analysed to see if they contain – now and again perhaps – a signal that shows sign of some kind of digital code. This project and others using similar radio telescopes are being carried out by the SETI Project. Anyone with a home computer can help to look for a 'meaningful' signal by downloading a program from their website which carries out the analysis in the background while the computer is working on its ordinary everyday tasks. Recently astronomers have also started to look for messages carried by laser beams. So far no such signals has been discovered. In the next few years the SETI Project will build a more suitable radio telescope made of an array of dishes, which will be steerable.

About 4% of nearby stars of about the same size and brightness as the Sun have been found to have planets. These planets are as large or larger than Jupiter and so may be unsuitable for life. We have checked just some stars up to 1000 light years away. But so far astronomers can only find such large planets – Earth-like planets are too small for the change in movement of the star to be detected at present. This means that there is a good chance that many more Sun-type stars do in fact have planets suitable for life. So – watch this space!

Picture 3 The Arecibo Radio telescope is built in a natural hollow in a hillside. It is not steerable so has a limited view of the sky.

Picture 4 The proposed telescope is an array of smaller steerable dishes, funded by Paul Allen, the co-founder of Microsoft. It will be built in California.

Finding an invisible planet

Distant stars are too small for us to see their surfaces as a disk, even with the best telescopes. Planets are even smaller – and dark. So how can astronomers find them?

One way is to measure the tiny amount of light that we can collect from a star. If we are lucky, the planet's orbit is edge on to the Earth so that the planet will move across the face of the star. As it does so the light from the star is cut down and this tiny effect can be detected. Careful measurements can even tell us the size of the planet. See picture 1.

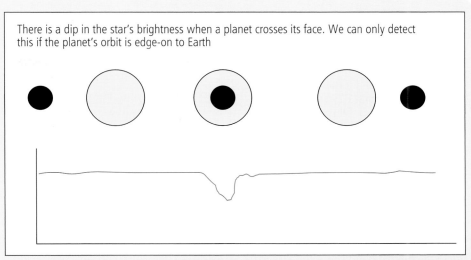

There is a dip in the star's brightness when a planet crosses its face. We can only detect this if the planet's orbit is edge-on to Earth

Picture 1 Planets are not hot and so do not emit light of the own. As a planet moves across the face of its star it will cut down the light emitted from the star, and its brightness appears to get less.

The most common way is to show that the star is *wobbling*. Both the star and its planets actually orbit around the centre of mass (sometimes called centre of gravity) of the star plus planet system. This is shown in picture 2. Astronomers can detect the movement of the star around the centre of mass using the Doppler Effect. When the star is moving towards Earth the lines in its light spectrum shift towards the blue end. When it is moving away the lines shift towards the red. The amount of shift tells us the speed of the star in its orbit. From this it is possible to calculate the mass of a large planet in its planetary system.

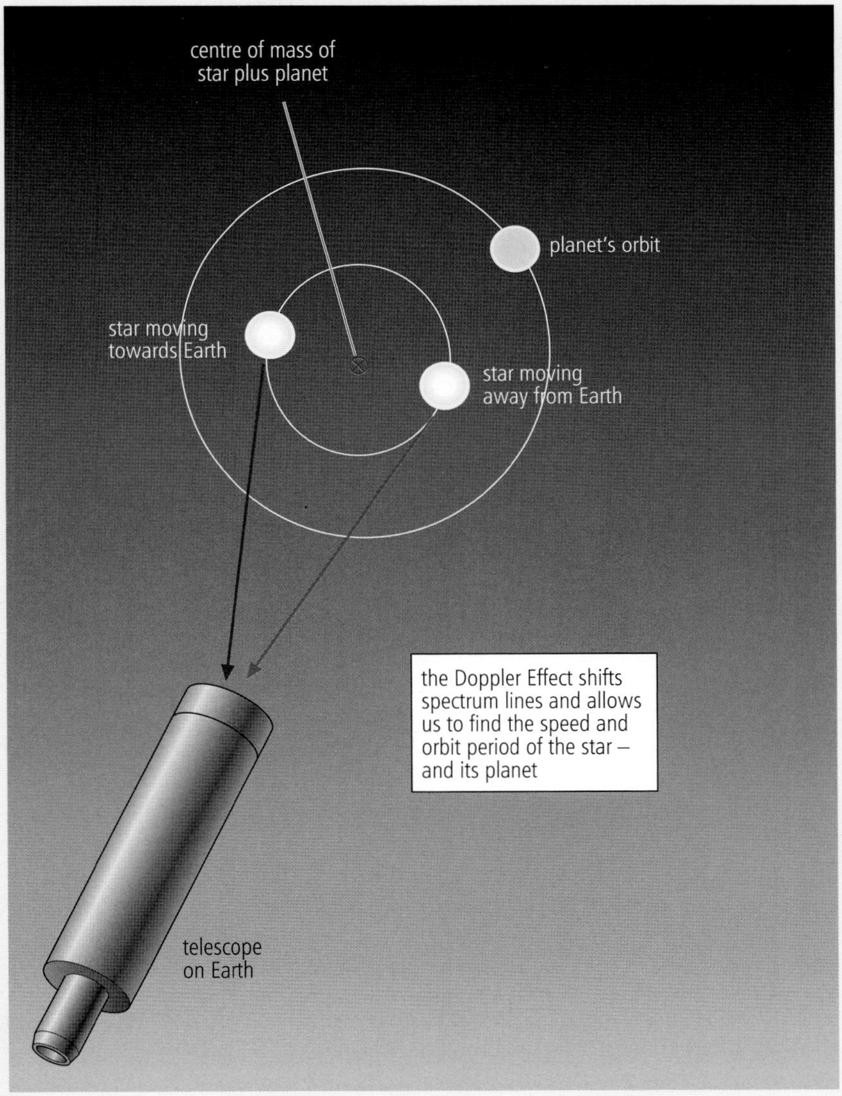

centre of mass of
star plus planet

planet's orbit

star moving
towards Earth

star moving
away from Earth

the Doppler Effect shifts
spectrum lines and allows
us to find the speed and
orbit period of the star –
and its planet

telescope
on Earth

Picture 2 Finding an invisible planet.

The Drake Formula

This includes the factors that decide whether we might be able to detect meaningful signals from intelligent beings somewhere in the Universe. N is the number of such detectable signals and the other probability factors multiply together to give the value of N:

$$N = R \times f_p \times n_e \times f_e \times f_I \times f_c \times L$$

R is the rate at which suitable stars (e.g. like the Sun) form in the Universe

f_p is the fraction of those stars that have planets

n_e is the fraction of those planets which have conditions suitable for life to develop

f_e is the fraction of those planets on which life actually develops

f_I is the fraction of these life-bearing planets that produce intelligent civilisations

f_c is the fraction of these intelligent civilisations that bother to send out messages

L is the length of time that they have been sending out messages

The value of R in our galaxy is about 10 per year – it has 100 billion stars and has existed for about 10 billion years. Guess at about 0.1 for f_p. Experts put n_e at 2 and f_e at 1. The chances of life progressing beyond simple forms is quite small, and even smaller that complex forms become intelligent enough to send out messages, so $f_I f_c$ is rated at 0.01. How large is L likely to be? We have avoided nuclear wars on Earth and so our advanced messaging civilisation has so far lasted 50 years.

Task

Use the Drake formula to calculate how many signals we are likely to be able to detect if L is

(a) 10 years (b) 50 years (c) 1000 years.

Distance and time

Our own galaxy, the Milky Way, is 120 000 light years across. The Sun is 30 000 light years from the centre. If we imagine a twin Earth near a star at the furthest edge of the Milky Way it would have had to send its signal 90 000 years ago to reach us at a time when humans are able to detect it. A reply would also take 90 000 years. Our imaginary civilisation might well have lost patience by now!

H

Sensing and control

Sensing – human and artificial

We get information from our surroundings by using our senses. More and more, we use artificial sensors to gain information – and to help make decisions.

The human body is covered with sensors. They are special kinds of living cells, which biologists call receptors. They share between them the task of sensing the outside world. They can sense temperature, pain, pressure and touch. Certain parts of the body are even more specialised. Cells are grouped together into sense organs – for example, the eye and the ear, the nose and the tongue.

■ Sensors as transducers

The sensor cells of an animal are triggered by a **stimulus** of some kind. The stimulus may be a sound, or a change in temperature or light, for example. But before the animal can react to it, the stimulus has to be changed into an electrical signal. This is what the sensor cells do. The electric pulse is then carried along one or more nerve cells into the brain, or some other part of the **nervous system**.

Picture 1 shows an athlete undergoing tests in a sports laboratory. The devices connected to his body take messages to a computer, just as his body sensors are taking messages to his brain.

Devices which change a stimulus, signal or message from one energy type to another are called **transducers**. Transducers are also dealt with in topic A4.

MICROELECTRONICS AND SENSORS

The modern world relies more and more on machines of one kind or another. Many of these are 'automatic': they are designed so that they **control themselves**. To do this, they need information about themselves and the surroundings – just as an animal would.

■ Car engines

A car engine works best at a certain temperature. If it gets too hot it will be inefficient, or seize up altogether. But it is also inefficient if it is too cold – it uses up too much fuel and may also cause extra pollution. The cooling system of the car relies on the flow of water inside the engine (the 'coolant'), and the flow of air over the engine.

When the engine is first switched on it needs to warm up. At this stage the cooling system is not needed. A **temperature sensor** checks the temperature. The circuit decides that it is too cool, and prevents the water from flowing.

When the engine is hot enough the sensor sends a message to allow water to flow. When the engine works harder the water flows more quickly, so that it is kept at the best working temperature. Picture 2 shows the cooling system in a car.

When the car is moving at a normal speed the flow of air over the engine helps to cool it. It also cools the water, by means of the 'radiator' at the front of the engine. In slow-moving traffic the cooling effect of the air may not be enough. The engine temperature rises towards danger. The sensor then switches on an air fan to increase the flow of air. If this isn't enough the sensor may switch the engine off altogether, to avoid damage.

A modern car uses **microelectronic** circuits to switch the cooling systems on and off. These circuits are able to measure and compare the signals coming into them. They use the signals to make decisions. And then they can switch parts of the engine system on or off.

The next topic is about how these circuits work.

■ Sensing temperature

A temperature sensor is usually made of a piece of material which is a good conductor of electricity when it is hot, but a poor conductor when it is cold. Heating the material gives energy to electrons which are normally trapped in atoms. The electrons are freed, so they can now move and so more charge can move through the material. In other words, the resistance of the material gets less as it gets hotter. Materials like this are called **semiconductors**.

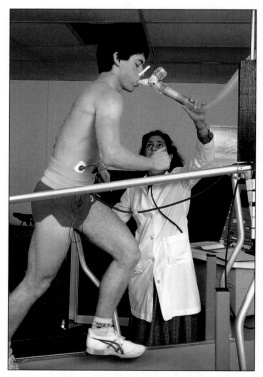

Picture 1 The body of this athlete is being monitored by electric sensors.

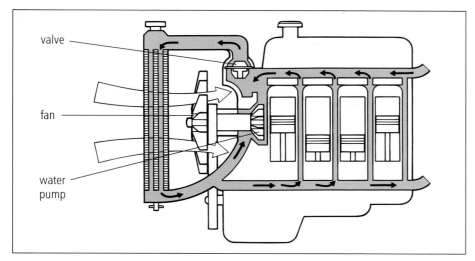

valve

fan

water pump

Picture 2 A car cooling system. A sensor turns on the air fan.

These temperature-sensitive materials are used to make devices called thermistors. See picture 3.

Think about a thermistor connected in a circuit. As the temperature rises its resistance gets less, and the current through it will increase. The current gets less when it gets colder. The changes in current can be used to switch other circuits on or off. Thus thermistors can be used to convert temperature changes into electrical signals.

Thermistors are used as electric thermometers, central heating controls and fire alarms. They are also used to protect lamps and motors from sudden surges of current when they are first switched on. They start off cold, and provide a protective resistance which stops too much current flowing. After a while the current through them warms them up and they let more current through.

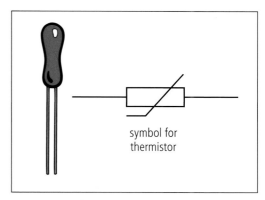

symbol for thermistor

Picture 3 A thermistor – a temperature-dependent resistor.

■ Light sensors

Heating a semiconductor material can free electrons and change its resistance. The same effect can be produced by the energy carried by radiations. *Light* can free electrons from some materials and they can be used to make **light-dependent resistors**, or **LDRs**. Picture 4 shows a typical LDR. In the dark its resistance might be 100 000 ohms (100 kΩ). In bright sunlight so many electrons are freed that its resistance falls to about 100 ohms.

So, by connecting them in the right circuits, we can use LDRs to convert changes in light intensity into electrical signals.

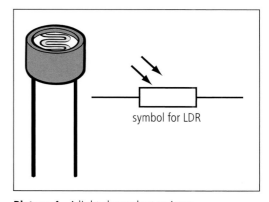

symbol for LDR

Picture 4 A light-dependent resistor.

■ Sensors for sound

We have met these already – they are **microphones**. These convert pressure changes – sound waves – into a changing electric current. See topic A4.

■ Force and movement

There are many devices that can sense movement. For example, the moving object can be linked to a sliding contact moving over a wire resistor. This is like a rheostat or potentiometer (see topic E3). Many computer games use movement sensors like this as 'joysticks'. As they are moved they alter the resistance and so the voltage applied to the input (sensing) circuit. A computer 'mouse' uses the same principle (see picture 5).

Picture 5 A computer mouse is a movement sensor. Movements are changed to voltages.

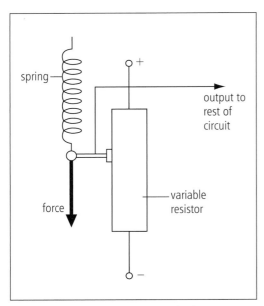

Picture 6 A potential divider attached to a spring can monitor a force.

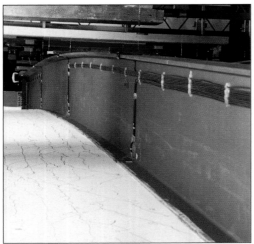

Picture 7 Strain gauges being used to test a girder. The gauges are covered by a layer of plastic glue.

Devices that sense force and movement often use the same idea – after all, a force can produce a movement. The force can be made to stretch or compress something and so change the resistance of an object. This could be a sponge made of conducting material, or grains of carbon (as in the carbon microphone, page 18), or a special **strain gauge**.

For example, a spring could be connected to a variable resistor, used as a potential divider, as in picture 6. When a force is applied to the spring it stretches and moves the sliding connection of the resistor. This changes the current, or the voltage applied to another circuit.

Strain gauges use this principle. They combine the spring and the resistor together, in one length of thin wire. The wire can stretch like a spring. As it stretches it gets thinner, so its resistance increases. Again, this change can be used to change a current or a voltage. These devices are useful because they can detect very small movements. They may be connected to the foundations of a bridge to monitor what happens as loads of different sizes cross over it, or when strong winds blow (see picture 7).

■ Other sensors

Automatic sensing is so useful in modern science and industry that many types of sensor have been developed. Temperature can be sensed by bimetallic switches, thermocouples and special diodes. Magnetic fields can be sensed by Hall Effect probes, search coils and resistors that change in magnetic fields. Ultrasound, infra-red and radar can detect movement and position. Capacitors and electrets can also detect movements. Light can be sensed by photodiodes and photocells. There are far more than you have time to learn about – but you are bound to have several of them somewhere at home!

ANALOGUE TRANSDUCERS

Most of the sensors described above produce an electric current or voltage which is a *copy* of the change they are sensing. The changes occur gradually, and the sensor output also changes gradually. This is illustrated in picture 8, which shows graphs of changing temperature and the changing current this produces in a thermistor.

The electric current is said to be an **analogue** of the changing temperature. Most transducers, in fact, produce an output which is an analogue of what they are sensing. But ordinary computers, and the microelectronic devices dealt with in the next topic, can't cope with these gradually changing, analogue signals. They respond only to numbers. In other words, they need a digital input. Topic A4 has explained how analogue signals are changed to digital ones.

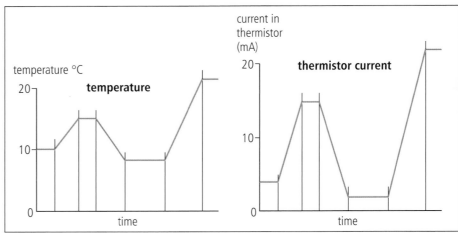

Picture 8 The current in a thermistor follows the pattern of temperature changes. It is an analogue of them.

Activities

A Sensing light

Light meters are useful for, say, taking photographs or for checking on how light intensity affects the growth of plants.

Design an investigation to find out how a light-dependent resistor might be used as a 'light meter'.

Check your plan with your teacher. (Hint: One problem you will have to solve is how to make this a fair test, i.e. produce 'equal units' of light.)

B Strain gauges

Use a library to find out more about strain gauges. Use a good encyclopaedia. Where are they used? And by whom?

C Sensors at home

Find as many examples as you can of household devices that use sensors of some kind. Describe what each sensor does, and what physical quantity it is sensing.

Questions

1 a Make a list of the kinds of stimulus that a human body can sense. For example, one would be touch. We talk about the 'five senses', but you should be able to think of more than five.

  b Can you think of any stimulus that can be sensed by machines but not by human beings?

2 What advantages or uses can you think of for being able to sense each of the following at a greater distance than normal? (a) temperature, (b) movement, (c) sound.

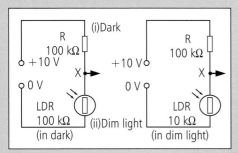

Picture 9

3 Picture 9 shows a circuit that includes an LDR. When light shines on the LDR its resistance becomes a lot less than what it was in the dark.

  a The resistor R and the LDR are connected in series. Jamal says, "Whatever the resistances of R and the LDR, the same current will flow in both." Do you agree with this? Give a reason for your answer.

  b In the dark the LDR has the same resistance as the resistor R. What is the voltage at point X?

  c In dim light the resistance of R stays unchanged but the LDR's resistance decreases to 10 000 ohms. What is the voltage at point X now?

  d In bright light the resistance of the LDR becomes less than a hundredth of its dark value. Which of the following is a reasonable (nearest) guess at the voltage at point X in bright light?

  (i) 10 V (ii) 5 V (iii) 1 V (iv) 0 V

(Hint: you need to know that the voltage across a conductor is proportional to the current in it.)

4 Two students did an experiment in which they measured the resistance of a thermistor at different temperatures. The results they got are shown in the table.

  a Plot a graph of resistance against temperature for this thermistor.

  b The students wanted to use the thermistor as a 'remote thermometer', to measure the temperature in a bird's nest from a distance. Draw a simple circuit they could use to do this.

  c They found that the resistance readings they obtained varied between 85 ohms and 110 ohms. What range of temperatures did this give for the nest?

  d Suggest what made the temperature in the nest change like this.

Temperature, T/°C	0	10	20	30	40	50	60	70	80
Resistance, R/ohms	300	200	140	100	70	50	35	25	18

Picture 1 Life is full of decisions!

LOGIC – AND DECISIONS

'If it's Tuesday today then it must be Wednesday tomorrow' is a **logical** statement. But it is only true as long as we keep the same order for the days of the week! Logic uses words like IF and THEN, and tries to end up with a TRUE statement. If you've ever tried computer programming you will have learned a lot about logic.

Logic is a way of thinking based on clear rules. If we follow the rules, we get the right answer. It is like mathematics, without the numbers. Of course, making decisions isn't always easy – and the ones we humans make aren't always logical (picture 1).

■ Logic words

Logic words are short and simple, like AND, NOT and OR. Let us think about using logic to make some decisions.

AND DECISIONS

For example:
Decision needed: Do I have to carry an umbrella?
Input facts: A It is raining and **B** I have to go out.
Decision (output): Yes, this means I must carry an umbrella. This decision would only be correct if both of the input facts (A *and* B) were correct. Of course there's no law against carrying an umbrella on a fine day. But you would look a bit silly carrying one to bed with you, even if it was raining outside.

OR DECISIONS

OR decisions are like this:
Decision needed: Shall I go to the school disco?
Input condition: I will go to the disco if either: **A** Jane invites me *or* **B** Tracy invites me.
This means that if neither girl invites me I don't go. (But what if *both* girls invite me? See below!)
Decision: Jane has invited me. Yes, I go.
These are simple decisions to make once you have decided on the 'rules'.
Microelectronic devices use simple logic like this. Even so, things can get quite complicated. One way of keeping track of everything is to use a **truth table**.

TRUTH TABLES

If a statement, fact or condition is *true* we give it the value one (**1**). If not, we give it a zero (**0**). These are the things we have to put into the electronic device so that it can make a decision, so we call them **inputs**. In the above examples these have been labelled **A** and **B**.

The decision is about *doing something*. It is an **output**. If the decision is *yes* we call the output **1**, if *no* the output is **0**. The truth table for the umbrella decision is shown in table 1: each row represents a possible situation. In the 'output', **0** = no umbrella; **1** = carry umbrella. You only carry an umbrella if it is raining *and* you are going out.

For the disco decision, table 2 says that if neither girl invites me then I don't go to the disco. If any *one* girl does then I do go.

Depending on how we all feel about it, I might decide to go when *both* girls invite me. If I do then we have what is called an **INCLUSIVE OR** kind of logic. The condition is 'A **OR** B **OR** both'. The decision in column three is then **1**.

If I feel it would be unwise to go when both girls invite me, then I don't go. I am using an **EXCLUSIVE OR** logic. This would be spelled out as 'A **OR** B but **NOT** both'. The decision is then **0**.

The questions at the end of the topic give you some practice in using truth tables.

LOGIC GATES

A gate is something that lets you through, or keeps you out. It depends on whether it is open or shut. Microelectronics devices use gates which 'open' or 'close' depending on what their inputs and the logic tells them. They are quite complicated circuits containing resistors and transistors. Picture 2 shows part of a logic chip containing many thousands of gates. You would need a course in quite advanced electronics to understand how they are made to work. But we can use them for all sorts of things without needing to know exactly what is going on inside.

Gates can be used to open and close other circuits. In other words they act like switches, and their output is either ON or OFF. For example, an AND gate has two inputs. Its output will be ON only if both of its inputs are ON. If we call its inputs A and B, and its output C, then its truth table is like table 1.

The output is ON only if both A *and* B are ON.

If we represent ON by **1**, and OFF by **0**, then this is exactly the same as the umbrella decision above.

Using the **1** or **0** system, the **INCLUSIVE OR** gate produces a truth table like table 2. This is like the disco decision.

In some books you will find that **1** is called **high**, and **0** is called **low**.

■ Sensors plus gates = decisions

The fan in some car cooling systems switches on only when the engine gets too hot. But it only works when the engine is running. This means that it must have an AND gate in it. One input to the gate is the engine on/off switch (ignition switch). The other is the temperature sensor.

The output from the AND gate makes the fan switch on when the engine is running AND the temperature is high. The car manufacturer has to set the temperature sensor to the right value so that it gives its '**1**' at a sensible temperature.

Table 1 The umbrella decision – this is like an AND gate.

Inputs		Output
A	B	
0	0	0
1	0	0
0	1	0
1	1	1

Table 2 The disco decision – an OR decision. It's an INCLUSIVE OR gate when the output decision is YES (1) but an EXCLUSIVE OR gate when the decision is NO (0).

Input		Output
A	B	
0	0	0
1	0	1
0	1	1
1	1	1? or 0?

Picture 2 A logic chip.

In the diagram (picture 3) input B is from the thermistor. Input A is connected to the ignition switch, so that when the engine is running A is ON.

When the temperature is low, say 20°C, the thermistor has a resistance of 2000 ohms. The standard resistor R has a resistance of 1000 ohms. The same current goes through both the thermistor and the resistor. This means that the voltage across them is proportional to their resistances.

By simple proportion the voltage across R is just one-third of the supply voltage (12 V). The voltage is shared, with one-third across the 1000 ohm fixed resistor and two-thirds across the 2000 ohm thermistor. Thus the 'input' voltage at X is 4 volts. This is not high enough to turn input B ON – it needs 10 volts. The output of the AND gate is zero, because only one input is 'ON'.

A	B	C
1	0	0

When the cooling water temperature reaches, say, 70°C, the thermistor resistance decreases to 200 ohms. The voltage across R changes to be 5/6 of 12 volts. This is just 10 volts, so input B goes ON and the output is now ON:

A	B	C
1	1	1

Thus the cooling fan is now switched on.

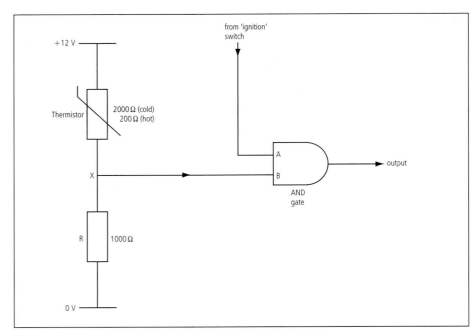

Picture 3   A decision circuit for temperature control.

Picture 3 shows a simple circuit for doing this. It uses a thermistor as part of a potential divider (see page 164), and one gate input (say **B**) is connected to point X. The resistor R is chosen so that at the 'danger' temperature the voltage input to B is high enough to trigger it. This might be 10 volts.

With the values given this will happen when the temperature is high enough to make the thermistor have a resistance of 200 ohms. The box shows how this is worked out.

■ Some more gates

THE NOT GATE
A NOT gate is a very contrary sort of gate. It only has one input connection. When its input is **1 (high)** its output is **0 (low)**. As you might expect, when its input is **0 (low)** its output is **1 (high)**.

It is also called an **inverter**. It is quite a useful device, especially when used with other gates, as described below.

THE NAND GATE AND THE NOR GATE
These gates are AND gates and OR gates with a NOT gate added to them. That is, they are NOT-ANDs and NOT-ORs.

This means that while an AND gate gives a **1** output when both inputs are **1**, the NAND gate gives a **0** output when both of its inputs are **1**. Similarly, a NOR gate gives a **0** output if any input is **1**. This is the opposite (or inverse) of what the OR gate does.

Picture 4 shows the truth tables for the main logic gates that you are likely to meet. It also shows their circuit symbols.

Activity A is about applications of microelectronics which make decisions using simple logic gates with two inputs.

Picture 4   Truth tables for some gates.

The NOT gate

Symbol	This is an inverter. It has only one input. Output is opposite to input.	Input at A	Output at Y
A —▷o— Y		0	1
		1	0

The AND gate

Symbol		input at A	Input at B	Output at Y
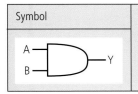	The AND gate has two inputs. The output is high only when input A **AND** input B are high.	0	0	0
		0	1	0
		1	0	0
		1	1	1

The OR gate

Symbol		input at A	Input at B	Output at Y
	There are two kinds of OR gate. This in the INCLUSIVE OR type. The output is high if **either** or **both** inputs A and B are high. An EXCLUSIVE OR type would show zero when both inputs are high.	0	0	0
		0	1	1
		1	0	1
		1	1	1

The NOR gate

Symbol		input at A	Input at B	Output at Y
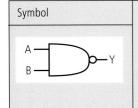	The NOR gate is the opposite of an OR gate. Its output is high when neither input is high. It's like an OR gate with a NOT gate attached at Y.	0	0	1
		0	1	0
		1	0	0
		1	1	0

The NAND gate

Symbol		input at A	Input at B	Output at Y
	The NAND gate is the opposite of an AND gate. Its output is high when inputs A and B are not both high. It's like an AND gate with a NOT gate attached at Y.	0	0	1
		0	1	1
		1	0	1
		1	1	0

Activity

A Pooling your knowledge

As a group, think of as many household devices or other kinds of everyday 'machines' as you can that might use microchips, with sensors and logic gates.

Discuss whether they actually do or not, and list them under three headings:

1 definitely use microelectronics,

2 might use microelectronics,

3 definitely don't use microelectronics.

For each of the items you put in list 1, one of the group should be prepared to give the reasons for putting it there.

Questions

1 You don't need microelectronics to make simple gates. Picture 5 shows two simple circuits using ordinary switches. One of them behaves like an AND gate, the other like an OR gate. Which is which? Explain your answer.

2 Explain the difference between an OR gate and an AND gate.

3 What is the difference between an AND gate and a NAND gate?

4 a Describe what a NOR gate does.

b Picture 6 shows a circuit with a NOR gate in it. The indicator lamp goes on when the NOR gate sends it a **1**. The light sensor is set to give a **1** when it is light, the temperature sensor gives a **1** when it is warm. What happens to the lamp when:

(i) it is dark and cold? (ii) it is light and cold? (iii) it is light and warm?

c Think up a practical application of this circuit. Describe it, briefly.

d Write out the truth table for this circuit.

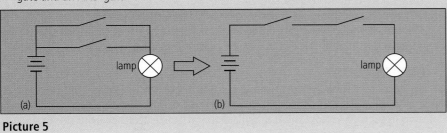

Picture 5

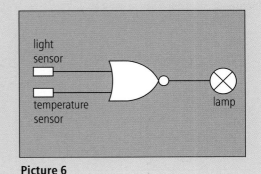

Picture 6

Solving problems with microelectronics

To solve problems with microelectronics you have to be quite logical…

Picture 1   Cats like cat flaps.

THE CAT FLAP PROBLEM

Suppose we want to design an automatic 'cat flap'. This is a small wooden flap cut into the back door. It can be pushed open by the cat (see picture 1). But you can lock it shut, if you want to.

To do this we want to use an electrically operated lock that is opened and closed by a small electric motor. This motor – **the driver** – can be switched on or off.

■ Keep the cat out at night!

At first you decide that the cat can only come in during the day time, so the lock can be controlled by a simple sensor. You make a circuit as shown in picture 2. The light sensor can be a light-dependent resistor (LDR). It makes a **1** output when it is light. This lets the door open.

– UNLESS IT IS RAINING!

Then you take pity on the poor animal and agree to let it in at night, *provided it is raining*. So we need a 'wet sensor'. The wet sensor can be two bare wires very nearly touching. A current flows to give a **1** when they get wet.

Picture 3 shows how these two sensors might be fitted to an OR gate. The cat can get in if it is light OR if it is wet. But not if it is dark and dry.

– OR VERY COLD!

Then you are persuaded that the cat ought to be let in if it is *cold* at night. This needs a temperature sensor. It is connected to another OR gate, connected as shown in picture 4. Now the flap will open if it gets a **1** either from the first OR gate or from the temperature sensor.

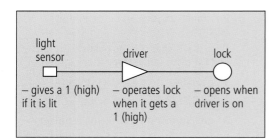

Picture 2   A first attempt.

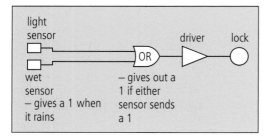

Picture 3   Cats don't like to get wet.

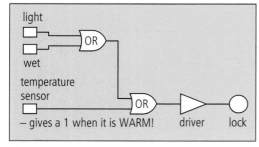

Picture 4   – or to get cold!

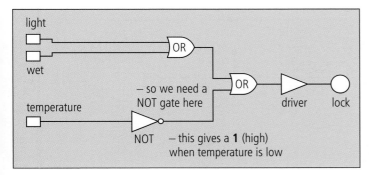

Picture 5 This is better!

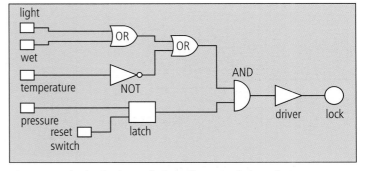

Picture 6 The final solution (but see if you can do better).

But there is something wrong with this! When it is cold the sensor you happen to have sends a **0**, and this would not open the flap. Both you and the cat want it to send a **1** when it is cold. This can be done by putting a NOT gate between the temperature sensor and the input (picture 5).

A **0** signal from the temperature sensor is changed by the NOT gate to a **1**. The cat is happy because a **low** temperature sends a **1** to the lock, to open it. Thus the flap will now open on a cold, dry night, as well as on a wet night.

OH NO!

One cold night you wake up to a terrible noise and find that the kitchen is full of cats. What can you do now?

Quite simple – put a **latch** on the cat flap. This means that once the door has closed again it stays closed. But it has to be an electronic latch, which closes the cat flap permanently when *one* cat has got in. It might be the wrong cat, of course, but that's your cat's problem!

You should be able to reset this latch when the cat has been put out each night.

You could fit a latch into the circuit as shown in picture 6. The AND gate unlocks the cat flap only if *both* of its inputs are **1**. The latch is set at **1** and stays there until one cat comes in. Then it switches to **0** and stays at **0** until you come along and reset it again, using a special reset switch. As long as the latch sends a **0** to the AND gate the cat flap locks cannot be opened.

You could set it off like this. The first cat through the cat flap steps on a pressure sensitive mat. This makes the latch go to **0**, and it stays at **0**. It is now locked, and will stay locked. This is the key point about a latch – it stays in one state, whatever else happens, until it is reset.

Other names for a latch circuit are:

● flip flops – because its output flips from one state to another and stays there; then it flops back again when somebody changes it,

● **bistable** – because it has *two* states (on or off) and stays in one (i.e. it is stable) until it is changed.

Latches are one of the most useful microelectronic circuits of all. They are the basis of **memory** devices. Because it stays in one state until it is deliberately changed we say that it remembers which state it is in. Computers would be useless without their memories, which use millions of bistable circuits in their memory chips.

The rest of this topic explains in more detail how a simple latch can be made from two gates. It is not easy to understand, but it is worth making an effort.

■ A bistable unit – or electronic latch

A simple latch or bistable can be made from just one gate. Picture 7 shows an OR gate connected to do this. The output (C) is fed back to one of the inputs (R). Both inputs, S and R, are **0** so the output is also **0**. What happens when input S is made a **1**?

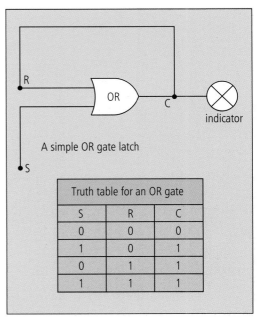

A simple OR gate latch

Truth table for an OR gate		
S	R	C
0	0	0
1	0	1
0	1	1
1	1	1

Picture 7 A simple OR latch gate.

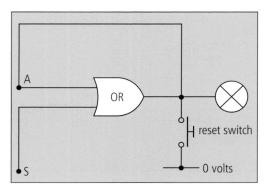

Picture 8 An OR latch gate with reset switch.

Table 1

S	R	X	Y
0	0	stable	
1	0	0	1
0	1	1	0
1	1	anything can happen! Avoid doing this!	

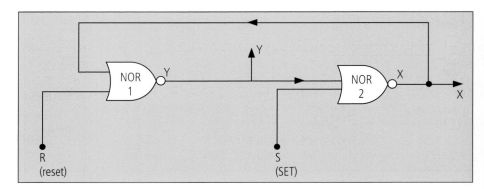

Picture 9 Circuit of a two-NOR bistable.

The truth table in picture 7 shows that the output C now goes to **1**. The indicator lamp will light. This also makes the fed-back input R go to **1**. We are now at line 4 of the truth table.

Now we take away the **1** from input S, and the output *stays at* **1**.

Check this with the truth table. In fact, whatever we do to S the output stays the same. The system is **stable**, with the output **latched** to **1**. The lamp stays on.

We have used input S to **set** the value of the output. What can we do to **reset** it to **0**, to **clear it**? Remember, we have made S to be **0** (off). The gate is latched to **1** because R is **1**. So to change it we have to make R a **0**.

This can be done by having a switch which is able to connect R, just for a moment, to a low voltage (e.g. earth). Picture 8 shows how this might be done. At this point both inputs are **0**, the output is **0**, and the system will stay like this until input S is given a **1**. This is where we started.

A TWO-GATE BISTABLE

Using just one gate means that a mechanical switch has to be used. This might be inconvenient. In most latching or bistable applications two gates are used so that the latching and clearing can be done by electrical signals. NAND or NOR gates are normally used for this.

Picture 9 shows a two-gate bistable. It has two 'free' inputs labelled S and R. S is used to **set** the output X to what is wanted – it will **latch** it. The output stays the same at X until it is changed (or **reset**) by input R.

The key point about the bistable is that the output of one NOR gate is fed to the input of the other. These **feedback** outputs are labelled X and Y.

The relevant truth table for this system is given in table 1. (You can check this using the separate truth tables for the two NOR gates, but it's tricky!).

Let's work this out in terms of the cat flap problem. To start suppose both S and R are **0**, and output X is **1**. This is fed to the AND gate (see picture 6) so that if any of the other conditions are met (it's light, cold or wet) the motor can work to open the lock of the cat flap. The cat can get in.

Then a cat comes in and the flap closes behind it. The cat then steps on a mat just in front of the cat flap. This triggers a pressure switch and sends a **1** to input S.

Immediately we are in line 2 of the truth table. Output X goes to **0** and the motor can no longer open the lock. Remember, for the motor to work it needs a **1** at both inputs to the AND gate. So ony one cat gets in.

As the pressure switch goes back to OFF when the cat leaves the mat, input S goes back to zero. This puts us in line 1 of the truth table – which is a STABLE line. This means that output X stays at **0**. The cat flap is **latched** shut.

Now next evening, when we put the cat out, we want to reset the latch. To do this we push another press switch, R. This is the **reset**. Pushing the switch sends a **1** and puts us into line 3 of the truth table. X is now **1** and the lock can be opened.

When we take our finger off it the press switch R goes back to **0**. S and R are now both **0** so we are back at a STABLE condition. This is shown in line 1 of the truth table. X is now **1**, which is where we started.

USING MICROELECTRONICS

This topic has explained just some of the main ideas about logic gates and how they can be used to solve problems. In your science lessons you should have plenty of chances to use **microelectronics kits** to solve problems. This is the best way to learn what the sensors and gates can do, and how they are used in everyday life. Picture 10 shows some typical microelectronic equipment that you might use in school.

Microcomputers use millions of gates, especially the 'latch' or bistable, which is the basic logic gate in the computer's memory. Most factories now use microelectronic control systems to operate machinery, or to check that it is safe and working properly.

More and more cars use electronic ignition. Cookers and ovens are checked and controlled using logic gates – especially microwave ovens, which even have memories. Cheap calculators use pressure sensors, binary counters and bistables to do arithmetic very quickly. They have made life a lot easier for those of us who need to do quick and accurate calculations. Most of us wear digital watches, which use similar kinds of circuits.

The next topic looks at some of these applications in more detail – especially the way microelectronic devices are used to collect, store and transmit **information**.

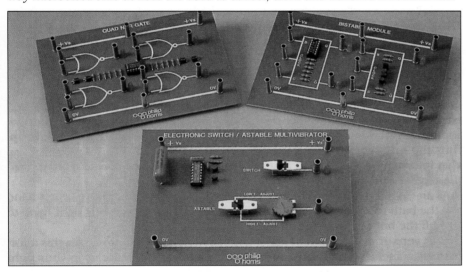

Picture 10 Some gates and sensors that you might use.

■ Decision systems

In all microelectronics applications the system can be split into three sections: INPUT, PROCESSOR and OUTPUT. The table shows some examples.

Table 2 Decision systems.

INPUT	PROCESSOR	OUTPUT
Human being Senses – eyes, ears, skin	brain	muscular activity, e.g. crossing a road when the light is green
Computer keyboard and mouse	central processing unit (CPU)	e.g. screen display, printer operation, etc
Car alarm movement or pressure change sensor	microelectronic unit (integrated circuit chip)	sound and flashing light alarm set off
Washing machine Water level and temperature sensors	microelectronic unit (integrated circuit chip)	motor starts

A   Using logic gates

You will get a much better understanding of how logic gates and sensors are used by trying to solve some problems with a microelectronics kit. You may already have done this in previous years, but if you find the following problems too easy your teacher can probably think up some harder ones! Design systems that can do the following:

1 Let you know if your pot plants need watering on a hot day.

2 Sound an alarm in your parents' bedroom if someone opens the door of your refrigerator at night.

3 Sound an alarm if it is windy or raining – but must only work when you have switched it on.

4 A fire alarm which will sound an alarm when it senses smoke or it gets too hot.

5 Switches on a fan when a light is switched on, but only when the window is closed.

Questions

1 Explain what an electronic **latch** is for. Why is it also called a **bistable**?

2 Draw a simple logic circuit that you could use to solve the following problems. Write out the truth table for your solution.

a For a deaf person: who wants a light signal to come on when someone presses a door bell switch during the day only.

b For a blind person: who wants a sound to be made when a teacup is filled to the right level.

c For a gardener: who wants a buzzer to sound when the soil in a plant pot gets too dry – but who doesn't want to be woken up at night!

3 Write out the truth tables for each of the 'cat flap' circuits drawn in pictures 3, 4 and 6.

4 What would happen in the circuit of picture 11 when:

a it was cold and light,

b it was cold and dark,

c it was warm and light?

Suggest a use for this circuit.

5 A home music system has the following devices: radio tuner, amplifier, CD player, tape deck, loudspeakers. Draw a block diagram of the system when it is assembled, organising it into the three sections: input, processor, output.

6 Name three simple input devices or sensors and explain how any one of them works.

7 Name three output devices and describe their use.

8 The block diagram (picture 12) shows the logic system that a gardener might use to turn on a water sprinkler on a hot day.

a Copy the diagram and draw lines to show which parts are input, processor and output devices.

b What change would the gardener have to make if she wanted the sprinkler to come on on a warm night rather than during the day?

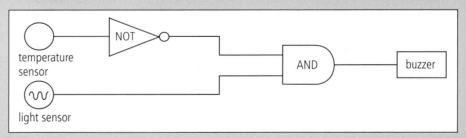

Picture 11

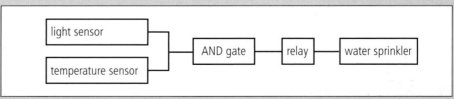

Picture 12

Transistors – the heart of the processor

Transistors are very small devices which are at the heart of electronic decision and computing systems. A computer CPU may contain millions of them – too small to be seen without a microscope.

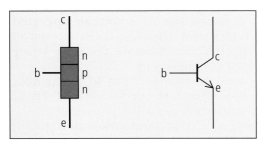

Picture 2 An npn transistor.

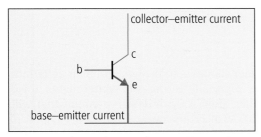

Picture 3 Current flow in a transistor.

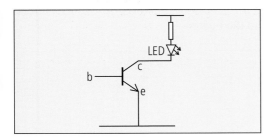

Picture 4 Using an LED as an indicator.

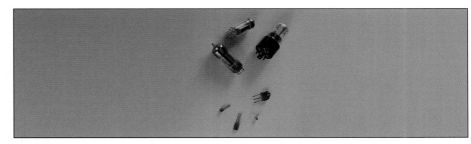

Picture 1 Large valves and small transistors.

■ Transistors and semiconductors

The transistor is one of the most significant inventions of the 20th century. Before its development, electronic devices such as radios and televisions contained large fragile components called **valves**, which were made of glass and metal. By contrast, transistors are small solid components made from materials called **semiconductors**.

As the name suggests, semiconductors are neither good conductors nor complete insulators, but fall between these two categories. The two most common examples are **silicon** and **germanium**. Semiconductor materials can be specially treated to improve their conducting properties, by introducing small amounts of impurities. This process is known as **doping**.

If a semiconductor is given extra *negative* charges, it is called **n–type**. If the doping creates a shortage of negative charges, leaving a surplus *positive* charge, the material is **p–type**. Picture 2 shows how these materials can be arranged in a three layer 'sandwich' – either **pnp** or **npn**. The outside layers of the sandwich are the **collector** and **emitter**; the central 'filling' is called the **base**.

■ How a transistor works

When the transistor is connected into a circuit, nothing happens, because no current can flow across the different layers from the collector to the emitter. Yet, as shown in picture 3, if a voltage is applied in the correct way across the **base–emitter** terminals, a small current flows between them. This has the effect of breaking down the 'barrier' in the layers, and current flows from the **collector** to **emitter** in the main part of the circuit: the transistor has been **switched on**.

This can be indicated, as in picture 4, by connecting an LED in the collector–emitter circuit, so that whenever the transistor conducts, the LED is *on*.

Note that although the current in the base triggers the flow of current in the main part of the circuit, in practical terms they are entirely separate. The base current can be much smaller than the collector–emitter current.

Even the tiny amount of electrical activity in the human body can be enough to switch the transistor on. If the base of the transistor in picture 5 is touched by the person's thumb, the transistor allows a current to flow from the battery and through the bulb.

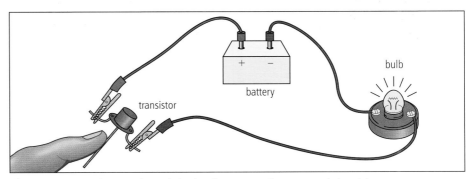

Picture 5 A transistor can be switched on by very small amounts of electricity.

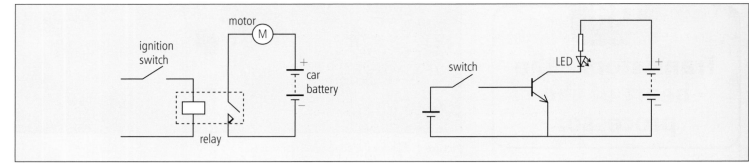

Picture 6   A transistor can be used as a switch.

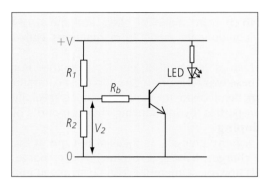

Picture 7   Using a voltage divider to switch a transistor on.

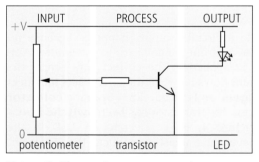

Picture 8   The transistor processes an input.

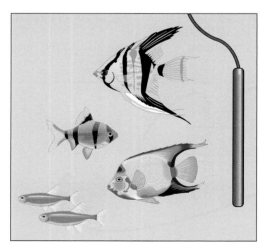

Picture 9   An aquarium heater.

■ The transistor as a switch

In picture 6, a relay switch is being used to switch on the starter motor of a car. When the ignition key switch is closed, a small current flows in the relay switch. It closes and completes the circuit that supplies a large current to the motor.

The transistor can be regarded as a switch which operates in a similar manner. A current *only* flows in the main part of the circuit if an **input voltage** produces a **base–emitter current**. We can use the transistor as a **voltage operated switch**. The advantage of such an electronic switch is that it can switch on and off millions of times every second. Computers can therefore do rapid binary calculations, using integrated circuits filled with transistors.

A voltage divider circuit can be used to provide input to a transistor (picture 7). The values of R_1 and R_2 must be chosen to give the required voltage across R_2. The resistor R_b is included to control the size of the base current.

If we connect the base to the variable contact on a **potentiometer**, we can increase the input voltage gradually until the transistor switches on. We find that the transistor starts to work when $V_2 = 0.7$ V.

The transistor is an example of a process device; if it receives the appropriate input signal, it can activate an output device.

■ Keeping warm

Tropical fish come originally from warmer climates, so the water in their aquarium must be kept at a suitable temperature, especially during cold winter nights. If we include a thermistor in a voltage divider, then we can design a circuit that will operate when the temperature drops below a certain level.

In picture 10, as the temperature falls, the resistance of the thermistor increases and so the voltage across it rises. At a certain point, the transistor will operate a relay, switching on a heater. When the temperature of the water has risen to an acceptable level, the voltage across the thermistor drops, which causes the transistor to switch off the relay and the heater.

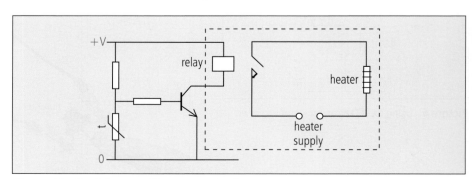

Picture 10   Circuit for controlling an aquarium heater.

■ Getting dry

A restaurant owner installs a hot-air dryer in the toilet (picture 13). Customers can push a button on the machine and dry their hands in the stream of warm air.

When the machine is off, as in picture 11, the capacitor, C is fully *charged*, so the voltage across it is equal to the supply voltage. The transistor is on, and operates a relay which holds the dryer switch *open*.

When the button switch S is pushed, the capacitor is *discharged*, the transistor switches *off*, and the relay *closes*, starting the blower. As soon as the button is released, the capacitor starts to charge up. The customer dries his hands until the capacitor has reached a voltage which activates the transistor, opening the relay switch and stopping the blower.

The owner finds that the blower is staying on long after the customers have dried their hands, and so adding to his electricity bill. He calls the company which supplied the dryer, and they send a technician. What *two* alterations could the technician make to the circuit?

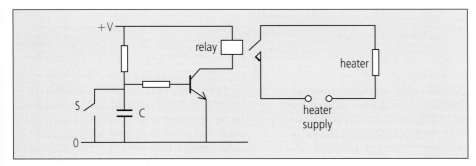

Picture 11 Controlling a hand dryer.

■ Staying bright

The owner of a house wishes his front room curtains to close automatically when it becomes dark outside. When he is on holiday, it will not be obvious to burglars that the house is empty. He designs a circuit as shown in picture 12. The LDR is fitted to the outside wall of the house, as a light sensor. When the light outside the window falls to a certain level, the voltage across the LDR has increased sufficiently to switch the transistor on. The small motor turns a pulley that draws the curtain cords, moving the curtains across.

When he first assembles the system there is a problem: the curtains shut during the day every time a dark cloud crosses the Sun. He adjusts the variable resistor until the circuit only operates when the light level outside is very low.

In real life, of course, things would not be as simple as our example suggests. For example, how would you switch the motor off when the curtains had closed fully? How do you make the circuit reverse the motor to open the curtains in the morning? To produce systems that deal with complicated situations, where events depend on combinations of circumstances, we need more sophisticated processing devices. This is dealt with in topics H2 and H3.

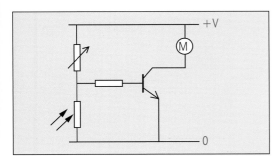

Picture 12 A light sensor circuit.

Questions

1 The diagram below shows an automatic hand washing unit in a restaurant.

Inserting the hands into the unit breaks a light beam and causes a stream of water to be turned on for ten seconds.

Picture 13

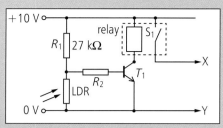

Picture 14

a The light beam is directed at a light dependent resistor (LDR) which is part of the circuit shown below.

i) When hands are inserted into the unit, the circuit causes the switch S1 in the relay to close. Explain why this happens.

ii) Calculate the voltage across the LDR when its resistance is 9.0 kΩ.

b When the relay switch in the picture 14 is closed, another circuit connected to X and Y as shown in picture 15 opens a water valve for ten seconds.

Complete the diagram to show the component which should be connected between P and Q so that the water is turned on for ten seconds.

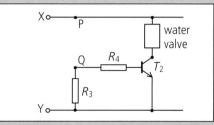

Picture 15

The history of the transistor

The transistor was developed during the 1940s at the Bell Telephone Laboratories in the United States, where research was being carried out into the properties of semiconductors.

It had long been known that certain crystals would only allow a current to flow in one direction, and such crystals were used in early radios. This is why the first radios were sometimes known as 'crystal sets'. Crystals were eventually replaced by the much more efficient vacuum tubes, or 'valves'.

William Shockley, Walter Brittain, and John Bardeen found that germanium crystals containing certain impurities were far more reliable than the early crystals, and had many advantages over fragile glass valves.

By combining different layers of material, it was possible to *transfer* a signal across the resistor formed by the germanium crystals – hence the name *transistor*. Unlike valves, these components were completely solid, and so the term *solid-state electronics* came in to use. Further advantages were that there could be extremely small and did not need time to warm up before beginning operation.

In 1948, Shockley and his co-workers produced a transistor which could act as an amplifier. The techniques for manufacturing semiconductor crystals quickly improved, and by 1953 tiny transistors were being used in hearing aids which could fit inside the ear.

Shockley, Brittain and Bardeen received the Nobel Prize for Physics in 1956.

GCSE exam questions
SECTION A Messages

1 The electromagnetic spectrum is the name given to a family of waves that includes light, infra red and ultra violet radiations. All members of the family can travel through a vacuum with the same high velocity. Electromagnetic waves are produced when the energy of electrically charged particles is changed in some way. The greater the change in energy, the shorter the wavelength of the electromagnetic waves produced. Radio waves, with a wavelength of up to 10 km and gamma (γ) rays with wavelengths of a thousand millionths of a millimetre are found at opposite ends of the electromagnetic spectrum.

  a Name **one** part of the electromagnetic spectrum
  i that is **not** mentioned in the above passage *[1]*
  ii that has a wavelength shorter than that of visible light. *[1]*

  b Give one reason why radio waves have a longer wavelength than gamma (γ) rays. *[1]*

  c State **one** practical use of
  i infra red radiation *[1]*
  ii ultra violet radiation *[1]*

Total 5 marks

(WJEC)

2 a An endoscope is an instrument used by doctors for looking inside patients. A bundle of thin optical fibres pass light into the patient's body, a second bundle of fibres carry reflected light back to the doctor.

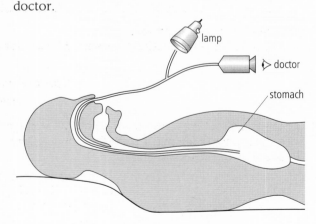

  i Complete a copy of the diagram below to show how an optical fibre is able to pass light into a patient's body. *[2]*

narrow beam of light

  ii Give **one** advantage of using lots of thin fibres to make the bundles, rather than a few thick fibres *[1]*
  iii Give **one** further example of the use of an optical fibre. *[1]*

  b The diagram shows a wave travelling through a stretched spring.

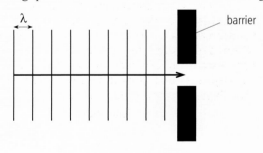

In what way is this wave the same as a sound wave? *[1]*

  c Sound waves travel faster in liquids than gases. Why? *[1]*

  d A bat uses ultra sound to find its way around. Explain how. *[2]*

Total 8 marks

(AQA)

3 Sound waves are diffracted when they pass through a gap in a barrier.

  a i Complete copies of the diagrams below to show how the effect of diffraction depends on the size of the gap. *[5]*

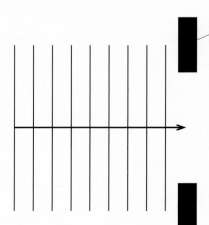

ii What other factor affects the diffraction that occurs when a wave passes through the gap? *[1]*

b When a person speaks onto a loudhailer, the sound is first amplified before passing out through a cone.

A typical frequency of sound for speech is 1000 Hz. The speed of sound in air is 330 m/s.

i Show that sound with a frequency of 1000 Hz has a wavelength of 0.33 m in air. *[2]*

ii The diameter of the loudhailer is 0.30 m. Explain whether it is suitable for a person speaking to a crowd of people. *[2]*

iii When listening to music, the ear needs to detect frequencies over a wider range. A typical frequency of a high-pitched sound is 4000 Hz. Explain why the loudhailer is not suitable for use by a female singer who is singing to an audience. *[2]*

Total 12 marks

(Edexcel)

4 Radio waves can travel from the transmitter to a receiver in three different ways.
Space waves can only be received if the transmitter is within sight of the transmitter.
Sky waves are reflected by the ionosphere.
Ground waves follow the Earth's curvature.
The diagrams show these waves.

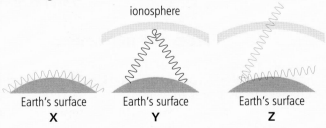

a Which type of radio wave is used for communication with satellites? *[2]*

b In 1901, Marconi sent a radio message from Canada to Cornwall.

i Explain why a space wave cannot travel from Canada to Cornwall. *[1]*

ii Suggest why the first radio transmissions were called 'wireless'. *[1]*

Total 4 marks

(Edexcel)

5 a Sound and video recordings can be stored in analogue or digital form.
Which method is used by:

i A vinyl disc (record). *[1]*

ii A compact disc (CD)? *[1]*

b Magnetic tape can be used to store information in either analogue or digital form. The tape passes over an erase head before a recording is made. This removes any previous recordings.
The diagram shows an erase head.

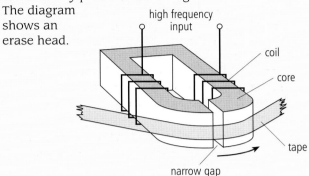

i Name a suitable material for the core. *[1]*

ii Explain why this material is suitable. *[2]*

iii The diagram shows the magnetic regions in a tape after it has been passed over the erase head. *[2]*

Copy and complete the diagram below to show how the magnetic regions are arranged when the tape stores a signal of constant frequency.

c Magnetic tape can stretch.
Explain how this can affect the sound heard during the playback. *[2]*

Total 9 marks

(Edexcel)

6 a The graph below shows how the output voltage from a microphone depends on the frequency of the sound being detected.

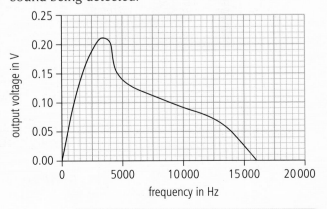

    i In testing a microphone, why is it important to keep the amplitude of the sound the same? **[1]**

    ii What is the frequency of the highest pitched sound that the microphone can detect? **[1]**

    iii Estimate the frequency at which the microphone is most sensitive. **[1]**

    iv The range of human hearing is 20 Hz to 20 000 Hz. Explain whether this microphone would be suitable for use in a recording studio. **[2]**

b Studio recordings are made on magnetic tape. The information can be transferred onto other tapes, vinyl discs (records) or compact discs (CDs). Describe the differences in the ways that information is stored on records and CDs. **[2]**

Total 7 marks

(Edexcel)

7 a A moving coil microphone is a transducer. Explain what is meant by a **transducer**. **[2]**

b i A moving coil microphone produces an analogue signal.
Explain the difference between an analogue signal and a digital signal.
You may use diagrams if you wish. **[2]**

    ii State and explain ONE advantage of using digital signals for transmission of information. **[2]**

c The diagram below shows the construction of a moving coil microphone.

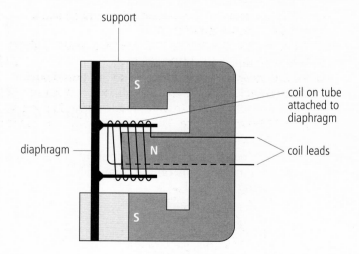

support

coil on tube attached to diaphragm

coil leads

diaphragm

When a variable sound wave signal arrives at the diaphragm, an analogue voltage is produced across the coil.

i Explain how an analogue voltage is produced. **[3]**

ii State ONE way to increase the sensitivity of the microphone. **[1]**

Total 10 marks

(Edexcel)

8 The diagram shows a simple AM (amplitude modulation) radio system for generating a radio signal.

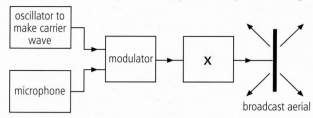

oscillator to make carrier wave

modulator

X

microphone

broadcast aerial

a What does the microphone do? **[1]**

b What is required in box **X** to make the signal strong enough to be received over a wide area? **[1]**

c The wave trace for the carrier is shown below.
In a copy of **Box 1** sketch a possible wave trace for the audio wave.
Now, in a copy of **Box 2**, show how the carrier wave is reshaped by the modulator. **[2]**

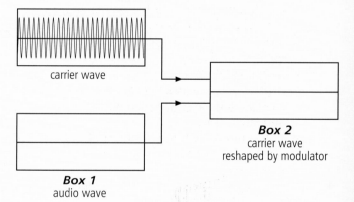

carrier wave

Box 2
carrier wave
reshaped by modulator

Box 1
audio wave

d Each radio station sends out a modulated carrier wave in this way.
How is it possible to listen to the signal from just one radio station at a time? **[2]**

Total 6 marks

(OCR)

SECTION B Forces and movement

1 The diagrams at the top of the next page show the forces acting on a car of mass 800 kg when its speed changes from 20 m/s to 25 m/s.
Diagram A shows the forces acting when the car travels at a constant speed of 20 m/s.
Diagram B shows the instant when a new driving force of 3600 N is applied.
Diagram C shows the forces acting when the car travels at a new constant speed of 25 m s.

a Write down the size of

    i drag force **D₁** **[1]**

    ii the resultant force on the car in B **[1]**

    iii drag force **D₂** **[1]**

b i Write down, **in words**, an equation connecting acceleration, mass and force. **[1]**

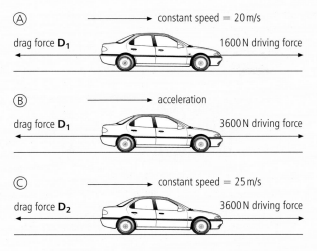

(A) constant speed = 20 m/s
drag force **D₁** ← → 1600 N driving force

(B) acceleration
drag force **D₁** ← → 3600 N driving force

(C) constant speed = 25 m/s
drag force **D₂** ← → 3600 N driving force

ii Calculate the initial acceleration of the car in B. (The mass of the car is 800 kg.) **[2]**

c i Explain why the resultant force and the acceleration of the car between stages B and C will gradually fall to zero. **[1]**

ii What is the average resultant force between stages B and C? **[1]**

d i Use the equation

$$kinetic\ energy = \tfrac{1}{2}mv^2$$

to calculate the change in kinetic energy of the car between stages A and C. **[2]**

ii Use your answers to **c ii** and **d i** to calculate the distance travelled by the car whilst it was accelerating. **[2]**

Total 12 marks

(WJEC)

2 The data in the table shows how the stopping distance of a car depends on its speed.

Stopping distance (m)	0	4	12	22	36	52	72
Speed (m/s)	0	5	10	15	20	25	30

a Write down TWO factors, apart from speed, that affect the stopping distance of a car. **[2]**

b Use the data to draw a graph of stopping distance against speed. **[3]**

c The speed limit in a supermarket car park is 7.5 m/s. Use the graph to estimate the stopping distance of a car travelling at this speed. **[2]**

d Describe how the stopping distance changes as the speed of a car increases. **[2]**

e Explain why the stopping distance is reduced if a driver is made aware of possible hazards. **[2]**

f The speed limit on roads in towns is 15 m/s. Some road safety campaigners are asking the government to change this to 10 m/s. Suggest why this may be a good idea. **[2]**

Total 13 marks

(Edexcel)

3 a The table below shows the velocity and time for an athlete running in a race.

Velocity in m/s	0	3.5	7.1	8.2	9.1	9.5	9.8	10.0	10.1	10.2	10.0
Time in s	0	1	2	3	4	5	6	7	8	9	10

i Plot a graph of these results with velocity in m/s on the y-axis and time in s on the x-axis. **[3]**

ii Use the graph to describe, in detail, the motion of the athlete during the race. **[3]**

iii Calculate the average acceleration of the athlete in the first 2 seconds. **[3]**

b i The athlete has a mass of 55 kg. Calculate the average resultant force on her in the first 2 seconds. **[2]**

ii The gravitational field strength is 10 N/kg. What is her weight? **[2]**

iii Calculate her increase in kinetic energy during the first 2 seconds of the race. **[3]**

iv Calculate her useful power output during the first 2 seconds of the race. **[2]**

v Her total power output is likely to be greater than that which you have calculated. Explain why. **[2]**

Total 20 marks

(Edexcel)

4 In recent years there has been a rapid growth in the number and use of mobile telephones. Mobile telephones use radio waves for transmitting speech. They have to use frequencies that are not already used by radio stations.

a Radio waves used for mobile telephones have a typical wavelength of 0.30 m. Calculate the frequency of these radio waves, given that there speed is 3.0×10^8 m/s. **[3]**

b Mobile telephones can be used to communicate throughout Europe using satellite links. A set of three satellites, each in an elliptical orbit, is used to give 24 hour coverage. The diagram below shows the orbit of one of these satellites.

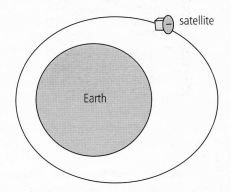

i On a copy of the diagram, draw an arrow on the diagram to show the gravitational force acting on the satellite. **[2]**

ii Describe how the size of this force changes as the satellite makes one orbit of the Earth. **[2]**

iii Place an M on the copy of the diagram where the acceleration of the satellite is greatest. **[1]**

c The diagram below shows how a dish aerial is used to focus waves and transmit them to the satellite. Focusing the radio waves minimises the effects of diffraction.

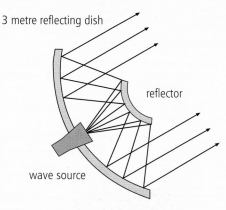

3 metre reflecting dish

reflector

wave source

i Explain why it is important to minimize the effects of diffraction. **[2]**

ii What TWO factors affect the amount of diffraction that takes place when a wave passes through an opening? **[2]**

iii The waves used for satellite transmission have a much shorter wavelength than 0.30 m used by mobile telephones.

Suggest why a wavelength of 0.30 m is unsuitable for satellite transmission. **[2]**

d Transatlantic telephone calls can be carried either using satellite links or by optical fibres on the seabed. Describe how optical fibres can be used to carry telephone calls. Suggest ONE advantage and ONE disadvantage of using optical fibres rather than satellite links. **[5]**

Total 19 marks

(Edexcel)

5 a Telecommunication satellites are generally placed in geostationary orbit round the Earth.

i Explain what is meant by a geostationary orbit. **[2]**

ii Where does the centripetal force come from that keeps the satellite in orbit around the Earth? **[1]**

b A satellite is in geostationary orbit with a radius of 42 400 km (4.24 × 10⁷ m).

i Show that the orbital speed of the satellite is about 3100 m/s. **[3]**

ii Use this orbital speed to show that the centripetal acceleration of the satellite is 0.23 m/s². **[2]**

iii The mass of the satellite is 1000 kg. Calculate its weight in this orbit. **[2]**

Total 10 marks

(Edexcel)

6 a What is the principle of conservation of momentum? **[2]**

b The diagram shows a simplified aircraft jet engine.

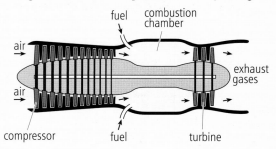

fuel   combustion chamber

air

exhaust gases

air

compressor   fuel   turbine

i What is the function of the turbine? **[1]**

ii Explain how the engine produces a forward thrust. **[4]**

c During the flight, air enters the engine at 175 m/s and leaves at 475 m/s. A forward thrust of 105 kN is produced.

Use the following equation to calculate the mass of air passing through the engine every second. (Ignore the mass of the burned fuel.)

force = change in momentum/ time **[2]**

Total 9 marks

(AQA)

SECTION D Energy

1 A room contains two electrically heated radiators. The radiators are exactly the same but contain different liquids.

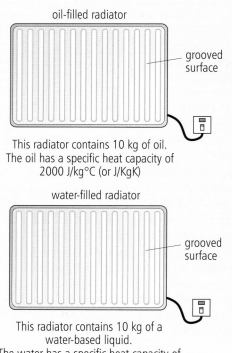

oil-filled radiator

grooved surface

This radiator contains 10 kg of oil. The oil has a specific heat capacity of 2000 J/kg°C (or J/KgK)

water-filled radiator

grooved surface

This radiator contains 10 kg of a water-based liquid. The water has a specific heat capacity of 4000 J/kg°C (or J/KgK)

a The radiators are switched on at the mains at 3 pm and left on for 4 hours. The graph shows how the temperature of the liquid in each radiator changes. The oil-filled radiator has taken 45 minutes to reach 60 °C.

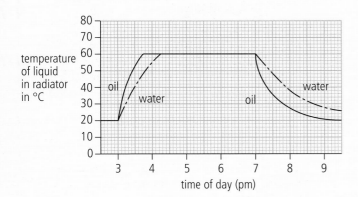

i How much longer does it take the water-filled radiator to reach 60 °C? *[1]*

ii The oil-filled radiator heats up faster than the water-filled radiator. *[1]*
What is the biggest difference between the temperatures of the two radiators during the heating-up time?

b Explain why it is a good idea for radiators to have grooved surfaces. *[2]*

c A radiator is heated by a 400 W electrical element. Calculate how much energy is given out by the electrical element in 120 s.
Use the equation below. You must show how you work out your answer
energy = power × time *[3]*

d Calculate the energy that needs to be transferred to raise the temperature of the water in the radiator by 20 °C.
The specific heat capacity of the water is 4000 J/kg °C. Use the equation below. You must show how you work out your answer. *[2]*

energy transfer = mass × specific heat capacity × temperature change

e The amount of energy needed to raise the temperature of the water-filled steel radiator is actually more than the correct answer to part **d**. Suggest why. *[1]*

f A student writes this
'The oil gives out more heat energy than the water between 7 and 8 o'clock because the slope of the line for the oil is steeper'.
Discuss whether the student is correct. Use you ideas about specific heat capacity and the rate of energy transfer. *[4]*

Total 14 marks

(OCR)

SECTION E Electricity and magnetism

1 a The diagram shows an electromagnet being used to lift some weight.

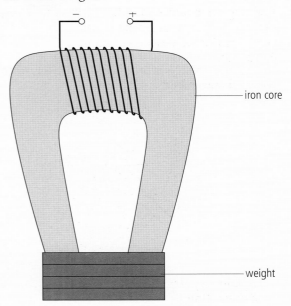

The graph shows how the weight lifted by the electromagnet depends on the current in the coil.

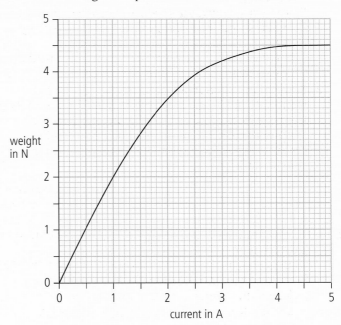

i What is the heaviest weight that the electromagnet can lift? *[1]*

ii Suggest how the electromagnet can be changed so that it will lift a heavier weight. *[1]*

b The electromagnet is used to pick up iron cans filled with fruit juice. Each can weighs 2 N.

i What current is needed for the electromagnet to lift one can? *[1]*

ii When this current is doubled, is the electromagnet able to lift two cans at the same time? Use data from the graph to give the reason for your answer. **[2]**

Total 5 marks

(Edexcel)

2 a When a coil rotates in a magnetic field, an alternating voltage is produced. Explain how the voltage is produced. **[2]**

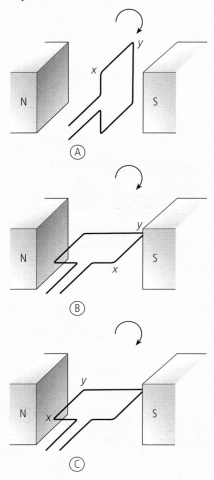

b The diagrams A, B and C show three positions of a coil as it rotates clockwise in a magnetic field produced by two poles.
The graph below shows how the voltage produced changes as the coil rotates.

When the coil is in the position shown by the diagram A, the output voltage is zero and is marked as 1 on the voltage–time graph.
State which point on the voltage–time graph corresponds to the coil position shown by

i Diagram B **[1]**
ii Diagram C **[1]**

c State **one** way of increasing the size of the voltage produced by **this** coil rotating in a magnetic field. **[1]**

d The diagram shows a transformer connected to a 230 V a.c. supply. It is used to operate a 5 V door bell.

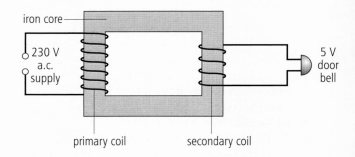

i Write down, **in words**, the equation connecting the number of turns in each coil to the voltages across them. **[1]**
ii If the primary coil of the above transformer has 920 turns, calculate the number of turns required on the secondary coil so that the door bell operates at 5 V. **[2]**

Total 8 marks

(WJEC)

3 Sam is investigating how the resistance of a lamp changes as she alters the current through it. She uses the circuit below.

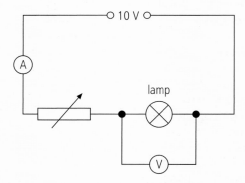

a She adjusts the setting of the variable resistor. Explain how this affects the current. **[2]**

b She records the values of the voltage across the lamp as the current changes. She plots the graph:

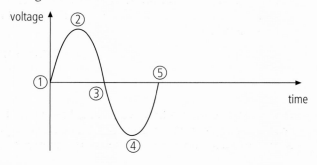

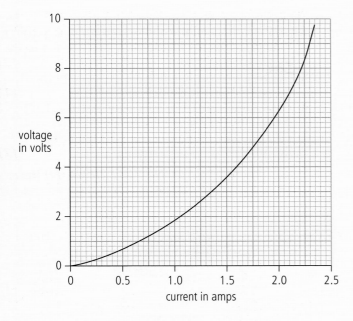

i Use the graph to find the value of the current when the voltage is 4.0 V. **[1]**
ii Calculate the resistance of the lamp when the voltage is 4.0 V. You **must** show how you work out your answer. **[3]**
c How can you tell from the graph that the resistance of the lamp increases between 4.0 V and 8.0 V? **[1]**

Total 7 marks

(OCR)

4 The diagram shows a circuit for emergency lighting. If the mains supply fails the relay switch closes and the lamps operate from the 12 V battery.

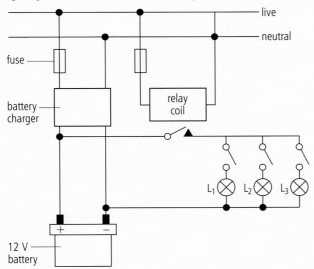

a Write down one reason for connecting the lamps in parallel. **[1]**
b When switched on, the current in each lamp is 5 A.
  i Calculate the current in the battery when all three lamps are switched on. **[1]**

ii Calculate the power of each lamp. **[3]**
c Lamps in emergency lighting circuits are connected to the battery using thick wires. Mains lamps of the same power are connected using thinner wires. Explain why. **[2]**

Total 7 marks

(Edexcel)

5 a One method of painting a car uses electrostatics. A paint spray produces paint droplets, all of which are given a positive charge. The car body is given a negative charge.

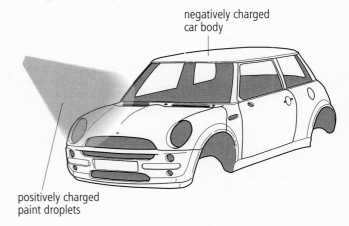

  i Explain why it is important to give all of the paint droplets a positive charge. **[2]**
  ii Explain why it is important to give the car body a negative charge. **[2]**
b The picture shows a light aircraft being refuelled after a flight.

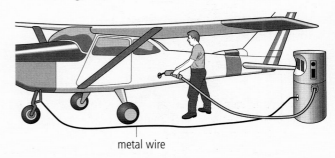

Explain why it is important that, before refuelling starts, the aircraft is first connected to the fuel pump by a metal wire. **[4]**

Total 8 marks

(AQA)

6 The diagram shows a long wire placed between the poles of a magnet. When a current I flows through the wire, a force acts on the wire causing it to move.

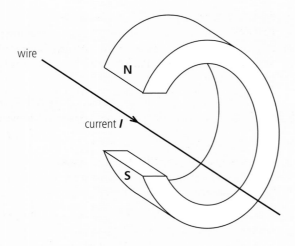

wire

N

current *I*

S

a Use Fleming's Left Hand Rule to find the direction of the force **on the diagram** with an arrow labelled **F**. **[1]**

b State what happens to the force on the wire when:

i The size of the current through the wire is increased. **[1]**

ii A weaker magnet is used. **[1]**

iii The direction of the current is reversed. **[1]**

c Name **one** practical device which uses this effect. **[1]**

Total 5 marks

(WJEC)

7 The diagram shows the construction of an X-ray tube. Electrons are emitted by the hot filament and fired at the tungsten anode where they are rapidly slowed down and produce X-rays.

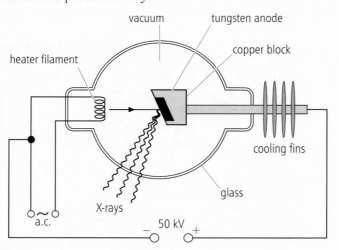

vacuum   tungsten anode

heater filament   copper block

cooling fins

glass

X-rays

a.c.   50 kV

a i Name the process in which electrons are emitted by a hot filament. **[1]**

ii Describe the energy transfers as the electrons move from the filament to the tungsten anode to produce X-rays. **[3]**

iii What is the source of energy for the electrons? **[1]**

b The current in the X-ray tube is 1.0 mA (1.0×10^{-3} A) when the voltage at the anode is 50 kV (5.0×10^{4} V).

i What total energy do the electrons transfer to the anode each second? **[2]**

ii Suggest why cooling fins are included in the design of the X-ray tube. **[1]**

iii The charge carried by 1 electron is 1.6×10^{-19} coulombs. How much energy does each electron gain in moving from the filament to the anode? **[2]**

Total 10 marks

(Edexcel)

8 The apparatus shown below can be used to investigate the production of electrons from a hot filament.

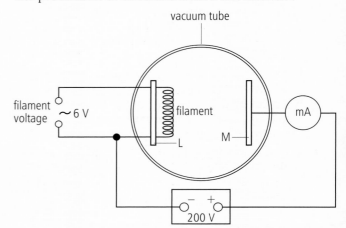

vacuum tube

filament voltage   ~6 V   filament

L   M   mA

200 V

When the filament is glowing, a current is measured by the milliammeter.

a i Explain fully why there is a current between L and M. **[3]**

ii When the filament voltage is reduced, the current decreases. Explain why this is. **[2]**

iii State and explain what would happen to the current if air entered in the vacuum tube. **[2]**

b The charge on the electron is 1.6×10^{-19} C.

i Calculate the kinetic energy of an electron arriving at plate M when the voltage between L and M is 200 V. Give your answer in Joules. **[3]**

ii The number of electrons arriving at M is 2.0×10^{16} per second. Calculate the current in the vacuum tube. **[3]**

Total 13 marks

(Edexcel)

9 The diagram at the top of the next page shows an electron beam. The beam is deflected as it passes between two metal plates.

a How can you tell from the diagram that the electrons have a negative charge? **[1]**

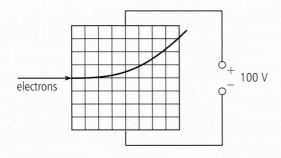

b Complete a copy of the diagram to show the paths of the electron beam when the voltage between the metal plates is changed as shown. *[4]*

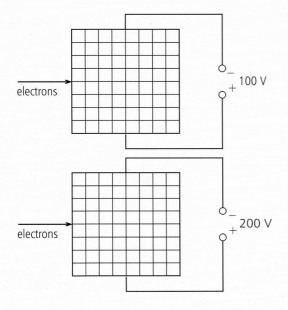

Total 5 marks
(Edexcel)

SECTION F Particles

1 The three main types of radioactive emission are called alpha, beta and gamma. The diagram shows the penetrations of alpha, beta and gamma radiation.

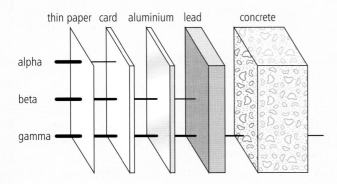

a Which type of radiation has the greatest penetration? *[1]*

b The diagram shows how aluminium sheet is rolled to form foil of constant thickness.

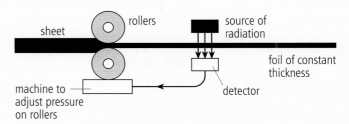

i Which type of radiation should be used to check the thickness of the foil? *[1]*

ii Explain why the other TWO types of radiation are **not** suitable. *[2]*

Total 4 marks
(Edexcel)

2 a The table gives information about five radioactive isotopes.

Isotope	Type of radiation	Half-life
Californium-241	alpha (α)	4 minutes
Cobalt-60	gamma (γ)	5 years
Hydrogen-3	beta (β)	12 years
Strontium-90	beta (β)	28 years
Technetium-99	gamma (γ)	6 hours

i What is an alpha particle? *[1]*

ii What is meant by the term half-life? *[1]*

iii Which **one** of the isotopes could be used as a tracer in medicine? Explain the reason for your choice. *[3]*

b The increased use of radioactive isotopes is leading to an increase in the amount of radioactive waste. One method for storing the waste is to seal it in containers, which are then placed deep underground.

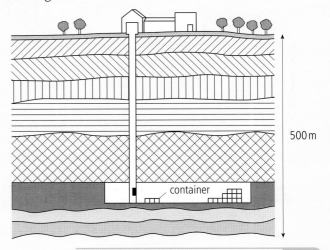

Some people may be worried about having such a storage site close to the area in which they live. Explain why. **[3]**

Total 8 marks

(AQA)

3 Radioactive carbon-14 emits a **β (beta) particle** when it decays. It has a **half-life** of 5600 years.

a Explain what you understand by the terms in bold print. **[3]**

b Living trees absorb carbon in the form of carbon dioxide and the amount of radioactive carbon-14 remains at a constant level within the tree. When the tree dies, the amount of carbon-14 decreases with time.

The decay curve for carbon-14 shows how the count rate would change over the next 16 000 years.

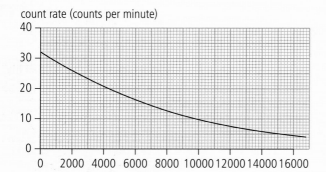

The carbon-14 from a sample of living wood near an ancient village gave a count rate of 32 counts per minute.

Carbon-14 from a sample of wood taken from one of the huts gave a lower count rate of 14 counts per minute.

i Suggest a reason why the wood from the hut gave a lower count rate than from the trees nearby. **[1]**

ii **Use the graph** to estimate the age of the village. **[1]**

c Explain why the safe disposal of radioactive waste from nuclear power stations is so expensive. **[3]**

Total 8 marks

(WJEC)

4 a The graph shows how a sample of a barium-143, a radioactive *isotope* with a short *half-life*, decays with time.

i What is meant by the term *isotope*? **[1]**

ii What is meant by the term *half-life*? **[1]**

iii Use the graph to find the half-life of barium-143 **[1]**

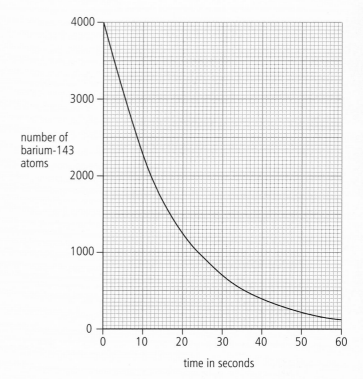

b Humans take in the radioactive isotope carbon-14 from their food. After death, the proportion of carbon-14 in their bones can be used to tell how long it is since they died. Carbon-14 has a half-life of 5700 years.

i A bone in a living human contains 80 units of carbon-14. An identical bone taken from a skeleton found in an ancient burial ground contains 5 units of carbon-14. Calculate the age of the skeleton. Show clearly how you work out your answer. **[2]**

ii Why is carbon-14 unsuitable for dating a skeleton believed to be about 150 years old? **[1]**

c The increased industrial use of radioactive materials is leading to increased amounts of radioactive waste. Some people suggest that liquid radioactive waste can be mixed with water and then safely dumped at sea. Do you agree with this suggestion? Explain the reason for your answer. **[3]**

Total 9 marks

(AQA)

5 The graph at the top of the next page shows data about the number of neutron and protons in stable nuclei. An atom of phosphorus-32 has 17 neutrons.

a Calculate the number of protons in the nucleus of phosphorus-32. **[1]**

b Mark an X on a copy of the graph to show the position of phosphorus-32. **[1]**

c How can you tell from the graph that phosphorus-32 is radioactive? **[1]**

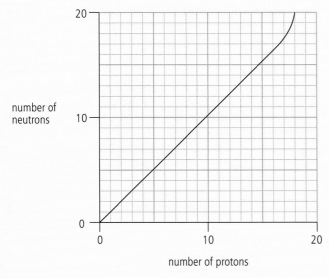

number of neutrons

number of protons

d The diagram below shows the changes which take place in the nucleus during β^- decay.

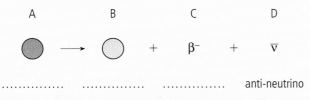

A   B   C   D

.... anti-neutrino

i Complete a copy of the diagram to give the names of the particles A, B and C. **[3]**

ii Explain why particles A and B are **not** fundamental particles. **[2]**

iii By calculating the n/p ratios, show that when phosphorus-32 undergoes β^- decay, the resultant isotope is stable. **[3]**

Total 11 marks

(Edexcel)

6 Natural uranium is a mixture of $^{235}_{92}U$ and $^{238}_{92}U$.

a What name is given to two different forms of the same element? **[1]**

b A nucleus of $^{235}_{92}U$ consists of 92 protons and 143 neutrons.
Write down the number of protons and neutrons in $^{238}_{92}U$. **[2]**

c Uranium-235 is used a fuel in nuclear reactors. The diagram illustrates the process.

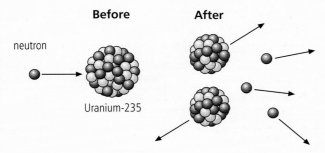

Before   After

neutron

Uranium-235

i Name the process shown in the diagram. **[2]**
ii Describe the process shown in the diagram. **[3]**

d Nuclear power stations produce highly radioactive waste. Metal cases containing the waste are kept in an air-cooled store for 50 years. They can then be disposed of safely.

i Suggest why the metal cases need to be kept cool. **[2]**

ii How should the store be designed so that as little as possible is released into the surroundings. **[1]**

Total 11 marks

(Edexcel)

7 Evidence for the structure of the atom comes from alpha particle scattering. The diagram below represents alpha particles from a radioactive source being directed directly at thin gold foil.

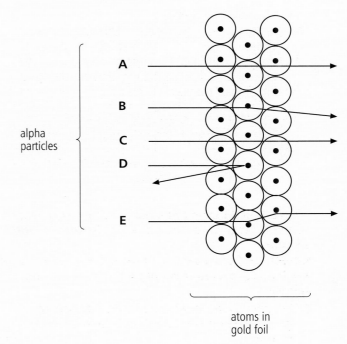

alpha particles

A
B
C
D
E

atoms in gold foil

a i Explain why particle B is deflected but particles A and C are not. **[2]**

ii What does the deflection of particle D show about the charge on the nucleus? Explain your answer. **[2]**

iii Only a very small number of particles are deflected in the same way as particle D. What does this show about the structure of a gold atom? **[2]**

b Suggest the likely result of an experiment using thick gold foil instead of thin gold foil. **[2]**

c The results of alpha particle scattering experiments led to an atomic model that describes the atom as being made up of protons and neutrons and electrons.

i Explain why the electron is described as a fundamental particle.

Protons and neutrons are each made up of quarks. The charge on an up quark is equal to two-thirds that on a positron, +e. The charge on a down quark is equal to one third that on an electron, -e. **[1]**

ii The diagram below represents the decay of a neutron.

Copy and complete the diagram by writing the name AND symbol of the particle on the right hand side of the decay equation. **[2]**

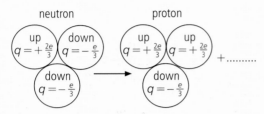

iii The diagram below represents the decay of a proton.

Copy and complete the diagram by writing the name AND symbol of the particle on the right hand side of the decay equation. **[2]**

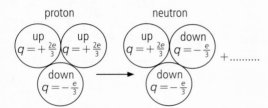

Total 13 marks

(Edexcel)

8 a The diagram shows some of the electron energy levels in an atom.

_____ level 3

_____ level 2

_____ level 1

An electron drops from level 3 to level 1.

i What is emitted when this happens? **[1]**

ii How can an electron in level 1 be made to go up to level 3? **[1]**

iii Draw on a copy of the diagram the different energy jumps possible for an electron which starts in level 3 and finishes in level 1. **[2]**

iv What evidence could you look at to see how many energy jumps there are? **[1]**

b Thorium-228 decays by alpha particle emission to radium-224.

Explain why the mass number decreases by 4 when an alpha particle is emitted from a thorium-228 nucleus. **[1]**

c Alpha particles of five different energies are produced in the decay of thorium-228.

i How could you show that alpha particles emitted have different energies? **[2]**

ii When an alpha particle of low energy is emitted, the radium-224 nucleus formed is left with to much energy.

How does this explain why gamma rays are emitted from the radium-224 along with an alpha particle? **[1]**

iii Gamma rays of different energies are produced in the decay of radium-224.

Suggest a reason for this. **[1]**

Total 10 marks

(Edexcel)

9 Anna investigates whether a trapped column of air in a thin glass tube acts like a thermometer. The tube is sealed at the bottom and open at the top. The air is trapped by a short length of coloured liquid. She measures the length of the column of air. She plots these results on a graph.

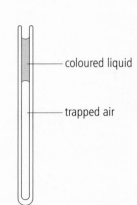

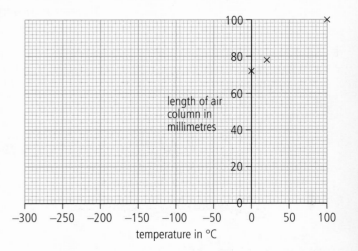

	temperature	length of air column
at room temperature	20 °C	78 mm
when the tube is in melting ice	0 °C	73 mm
when the tube is in boiling water	100 °C	100 mm

a i Use the graph to find the temperature at which the length of the air column is zero. **[2]**
ii What do we call this temperature? **[1]**
iii Explain why the pressure of a gas at this temperature is zero. **[1]**
b Use your ideas about particles in air to explain why the column of liquid does not fall to the bottom of the tube at room temperature. **[4]**

Total 8 marks

(OCR)

10 A radioactive isotope (radioisotope) can be used to treat a patient who has a cancerous tumour inside their body. In this treatment the radioisotope is held directly above the tumour as shown.

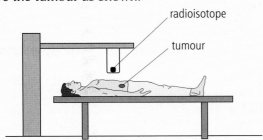

a Why are radioisotopes used in the treatment of cancer? **[2]**
b The radioisotope used is a gamma (γ) emitter. Why is it important to use a gamma emitter in the treatment of the tumour shown above? **[2]**
c The diagram below shows how the tumour is treated when viewed from one end.
During the treatment the radioisotope is moved from A to B and back to A again continuously. Why is this done? **[2]**

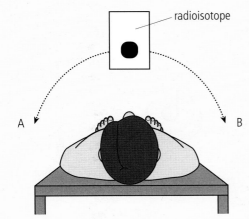

d The radioisotope use in the treatment of this cancerous tumour has a half-life of several years. Give a reason why a long half-life radioisotope is used. **[3]**

Total 9 marks

(CCEA)

11 a The diagram shows a sealed gas syringe in a heated water bath.
Explain in terms of molecules, why, if the pressure inside the syringe is to remain constant the gas must expand as its temperature rises. **[3]**

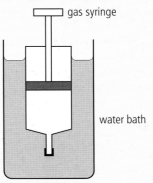

b A student was asked to investigate the relationship between the volume and pressure of a gas. The student used a fixed mass of oxygen kept at a constant temperature of 300 kelvin. The results of the investigation were used to plot a graph.

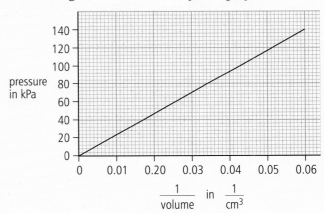

i Write down the relationship between the volume and pressure of a gas as found by this investigation. **[1]**
ii On a copy of the graph draw the line that would be obtained if it were possible to repeat the investigation at a temperature of 600 kelvins. **[1]**
c A gas cylinder contains 0.05 m³ of helium at a pressure of 16 000 kPa. The gas is used to blow up balloons. Each balloon when fully inflated contains 0.04 m³ of helium at a pressure of 102 kPa. The temperature of the helium inside both the cylinder and the balloons is the same.
Use the following equation to calculate the maximum number of balloons that can be fully inflated using this gas cylinder. Show clearly how you work out your final answer.

$$\frac{PV}{T} = \text{constant}$$ **[4]**

Total 9 marks

(AQA)

SECTION G   Earth and space

1 The graph shows the orbit time and average distance from the Sun of some planets and some asteroids. Asteroids are sometimes called minor planets.

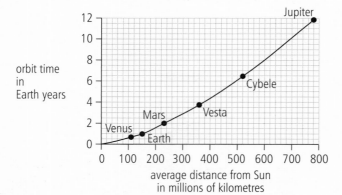

a Suggest why Jupiter takes longer than Mars to orbit the Sun. **[2]**

b The asteroid Ida is in orbit at an average distance of 430 million km from the Sun.
Use the graph to find out how long it takes to orbit the Sun. You must state clearly, how you got your answer. **[2]**

c The orbit of Ida about the Sun is, in fact, elliptical. This means its speed varies during the orbit, like a comet.

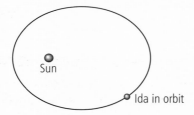

   i Write an X on a copy of the diagram to mark the place where Ida will be travelling at its highest speed. **[1]**

   ii Explain why it will be travelling at its highest speed at this place. **[1]**

d The light from distant galaxies is observed to be **red shifted**. Measurements of red shift allow astronomers to calculate the speed that the galaxies are travelling away from us. The graph shows how the speed that galaxies move away from us varies with their distance from us.

   i What is meant by **red shift**? **[1]**

   ii What type of shift would be observed in the light from stars travelling **towards** us? **[1]**

   iii What does the graph suggest about the link between the speed of a galaxy and its distance from us? **[1]**

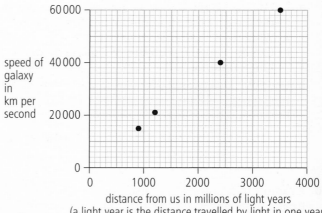

   iv A galaxy moves away from us at 30 000 km/s
Use the graph to estimate how far away the galaxy is.
You must state clearly how you get your answer. **[2]**

   v How long would it take light to travel this distance? **[1]**

   vi The galaxy, moving at 30 000 km/s is travelling at one tenth (0.1) of the speed of light. Assuming that all matter in the Universe was originally in one place, how long has it taken for the galaxy and us to be this distance apart? You must show how you work out your answer. **[2]**

   vii What is the significance of this value? **[1]**

Total 15 marks

(OCR)

2 a The Cassini spacecraft launched in 1997 will take seven years to reach Saturn. The journey will take the spacecraft close to several other planets.

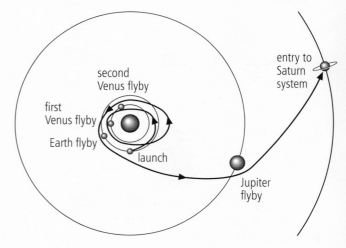

Each time the spacecraft approaches a planet it changes direction and gains kinetic energy. Explain why. **[2]**

b Cassini carries a probe, which will travel to Titan, Saturn's largest moon. The 320 kg probe will enter

Titan's atmosphere at 6 km/s. After plunging 100 km, parachutes will open to reduce the speed of the probe before it lands on Titan's surface.

i Use the equation below to calculate in joules, the kinetic energy of the probe as it enters Titan's atmosphere. Show clearly how you work out your answer.

$$\text{Kinetic energy} = \frac{1}{2}mv^2 \qquad \textbf{[2]}$$

ii The outside of the probe is fitted with a heat shield designed to withstand very high temperatures. Explain why. **[2]**

iii Why do parachutes reduce the speed of falling objects? **[1]**

c The Big Bang theory attempts to explain the origin of the Universe.

i What is the Big Bang theory? **[1]**

ii What can be predicted from the Big Bang theory about the size of the Universe. **[1]**

d i Explain how stars like the Sun were formed. **[2]**

ii The Sun is made mostly of hydrogen. Eventually the hydrogen will be used up and the Sun will die. Describe what will happen to the Sun from the time the hydrogen is used up until the Sun dies. **[3]**

Total 14 marks

(AQA)

3 When an earthquake occurs, shock waves travel through the Earth. The diagram shows the passage of two types of wave, called P and S waves.

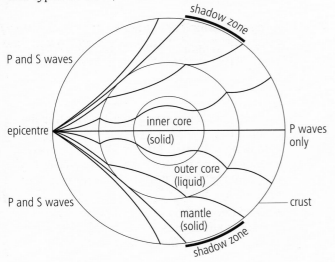

a i The waves from the epicentre change direction as they go further into the mantle. Suggest what causes this. **[1]**

ii The diagram shows that both S waves and P waves can travel through the solid mantle. The inner core of the Earth is also thought to be solid. Explain why S waves do not reach the solid inner core. **[2]**

iii Under water, energy can be transmitted as longitudinal waves. What types of wave are S waves and P waves? **[1]**

b The waves from earthquakes are detected by instruments called seismometers. The diagram shows a simple seismometer.

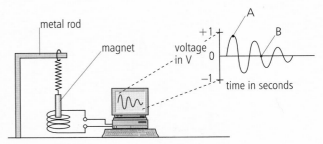

It consists of a bar magnet suspended on a spring. The spring hangs from a metal rod that transmits vibrations from the Earth. A computer monitors the voltage across the coil. There is an earthquake, the magnet moves in and out of the coil.

i Explain why a voltage is induced in the coil **[1]**

ii Why is the induced voltage alternating? **[1]**

iii Describe the movement of the magnet when the induced voltage has its greatest value, at the point labelled A. **[1]**

iv Describe the movement of the magnet when the induced voltage is zero, as at the point B **[1]**

v Suggest TWO ways in which the seismometer could be made more sensitive, so that it can detect smaller earthquakes. **[2]**

Total 10 marks

(Edexcel)

SECTION H   Sensing and control

1 It is dangerous for aircraft to take off or land when there is a strong wind across the runway. Neil's airport has installed this device to detect these dangerous cross winds.

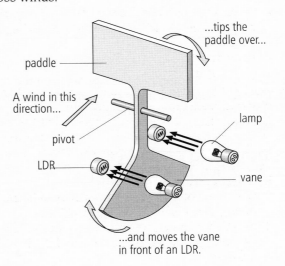

The lamps shine light onto the LDR. Any cross wind pushes the vane between the lamp and one of the LDRs. Here is the circuit for **one** of the LDRs.

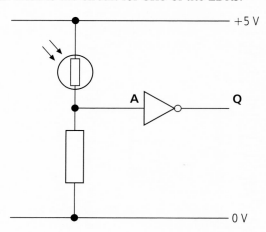

a Write out these sentences with the words HIGH or LOW correctly used:
When there is no wind, there is lots of light on the LDR. It has a … resistance.
In a strong wind, there is no light on the LDR. So it has a … resistance. **[2]**

b The graph shows how the voltage at A changes during the day.
On a copy of the **graph**, show how the voltage at Q changes during the day. Use the data in the table. **[3]**

voltage at A	voltage at Q
less than 2.0 V	4.5 V
more than 2.0 V	0.5 V

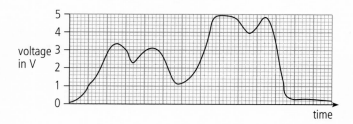

c A logic gate Z combines the signals from the sensors. The LED must glow if the crosswind is dangerous. The output from each sensor is LOW when there is no wind.

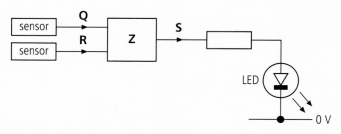

i Copy and complete the table. **[2]**

R	Q	S
LOW	LOW	
LOW	HIGH	
HIGH	LOW	
HIGH	HIGH	HIGH

ii Name the logic gate Z. **[1]**

Total 8 marks
(OCR)

2 Anita uses a remote control to operate her compact disc (CD) player. The remote control uses a beam of infra-red light from an LED to operate the CD player.

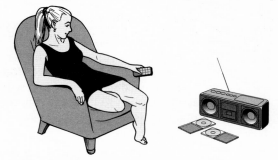

a The LED is turned on and off by a NOT gate.

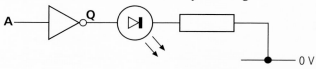

i Copy and complete the table. **[2]**

A	Q (HIGH or LOW)	LED (ON or OFF)
HIGH		
LOW		

ii Copy the sentence using words from this list to complete it:
electrical   heat   kinetic   light   nuclear
… energy from the NOT gate is transferred to … energy in the LED and … energy in the resistor. **[3]**

b The graph shows the pattern of pulses emitted by the LED when a key is pressed on the remote control. Each key makes a different pattern.

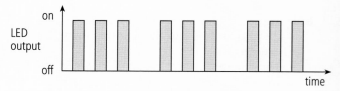

i This is a digital signal. How can you tell from the graph? **[1]**
ii Explain the advantage of using a digital signal. **[1]**

c The semiconductor which emits the infra-red light is embedded in solid plastic. As the infra-red light passes from the plastic into the air it is refracted.

   i What is meant by refraction? *[1]*

   ii The diagrams show rays of infra-red light in two different types of LED. Draw lines on a copy of each diagram, to show the path of light in the air. *[3]*

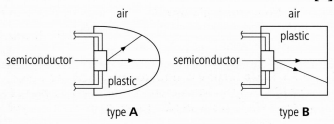

   iii Copy and complete the sentence:
   The remote control uses LED type ... because ...
   (explain) *[2]*

Total 13 marks

(OCR)

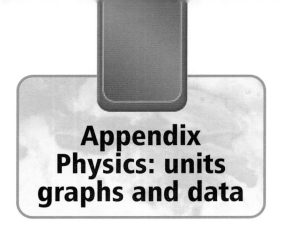

Appendix
Physics: units graphs and data

UNITS

All physical measurements are in units linked to a few basic **SI** (Système International) units. These base units are:

length: **metre**; time: **second**; mass: **kilogram**; electric current: **ampere**; temperature: **kelvin**; luminous intensity: **candela**; amount of substance: **mole**.

For example, **speed** is defined as *distance covered per unit of time*. **Velocity** is speed in a given direction. Thus the unit for speed is metre per second, written as m/s or m s^{-1}. Acceleration is speed change per second, so its units are m/s^2 or m s^{-2}.

Force is defined in terms of how much a mass is accelerated:

$$\text{force} = \text{mass} \times \text{acceleration}.$$

Thus the units of force are kg m s^{-2}. This unit has its own name the newton (N). You should always quote the units when you write down the value of a physical quantity. The most common units have names chosen from the famous physicists who either invented the concept or investigated it well:

frequency hertz (Hz)
force newton (N)
current ampere (A)
electrical capacitance farad (F)
energy joule (J)
power watt (W)
potential difference volt (V)
pressure pascal (Pa)
electric charge coulomb (C)
resistance ohm (Ω)

■ Large and small

Prefixes are used to multiply units, always in powers of 10. The ones in common use are:

multiplying factor	power of 10	prefix
one billionth	10^{-9}	nano n
one millionth	10^{-6}	micro μ
one thousandth	10^{-3}	milli m
one hundredth	10^{-2}	centi c
one thousand	10^{3}	kilo k
one million	10^{6}	mega M
one billion	10^{9}	giga G

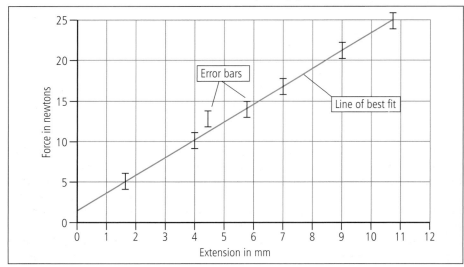

Picture 1 A well-drawn graph.

FUNDAMENTAL FORMULAE IN PHYSICS

The fundamental formulae in physics are those that define important ideas in terms of simpler ones, for example, momentum is defined as mass × velocity. There many other important formulae but they are 'discovered' relationships (like the Hooke Law) or are derived from more fundamental ones (like $s = ut + \frac{1}{2}at^2$). The fundamental formulae you have met in this book are:

speed (velocity): $v = \dfrac{s}{t}$

acceleration: $a = \dfrac{v}{t}$

force: $F = ma$

work $W = Fs$

momentum: $p = mv$

gravitational potential energy: $E = mgh$

kinetic energy: $E = \frac{1}{2}mv^2$

pressure: $p = \dfrac{F}{A}$

resistance: $R = \dfrac{V}{I}$

power: $P = \dfrac{E}{t}$

electric charge: $Q = It$

electric potential difference: $V = \dfrac{E}{Q} = \dfrac{P(\text{power})}{I}$

GRAPHS

Graphs can show us the relationship between quantities, how one thing affects another. We can also make calculations from graphs. Most graphs in physics are line graphs. A useful line graph must have

- a clear, numbered scale, with correct units
- points clearly plotted showing the data which were used to draw it (with error bars if possible)
- a line of best fit

These features are illustrated in picture 1.

A **straight line** graph shows that one quantity is proportional to another. The two quantities (say x and y) will be related to each other by the relationship.

$$y = mx + c$$

where m is the slope (gradient) of the graph and c is the intercept on the y axis (picture 2). In this formula the value of y is decided by the value of x. y is thus called a dependent variable. x is the independent variable. As a general rule we use the vertical (y) axis to show what happens to a quantity when we vary another one, plotted on the horizontal (x) axis. The vertical axis is for the dependent variable, the x for the independent one.

A graph of two quantities related by a formula such as $y = k/x$ is an **inverse** relationship. It will be like picture 3, which was obtained by plotting volume against pressure for a gas (Boyle's Law – page 209). If you suspect a relationship

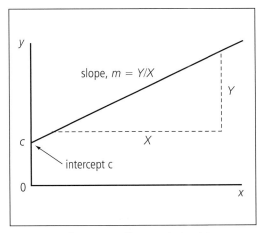

Picture 2 Illustration of linear relationship.

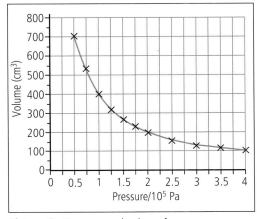

Picture 3 Pressure and volume for a gas.

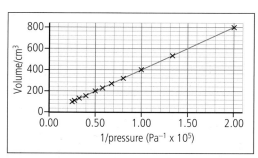

Picture 4   An inverse plot.

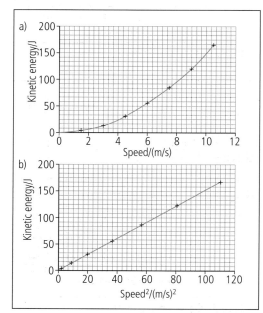

Picture 5   (a) and (b) changing a curve to a straight line.

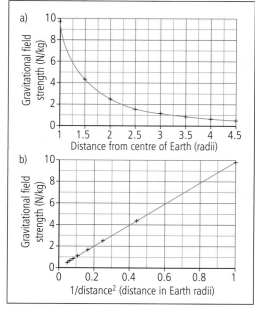

Picture 6   Inverse square plots.

like this you can test it by plotting y against $\frac{1}{x}$. This produces a straight line, as in picture 4, which is based on the same data as the graph in picture 3.

Some relationships involve the **square** of the independent variable: for example, the kinetic energy (E_k) of a car is proportional to the speed squared. Picture 5a shows that E_k increases very rapidly as speed v increases. If you suspect that a set of results show this kind of relationship you can plot the dependent variable against the square of the independent one. This will give a straight line graph if your suspicion is correct (picture 5b).

Another common relationship in physics is an **inverse square** relationship: e.g. the gravitational law:

$$F = G\frac{Mm}{r^2}$$

This will also give a curved line when you plot F against r. A graph of F against $\frac{1}{r^2}$ will give a straight line (picture 6).

■ Graphs of growth and decay

Picture 7 shows how the activity (emission rate) of a sample of a radioactive isotope changes with time. The activity falls off with time, at first rapidly and then more slowly. This is typical of radioactive decay (see topic F2). Remember that the nucleus of a radioactive isotope is unstable. It is liable to emit some radiation and become a different nucleus as a result. The activity is always proportional to the number of undecayed nuclei present. The graph is due to a simple physical effect: when radiation is emitted from the first nucleus it stops being radioactive.

Thus the activity is high at the start because there are a lot of radioactive nuclei present. But as time goes on the number of active nuclei gets less, and so does the activity. This process is an example of what is called **exponential decay**.

Picture 8 shows what might happen to a population of rabbits when a small number are put on an island where there is plenty of food and no predators. The growth of the population is quite small at the start, but then rapidly increases. This is because the number of young rabbits added to the population each season is proportional to the number of mature rabbits present. As the offspring grow up, so they produce even more young rabbits. This is an example of an **exponential growth**.

Both examples have one thing in common: the change in a variable is proportional to the value of the variable itself at any time. The graphs also have a constant feature related to the time it takes for things to change. In exponential decay there will be a constant half life – this is the time it takes for the dependent variable to fall to half of any given value. In exponential growth we have a constant doubling time – this is the time it takes for the dependent variable to become twice what it was at any given time.

These values are shown on the graphs in pictures 7 and 8.

■ Using graphs

Graphs can be used to make predictions. For example, we can guess that in picture 9 the value of current at a voltage of 7 V is likely to be 0.29 A. It is unlikely that a well-behaved piece of metal will suddenly do something odd between 6 V and 8 V. We have no real evidence that it does behave well, of course. This trick of guessing a value we haven't actually measured is called **interpolation**.

We can even predict what should happen if we increased the voltage. If the wire carries on behaving as it did up to 12 V than it should carry a current of 0.67 A at 16 V. This kind of prediction from a graph is called **extrapolation**.

Both methods usually work well when the graph is linear, but it would be dangerous to rely on them for accurate predictions when the graph is like that in picture 10. Nevertheless predictions were made and later measurements showed them to be correct. This graph was of early results that showed that the Universe had an average temperature of about 3 K, and was the main evidence for the Big Bang Theory of the origin of the Universe (pages 292–3).

THE AREA UNDER A GRAPH
The area under a graph can give useful information. Picture 11a shows force plotted against extension when a spring is stretched. The shaded area under the graph is equal to the work done in stretching the spring. Why? The definition of work done is

$$\text{work} = \text{force} \times \text{distance moved by force}$$

The force increases as the spring extends, so that the work done per mm of extension changes continuously. The maximum force is F, the minimum is zero. Thus the average force is $\dfrac{F}{2}$

So we can say that the work done = average force × distance moved.

$$= \frac{1}{2}Fx \text{ which is also the geometrical area under the graph.}$$

This rule applies even when the force–distance relationship is not linear (picture 11b).

This idea is used on page 76 to derive formulae for distance moved by an accelerating object.

EXAMPLE
The table shows the results of a test on the performance of a model car.

time/s	4	6	8	10	12	14	16	18	20
speed/ms⁻¹	1.0	1.2	1.4	1.6	1.8	2.0	2.2	2.4	2.6

These results are plotted on a graph (picture 12). By extrapolating backwards the intercept on the speed axis shows us that at time zero the model was travelling at 0.6 m s^{-1}. We might guess that the car would be travelling at 3 m s^{-1} – 24 seconds after the start of timing (by extrapolating forwards). The slope of the graph gives the acceleration: 0.1 m s^{-2}. The area under the graph gives the distance travelled in the first 20 seconds: 32 m.

Query: would it be sensible to predict by extrapolation that the model car would reach a speed of about 60 m s^{-1} after a total elapsed time of 10 minutes (600 s)?

USEFUL DATA

■ Fundamental physical constants
speed of light in a vacuum, $c = 3 \times 10^8 \text{ m s}^{-1}$
charge on electron, proton, $e = 1.6 \times 10^{-19} \text{ C}$
Universal gravitational constant $G = 6.67 \times 10^{-11} \text{ N m}^2 \text{ kg}^{-2}$
acceleration of free fall, $g = 9.8 \text{ m s}^{-2}$

■ Other constants
radius of Earth $= 6.4 \times 10^6 \text{ m}$
mass of Earth $= 6 \times 10^{24} \text{ kg}$
Earth–Sun distance $= 1.5 \times 10^{11} \text{ m}$
mass of Sun $= 2 \times 10^{30} \text{ kg}$

■ Speeds
sound in air $= 330 \text{ m s}^{-1}$
sound in water $= 1410 \text{ m s}^{-1}$

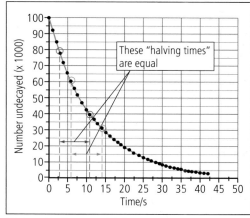

Picture 7 Exponential decay.

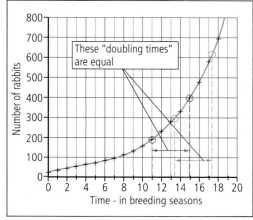

Picture 8 Exponential growth

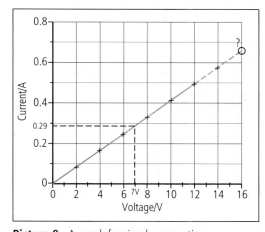

Picture 9 A graph for simple proportion.

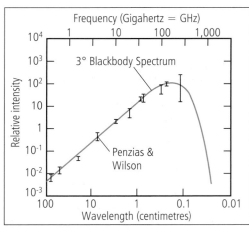

Picture 10 Early graph of 3 K background, with error bars.

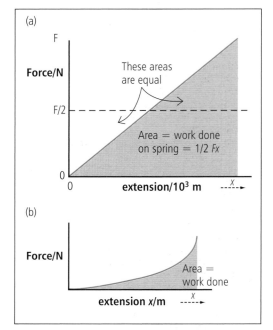

Picture 11 Areas under graphs: work.

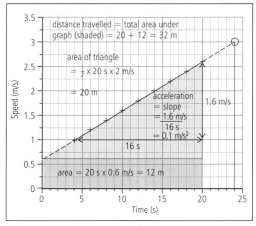

Picture 12 Areas under graphs: distance.

	Specific heat capacities ($J\ kg^{-1}\ K^{-1}$)	Densities ($kg\ m^{-3}$)
aluminium	886	2700
brass	372	8500
copper	380	8930
glass	about 600	about 2500
ice	210	920
rubber	113	920
iron	490	7870
lead	127	11370
marble	880	2700
water	4180	1000
paraffin	2140	800

USEFUL FORMULAE

$$pressure = \frac{force}{area} \quad P = \frac{F}{A}$$

$$speed = \frac{distance}{time\ taken}$$

$$for\ an\ ideal\ gas, \frac{P_1 V_1}{T_1} = \frac{P_2 V_2}{T_2}$$

$$work\ done = force \times distance\ moved\ in\ direction\ of\ force$$

$$W = Fs$$

$$power = \frac{energy\ transferred}{time\ taken} = \frac{work\ done}{time\ taken} \quad P = \frac{W}{t}$$

$$electrical\ energy\ (in\ kWh) = power\ (in\ kW) \times time\ (in\ h)$$

For a body in equilibrium

$$sum\ of\ clockwise\ moments\ about\ any\ point\ in\ a\ plane$$
$$= sum\ of\ anticlockwise\ moments\ about\ that\ point$$

$$moment\ of\ a\ force\ about\ a\ pivot = force \times perpendicular\ distance\ from$$
$$force\ to\ pivot$$

$$energy = potential\ difference \times current \times time \quad W = VIt$$

$$energy\ supplied\ to\ raise\ temperature = mass \times specific\ heat\ capacity$$
$$\times temperature\ change$$

$$force = mass \times acceleration \quad F = ma$$

$$acceleration = \frac{change\ in\ velocity}{time\ taken} \quad a = \frac{v-u}{t}$$

$$wave\ speed = frequency \times wavelength \quad v = f\lambda$$

$$charge = current \times time \quad Q = It$$

$$potential\ difference = current \times resistance \quad V = IR$$

$$electric\ power = potential\ difference \times current \quad P = VI$$

$$weight = mass \times gravitational\ field\ strength \quad W = mg$$

For a body of mass m moving with velocity v, kinetic energy $= \frac{1}{2}mv^2$

For a body of mass m raised through a height, h,

$$increase\ in\ gravitational\ potential\ energy = mgh$$

$$momentum = mass \times velocity$$

Index

Acknowledgements

The authors and publisher are grateful to the following for permission to reproduce photographs. While every effort has been made to trace copyright holders, if any acknowledgement has been inadvertently omitted, the publisher will be pleased to make the necessary arrangement at the first opportunity.

AEA Technology: 240.1;
AKG London: 92.2c (Erich Lessing);
Allsport: 64, 77, 144;
Alton Towers: 103;
American Institute of Physics: 221.2 (1969 Marsden Booklet Editorial Panel);
Anglo-Australian Observatory: 1;
Ann Ronan Picture Library: 70.2 (top), 92.2b, 215;
Axon Images: 41;
Barnaby's Picture Library: 13, 63.2
Birmingham Symphony Hall: 15;
Bridgeman Art Library: 160.1 (Portrait photograph of Michael Faraday (1791–1867) and John Frederick Daniell (1790–1845), The Royal Institution, London, TRI), 160.2 (Sir Humphry Davy, 1815 by Sir Thomas Lawrence (1769–1830), The Royal Institution, London, UK);
British Steel: 113;
Bruce Coleman: 159, 189.2;
Carrington Counter Associates: 177;
CEGB: 193.1;
Chris Ridgers: 21.6, 21.7, 22, 24, 25, 26, 59.3, 83, 132, 138.1, 138.2, 145, 152.1, 152.2, 153abde, 167, 170.2, 178.3, 181, 182.7, 183, 202.4, 202.6, 203.8, 260.9, 260.10, 301.5, 304, 308;
Corel (NT): 57, 58, 60, 299;
DETR: 66 (Crown Copyright 1999);
Digital Vision (NT): 100.8, 151;
Ever Ready: 190;
Eye Ubiquitous: 92.2a (Brian Harding);
Frank Lane Picture Agency: 98;
Getty Images: 300, 305 (Telegraph Colour Library);
Glynn Millhouse: 42;
Griffin: 31, 163, 164;
Hawker Siddley: 114.3;
Holt Studios International: 134.9, 134.10;
Hulton Getty: 4.5, 70.2 (bottom), 208.1, 221.1, 222, 230, 245;
Hutchinson Picture Library: 124;
Imperial War Museum: 39;
J Allen Cash photolibrary: 44, 84, 126, 162.1, 290.4;
JET: 205;
Jim Breithaupt: 40.3;
John Urling Clark: 18, 19.3, 19.4, 108.8, 156.1 (right), 166, 182.5, 187, 188.9, 257, 260.8;
JVC: 153c;
Last Resort Picture Library: 117;
Martin Sookias: 313;
Martyn Chillmaid: 59.3, 110.2, 120.11, 179.7;
Michael Holford Picture Library: 106.3;

NASA: 99.6, 198.1, 256, 273.8, 285;
Natural Visions: 189.1 (Heather Angel);
Naval Research Laboratory, Washington DC: 121;
NNRC: 238.6;
Rex Features: 17.16 (Ray Tang), 111, 118;
Richmond College: 40.1, 47, (Department of Photography);
Robert Harding Picture Library: 55 (Tom Caroll, Phototake);
Rowenta: 184.1, 184.2;
Royal Observatory: 271, 291.8, 291.9;
Salters: 112.6;
Science and Society Photolibrary: 160.3, 161.4, 161.5;
Science Photolibrary: 21.8, 33.14, 46, 48, (Richard Folwell), 49, 50.2, 51.1, 53.3 (NRAO), 63.1, 70.1, 71, 93, 95.1, 96, 97, (NRSC), 99.5 (Geospace), 100.7, (Royal Observatory, Edinburgh), 105, 106.4, 107.5, 107.6, 107.7, 108.9, 110.1, 122, 169, 170.1, 170.4, 171, 172, 178.4, 188.10, 193.3, 198.12 (Martin Bond), 198.13, 198.14, 203.10, 204, 208.2, 216, 223, 235, 236.2, 240.3 (Geoff Tompkinson), 240.4 (CNRI), 241.1 (Stanford Linear Accelerator Center), 241.2 (CERN), 241.3 (CERN), 250.4, 253 (Georg Gerster), 272, 273.7, 275.1, 275.2 (Pekka Pavainen), 276.4, 277.6, 277.7, 280.2, 280.3, 281.4, 281.6, 282, 283 (Hale Observatories), 289.2, 289.3, 290.6, 291.7, 294.1 (Eckhard Slavik), 294.2 (NOAO), 296.3 (David Parker);
Scope Optics: 33.13;
SETI Institute: 296.4;
Sheffield University: 240.2;
Shout Pictures: 89;
Southern Electric: 179.6;
Spectrum: 140, 212.136;
Stuart Boreham: 14, 120.9, 134.11, 135;
Surrey Space Centre: 95.2;
UKAEA: 238.5;
Volvo: 67, 109;
Wild Leitz, Heersburg, Germany: 34

Picture research by johnbailey@axonimages.com

Thanks are also due to the following awarding bodies for kind permission to reproduce examination questions:

Assessment and Qualifications Alliance (AQA)
Edexcel
Northern Ireland Council for the Curriculum Examinations and Assessment (CCEA)
Oxford Cambridge and RSA Examinations (OCR)
Welsh Joint Education Committee (WJEC)